THE CATHEDRALS OF ENGLAND AND WALES

NORWICH CATHEDRAL FROM THE SOUTH-EAST

THE CATHEDRALS OF ENGLAND AND WALES

BEING A FOURTH EDITION OF
ENGLISH CATHEDRALS ILLUSTRATED

BY

FRANCIS BOND

M.A., LINCOLN COLLEGE, OXFORD; HONORARY ASSOCIATE OF THE
ROYAL INSTITUTE OF BRITISH ARCHITECTS; FELLOW OF THE
GEOLOGICAL SOCIETY, LONDON; AUTHOR OF "GOTHIC ARCHITEC-
TURE IN ENGLAND," "WESTMINSTER ABBEY," "SCREENS AND
GALLERIES IN ENGLISH CHURCHES," ETC. ETC.

Illustrated by over 200 reproductions from photographs and a series of ground plans to a uniform scale

This edition digitally re-mastered and
published by JM Classic Editions © 2007
Original text © Francis Bond 1912

ISBN 978-1-905217-82-3

All rights reserved. No part of this book subject
to copyright may be reproduced in any form or
by any means without prior permission in writing
from the publisher.

PREFACE

THE first edition of "English Cathedrals Illustrated" was published in 1899; in the second edition a few verbal corrections were inserted; the third edition was published without revision. In the present edition many important changes have been made. In its original form the book had two grave defects. One was that it contained no ground plans, which are indispensable to reader and visitor alike, and have been supplied in the present volume; they are reproduced to a uniform scale of 100 ft. to the inch. One or two plans of parish churches now forming cathedrals, such as Newcastle, are omitted, being of parochial rather than cathedral type. Secondly, in conformity with Mr Rickman's nomenclature, the attempt was made to thrust the history of every cathedral into his Procrustean framework of Norman, Early English, Decorated and Perpendicular periods. The result was disastrous. Such an arrangement is a wholesale perversion of architectural history. No cathedral was ever built in just four building periods—these and no other. In some cathedrals, e.g., Salisbury, there are less than four building periods; in most cases there are seven, eight, or even more. In this volume the actual building periods are treated separately, and no attempt is made to cram them into arbitrary imaginary compartments.

PREFACE

The book has been re-illustrated in a much more comprehensive manner, only a few examples of detail being retained from the earlier editions. With the exception of the ground plans, the illustrations are from photographs, the sources of which are given in the note of acknowledgment. The more important features of each cathedral are represented, and it is hoped that this will tend materially to elucidate and increase the interest of the text: neither the text, however, nor the illustrations are intended as a substitute for personal study of the cathedrals on the spot, which it is the purpose of the book to foster and facilitate.

Short bibliographies are appended to the accounts of the various cathedrals. In addition, the student is referred to the following: Browne Willis' *Survey of the Cathedrals of York, Durham, Carlisle, Chester, Lichfield, Hereford, Gloucester, Bristol, Lincoln, Ely, Oxford, and Peterborough*, 2 vols., 8vo, London. 1730; Britton's *History and Antiquities of Canterbury, York, Bristol, Exeter, Gloucester, Hereford, Lichfield, Norwich, Oxford, Peterborough, Salisbury, Wells, Winchester, Worcester Cathedrals*, London, 1821-1836; *Cathedrals of England and Wales*, published by "*The Builder*," London, 1904; Murray's *Handbooks to the Cathedrals of England and Wales*, 8 vols., 3rd edition, London, 1903. In *English Minsters* by Rev. M. E. C. Walcott, pages xv. to xix., is a bibliography of each cathedral.

All the cathedrals were visited by the writer when the first edition of this work was in preparation, and in recent years they have been revisited again and again. The result of continuous and comparative study of the English churches in general has been to shew the writer that in many cases conclusions originally accepted by himself and others are untenable: to a large extent, therefore, it has been found necessary to rewrite the book; the changes made in the account of the architectural history of the cathedrals of Lincoln, Worcester, Llandaff, Exeter, and Hereford are very considerable. That a higher standard of accuracy has been reached than in the earlier editions of the book may be fairly assumed. Complete accuracy, however, is impossible in dealing with a subject so vast. It is impossible even to know a single cathedral. As has been finely said by Mr Fergusson: "Not only is there built into a mediæval cathedral the accumulated thought of all the men who had occupied themselves with building during the preceding centuries, but you have the dream and aspiration of the bishop, abbot, or clergy for whom it was designed; the master-mason's skilled construction; the work of the carver, the painter, the glazier, the host of men who, each in his own craft, knew all that had been done before them, and had spent their lives in struggling to surpass the works of their forefathers. It is more than this: there is not one shaft, one moulding, one carving, not one chisel-mark in such a building, that was not designed specially for the place where it is found, and which was not the best that the experience of the age could invent for the purposes to which it is applied; nothing was borrowed; and nothing that was designed for one purpose was used for another. A thought or a motive peeps out through every joint; you may wander in such a building for weeks or for months together, and never know it all."

FRANCIS BOND.

June 1912.

NOTE OF ACKNOWLEDGMENT

THE writer has had the good fortune to secure the assistance of numerous local experts in revising the proofs of various chapters: acknowledgments are due to Rev. A. E. Alston, M.A., Rev. John Bailey, M.A., Miss Maude E. Bull, George Benson, Esq., A.R.I.B.A., Canon Church, F.S.A., W. Eaton, Esq., A.R.I.B.A., the Dean of Ely, Rev. Edward Forse, M.A., Rev. J. T. Fowler, D.C.L., W. Francis, Esq., Miss Edith Hoskyns, P. M. Johnston, Esq., F.S.A., the Dean of Lichfield, the Hon. Mrs O'Grady, H. Plowman, Esq., Miss Edith K. Prideaux, Professor S. H. Reynolds, the Dean of Ripon, C. B. Shuttleworth, Esq., W. Wheeler, Esq., and Canon J. M. Wilson, D.D.

For photographs the author is indebted to the following: to H. W. Bennett, Esq., for the illustrations given on pp. 5, 59, 61, 87, 109, 374; W. M. Dodson, Esq. (Bettws-y-Coed), pp. 112, 469; W. Francis, Esq., pp. 243, 250, 254; Messrs F. Frith & Co., Ltd., pp. 216, 224, 484; J. Gale, Esq., p. 28; J. P. Gibson, Esq., pp. 85, 88, 208; The Herefordshire Photographic Society, pp. 156, 160, 165, 169; The London Stereoscopic Co. Ltd., p. 215; C. F. Nunneley, Esq., pp. 101, 103, 138, 230, 233, 307; The Photochrom Company Ltd., the frontispiece and pp. 31, 47, 48, 50, 80, 96, 99, 117, 123, 145, 148, 153, 174, 188, 220, 226, 260, 261, 263, 270, 277, 297, 313, 315, 346, 363, 381, 386, 387, 394, 407, 485; S. Smith, Esq. (Lincoln), pp. 195, 197, 203; the Rev. F. Sumner, pp. 68, 75, 77, 168, 247, 302, 306, 326, 329, 375, 376, 392, 400; F. R. P. Sumner, Esq., pp. 6, 71, 151, 249, 304, 305, 308, 328, 330, 377, 402; Aymer

Vallance, Esq., M.A., F.S.A., pp. 25, 35, 38, 40; and A. E. Walsham, Esq., pp. 248 and 253. To Sir Arthur Blomfield & Sons the author is indebted for the plan of Southwark Cathedral, and to G. Gilbert Scott, Esq., for the plan and two views of Liverpool Cathedral. The illustrations on pp. 26, 44, 45, 46, 65, 104, 161, 163, 183, 365, 421, 463, and 474, are from photographs by the author. Thanks are also due to Mr G. E. Kruger for his design of the cover.

CONTENTS

	PAGE
CLASSIFICATION OF CATHEDRALS - - -	xxii

INTRODUCTION - - - - - - - 1
    Methods of studying Cathedrals—Influences which lead to structural changes—Ritualistic divisions of Cathedrals.

BRISTOL—The Cathedral Church of the Holy Trinity - 9
    Augustinian Establishment, 9; FIRST BUILDING PERIOD (Norman Church), 10; Norman Remains, 11; SECOND PERIOD, 12; Elder Lady Chapel, 12; THIRD PERIOD, 13; rebuilding, 13; lighting problems, 13; Vaulting, 14; Lady Chapel, 17; Choir, 17; Berkeley Chapel, 17; Chancel, 18; decorative detail, 18; Newton Chapel, 19; FOURTH PERIOD, 19; Transepts remodelled, 19; FIFTH PERIOD, 20; modern executions, 20.

CANTERBURY—The Cathedral of Christ Church - 22
    FIRST PERIOD, 22; Pre-Conquest remains, 22; Lanfranc's Cathedral and Benedictine Monastery, 22; site of Becket's martyrdom, 24; SECOND PERIOD, 24; Anselm's work, 24; Chapels, 26; Presbytery, 27; the Choir, 27, 30; THIRD PERIOD, 28; Destruction and Restoration of Choir, 28; Becket's Corona, 30; French Influences, 32; Stained Glass, 33; FOURTH PERIOD, 34; Crypt, 35; FIFTH PERIOD, 35; Norman Work Removed, 35; Clerestory, 36; SIXTH PERIOD, 37; Cloisters, 37; SEVENTH PERIOD, 37; Central Tower, 37; Chapter House, 38; West Front, 40.

CONTENTS

CARLISLE—The Cathedral Church of the Holy Trinity   43

Augustinian Establishment, 43; FIRST PERIOD, 43; the Norman Church, 43; SECOND PERIOD, 44; Gothic Chancel Built, 45; THIRD PERIOD, 46; destruction by fire, 46; the East Front, 47; FOURTH PERIOD, 49; Central Tower and Nave, 49; FIFTH PERIOD, 50; Gondebour's illuminations, 50; SIXTH PERIOD, 51.

CHESTER—The Cathedral Church of Christ and the Blessed Virgin   52

Benedictine Monastery, 52; FIRST PERIOD, 52; Norman Work extant, 52; Cloisters, 55; SECOND PERIOD, 55; THIRD PERIOD, 55; Lady Chapel, 57; the Choir, 57; FOURTH PERIOD, 58; extensive rebuilding, 58; St. Oswald's Church, 59; Central Tower and Nave, 60; FIFTH PERIOD, 62; Nave, High Altar, and Cloisters, 62; Minor Works, 63; Stalls, 63.

CHICHESTER—The Cathedral Church of the Holy Trinity   65

Foundation of the See, 67; the Norman Church, 68; the Lady Chapel, 70; destruction by fire and restoration, 71; the Towers, 76; Chapels, 76; Window Tracery, 78; detached Campanile, 79; Bernardi's paintings, 80; rebuilding of the Towers and Spire, 81.

DURHAM—The Cathedral Church of Christ and the Blessed Virgin Mary   82

Foundation of the See, 82; Benedictine Establishment, 84; Episcopal Jurisdiction, 84; FIRST PERIOD, 86; the Norman Cathedral, 86; Vaulting, 88; Internal Elevation, 89; SECOND PERIOD, 89; Gothic spirit, 90; THIRD PERIOD, 90; "Chapel of the Nine Altars," 91; FOURTH PERIOD, 93; Window Tracery, 93; Altar Reredos, 93; FIFTH PERIOD, 93; the Central Tower, 93; SIXTH PERIOD, 94; the Sanctuary Knocker, 94.

CONTENTS

ELY—The Cathedral Church of the Holy and Undivisible Trinity - - - - - - 96

Benedictine Establishment, 98; FIRST PERIOD, 98; Plan and Construction of Norman Cathedral, 98; SECOND PERIOD, 102; The Galilee Porch, 102; Reconstruction of East End, 102; THIRD PERIOD, 104; the Lady Chapel, 105; Collapse of Central Tower, 106; Construction of the Octagon, 106; the rebuilt Choir, 108; Stalls, 110; FOURTH PERIOD, 110; Lighting improvements, 110; Chantry Chapels, 110; FIFTH PERIOD, 111; Wren's Classical Doorway, 111; MINOR WORKS, 111.

EXETER—The Cathedral Church of St. Peter - - 114

Foundation of the See, 114; FIRST PERIOD, 116; construction of the Norman Cathedral, 111; SECOND PERIOD, 118; the Chapter House, 118; THIRD PERIOD, 119; the Chapels, 119; FOURTH PERIOD, 121; various completions, 121; the Arcades, 122; FIFTH PERIOD, 123; the Choir remodelled, 123; SIXTH PERIOD, 124; completion of the Choir, 124; the Bishop's Throne, 125; the High Altar, 126; SEVENTH PERIOD, 127; the design of the Cathedral, 130; Interior Problems, 130; Window Tracery, 131; symmetry of the design, 131; EIGHTH PERIOD, 133; the Chantries, 134.

GLOUCESTER—The Cathedral Church of St. Peter - 136

Benedictine Establishment, 136; FIRST PERIOD, 136; the Crypt, 136; SECOND PERIOD, 138; the rebuilding, 138; the Choir and Nave, 140; THIRD PERIOD, 142; Towers, 142; destruction by fires, 143; FOURTH PERIOD, 143; Strengthening by Buttresses, 143; Windows, 144; FIFTH PERIOD, 144; Tomb of Edward II., 144; SIXTH PERIOD, 146; Lighting improvements, 146; South Transept, 146; Vaulting, 149; The East End, 150; SEVENTH PERIOD, 151; rebuilding of Cloisters, 151; EIGHTH PERIOD, 151; West Front, 151; NINTH PERIOD, 152; Central Tower, 152; TENTH PERIOD, 152; rebuilding of Lady Chapel, 152; The Cloister, Chapter House, etc., 153; Minor Works and Monuments, 154.

xvi CONTENTS

PAGE

HEREFORD—The Cathedral Church of St. Mary and
St. Ethelbert - - - - - 156

FIRST PERIOD, 158; the Norman Church, 158; SECOND PERIOD, 160; Nave and renovation of Choir, 161; THIRD PERIOD, 161; the Chapels, 162; FOURTH PERIOD, 162; completion of Lady Chapel, 163; FIFTH PERIOD, 164; Lighting Problems, 164; SIXTH PERIOD, 164; North Transept rebuilt, 164; SEVENTH PERIOD, 165; St. Cantelupe's Shrine, 166; various improvements, 166; EIGHTH PERIOD, 167; Central Tower rebuilt, 167; S.E. Transept rebuilt, 168; NINTH PERIOD, 168; South Transept Windows, 168; Chantry Chapels, 169; TENTH PERIOD, 170; Modern Restorations, 170.

LICHFIELD—The Cathedral Church of St. Mary - 172

Foundation of the See, 172; story of St. Chad, 173; History of the See, 175; the Cathedral during the Civil War, 176; Puritanical Devastations, 177; Re-erection of Central Tower, 178; FIRST PERIOD, 178; the Norman Cathedral, 178; SECOND PERIOD, 179; the Norman Cathedral rebuilt, 179; THIRD PERIOD, 182; the Transepts and Chapter House, 182; FOURTH PERIOD, 183; the Nave, 183; FIFTH PERIOD, 185; the West Front, 185; the Lady Chapel, 185; SIXTH PERIOD, 186; St. Chad's Shrine, 186-7; Lighting improvements, 186; SEVENTH PERIOD, 187; Altar Screen, 187; completion of St. Chad's Shrine, 188; Minor Works, 189.

LINCOLN—The Cathedral Church of St. Mary - - 191

FIRST PERIOD, 191; Norman Remains, 191; SECOND PERIOD, 193; the Towers, 193; THIRD PERIOD, 194; the rebuilding, 194; St. Hugh's Work, 196, etc.; FOURTH PERIOD, 198; FIFTH PERIOD, 198; the Nave, 198; the West Front, 201; SIXTH PERIOD, 201; collapse and re-erection of Central Tower, 201; Choir and Transepts, 202; SEVENTH PERIOD, 204; the Angel Choir, 205; the Central Tower and Spire, 205; EIGHTH PERIOD, 206; Bishop Dalderby's Shrine, 206; NINTH PERIOD, 207; Choir Stalls, 207; TENTH PERIOD, 207; West Windows, 207; Chantries, 208; ELEVENTH PERIOD, 209.

CONTENTS

LONDON—The Cathedral Church of St. Paul - - 210
Sir Christopher Wren, 210; the original design, 212; the Dome, 214-221; the Interior, 217; the Exterior, 217.

MANCHESTER—The Cathedral Church of St. Mary - 224

NEWCASTLE—The Cathedral Church of St. Nicholas - 226

NORWICH—The Cathedral Church of the Holy Trinity 227
The See, 227; commencement of present Cathedral, 227; the Plan, 229; damage by fire and storm; improvements to Lighting, 235; making the Cathedral fireproof, 237; Vaulting, 238; the Interior, 240.

OXFORD—The Cathedral Church of Christ - - 243
St. Frideswide, 243; FIRST PERIOD, 245; Saxon Remains, 245; SECOND PERIOD, 245; Augustinian Establishment, 245; the Twelfth-Century Cathedral, 246; the East End, 247; THIRD PERIOD, 250; Tower and Chapter House, 250; FOURTH PERIOD, 251; Lighting, 251; St. Catherine's Chapel, 252; FIFTH PERIOD, 252; Vaulting the Choir, 253; SIXTH PERIOD, 254; Foundation of Bishopric, 254; Chronological Notes, 255.

PETERBOROUGH—The Cathedral Church of St. Peter 257
Establishment of the Monastery, 257; Legendary History, 257; FIRST PERIOD, 259; destruction of Saxon Church by Fire, 259; SECOND PERIOD, 260; commencement of Present Cathedral, 260; THIRD PERIOD, 261; Transepts and Nave, 262; FOURTH PERIOD, 264; extension of Nave, 264; New West Transept, 265; FIFTH PERIOD, 265; SIXTH PERIOD, 265; the West Front, 266; SEVENTH PERIOD, 268; Lady Chapel, 268; EIGHTH PERIOD, 268; Norman Tower, 268; Lighting, 268; NINTH PERIOD, 269; Windows, 269; TENTH PERIOD, 270; Procession Path and Chapels, 270; ELEVENTH PERIOD, 271; Parliamentarian mal-treatment, 271.

xviii   CONTENTS

                                                                                  PAGE

RIPON—The Cathedral Church of St. Peter and St. Wilfrid - - - - - - -   272

FIRST PERIOD, 272; the Seventh-Century Church, 272; SECOND PERIOD, 273; the Norman Church, 273; THIRD PERIOD, 274; the Cathedral rebuilt, 274; St Wilfrid's Shrine, 275; the Nave, 275; Central Tower and Choir, 276; FOURTH PERIOD, 279; the West Front, 279; FIFTH PERIOD, 279; the East End, 279; SIXTH PERIOD, 280; Sedilia and Lady Chapel, 280; SEVENTH PERIOD, 280; collapse of Central Tower, 281; Woodwork, 282; EIGHTH PERIOD, 282; addition of Aisles, 282; NINTH PERIOD, removal of Spires, 282.

ROCHESTER—The Cathedral Church of St. Andrew -   283

St Augustine's Mission, 283; FIRST PERIOD, 284; the Early Church, 284; SECOND PERIOD, 284; the Norman Cathedral, 284; THIRD PERIOD, 286; the Nave, 287; the West Front, 287; FOURTH PERIOD, 288; Eastern Limb Rebuilt, 288; FIFTH PERIOD, 290; extension of Choir, 290; SIXTH PERIOD, 290; SEVENTH PERIOD, 290; Central Tower, 290; EIGHTH PERIOD, 290; NINTH PERIOD, 290; removal of Southern Tower, 290; St. William, 291; TENTH PERIOD, 292; various Works, 292; ELEVENTH PERIOD, 292; Lighting Improved, 292; TWELFTH PERIOD, 293; Enlargement of Lady Chapel and South Transept, 293; THIRTEENTH PERIOD, 293; Tower and Spire replaced, 293.

ST. ALBANS—The Cathedral Church of St. Alban -   294

General Survey, 294; Benedictine Foundation, 298; the Ritualistic Divisions, 299; FIRST PERIOD, 301; Norman Work, 301; Norman Nave, 302; Aisles and Transepts, 303; SECOND PERIOD, 304; Arcade and Doorway, 304; THIRD PERIOD, 305; the West Front, 305; FOURTH PERIOD, 305; Westernmost Bays, 305; FIFTH PERIOD, 306; Sanctuary, 306; Chapels, 307; SIXTH PERIOD, 307; the Lady Chapel, 307; SEVENTH PERIOD, 307; collapse of Nave and restoration, 307; EIGHTH PERIOD, 307; Minor Works, 308.

CONTENTS xix

PAGE

SALISBURY—The Cathedral Church of St. Mary - 310

The Norman Cathedral, 310; commencement of the Present Cathedral, 312; comparative Survey of the Cathedral, 312-316; the Plan, 316; the Tower and Spire, 317; the External Aspect, 320; the Lighting, 325; the Interior, 326; the East End, 328.

SOUTHWARK—The Cathedral Church of St. Saviour - 331

Foundation of St. Mary Overie, 331; Establishment as Augustinian Priory, 331; FIRST PERIOD, 332; Norman remains, 332; SECOND PERIOD, 333: rebuilding Eastern and Western Limbs, 333; the Presbytery, 334; the Nave, 335; THIRD PERIOD, 335; FOURTH PERIOD, 336; the Lady Chapel, 336; FIFTH PERIOD, 337; Tracery, 337; SIXTH PERIOD, 338; Reredos and Western Façade, 338; MINOR DETAILS, 338.

SOUTHWELL—The Cathedral Church of St. Mary - 342

Foundation of the See, 342; FIRST PERIOD, 343; SECOND PERIOD, 343; THIRD PERIOD, 344; the Norman Church, 344; FOURTH PERIOD, 348; the Exterior of the Eastern Limb, 348; the Choir, 349; FIFTH PERIOD, 353; SIXTH PERIOD, 353; Cloister, 353; SEVENTH PERIOD, 353; Chapter House, 353; EIGHTH PERIOD, 354; Choir Screen, 354; NINTH PERIOD, 355; Tracery, 355; TENTH PERIOD, 355; Minor Works, 355.

WAKEFIELD—The Cathedral Church of All Saints - 357

WELLS—The Cathedral Church of St. Andrew - 360

Its Charming Aspect, 360; FIRST PERIOD, 364; Norman remains, 364; SECOND PERIOD, 364; commencement of Present Cathedral, 364; the Design, 366; Vaulting, 367; the Lighting System, 369; order of execution, 372; THIRD PERIOD, 373; the Western Façade, 374; Western Chapels, 376; FOURTH PERIOD, 376; the Chapter House, 377; FIFTH PERIOD, 377; extension of Choir, 378; Lady Chapel, 379; Central Tower heightened, 381; SIXTH PERIOD, 382; the Western Towers heightened, 382; the present Cloisters, 382.

CONTENTS

WINCHESTER—The Cathedral Church of the Holy and Indivisible Trinity - - - - - 384
Proportions of the Cathedral, 384; FIRST PERIOD, 387; Remains of the Early Church, 387; the Crypt, 390; South Transept, 390; the Central Tower, 391; SECOND PERIOD, 391; Norman Doorway and Font, 391; THIRD PERIOD, 392; Retro-Choir, 392; Chapel of Holy Sepulchre, 393; Stalls, 393; FOURTH PERIOD, 393; restoration of Presbytery, 394; FIFTH PERIOD, 395; Re-erection of Nave, 395; SIXTH PERIOD, 401; the East End, 401; Langton's Chantry, 402; the Ritualistic Division, 403.

WORCESTER—The Cathedral Church of Christ and the Blessed Mary the Virgin of Worcester - - 404
Establishment of Benedictine Order, 404; FIRST PERIOD, 406; Anglo-Norman Church, 406; SECOND PERIOD, 408; CHAPTER HOUSE, 408; THIRD PERIOD, 409; completion of Nave, 409; FOURTH PERIOD, 412; repairs through damage by fire, 412; FIFTH PERIOD, 413; St. Wulfstan, 413; The Presbytery, 414; Lady Chapel, 415; completion of East End, 417; SIXTH PERIOD, 418; lower part of Tower rebuilt, 419; SEVENTH PERIOD, 419; Bishop Cobham's minor Works, 420; EIGHTH PERIOD, 421; Cloisters and upper part of Tower rebuilt, 421; NINTH PERIOD, 421; Vaultings, 422; TENTH PERIOD, 422; remodelling of Chapter House, 423; Prince Arthur's Chantry, 423; ELEVENTH PERIOD, 423; Jacobean Pulpit, 423; TWELFTH PERIOD, 423; Modern Furniture, etc., 423; tour of the Cloister, 424.

YORK—The Cathedral Church of St. Peter - - - 426
FIRST PERIOD, 428; South Transept, 428; SECOND PERIOD, 430; the Nave, 430; THIRD PERIOD, 433; Chapter House, 433; FOURTH PERIOD, 433; extensions to the East, 433; the exterior aspect, 437.

THE WELSH CATHEDRALS—
BANGOR - - - - - - - 442
The Norman Church, 442; work of Bishop Anian, 442-3; destruction by fire, 445; Restorations, 445.

CONTENTS

THE WELSH CATHEDRALS—*Continued*

LLANDAFF - - - - - - - 446

FIRST PERIOD, 447; Urban's Norman Cathedral, 447-456; SECOND PERIOD, 456; completion of Urban's Cathedral, 456; THIRD PERIOD, 460; Campanile and Chapter House, 460; FOURTH PERIOD, 460; Lady Chapel, 460; FIFTH PERIOD, 461; Improvements to Lighting, 461; SIXTH PERIOD, 462; New Doorways, 462; SEVENTH PERIOD, 462; North-West Tower, 462; EIGHTH PERIOD, 463; Restorations, 463.

ST. ASAPH'S - - - - - - - 464

ST. DAVID'S - - - - - - - 466

FIRST PERIOD, 466; commencement of the Present Church, 466; the Aisles, 468; SECOND PERIOD, 468; Presbytery and Transepts remodelled, 469; THIRD PERIOD, 470; De Leia's Church, 470; FOURTH PERIOD, 471; Chapel of St Thomas the Martyr, 471; Shrines, 471; FIFTH PERIOD, 471; the Chantry, 471; SIXTH PERIOD, 471; the Chapels, 472; SEVENTH PERIOD, 473; Woodwork, 473; EIGHTH PERIOD, 473; completion of Eastern Chapels, 473; Exterior, 474.

MODERN CATHEDRALS—

BIRMINGHAM - - - - - - - 477

LIVERPOOL - - - - - - - 479

TRURO - - - - - - - 483

INDEX - - - - - - - - 487

CLASSIFICATION OF THE CATHEDRALS

THIRTEEN CATHEDRALS OF THE OLD FOUNDATION (Pre-Conquest).—Bangor, Chichester, Exeter, Hereford, Lichfield, Lincoln, Llandaff, London, St. Asaph, St. David's, Salisbury, Wells, York. These were served by secular canons. Not being served by monks, they required none of the monastic buildings, except the chapter-house. Some, however, have cloisters. The establishments of these cathedrals were not suppressed, as were other ecclesiastical colleges, at the Reformation.

THIRTEEN CATHEDRALS OF THE NEW FOUNDATION.—
(*a*) *Pre-Reformation Sees.* Seven cathedrals attached to Benedictine monasteries—viz., Canterbury, Durham, Ely, Norwich, Rochester, Winchester, Worcester; one, Carlisle, attached to a house of Augustinian canons.

(*b*) *Sees founded by Henry VIII.*, who converted into cathedrals three Benedictine churches—viz., Chester, Gloucester, and Peterborough; and two Augustinian churches—viz., Bristol and Oxford.

All the above thirteen churches ceased at the Reformation to be served by monks or regular canons, and received a new foundation of dean and secular canons.

TEN CATHEDRALS OF MODERN FOUNDATION.—Birmingham, Liverpool, Manchester, Newcastle, Ripon, St. Albans, Southwark, Southwell, Truro, Wakefield.

ELEVEN CHURCHES OF BENEDICTINE MONKS.—Canterbury, Chester, Durham, Ely, Gloucester, Norwich, Peterborough, Rochester, Winchester, Worcester, St. Albans.

FOUR CHURCHES OF REGULAR CANONS OF THE AUGUSTINIAN ORDER.—Bristol, Carlisle, Oxford, Southwark.

THREE COLLEGIATE CHURCHES OF SECULAR CANONS.—Manchester, Ripon, Southwell; in addition to the thirteen cathedrals of the Old Foundation.

THE CATHEDRALS OF ENGLAND AND WALES

INTRODUCTION

THE following pages are an attempt to make the study of the English cathedrals more interesting. Every ancient building has a life-history of its own, and should be studied biographically But open a guide-book, or visit the different portions of a cathedral (Winchester, for example) in the regulation order, and what you read of or see will probably be, first, what was done in the nave in the latter part of the fourteenth and in the fifteenth century; then the work done in the crossing in the twelfth century; then work done in the transepts in the eleventh century; then the work in the choir in the first half of the fourteenth century; then the work done in the retro-choir early in the thirteenth century; finally, sixteenth-century work in the Lady chapel. To the reader this hop, skip, and jump method—if it deserves to be called a method—is simply maddening. For the visitor it has one merit, and one merit only: it saves his legs. It is not desired, however, to save the visitor's legs; it must candidly be confessed that the biographical method of studying a cathedral involves a certain amount of marching and countermarching. It is to be hoped that there are some visitors who will not be deterred by a little additional bodily fatigue from studying the cathedrals aright. With what horror a reader would study a biography of the Great Duke which commenced with the Peninsular War, then described his school-days at Eton, followed these up by the battle of Waterloo, digressed into a description of his childhood and ancestry, described his career as a Tory Prime Minister, and wound up with his campaigns in India! Yet that is how the English cathedrals are studied.

But it is not sufficient to study the different parts of a cathedral in chronological order. It would be a dull biography of a man, and a dull history of a people, which put events correctly in chronological order, but did not point out the causal connection between them. It is just when we reach this point that the real interest begins. It does not interest one much to hear that an acquaintance whom we saw in London in the spring is now in the Australian bush: it does interest one when one hears that he had to leave the country because three months ago he was detected cheating at cards. So, in a cathedral, it is not enough to know that such a vault was put up or such a row of windows inserted in the fifteenth century. We want to know why the cathedral people constructed the vault or the windows just then; also, why they were not satisfied with what was there before; also, what was there before. And with the latter query comes in a fine field of action for what is called the "constructive imagination."

On the motives which influenced mediæval builders considerable stress is laid throughout the book, simply because, if it has occurred at all to writers to ask why such and such a change was made, the answer usually has been —the quotation is from an article on one of the cathedrals— "simply a desire for what was thought a far superior kind of beauty led to the alteration of this work": *i.e.*, the Gothic builders were æsthetic dilettanti, striving after prettiness for prettiness' sake; on a level with painters and poets and musicians. Now, some changes were due, it must be admitted, to æsthetic considerations simply: *e.g.*, the substitution of the present choir for the former twelfth century choir at York; so also one of every pair of towers at the west end of a cathedral; and every spire in the country.

But the more the history of the cathedrals is studied, the more clearly it will be seen that the great majority of

INTRODUCTION 3

the alterations in the structure were forced on the ecclesiastical authorities of the day by practical considerations. The monastery was large, as at Canterbury, and the church the seat of an archbishop; Lanfranc's short choir had to

YORK CHOIR

be replaced by a longer one. Saint-worship increased; pilgrimages increased; pilgrims came in thousands and tens of thousands. They could not be accommodated in the crypts as before; room had to be found on the floor of the choir for shrines transferred from the crypt; and aisles had to be constructed round the shrines, that there might be a free passage, and no dangerous block in the stream of pilgrims. For the local saint—the St. Thomas of Canterbury, the St. Hugh of Lincoln—accommodation on a vast scale had to be provided. But beside the local saints, there were the great saints of the Church; for them special chapels, with altars, had to be provided, either in a new eastern transept or in the aisles of a central transept. There was, moreover, especially in the first half of the thirteenth century, a great increase in the number and dimensions of Lady chapels. For these reasons, then —what we may call ritualistic reasons— vast eastern extensions were made in nearly every cathedral.

CLERESTORY OF SOUTH SIDE OF CHOIR, NORWICH

But the original Norman cathedrals were not only small and inconvenient to the east, but were throughout very badly lighted; a very large amount of history, as is pointed out in speaking of Gloucester, Hereford, and Norwich, consists of attempts to improve the lighting of the cathedral. Sometimes, indeed, the improvement took the shape of total destruction of the old gloomy church, and its replacement by a brilliantly illuminated successor, as at York. Connected with this was the mania for an increased acreage of stained glass—an æsthetic motive, which, however, had its practical side; the stained glass justifying itself to the monks and canons as providing a series of lessons in Scripture history or Church history.

Many changes were due to damage from fire or storm,

ELY CHOIR

or to jerry building. The clerestory of Norwich had to be rebuilt because it had been crushed by the fall of the spire. The Norwich monks were driven to fire-proof the whole church, because fires in 1463 and 1509 shewed them the necessity of it, by burning down successively the wooden roofs, first of the nave and choir, then of the transept. If our documentary evidence were not so deplorably incomplete, we should find that very many other alterations were due to the effect of fire and tempest: in which case the list of æsthetic changes would be yet further cut down.

ST. ALBAN'S NAVE

Add to these causes the frequent collapses due to mediæval jerry-building, both Norman and Gothic. Many central towers collapsed—e.g., at Winchester, Ripon, Ely, Peterborough, Lincoln; and doubtless there were collapses of many other towers, of which we have no record. Hence, for example, the fourteenth-century choir of Ely. Whole sections of a cathedral tumbled down—e.g., in St. Alban's nave. The early masonry was but skin-deep; inside the thin casing of ashlar the core of piers and walls alike crumbled into powder; foundations were insufficient, or were omitted altogether. The object was, but too often, not to build soundly, but to build as quickly as possible.

As regards the nomenclature of the parts of a cathedral,

it may be useful to mention that the high altar is to the east; and that, facing the east, the visitor has the south transept and south aisles on his right, and the north transept and north aisles on his left hand. Standing at the altar or the choir-screen, and looking down the nave to the great doors, he has the north transept and north aisle of the nave on his right, and the south transept and south aisle of the nave on his left.

The western limb of the cathedral is called the nave. The term "choir" is sometimes loosely applied to the whole of the eastern limb. Strictly it applies just to that part of the church where the stalls are; and that part, as in St. Alban's and Norwich, need not necessarily be in the eastern limb at all, but in the crossing and in the easternmost bays of the nave. In a cathedral with a fully developed plan—e.g., St. Alban's or Winchester—the following ritualistic divisions will be met with in passing from west to east:—
(1) The nave; (2) the choir; (3) the presbytery or sanctuary;

THE TRIFORIUM OF LINCOLN RETROCHOIR

(4) the retrochoir, containing (a) Saint's chapel or feretory, (b) procession path, (c) Lady chapel. Sometimes these ritualistic divisions correspond with the architectural divisions of the church; sometimes they do not: e.g., the ritualistic divisions of the eastern limbs of York and Lincoln were not shown in the structure, but merely marked off by screens, most of which have been destroyed.

As a rule, architectural detail is not described. The visitor to the cathedral does not need the description; the reader does not need it, if he has an illustration before him; if he has not, no amount of verbiage will make clear to him what, for instance, a bay of the Angel triforium of Lincoln is like.

The writer has followed the convenient custom of ascribing the design of different parts of the cathedrals to various bishops and abbots and priors. Such names, however, are merely convenient chronological fixtures, not intended to signify that the dignitaries of the church personally designed and erected them, but simply that they were in office when the work was done.

THE CATHEDRAL CHURCH OF THE HOLY AND UNDIVIDED TRINITY, BRISTOL

BUILT FOR AUGUSTINIAN CANONS

BRISTOL CATHEDRAL was originally a church of the Regular Canons of the Augustinian Order, who settled at Bristol in 1142. These canons were Regulars; *i.e.*, they lived in accordance with a *regula* or code, which in their case was based on the precepts of St. Augustine of Hippo. Like monks, they lived a cœnobitic life; but unlike monks, they are found taking part in parochial work, and the naves of their churches were open, much more than those of monks, for lay use; moreover, they were all of them priests, whereas at this period monks as a rule were laymen. The staircase in the south transept is that by which they descended from their dormitory into church for the service of matins at or soon after midnight. Their chapter house remains on the east side of the cloister; and on the south side the fine thirteenth-century doorway to their refectory. The principal entrance to their precincts was by the great gateway, which appears to have been rebuilt, but with the same Norman detail, *c.* 1515. Another rich Norman gateway, strengthened about the same time, in Lower College Green led to the Abbot's hall. The good lord Sir Robert and Lady Eva his wife, up to the Dissolution, had an anniversary with special services and great giving of alms to the canons, their servants, and to poor men and prisoners; also daily intercession was made for them both in church and chapter house.

In 1542, like the Augustinian churches of Carlisle and Oxford, it became a cathedral. In 1836 the diocese was united to that of Gloucester; in 1897 it resumed its independent status.

FIRST PERIOD.—The Norman church, begun in 1142, is said, somewhat doubtfully, to have been consecrated in 1148. In 1155 its founder, Robert Fitzharding, ancestor of the Fitzhardings of Berkeley castle, received a grant of the forfeited estates of Roger de Berkeley, and with these additional resources would be able to carry out the work with the increased richness of detail which is noteworthy in the Chapter house. The church had an aisled nave which, internally, was 109 ft. long, and, including the aisles, 56 ft. broad; a transept; and a presbytery with aisles which were about one-third narrower than at present. The presbytery was three bays long. At the end of the third bay from the central tower a straight wall was found beneath the pavement in 1894; but as no measurements were taken, it is impossible to say whether it was the foundation of the main east wall of the church, or merely the sleeping wall of

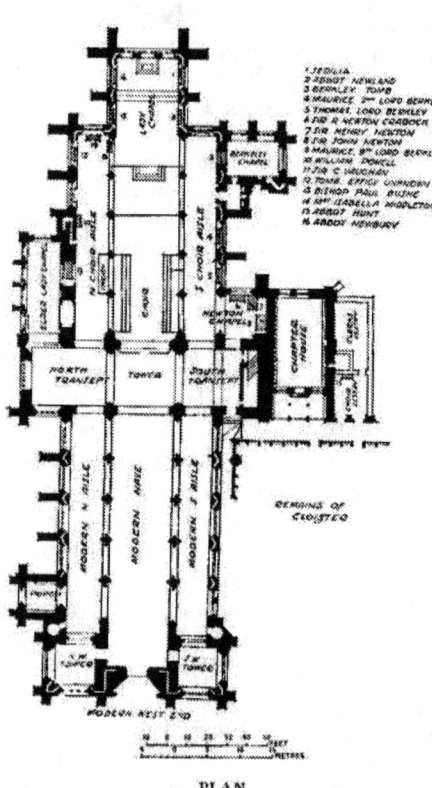

PLAN

a central apse or of an arch or arches leading into a procession path. The church provided a spacious nave for the laity; as well as a choir, probably placed in the crossing, and a presbytery, for the daily services of the canons. In 1491 there were ten canons in priest's orders and eight novices.

Here and there the work begun by the founder, Robert Fitzharding, survives. This includes (1) the end wall of the south transept. Inside the transept are two Norman cushion-corbels supporting later capitals. (2) Outside the south transept are flat pilaster buttresses at the angles; the set-off of the ancient parapet; and a plain gable window, set in a rough wall, on which may be seen the weathering of the original steep roof. (3) The coursed masonry below the big window of the north transept. (4) The lower part of the tower-piers; for their moldings, as in the earlier remodelling of Winchester nave, are those of a Norman compound pier. (5) The corbels reused in the staircase on the north side of the choir. (6) The two gatehouses. (7) The Chapter house, which is said to have been one bay longer to the east, and to have had an eastern apse; but Archdeacon Norris had a hole dug, 6 ft. deep, in a line with the south wall, and no foundations of an eastern wall were found. (8) In the vestibule to the Chapter house, the bays being oblong, pointed arches were used on the short sides of each bay, so

THE CHAPTER HOUSE

that their crowns might rise to the same height as those of the semicircular arches on the longer sides, as the builders thought was demanded by the requirements of vaulting. In the same way, beneath the central towers of Oxford Cathedral and Bolton Priory, pointed arches were built over the narrow transepts; while over the broader nave and choir the semicircular arch was employed. The vestibule must be well advanced in the third quarter of the twelfth century.

THE ELDER LADY CHAPEL.

SECOND PERIOD. —The Norman church must have been dark, and preparations were made to improve the lighting of the north transept by the insertion of a big window in its north wall. The tracery of the present window is later; but its inner jambs, moldings, and shafts, and the external cill and string, as well as a great part of the buttresses, seem to have been executed $c.$ 1250. In the same century a beautiful Lady chapel was built, projecting eastward from the north transept, and separated by a few feet from the north wall of the choir. The same position was adopted later for the Lady chapels of Peterborough and Ely. This chapel is the artistic gem of the cathedral; it is surrounded by arcades of the greatest beauty, with sculptured grotesques interspersed among the scrolls of the foliage. Later on it received the name of the elder Lady chapel; another Lady chapel having been built in the more normal position at the extreme east of the choir. The chapel is earlier than 1253, for in that year ex-abbot David was buried in it. Abbot Bradeston (1234-1236) founded a chantry in it, and may have built the chapel; or it may be the work of his predecessor, David (1225-1234). It was originally without a vault. The present vault has a ridge rib, the ribs are molded on the chamfer plane, and the bosses are some of naturalistic, and some of undulatory foliage. The east window has tracery of rather advanced geometrical type; it is of earlier type than in Knowle's work, begun in 1298; probably both vault and window are *c.* 1290. The addition of the vault ultimately necessitated the reconstruction of the buttresses and the pinnacles, probably in the fifteenth century. Of the original pinnacles only one, at the north-eastern corner, remains. The southern entrance to the Lady chapel was probably added in 1491.

THIRD PERIOD.—The great building period at Bristol commences in 1298, when Edmund Knowle was Treasurer, and includes the abbacy both of Knowle himself (1306-1332), and of John Snow (1332-1341). In their time the canons set to work to rebuild the whole church from east to west. The Norman transepts do not appear to have been touched; but the whole of the eastern limb with its chapels was completed, and at least one bay of the nave; it is likely also that the foundations of the whole of a new nave were laid outside of and not interfering with the Norman nave, and that a new west front was commenced. The system of construction adopted is very remarkable and makes the church quite unique among our cathedrals. All other cathedral authorities had agreed long ago that the cardinal fault in the earlier vaulted churches was the bad system of lighting, but that the remedy was to be found mainly in improving the top-lighting—*i.e.*, in increasing the dimensions of the clerestory. Beverley clerestory had taller windows than Durham; Salisbury clerestory had three windows for every one of Beverley; Exeter spread out its windows in increasing breadth till they touched the buttresses on either side; the clerestories of the choir of Gloucester, now about to be erected, were a vast, lofty, continuous sheet of glass. But there was an alternative system of improving the lighting, which in parish churches, such as Grantham, Ledbury, and Leominster, was the result of fortuitous growth. It was to magnify the aisles at the expense of the nave, to lift them up so high that windows of vast height could be placed in their walls, to dispense with a clerestory altogether, and to give to the pier-arcade of the nave the additional height gained by the suppression of the clerestory. It was to substitute side-lighting for top-lighting; to rely exclusively on the flood of light passing from vast, lofty aisle windows into the nave through elevated arches. Hence the big windows of Bristol choir, each representing a pair of windows; the lower half the usual small window of an aisle, the upper half the larger window which elsewhere would be found in the clerestory.

But the new design had another merit, which probably weighed still more with the Bristol builders. The cardinal difficulty of the mediæval builders was how to keep up on the top of lofty clerestory walls a heavy stone vault which was always striving to push them asunder. They succeeded at length in keeping the clerestory walls from being thrust out by propping them up with flying buttresses, perilously exposed, however, to all the vicissitudes of English weather. But there was another solution of the problem. It was to stop the outward thrusts of the nave vault, not by the combined resistance of buttress, pinnacle, and flying buttress, but by bringing into play opposing thrusts—*i.e.*, the inward thrusts of vaults built over the aisles. But to make these outward and inward thrusts exactly balance and neutralise one another, the aisle vaults must be of the same height and span as those of the nave. The nave must be lowered or the aisles must be raised, or both. At Bristol the architect has preferred to raise the aisles. Then, the stability of the nave vault being secured, all the builder has to do is to stop the outward thrusts of the vaults of the aisles. This it is easy enough to do by a row of buttresses weighted with pinnacles. So Bristol Cathedral, to eyes

THE CHOIR

accustomed to contemporary cathedrals, presents the strange solecism of having neither triforium, clerestory, nor flying buttresses.

There was one further difficulty. Where nave and aisles were of the same span, the opposing thrusts of their vaults might be made to balance one another exactly. But at Bristol the nave is nearly twice as broad as each aisle, and the outward thrusts of its vaults, if no remedy were applied, would quite overpower the inward thrusts of the vaults of the narrow aisles. The latter vaults, therefore, had to be reinforced. This might have been done by inserting internal flying buttresses. The effect, however, would have been ugly. Instead of this, the architect puts a stone beam or transom across, and props it up with a pointed arch. This transom effectually prevents the piers from bulging towards the aisle. Here and there a similar system was adopted elsewhere, e.g., in the choir of the Temple church, London. In France one great architectural school, what the French call the Plantagenet school, because at the period of its dominance the English Plantagenets ruled in Anjou and Poitou, normally constructed their churches in this fashion, with parallel naves of similar height and span, and destitute of triforium and clerestory; one of the most important of these is the cathe-

THE SOUTH AISLE

dral of Poitiers, in which Eleanor of Guienne, Queen of Henry II., had a hand. But it is not necessary to go abroad for precedents. Many a monastic refectory and chapter house had two or three parallel aisles of the same height and span, and these were constructed without clerestories or flying buttresses, adequate light being obtainable from windows in the end and side walls.

In the new work the altar stood in the same position as at present; this is proved by the fact that over it is a vaulting arch more important than the rest, and that west of it the centre-pieces of the lierne vaults are cusped, while to the east they are not. The bay at the back of it formed the procession path; next came a new unaisled Lady chapel of two bays, with an axis deviating 5 ft. to the north. South of the Lady chapel is a double chapel, the Berkeley chapel. The molds and ornaments agree with those of Knowle's work, but it is an afterthought. It was built after the south aisle wall was erected, and so an entrance had to be contrived from the sacristy, and not direct from the aisle; its east wall does not line with that of the aisle, and it has a different external plinth. Probably Knowle's original plan was to have an altar in the eastern bay of each choir aisle; but as this would have blocked the procession path, a double chapel was built to hold the two altars. Knowle is specifically recorded to have built the sacristy, so we may perhaps attribute the Berkeley chapel to Snow. The latter is the only one of the abbots who was enrolled among the abbot-benefactors, and he was buried, like Knowle, in front of the rood screen; we may fairly conclude that he did a good deal of the work usually ascribed to Knowle, who is merely recorded in a vague way to have "built the whole area of the church." The choir screen of the *novum opus* stood as at present under the eastern arch of the tower, and there was a rood screen under the western arch. The two western bays of the chancel formed the choir; the two eastern the presbytery.

All this was the work of a man of the highest genius; only to be paralleled by that other architect who was to commence the great work at Gloucester *c.* 1330. The design is not only remarkable as an exhibition of sound and original engineering which has stood stable to this day, but because it reveals high artistic qualities. This chancel, with arches rising to the height of 52 ft., beyond those of any other of our cathedrals, full of light and spaciousness and atmosphere, is as interesting in detail as it is in its general *ensemble*. There is indeed no triforium or clerestory, but at the level of the window cills runs a continuous wall passage, as in Henry III.'s work at Westminster. Externally, the ground course, buttress and pinnacle are a vigorous and fresh composition; above, where is now a battlement, there seems originally to have reigned a pierced parapet of singular beauty. The piers as seen on plan, are an entire novelty, and were to be copied all over England in later Gothic. The capitals, corbels, and bosses are admirable examples of the transition from naturalistic to undulatory foliage. The skeleton vaulting of the sacristy is a novelty, speedily copied at St. David's. The stellate tomb-recesses, also reproduced at St. David's, are also original, though we may cite something similar in the western procession doorway of Norwich nave. The reredos and sedilia of the Lady chapel are of the richest and most novel design. So is the eastern window, from which were evolved the designs of the windows of St. Mary Redcliffe. (Unlike the rest of the windows, the mullions and tracery are not bonded into the cill, jambs, and arch, but were inserted subsequently.) Not content with further renderings of oak, maple, vine, and the like, the carver reproduces pomegranates, medlars, maple seeds, and ammonites. Ammonites occur in abundance at Keynsham a few miles away, and were believed to be snakes which had been turned into stone by St. Keyne, who had a hermitage there; one of the altars in the Berkeley chapel may have been dedicated to her. In the head of the east window and in the side windows of the Lady chapel fine original glass remains, which the heraldry shews was made between 1312 and 1322. In the sacristy there are three recesses; the eastern one has a well-built flue to carry off the charcoal fumes produced in baking the sacramental wafers on a brazier; or it may have been employed when the charcoal for the censers was being kindled. Its chimney may be seen outside. Opposite is a long cupboard for the abbot's crosier. Formerly there was a room for the sacristan above the Berkeley chapel; the stairs remain in the corner of the chapel, but the roof has been flattened and the room has gone.

The Newton chapel in the south aisle is also an afterthought; for though the masonry of its east wall is coursed exactly with that of the south wall of the aisle, there is a straight joint between the two. Knowle's string of ball flower appears within, but there is no ball flower in the tracery of the east window, and it has supermullions; it would seem that the east wall is part of the work of Knowle and Snow, but that the window was not inserted till late in the fourteenth century; to which date also probably belongs the simple quadripartite vaulting in the chapel and the adjoining bay of the aisle.

FOURTH PERIOD.—From the middle of the fifteenth century up to the Dissolution important work was going on. The bishop of Bath and Wells in 1466 leased to the canons a quarry at Dundry, Somerset; with this stone probably the central tower was built; old prints shew that it once had pinnacles. To the end of this century and the first part of the next belongs the remodelling of the transepts. Much was done by Abbot Nailheart or Newland, who ruled the abbey from 1481 to 1515; the best thing he did was to leave behind him a chronicle of the history of the abbey. He went on with the new nave begun by Knowle and Snow, both working at the west front and carrying up the walls of the north aisle to the cills of the windows. He is buried on the south side of the western bay of the Lady chapel; his rebus is, "a bleeding heart with three nails." Across the entrance of the Lady chapel originally there was a screen carrying an organ, like that remaining at Ottery St. Mary. (Near Newland's tomb is a brass plate in memory of Joseph Butler, the author of "The Analogy of

Religion"; he was bishop of Bristol from 1738 to 1750.) To the sixteenth century belongs the remodelling of the great gateway, c. 1515. To Abbot William Burton is due the cresting of the reredos in the Lady chapel, on which appear his initial and rebus, "burs on a tun." Between 1542 and 1547 was erected a handsome stone choir screen; this was demolished in 1860 by Dean Elliott, who did much work in the cathedral, both good and evil part of

EXTERIOR FROM THE NORTH-EAST

the screen has recently been re-erected as a parclose screen to the south side of the chancel.

FIFTH PERIOD.—At the Dissolution the original dedication to St. Augustine was abolished. Either at or after the Dissolution, all the nave walls were removed; both those of Snow and Newland as well as those of Fitzharding, if the latter were still standing. Between 1868 and 1888 was built the present nave with the west front; the interior is successful, but is greatly darkened by inferior local glass. In 1899 the reredos of the presbytery was erected, and in 1905 the choir screen; both designed by Mr Pearson.

BIBLIOGRAPHY. — Mr Godwin's paper on Bristol Cathedral in *Archæological Journal*, vol. xx.

Mr C. Winston in the Bristol volume of the *British Archæological Institute*.

Dallaway's edition of notes made by *William of Worcester*, c. 1480.

Mr R. H. Warren in *Clifton Antiquarian Society*, v. 167.

Mr T. S. Pope in *Clifton Antiquarian Society*, i. 251.

THE CATHEDRAL OF CHRIST CHURCH, CANTERBURY

BUILT FOR BENEDICTINE MONKS

OF all our cathedrals none is of such absorbing interest as Canterbury. It is vast in scale; the problems presented by the incorporation of fragments of its predecessors are fascinating to the antiquary; its eastern limb as set out in the eleventh century changed the whole direction of English church planning; its twelfth-century successor introduced into England important features of the Gothic architecture of France; and laid the foundations of the south-eastern school of English Gothic; in spite of much destruction its walls yet hold a wealth of noble monuments, unequalled except at Westminster; it has preserved treasures of early glass beyond compare; important portions of its monastic buildings survive; it has one of the noblest central towers in the world; like Gloucester, its masses group magnificently seen far away; finally great historical scenes have been enacted within its walls—above all, that greatest of all historical tragedies to the mind of the mediæval Englishman, the murder of Becket. To Canterbury, as in the days of old, every Englishman owes a pilgrimage.

FIRST PERIOD.—Of the pre-Conquest cathedrals of Canterbury nothing remains, unless it be fragments of rude masonry in crypt and cloister. In 1067 the last Anglo-Saxon cathedral was consumed by fire. Lanfranc, the first Norman archbishop, in 1070 commenced the rebuilding of the church and monastery, and is recorded to have finished the work in seven years.

Of Lanfranc's cathedral, built, together with the Benedictine monastery, between 1070 and 1077, there remains

REFERENCES TO MONUMENTS ETC
1 CARDINAL CHATILLION
2 ARCHBISHOP COURTNEY
3 EDWARD THE BLACK PRINCE
4 ARCH^P SIMON OF MEPHAM
5 ARCH^P SUDBURY
6 ARCH^P STRATFORD
7 ARCH^P KEMPE
8 ARCH^P HUBERT WALTER
9 ARCH^P REYNOLDS
10 ARCH^P STEPHEN LANGTON
11 LADY HOLLANDS TOMB
12 SIR J. HALES
13 F. GODFREY
14 ARCH^P PECKHAM
15 ARCH^P WARHAM
16 DEAN ROGERS
17 DEAN BARGRAVE
18 DEAN TURNER
19 DEAN BOYS
20 DEAN FOTHERBY
21 ARCH^P CHICHELE
22 ARCH^P BOURCHIER
23 HENRY IV's M^T
24 DEAN WOTTON
25 CARDINAL POLE
A BECKETS SHRINE
B ORGAN SCREEN
C GREAT TOWER
D ENTRANCE TO CRYPT
E STAIRCASE
F SPOT WHERE BECKET FELL
G MARTYRDOM
H LADY CHAPEL
J S^T ANDREWS TOWER
K CONDUIT
BECKETS CROWN
HENRY IV's CHANTRY CHAPEL
VESTRY
S^T ANSELMS CHAPEL
LIBRARY
ALTAR
N W TRANSEPT
S.E TRANSEPT
N CHOIR AISLE
CHOIR
S CHOIR AISLE
CHAPTER HOUSE
S TRANSEPT
CLOISTERS
N. AISLE
NAVE
S. AISLE
S PORCH
N W. TOWER
S.W. TOWER
WEST DOOR
0 50 100 200 300
SCALE OF FEET
0 5 10 20 30 40 50 60 70 80 90
SCALE OF METRES

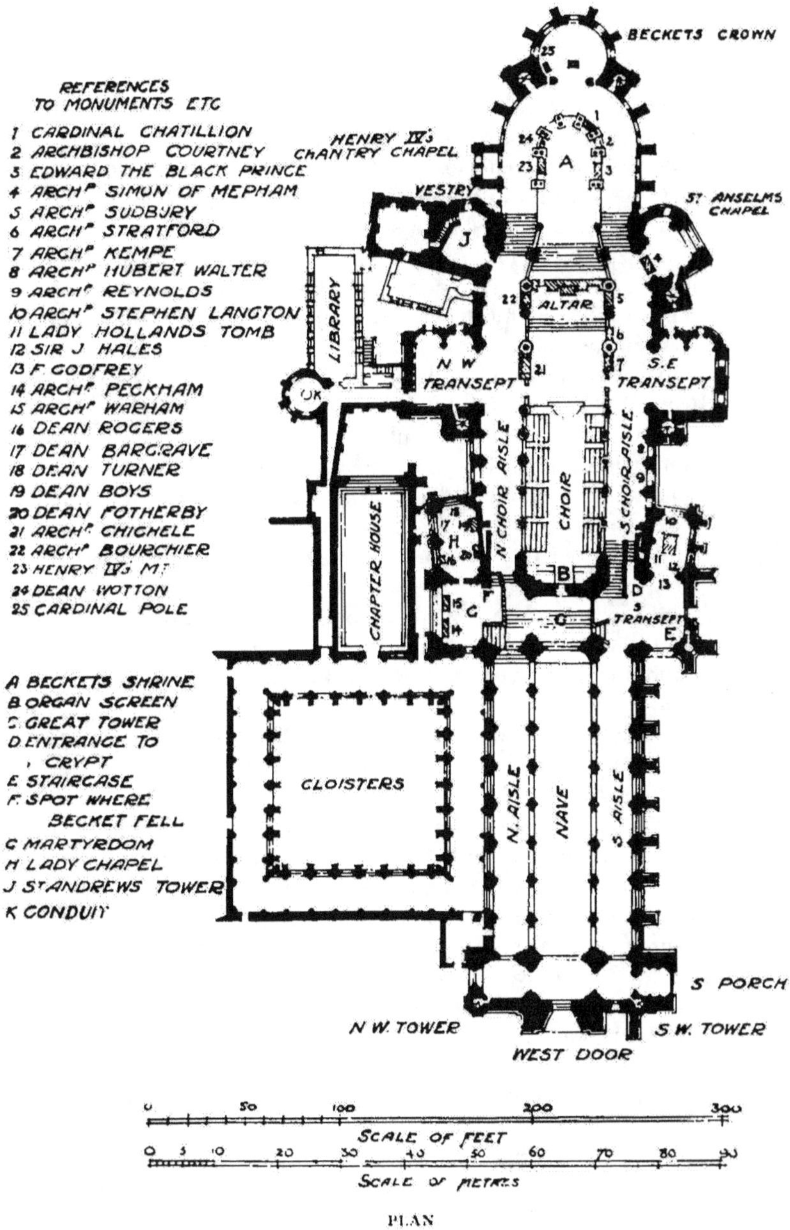

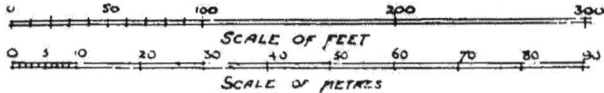

PLAN

the internal plinth of the walls of nave and transept. In the north transept some of his small square blocks of Caen stone are well seen close to the site of the martyrdom, as well as his turret in the north-west corner. (The site of the martyrdom is marked by a small square stone with a square sinking in the centre; it is near the south-east corner of the north transept). His nave and transepts were allowed to remain till the fourteenth century. Lanfranc's cathedral was an unambitious building, built in a hurry; closely copied, to save time probably, both in plan and dimensions, from William the Conqueror's abbey-church at Caen, from which Lanfranc came to rule at Canterbury. Its nave and transepts were of the same size as at present; in each transept was a vaulted gallery, as at Winchester, Ely, and the Confessor's church at Westminster; the eastern limb probably had but two bays and terminated, as also its aisles, in an apse.

SECOND PERIOD.—Such a building was altogether unworthy to be the seat of the Primate of all England and the church of a monastery in which Lanfranc had placed more than a hundred monks. The short eastern limb formed a presbytery, the transepts were without aisles, the nave was short, and a considerable part was occupied by the stalls of the monks. There was a great deficiency of chapels; and, above all, there was no procession aisle. Very soon, therefore, in 1096, the remodelling of the cathedral was undertaken, and was carried out, in the time of Archbishop Anselm, first by Prior Ernulph, and afterwards by Prior Conrad; the church, as enlarged, being finished in 1115 and reconsecrated in 1130. It was impossible to extend the church to the west, because of the western towers. The first thing to secure was that there should be no interruption in the daily services. This is expressly stated by the monastic chronicler. Accordingly, Lanfranc's eastern limb was not pulled down at first, but the new arcade was built outside the old one. This made the new presbytery considerably broader than its predecessor. Then the monks proceeded to build east of the central tower an extension which, in plan, was itself practically a complete cathedral—with nave, transept, presbytery, procession aisle, and three radiating chapels, of which the easternmost was rectangular. This vast eastern limb was longer than the nave. It was portioned out as follows. The western bays were utilised as choir, the monks' stalls being transferred to them from the crossing and eastern bays of the nave. In some churches they occupy the latter position to this day, *e.g.*, St. Alban's, Norwich, Westminster; but after this date most of the greater English churches transferred their choir to the eastern limb. This made the eastern limb of the normal English church excessively long, and differentiated it more than anything else from its continental brethren. Secondly, in each of the new eastern transepts two apsidal chapels were built, and three more larger chapels were set tangentially

NORMAN TOWER OF THE SOUTH-EAST TRANSEPT

to the procession path; thus seven eastern chapels were gained instead of the two in Lanfranc's eastern limb. Professor Willis was of opinion that the gradual acquirement of relics and the accumulation of canonised archbishops for whose shrines and tombs accommodation had to be provided was one of the principal reasons why the extension was made: this view has truth in it, but is put much too strongly. More important was the necessity

JUNCTION OF THE NORTH-EAST TRANSEPT AND CHOIR

of having numerous altars at which each of the hundred or more monks could say his individual mass each day, and the great use at all times in the English Church of processional ritual. Moreover, Canterbury was the most famous pilgrim church in England, and the procession path could be utilised to provide a way by which the crowded throng should be able to make the round of the eastern limb, viewing in turn the numerous relics exposed on the altars and the tombs of the many sainted archbishops. It is noteworthy that the north-eastern and south-eastern chapels are twisted round, so as to get the altar more nearly north and south; at Winchester they were made to point exactly due east. It is probable that the whole plan is a derivative from Lewes and ultimately from Cluny, of which the choir was begun in 1089 and consecrated in 1095, the year before Prior Ernulph began work at Canterbury. At Lewes, itself a Cluniac church, the eastern transept, procession path, and five tangential chapels were in progress between 1091 and 1098. A similar eastern extension was carried out in the thirteenth century at Bayham abbey, Sussex. Like the elongation of the eastern limb, the addition of the eastern transept found great favour in England, being reproduced at Lincoln, Rochester, Worcester, Salisbury, Beverley, and Bayham. The plan also provided what was regarded as a *sine qua non* in an English church of the first rank—a very long presbytery, long enough to hold the daily or matutinal altar as well as the high altar. So much was a spacious presbytery esteemed that even when an eastern limb had been greatly prolonged, the stalls were sometimes still left in the crossing and eastern bays of the nave, *e.g.*, at Ely. As regards planning, Ernulph's extension was by far the best in England; as regards progress in vaulting, it was far below Durham, having only groined, *i.e.*, unribbed vaults, in the aisles, and instead of a high vault merely a wooden ceiling.

Of "Conrad's glorious choir" (it was commenced by Prior Ernulph *c.* 1096 and finished *c.* 1115 by Prior Conrad) a considerable amount remains. The round-arched work in the crypt is nearly all of this date, except the carving of many of the capitals and shafts, which was executed later; and from the extent of his crypt one can plot out the exact shape and dimensions of the Norman choir. Much of his work is seen outside, especially in and near the south-east transept with its intersecting semicircular arcades, and the most charming little Norman tower imaginable. In the interior many Norman stones, "cross-hatched," may be seen in the aisle-wall immediately after entering the south choir-aisle by the flight of steps; the lower part of the vaulting-shaft in this wall, built of several stones and not of solid drums, as it is higher up, is also Norman. So also are those bases which do not possess the water-holding molding. The windows also are there, but have been heightened, their heads being reset. In the eastern transepts there are two clerestories; in the lower of the two the windows are those of Conrad's clerestory, on the top of which a second clerestory was built afterwards. To this period belongs the "Dark Entry" in the cloisters, the carved caps and bases in St. Anselm's chapel, the vaulted Treasury (now the vestry of the Chapter), the circular conduit tower, with early ribbed vaulting, the three upper courses of the transeptal towers, the infirmary chapel, the Green Court gateway, the porch and staircase of the *Aula Nova* or North Hall, and the Cemetery gate (the entrance to the present bowling green).

THE CRYPT

THIRD PERIOD.—Conrad's glorious choir was destroyed by a great fire in the year 1174, "men cursing God and his saints for the destruction of their church." Then the monks, instead of being satisfied with our home-bred English architecture, of which such beautiful examples were on the point of rising at Wells and Ripon, sent for a foreigner. The present choir of Canterbury, like that of Westminster, was "made in France." The only consolation one has is the fact—which is a fact—that with that stolid insularity which from the twelfth century has insisted on working out its own salvation in its own way—English architects largely ignored them both. The new French choir of Canterbury was to be a rock on which the main current of English art struck and parted asunder only to meet again on the other side. The one great church in which the influence of Canterbury choir was to be suspected is Lincoln, begun in 1192. In St. Hugh's work the obligations to the Canterbury design are great; but there are hardly any, with the exception of the omission of the hood mold, and the great projection of the buttresses, which are due to the French features in the Canterbury design; it is the English features that are copied, and they are very numerous. The coupled columns, the French arch-molds, the Corinthianesque capitals of Canterbury were un-English; no one would have anything to do with them anywhere, unless in the hall of Oakham.

The eastern limb, as rebuilt, was even longer than that of Conrad. The reason was precisely that which brought about the extensions at Lincoln, Durham, Westminster as elsewhere, viz., the enormous popularity of a great local saint, bringing to his shrine hosts of pilgrims, whose offerings were adequate and more than adequate to provide him with a stately mausoleum. This mausoleum or Saint's chapel was built on the site of Conrad's easternmost chapel, where Becket had sung his first mass and to the altar of which he at all times greatly resorted. It had been dedicated to the Holy Trinity, and it is possible that till 1220 the new Saint's chapel retained the old name. But in that year the relics of St. Thomas of Canterbury were translated from the crypt, where they had rested from the day of his murder in 1170, and were placed in a shrine on the Italian pavement, still existing, behind the high altar, where grooves in the stone made by kneeling pilgrims may be seen. (The pavement is *opus Alexandrinum* executed in foreign marbles, but put together by English workmen. Around are pillars of rare marble, probably presents from foreign potentates; others, also intended for this chapel, are said to have been detained at Marsala in Sicily, where they may still be seen.) From that time the chapel was known as St. Thomas' chapel till modern days, when, unfortunately, it has become usual to call it Trinity chapel once more. East of the processional aisle was built a circular chapel, intended to rise into a circular tower, which was begun but never completed. This circular chapel is called the Corona; it is probable that in it was placed a shrine containing a fragment of the skull, *corona*, of the martyr chopped off by the murderer's sword.

In the choir all the levels have been changed; the altar used to stand on the lower platform; the diaper work to the south probably is that of the backs of the sedilia.

The design of the choir is a close copy of the work at Sens, Noyon, Senlis, and the neighbouring cathedrals. Columns almost classical in proportion replace the heavy English cylinder. The coupled columns and Corinthian-esque capitals of Sens are faithfully reproduced in the Saint's chapel. The choir, as at Sens, is arranged in coupled bays with sexpartite vaulting; while principal and intermediate piers, single and compound vaulting-shafts occur alternately in either choir. In unstable French fashion the vaulting-shaft is perched on the abacus. The abacus is square, except in the eastern part of the crypt. The capitals of the choir are foliated; the English molded capital occurs only in the crypt. Each bay of the triforium in both cathedrals contains a couple of arches, each arch subdivided by a central shaft. Both cathedrals have round transverse arches in the vaulting of the aisles. The windows are not the tall slender lancets of England, but the broad squat lancets of France. The pointed arches of the apse of the Saint's chapel on their tall stilts have a thoroughly French look. French, too, is the wish to dispense with a hood-mold round the pier-arches. And, as at Noyon, flying buttresses emerge from the gloom of the triforium into the open air.

But there is another factor besides the personality of William of Sens. He had to deal with a British building committee and with British workmen; he was not given free scope. The groined vaults had saved the aisle walls from much damage by fire, and these were retained to the height of 12 ft. The monks wished to retain the

THE CHOIR, EAST

chapels of St. Anselm and St. Andrew, which had not been seriously damaged by the fire. But since they were almost in a line with his pier-arcades, he had to make the latter converge inwards, and then, after passing the two chapels, outwards, giving a most unpleasant twist to the lines of the presbytery. Again, the crypt had escaped the fire. In it were the piers on which the pillars of Conrad's arcades had rested. The monks wished to retain them as the supports of the new pillars. But it was also desired to throw the eastern transepts into the church. Till the fire each had been entered by two low arches with a pier between. This pillar was to be done away with, and a single lofty arch to be built, broader than the two arches together had been. The result was that all the western pillars had to be placed a little to the west of the positions formerly occupied, and all the eastern pillars a little to the east. Consequently all the piers in the crypt had to be strengthened either on their western or their eastern side. To the retention of the old supports is also due the unequal spacing of the arches. Some were narrow and were pointed; others were broad and were made semicircular; such a mixture of arch forms must surely have been distasteful to an architect accustomed to the advanced French design of 1174. (St. Denis had been begun in 1140, Sens c. 1155, Notre Dame, Paris, in 1163.) Again, since the lower part of the walls of the aisles was retained, while the position of the pillars was shifted, the supports of the vault in the aisle wall in many cases no longer faced the pillars; the result was that many of the bays of the new aisle-vaults were no longer rectangular, as those of the groined vaults had been, but trapezoidal, or else were truncated. Nor can the profuse use of barbaric zigzag and billet ornament be due to the French architect. On the other hand he cannot be credited with the lavish use of Purbeck marble. This was not in use in France, nor in England, except, perhaps a few years earlier, in St. Cross, Winchester. Before the century was out, the marble use passed from Canterbury to Durham, Chichester, and Christ Church, Dublin; and during the first half of the thirteenth century its detached shafts encircling the piers were adopted in almost every important church except those of the Western and Northern Gothic schools. It is interesting to watch the French William's experiments with the new shafts; working as he did from west to east, he is constantly trying new combinations of pier and shaft, and with increasing success. At the beginning of the fifth year of his work, William of Sens was seriously injured by a fall from the scaffold, and soon after returned to France. He had completed the eastern limb, including the high vault, as far as the east end of the eastern transepts, and all the upper parts of the external walls. An English William was appointed to succeed him. He completed St. Thomas' chapel, Becket's Corona, and the crypt beneath the two. It is usual to attribute to the English William an important part in the design of the eastern chapels and crypt. The facts seem to point the other way. These eastern portions are less English and more French than the western work. There is no trace of English influence in the design, except solely the rounding of the abacus and the molding of the capitals in the crypt. With these two minor exceptions, everything was completed in strict conformity with the French design.

THE CRYPT

More important even than the architecture is the ancient glass. Canterbury and York are the great treasure-houses of stained glass: Canterbury for early thirteenth-century glass, York for fourteenth-century glass. Three of the windows in the Saint's chapel illustrate the miracles of St. Thomas. On the north side, in the lower group of the eastern window, is the story of a child (1) who falls into the Medway, (2) the other boys tell his parents, (3) the body is drawn out of the water, *cætera desunt*. In the next group is the story of a boy who was brought to life by a draught of water mixed with the saint's blood. But the father omitted to pay the offerings promised to the saint. In the central medallion another son lies dead, struck by the sword of St. Thomas, who is seen through the ceiling. In another group a woman is being flagellated by way of penance. Two other windows describe miracles of healing: in a medallion in a lower part of the western window a madman comes up, "*amens accedit*," beaten with sticks and bound; in the next he is cured, "*sanus recedit*." In one is the only representation extant of the later shrine; the martyr, in a mauve vestment, appears in a vision to Benedict below. On the shrine is the box, as described by Erasmus, which contained the archbishop's sudary. In the east window of the Corona is portrayed Christ's Passion; in the two windows of the north aisle are types and antitypes from the Old and New Testaments; among them the three Magi, all asleep in one bed. The circular window in the northeast transept also contains the original glass; and many fragments are seen elsewhere.

FOURTH PERIOD.—For nearly two hundred years nothing structural was done in the church; the magnificent choir, presbytery, saint's chapel, procession aisle, and Corona looked down on Lanfranc's humble transepts and nave. To the first half of the thirteenth century belong two handsome doorways in the cloister and its north wall; also the south alley of the infirmary cloister between the conduit tower and the infirmary. In 1254 was built the west doorway of the Prior's chapel, now the library.

In 1305 Prior Eastry erected the stone parclose screens of the choir. About the same time was built the Chapter house, of which the lower part, as far as the cills of the present windows, remains; also the brewhouse, now the great school, with its porch and granary. In 1336 the great window was inserted in St. Anselm's chapel. In 1342 there was built the refectory of the infirmary, now forming the dining and drawing room of a canon's house. In 1363 a chantry was founded in the crypt by the Black

Prince, perhaps as a penalty for marrying his cousin, Joan of Kent. The whole of the crypt was dedicated to Our Lady, whose monogram may be seen here and there on the vault; about this time screens and reredos were put up round her special altar there. (There was another Lady chapel above ground in the eastern bays of the north aisle of the nave.)

FIFTH PERIOD.—At length Canterbury woke up, and removed the Norman nave and transept. The western bays were built first, so as to interfere with the services as little

THE TOMB OF HENRY IV.   THE TOMB OF THE
                           BLACK PRINCE

as possible (1379-1381). The rest of the nave and the transepts were rebuilt between 1382 and 1400. The south porch has the arms of Archbishop Sudbury (1375-1381). The new nave is imposing, but somehow no one seems to be a very ardent admirer of it. Its proportions are not good: Winchester nave is about the same height, but is 70 ft. longer. It was impossible to make it longer, for both the Norman western towers were still standing. The gravest fault is in the internal elevation. This is due to the lighting system adopted. Gloucester had taught the world that it

THE NAVE, LOOKING EAST

was on clerestory light a church should rely: and had shewn how magnificent was the effect of a lofty clerestory which was almost an unbroken sheet of glass. At Canterbury the clerestory is of the most exiguous dimensions; the architect has chosen to rely on side light, *i.e.*, from the windows of the aisle. The aisles therefore he had to build exceedingly lofty, with piers and arches to match. His ground story therefore is magnificent. But it is surmounted not only by an exiguous clerestory but by a closed triforium. Instead of the lovely open triforium arcades which had been elaborated from those of Ely choir in 1083 to those of Ely choir in 1322, there is now nothing left but a panelled wall, an evil precedent set in Winchester nave, and soon followed here, in Chester nave, Bath abbey-church, and elsewhere. Again, Gloucester, with marked success, had pointed the way to an internal elevation of one story; an attempt is made here to copy the Gloucester design; but the effect is spoiled by the banding of the vaulting-shafts. To the end of the fourteenth century belong also the upper part of the Chapter house with its boarded roof, and the great stone choir-screen.

SIXTH PERIOD.—To the fifteenth century belong the vaulting and window-screens of the cloisters (1397-1412); St. Michael's or the Warrior chapel, finished in 1439; this has an extraordinarily complicated lierne vault, following again a Gloucester precedent, that of the vault of the south transept; the chantry chapel of Henry IV. (1433-1435); the rebuilding of the south-west tower (1440-1452); a third Lady chapel, now called Deans' chapel, projecting from the north transept (1448-1455).

SEVENTH PERIOD.—Between 1495 and 1503 the central tower was raised to a total height of 235 ft.; the core of its lower walls is of the original Norman masonry. On its summit from Norman days there was a cherub or angel, and it was called the Angel steeple. At this period strainer-arches were inserted to prevent the piers of the tower bulging in under the additional work; similar ones may be seen at Rushden, Northants. In 1517 was built

THE CENTRAL TOWER

the Christ Church gateway, by which the cathedral is approached from the south-west; its doors were put up in 1662. The pretty Jacobean font and cover belong to the same year.

The *Chapter house* is rectangular, for a rectangular building fitted more easily into the east walk of a monastic cloister. Nearly all the monastic chapter houses are therefore rectangular, but sometimes had apses; the exceptions being the Benedictine chapter houses of Worcester, Westminster, Evesham, and Belvoir (which last was exceptional also in position, being placed in the very centre of the cloister), and the Cistercian chapter houses of Morgam and Abbey Dore,

THE EXTERIOR FROM THE SOUTH-WEST

sister designs. On the other hand the Secular Canons, having as a rule no cloister, preferred a polygonal chapter house, as at Lincoln, Beverley, Lichfield, Salisbury, Wells, Elgin, Southwell, York, Old St. Paul's, Hereford, Howden, Manchester, Warwick. So did the Regular Canons at Alnwick, Cockersand, Thornton, Carlisle, Bridlington, and Bolton. This beautiful polygonal form seems not to occur in France.

At the north-west corner of the cloister is the doorway through which Becket passed to the north-west transept, with his murderers in pursuit of him. Near here is a hole in the wall, the Buttery hatch. In the fifteenth century the south walk of the cloister was divided into "studies" for the monks by wooden partitions (at Gloucester they are of stone), and its windows were glazed.

From the cloister we pass to the *West Front*, and commence the tour of the exterior. The southwest tower was completed by Prior Goldstone, 1440-1452; the copy of it was put up in 1834: "it was an eyesore that the two towers did not match."

On the south side is seen the porch; the nave, whose clerestory is largely concealed by the excessive height of the aisles; and the charming pinnacle

CONDUIT TOWER

of the south-west transept. East of the Warrior's chapel is the projecting end of Stephen Langton's tomb. East of this, the two lower rows of windows are those of Conrad's choir; the upper row that of William of Sens. The middle windows in the south-east transept were the clerestory windows of Conrad; the windows above them are those of William of Sens. The three upper stages of the tower on the south of this transept are late Norman work; one of the prettiest bits in Canterbury. Farther east we have French design, pure and simple; here, for the first time in English architecture, the flying buttresses are openly displayed; notice how flat and plain they are; it had not yet occurred to architects to make them decorative. Then comes the broken, rocky outline of the Corona —the great puzzle of Canterbury. North-east of the Corona are two groups of ruined

THE NORMAN STAIRCASE

Norman pillars and arches discoloured by fire; once they were continuous, forming one very long building, the *Monks' Infirmary*, of which the west end was originally an open dormitory, open to the roof, and the east end, separated off by a screen, the Chapel; this has a window with geometrical tracery. A mediæval infirmary of this type is still in use at Chichester. The Canterbury infirmary had a north transept, called the Table Hall or Refectory (now part of the house of the Archdeacon of Maidstone), in which the inmates dined. On the north side of St. Thomas' chapel is seen the *Chantry of Henry IV.*; then *St. Andrew's Tower* and the barred *Treasury;* the lower part of the latter is late Norman work, largely rebuilt. The south alley of the *Infirmary Cloister* was built about 1236. Along this one passes to the so-called *Baptistery*, which is nothing but a mediæval water-tower; late Norman below, fifteenth-century work above. Returning towards the Infirmary, we turn to the north up the east alley of the Infirmary Cloister, now called the "*Dark Entry*," at the north end of which is the *Prior's Gateway*. On the left are some Norman shafts and arches of beautiful design. It was the Dark Entry that was haunted by Nell Cook of the "Ingoldsby Legends." West of the Prior's gateway are the two columns from the seventh-century church at Reculvers. On the north side of the Prior's or Green Court are the Brewery and Bakehouse; to the north-west is the famous Norman staircase, which originally led to a great North Hall; perhaps a Casual Ward—for tramps too found acommodation at the monasteries.

BIBLIOGRAPHY.—Professor Willis' *Architectural History of Canterbury Cathedral*.
Dean Stanley's *Historical Memorials of Canterbury*.
Canon Scott Robertson in *Archæologia Cantiana*, xiv. 281.
Field and Routledge's *Canterbury Official Guide* is an excellent guide-book both to the city and the cathedral, and contains good plans.
See also the bibliography in Willis' *Canterbury Cathedral*, 138.

THE CATHEDRAL CHURCH OF THE HOLY TRINITY, CARLISLE

BUILT FOR AUGUSTINIAN CANONS

CARLISLE CATHEDRAL, though but a torso, is of exceptional interest, both archæologically and artistically. Up to the Reformation it was the only cathedral served by the Austin or Black Canons; all the rest being either attached to monasteries of Benedictine monks, or served by Secular Canons. The church attached to the house of Austin Canons in Carlisle was dedicated to the Blessed Virgin Mary; it was re-dedicated to the Holy and undivided Trinity when placed on the New Foundation by Henry VIII.

FIRST PERIOD, 1101-c. 1150.—The Augustinian house was founded by Henry I. in 1101, at the instigation of Queen Matilda; Carlisle became the seat of a bishopric in 1133. The Norman church consisted of an aisled nave of seven bays, a transept with eastern apses, and an aisled presbytery of two bays,

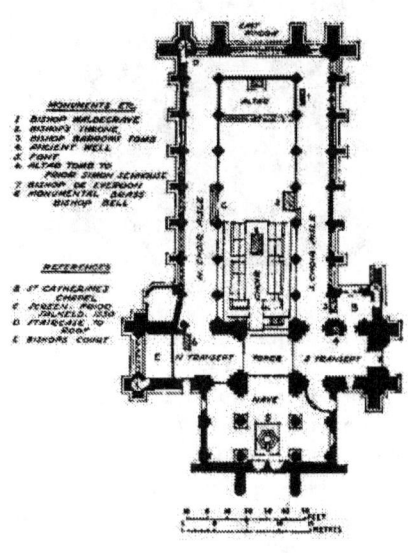

THE PLAN

which probably ended in an unaisled apse. Norman aisles were usually vaulted; but the aisle-walls of Carlisle nave are so thin that they can never have supported a vault. The work is singularly plain and heavy; in the nave the piers are low cylinders, like those of Hereford nave; from them rise the commencements of shafts intended to carry the roof.

PRIOR GONDEBOUR'S SCREEN, ST. CATHERINE'S CHAPEL.

The triforium has a single open arch, as at Norwich. The clerestory, as often, consists of a tall central arch containing a window, flanked by two low blind arches. The capitals, as usually in early twelfth-century work, are scalloped; all the arches are destitute of sculpture, of some not even the edges are molded, *i.e.*, rounded. The capitals of the tower arches have been reset lower down; formerly they supported the four lofty arches on which the Norman tower rested.

SECOND PERIOD, *c.* 1223-1246 onwards.—The lower parts of the northern and southern faces of the piers of the tower are flat: their shafts being stopped by corbels instead of descending to the ground. This was to allow the stalls of the Canons to be placed close up to the piers. The Canons sat in the crossing and the two eastern bays of the nave. Like the Benedictine monks of Canterbury, they wished to sit in the choir. And so the Norman chancel, being altogether inadequate to contain stalls and sanctuary, was pulled down as at Canterbury; and a beautiful early Gothic chancel of seven bays was built. Of this the vaulted aisles and the pier-arches still remain. The work appears to belong to the second quarter of the thirteenth century; for in the south aisle the Lancet windows are developing into plate-tracery, and the charming arcading on the aisle-walls is cinquefoiled. The new chancel was not only far in advance of its Norman predecessor in length and height; but it was also 12 ft. broader. The church could not be broadened to the south, because the cloister would prevent any removal of the wall of the south aisle, when the nave should be rebuilt. So the south wall of the choir was rebuilt on the old foundations: the southern row of piers probably also rests on the foundations of the Norman piers. The central aisle of the choir was made much broader than that of the nave, with which, therefore, it is out of axis; the same is the case with the north aisle of the choir.

PIERS ON THE NORTH SIDE OF THE CHOIR

At the same time the eastern apse of the south transept was rebuilt rectangular, with crisply carved conventional foliage. The northern transept was to have been rebuilt on a more extensive scale, not being cramped, like the south transept, by monastic buildings adjacent. It was to have had an eastern aisle; but when one pier of the aisle had been built, and part of its eastern wall (a fragment of which, with base-course and string-course, survives), the work was suddenly stopped.

THIRD PERIOD, 1292–c. 1382.—Hardly was the new choir completed when, together with belfry and bells, it was destroyed in 1292 by a great fire, with the exception of the aisles, which were protected by their stone vaults, and the pier-arches. The Canons, not a whit disheartened, resolved to rebuild the choir, and to rebuild it even longer than before. To its length they added an eastern bay, just wide enough to provide a processional path at the back of the high altar; and instead of a low east end, the choir was built full height up to the east, as at Ely and Lincoln. The thirteenth-century arches, between the choir and its aisles, which apparently were not much damaged by the fire, they managed in some inexplicable way to retain. A modern contractor would take the arches down, and then rebuild them with the old stones. A mediæval builder would be more likely to underpin the arches, take the piers away, and then rebuild them without disturbing the arches at all. The old builders revelled in such engineering feats. The capitals of the new piers are exceedingly rich and interesting;

THE SOUTH CHOIR ARCADE

they contain the best mediæval representation we possess of the Seasons; six capitals on the south side from east to west, six on the north side from west to east. The corbels also of the vaulting-shafts have rich naturalistic foliage. With that respect for good earlier work that is characteristic of the fourteenth century, and so rare at any other time, they carried the cinquefoiled arcading of the aisles round the east wall, introducing, however, the characteristic detail of the period, not to bewilder unfortunate antiquaries of later days.

Their *chef d'œuvre*, however, was the east front. On this they lavished all their wealth and all their art. It is a very poem in stone. Its only rival is the contemporary east front of Selby. "The great window," says Professor Freeman, "is the grandest of its kind in England." It certainly has no rival, unless it be that of York. The four lateral lights on either side of the Carlisle windows are gathered up into two pointed arches; at York these two arches are ogees: the free swing of the ogee arches contrasting most effectively with the pointed arch which embraces them both. The glass in the tracery of the Carlisle window represents Our Lord sitting in Judgment; the procession of the Blessed to the Palace of Heaven, shown in two silvery quatrefoils;

THE EAST END

and very realistic representations of Hell and of the General Resurrection. It contains a portrait of John of Gaunt; so that the window was probably glazed when he was Governor

THE CHOIR AND EAST WINDOW

of Carlisle, 1380-84. The lower lights are of modern glass by Hardman.

So far the Canons spared no expense; everything was of the best. But their resources were taxed too heavily; it was impossible to finish the choir with the magnificence with which it was commenced. Triforium and clerestory are thin and poor; the inner arcade of the latter of the barest character; on the other hand it has an exceptionally broad wall-passage; moreover, a vault was found too expensive, and was omitted. Then hammerbeams were constructed for a roof of the type of the magnificent roofs of March church and Westminster Hall. This in its turn was abandoned, and the present wagon roof of wood was put up. For similar economical reasons probably the south transept was rebuilt without the aisle commenced in the thirteenth century.

FOURTH PERIOD (c. 1400-1484).—But the misfortunes of the Canons were not over yet. Another fire destroyed the new north transept. This was rebuilt between 1400 and 1419 by Bishop Strickland. About this time also were executed the admirably carved stalls, with their interesting misericords; the tabernacled canopies overhead were put up by Prior Haithwaite in 1433; originally they were painted and gilded, and statuettes stood on the pedestal of every niche.

Then came the question of the central tower and the nave. The original plan had been that, when the choir was finished, a new central tower and a new nave should be built, both of the same width as the choir. But the courage of the Canons gave way; their troubles had been too much for them. They saw no prospect of ever being able to rebuild the Norman nave; so instead of pulling down the Norman tower and building one as broad as the choir, they left it standing; merely adding a new upper story to it. It is, of course, far too small for its position; and while ranging with the nave, is quite lop-sided when seen in connection with the roof of the choir; though the awkwardness is lessened, and even made picturesque, by the addition of a staircase-turret on the north side of the tower. One reason why the rebuilding of the tower was not attempted was no doubt the presence of springs beneath the crossing; as it is, the piers of the tower have sunk deep and unequally, distorting the neighbouring arches and leaving most unpleasant cracks in the walls.

FIFTH PERIOD, 1484-1538.—In 1484 an energetic Prior, Gondebour, came into office; a man with a liking for colour. He painted the roof of the chancel, and the pillars as well; and on the backs of the stalls depicted the lives of St. Augustine, St. Anthony, and St. Cuthbert: to him also are due the beautiful screens of St. Catherine's chapel. He built the great barn, still standing in part, open on one side, with beams nearly 2 ft. deep. He rebuilt the Refectory

THE EXTERIOR FROM THE NORTH-WEST

or Fratry, the dining-hall of the Canons, with vaulted cellarage of the fourteenth century below. In all mediæval refectories silence was imperative at meals, and a good book of some sort was read from a pulpit in one of the side walls. The Carlisle reading-pulpit with its staircase remains; illustrated by Billings as a *confessional box*. At the west end of the hall are the hatches through which the food was formerly passed from a kitchen on the other side of the wall. In the Fratry are preserved several curiosities; it should be visited. The Abbey Gatehouse, north-west of the nave, was built in 1527.

SIXTH PERIOD—POST-REFORMATION WORK.—Launcelot Salkeld, the last Prior and the first Dean of Carlisle, added the charming Renaissance screen on the north side of the presbytery (*c.* 1540). In the seventeenth century the western bays of the Norman nave were pulled down, during the Civil War, to provide materials for the repair of the city walls and guard-houses. Both in the north and south aisles there used to be windows of the fifteenth century; these were destroyed with their interesting history, and modern shams substituted in a destructive "restoration" by Mr Ewan Christian.

The cathedral possesses two very fine brasses; one, in the middle of the choir, of Bishop Bell (1478-1495); the other, in the north aisle, of Bishop Robinson (1598-1616).

BIBLIOGRAPHY.—Billings, R.W., *Carlisle Cathedral*, London, 1840.

THE CATHEDRAL CHURCH OF CHRIST AND THE BLESSED VIRGIN MARY, CHESTER

Built for Benedictine Monks

AT Chester there was originally an establishment of Secular Canons. The patron saint of the church was St. Werburgh, a niece of St. Etheldreda of Ely. In 1093 it was refounded as a Benedictine monastery by that great noble Hugh Lupus, Earl of Chester, who ruled the Welsh Marches with almost regal sway. Henry VIII. made t the seat of a bishopric, which, though but a part of the ancient Mercian diocese of Lichfield, extended northwards into Yorkshire and Westmorland. Nowadays the diocese and county of Chester are coextensive. The abbey church was rededicated, as a cathedral, to Christ and the Blessed Virgin Mary in 1541.

If we proceed to the west doors, we have before us a vista of exceptional beauty. The apparent length of the interior is greatly increased by the return stalls, which, however, are not so solid and lofty as to block up the vista entirely, as do the stone screens at Canterbury and York, nor so exiguous as the metal screens at Lichfield and Ely. The effect was even finer when the organ stood over the entrance to the choir.

First Period, 1093-c. 1260.—Passing under the new organ screen into the *north transept*, we come to the most ancient work to be found in the cathedral—genuine early Norman work of the eleventh century. It is to be compared with that of the south transepts of St. Alban's, Hereford, and Pershore. Below, in the east wall, is an arch, which once led into an apse. Above is a balustraded arcade, quite of the St. Alban's and Hereford type. Above, there must have been small clerestory windows, such as those built up in the opposite wall. The whole transept

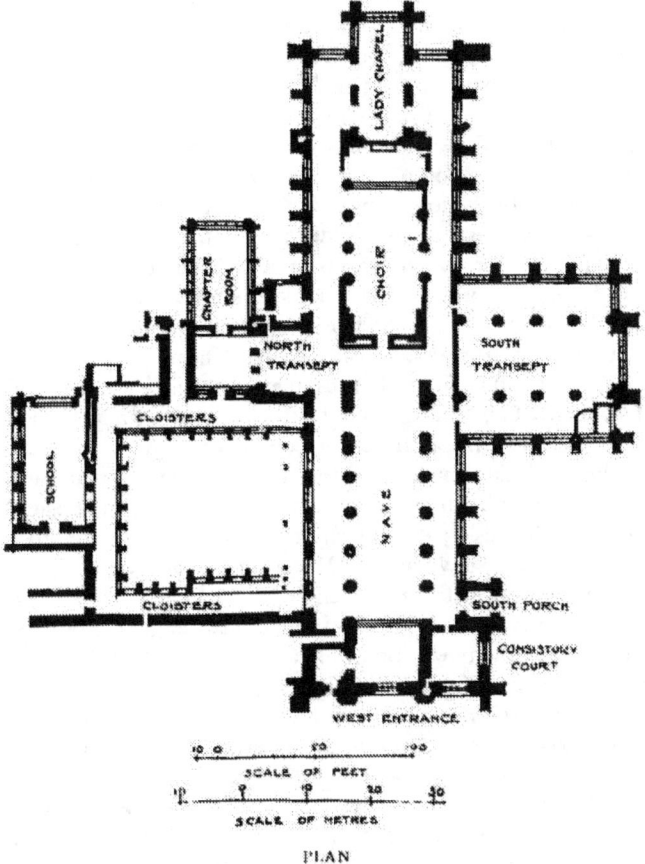

PLAN

must have been low and humble, and is invaluable as shewing us what early Norman work was really like, and of enabling us to realise the vast progress that had taken place in design, in masonry, and in carving by the time that

Durham, Romsey, and Norwich were begun. This early transept was of one bay only. Notice how small the stones are, the gaping joints, and the irregularity of the courses: it seems earlier than 1093.

Bearing in mind the character of this masonry, pass out of the transept into the *north aisle of the nave*, and proceed to the Norman tower at the west end of it. The work here, *c.* 1105, is clumsy and massive, but far superior to that of the north transept. The north wall of the nave (now covered with mosaics) is also Norman. Other traces of the Norman cathedral will be found in the *north aisle of the choir*, to which we retrace our steps. On the right will be seen a great circular capital upside down, which has been used as a foundation for the north-east pier of the tower. A few feet further is one of the original circular bases, proving that the Norman choir had vast circular piers like those of Gloucester, Carlisle, and St. John's, Chester. Two bays further east will be found in the pavement a semicircular band of dark marble, and another base of a pier which divided the north apse from the large central one; here the base moldings differ somewhat from those of the circular pier. This marks foundations that have been found of the apsidal ending of this aisle; one of the stones of this Norman apse remains in the pavement. Moreover, it has been found that the central aisle of the choir, at the end of the second bay from the tower, ended in a semicircular range of columns, like St. Bartholomew's, Smithfield. From these indications we can restore the plan of the original Norman cathedral with some certainty. It had a nave and aisles of the same dimensions as the present ones; unaisled transepts, each of a single bay, and an eastern apse to each transept; a low central tower; a choir of two bays, ending in a semicircular range of columns and arches, and surrounded to the east by a semicircular ambulatory or processional path. On either side were aisles, three and a half bays long, each terminating in an eastern apse. So that the Norman cathedral had five eastern apses, and resembled in plan Gloucester and Norwich, except that the chapels of the choir-aisles of Chester point, not north-east and south-east, but due east. It was about 300 ft. in length.

Norman Cloisters.—Returning to the north aisle of the nave we pass through the doorway at the east end of the aisle into the cloister. This doorway, as seen from the cloister, is, from its ornamentation, of later date than the north transept, and may also be about 1100. The *south wall* of the cloister on the left is now seen to be Norman; Norman abbots are buried in the recesses. Passing along the cloister westwards, we have in front another Norman door, and a very late Norman passage. Passing along the *west walk* of the cloister, a doorway on the left leads into a large Norman undercroft, with two aisles roofed with massive groined vaulting. Above, as the division in the vaulting and staircase shew, were a large and a small hall. These buildings on the west of the cloisters were originally the cellars, refectory, and guest-house in charge of the cellarer; afterwards they became the cellars and hall of the Abbot. To the south, above the late Norman passage, is the Episcopal chapel, also Norman, with a fine Jacobean plastered ceiling.

SECOND PERIOD, *c.* 1180.—We return by the cloister and north transept to the *north aisle of the choir*, and pass into the vestry to the left. The apse of the north transept was pulled down; but part of the foundation of this Norman apse may be seen in the pavement near the door; the arch in the west wall was formerly open to the transept; and a new chapel was built here late in the twelfth century, to which period the vaulting belongs. Later on, the east end of it was remodelled, and the western arch built up. In the vestry is a cupboard with delicate hammered and *stamped* ironwork; *c.* 1250, by Thomas de Leighton.

THIRD PERIOD, *c.* 1200-*c.* 1315.—This was one of the most extensive of the building periods of the abbey, and contains the most beautiful work. To get a large Lady chapel, a processional path, and an enlarged presbytery, the whole of the eastern limb of the church was rebuilt on a far larger scale, beginning at the east; and on the eastern and northern sides of the cloister the adjoining buildings, which hitherto probably had been of wood, were also rebuilt. First we return to the *north transept* and pass into the *east walk of the cloister*, straight in front. On our right is the *vestibule*, the architectural gem of the cathedral; before entering it, notice its trefoiled doorway, encircled with sprigs of conventional foliage; the piers have bases, but no capitals—a feature common enough in late Gothic, but very unusual in such early work, date 1240-1250. Then enter the *Chapter house*, which is of the same date as the vestibule. It is rectangular, as were most of the monastic Chapter houses originally; the windows have an inner arcade. Returning to the vestibule, and passing out of it by the modern north doorway, we cross the *Slype* with its elaborate vault; this is a passage which led to the monks' infirmary. Then we pass into a vaulted building of two aisles, each of four bays, restored at considerable expense, and then allowed to relapse into a coal-cellar: this is the so-called fratry; really it is what was called at Durham the *Common House*. Rooms in similar position occur at Fountains and Westminster; probably for the Novices. Then we return to the *cloister*, and proceed to the end of the east walk. Above the vestibule, slype and common house was the *dormitory* of the monks. It was reached in the daytime by a flight of steps from the *doorway* near the end of the east walk; the little quatrefoiled *window* to the right of the doorway lighted this staircase.

Next we enter the *north walk* of the cloister where the arms of Henry VII. and also those of Wolsey as Archbishop of York are seen. Along the whole of it extended the *Refectory* or Frater, the monks' dining-hall; now the west end has been lopped off, and a passage driven through the east of it. Towards the west end will be found a fine *doorway* by which it was originally entered. To the right of the doorway is a recess marking the site of the *lavatory*. Inside, in the south wall, is the original staircase and *pulpit* of the refectory. Another equally fine pulpit remains in the refectory of Beaulieu, Hampshire; another, in the open air, opposite Shrewsbury Abbey. The upper part of the refectory has rectilinear tracery inserted in the original windows.

Then we retrace our steps through the *cloister walks* to the *north transept*, and pass to the left along the *north choir aisle* to the far east of the cathedral. Here is the *Lady chapel*; much restored, of similar date and character to those of Hereford and Bristol. It was a remarkable specimen of mediæval "jerry-building," built without foundations of any sort or kind. One of the bosses, figured in Dean Howson's book on "The Dee," depicts the murder of

THE EXTERIOR FROM THE SOUTH-EAST

Thomas Becket; the other two, The Virgin and Child, and The Holy Trinity. Originally the Lady chapel had three windows, each triplets, on either side.

Leaving the Lady chapel, we return westward till we can enter the *Choir*. Here we see similar work on its eastern wall, and in the lower part of its two easternmost bays. The east wall is pierced by but one arch, as at Hereford and Chichester; an inferior ending to the triple eastern arches of the choirs of Wells and Salisbury. The moldings of the southern arches are a cheap imitation of the better work on the north.

Western Choir.—The remaining bays to the west have piers of an altogether different and later section. The choir aisles were lengthened to the east about 1500, though the capitals and vaulting-shafts are those of the semi-hexagonal apse which previously terminated the aisles. In digging, the foundations of the east ends of these aisles have been found. They turn out to have been polygonal. Sir G. G. Scott has been allowed to rebuild the south aisle in apsidal form, and to crown his work with a hideous "extinguisher" roof. He also pulled down the fifteenth-century choir aisle, and expelled the monuments of three ancient county families in favour of an eminent contractor. This is called "restoration."

All the above work stops at the top of the beautiful triforium, a trefoiled arcade; the clerestory is later work (1275-1300). The proportions of the choir as thus completed are not satisfactory; the tall clerestory, with its big broad windows, is ruinous to the effect of the low pier-arcade and the diminutive triforium: it looks top-heavy.

We now proceed to the south transept.

FOURTH PERIOD, *c.* 1315-*c.* 1492.—This falls into two parts: comprising respectively the work done before and after the Black Death.

We have seen that by 1300 or soon after, the monks had rebuilt all the work to the east and north of the cloister, as well as the Lady chapel and the whole of the choir. In the fourteenth century they set to work to rebuild the whole of the south transept, the central tower, and the nave. None of the upper parts of these, however, were finished till the following century. The *South Transept* is so vast that the old church of St. Oswald may have still remained in use while the transept was building around it. It has western as well as eastern aisles: which it is rare to find except in cathedrals of the first rank, such as Ely and York. Some of the aisle windows retain very beautiful flowing tracery. The springers of vaults remain, but no vaulting was executed, except one bay at the south end of the east aisle, till recently, when the remainder of this aisle was vaulted. The vast size of this transept—it is as large as the choir, and nearly as large as the nave—is in striking contrast to the diminutive north transept, and is the most remarkable

THE CHOIR

feature in the ground plan of the cathedral. Originally there stood here an independent church, belonging to the parish of St. Oswald. But in the fourteenth century, when the abbey was in possession of great wealth, the monks desired to enlarge their church. They could not enlarge it to the north, for on the north were their cloisters, chapter house, refectory, and dormitory. On the south was the parish church of St. Oswald; they therefore came to terms with the parishioners, in accordance with which they built a new parish church for them, where now stands the Music Hall. But in 1486 the parishioners were able to evade their bargain, and vindicated their claim to the whole of the new south transept, which the monks by this time had completed. "Sic vos non vobis." And to get into it they cut the fifteenth-century doorway, which is still to be seen at the south end of the west aisle of the new transept. And here they remained in possession till the present century, using the transept as their parish church. In 1824 the transept was actually blocked from the cathedral by a solid wall. But in 1874 a new church, St. Thomas, was once more built for the parishioners, and they were again ejected from the site of the old church of St. Oswald. The dividing wall was pulled down, and the transept has been again thrown into the cathedral. In the year 1902 it was restored as a memorial to the late Duke of Westminster, and a recumbent figure of his Grace placed on the west side; the ancient altar was also reinstated. This transept was not finished when the Black Death arrived in 1349; and when the work was resumed in the fifteenth century, the remaining windows of the transept were given rectilinear instead of flowing tracery.

Central Tower.—This also was probably commenced in the fourteenth and finished in the fifteenth century. It has been found that the north-west pier rests upon some floriated gravestones of the thirteenth century, which disposes of the idea that the piers of the tower have a Norman core. Notice the variation in the treatment of the tower-arches.

Nave.—A beginning was made also with the rebuilding of the south side of the nave in the first half of the fourteenth century; the pillars and arches are of simple and good

design, and the lower windows, like those in the south
transept, have flowing tracery. The northern pier-arcade is
later and somewhat different. It would seem that the
ground story of the nave was not finished till late in the

THE NAVE, LOOKING EAST

fifteenth century, for the initials of Abbot Simon Ripley
(1485-1492) are found on the first pier from the west. To
the latter part of this period may be assigned all those
windows with rectilinear tracery with cusps, in the transepts,
the nave, and elsewhere.

FIFTH PERIOD—*Nave.*—The final operations comprised all those windows which are without cusps—*e.g.*, the clerestory windows and the north aisle windows of the nave; also the south porch and west front and the commencement of a south-west tower, and the fine wooden roof of the north transept. All this was done early in the sixteenth century. Perhaps piety had waxed cold, and pilgrims' offertories may have become less productive. At any rate, all the upper part of the interior of the nave is bare, bald, and poverty-stricken. For the beautiful triforium of the choir we have here a blank wall; unhappy, too, in proportions, the nave of Chester is one of the least satisfactory designs of our cathedrals.

One other alteration had been made. The High altar originally stood one bay further to the west than it does now, and the bay where it now stands formed the processional path. But this bay was also wanted for a Saint's chapel, that of St. Werburgh, with her shrine in the centre, as at St. Alban's. So the eastern apses of the two choir aisles were pulled down, and two longer aisles were built, one on each side of the Lady chapel. (The one on the north is still allowed to exist; the one on the south was pulled down by Scott.) Then the west window on either side of the Lady chapel was converted into a doorway, and a convenient processional path was provided between the Lady chapel and the Saint's chapel. It should be added that the stalls of the choir were originally under the central tower, as at Gloucester.

To the last period belong the eastern, northern, and western walks of the cloister, which should be visited next. In part of the west walk, and in the new south walk, there is a double arcade; dividing the walks into a series of separate compartments or studies for the monks. An analogous arrangement occurs in the cloisters of Gloucester. Notice, also, the *insouciance* with which these Tudor builders dropped the ribs of their vaults down on earlier doors and arches. Similar reckless disregard of the good work of preceding builders occurs at Canterbury, where the most beautiful doorway in the cathedral is cut into by later vaulting.

In recent days the inner wall of the *north aisle of the nave* has been cased with mosaics which cannot be seen, and has been provided with rich vaulting; and to provide abutment for this new vault the south walk of the cloister has been rebuilt. The nave and choir have been vaulted in wood; following the precedents of York Minster and Selby Abbey. The exterior is, to all intents and purposes, nineteenth-century work. The original design had almost wholly disappeared through the decay of the soft sandstone. It is, however, very handsome and effective; especially in contrast with the exterior, also modern, of Worcester. As at Salisbury, Lincoln, and Hereford, there is a magnificent view of the whole of the exterior from the north-east; seen from the city wall towards sunset, this red sandstone cathedral makes an impression not soon effaced.

Of minor work the most important is the pedestal of St. Werburgh's shrine, now placed west of the Lady chapel; it had long stood in the choir, converted into a bishop's throne. It should be compared with the shrine-pedestals at St. Alban's, Oxford, and Hereford; its date may be *c.* 1330. There is also a Byzantine font, brought from the East, perhaps of the eighth century. The stall work, *c.* 1390, is magnificent; tabernacled canopies, bench ends, elbow rests, and misericords deserve minute prolonged study. Besides these there are Renaissance gates of Spanish ironwork; and the epitaphs of John Lowe, tobacconist, John Paul, publican, and John Phillips, merchant, in the south transept; those of Mayor Green, and an American loyalist, on the south-west pier of the tower; the tablet of Randolph Caldecott and the pretentious monument of Bishop Pearson in the north transept; the tablet of Dean Arderne in the south aisle of the choir, which should not be missed; and in the north aisle those of Subdean Bispham and Bishop Jacobson, and the epitaph on the gravestone of E. P. Gastrell. The new organ rests on five Renaissance columns brought from Italy; the communion table is of wood from the Holy Land. On the wall near the west door is a tablet to Bishop Hall, and another

To the Memory of

JOHN MOORE NAPIER

Captain in Her Majesty's 62nd Regiment
Who died of Asiatic Cholera
in Scinde
on the 7th of July, 1846,
Aged 29 years.

> The tomb is no record of high lineage;
>   His may be traced by his name;
>   His race was one of soldiers.
> Among soldiers he lived; among them he died;
> A soldier falling, where numbers fell with him,
>   In a barbarous land.
> Yet there was none died more generous,
> More daring, more gifted, or more religious.
>   On his early grave
> Fell the tears of stern and hardy men,
> As his had fallen on the graves of others.

There is not much in verse that rings like these few lines of prose.

BIBLIOGRAPHY.—Mr Hussey in *Archæological Journal*, v.
  Mr Ayrton in *Chester Arch. Society*, i., and Sir Gilbert Scott in ditto, ii.
  Mr J. H. Parker in *Mediæval Architecture of Chester*.
  Dean Howson in *Handbook to Chester Cathedral*.

FROM THE WEST

THE CATHEDRAL CHURCH OF THE HOLY TRINITY, CHICHESTER

BUILT FOR SECULAR CANONS

CHICHESTER CATHEDRAL, though one of the smallest, is to the student of mediæval architecture one of the most interesting and important of our cathedrals. At Salisbury one or two styles of architecture are represented; at Canterbury two or three; in Chichester cathedral building was going on practically continuously from c. 1091 till the fourteenth century, and again, intermittently, up to the Dissolution. For the eleventh, twelfth, and thirteenth centuries it is an epitome of English church architecture. We have many other composite and heterogeneous cathedrals, but nowhere, not even at St. Alban's and Hereford, is such an unbroken sequence of mediæval building to be studied as at Chichester.

The last kingdom, says Canon Bright, that remained outside the Church, was that of the South Saxons, hemmed in by a thick line of well-nigh impenetrable forest, and so

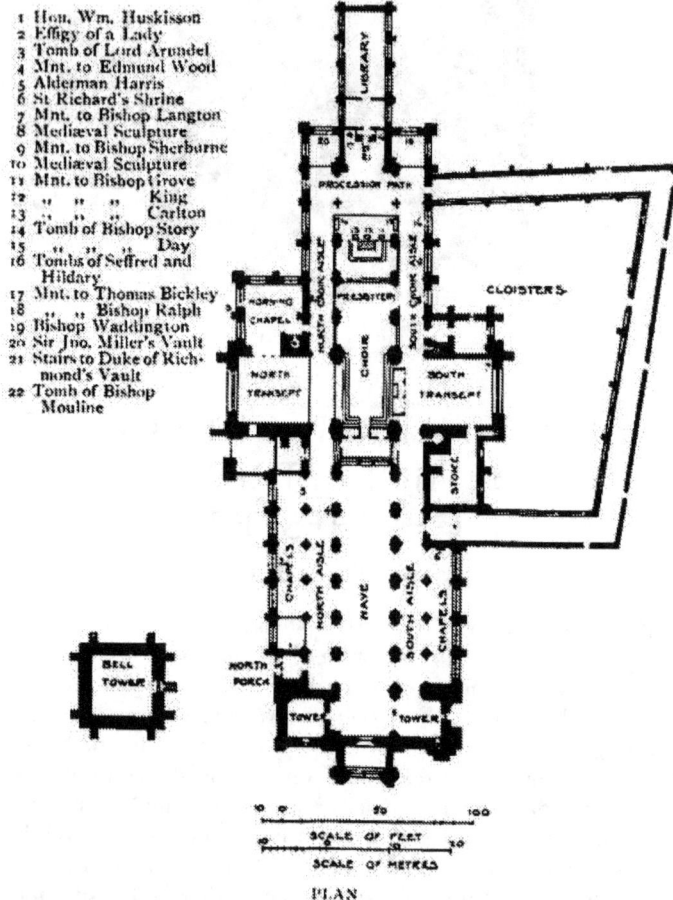

1 Hon. Wm. Huskisson
2 Effigy of a Lady
3 Tomb of Lord Arundel
4 Mnt. to Edmund Wood
5 Alderman Harris
6 St Richard's Shrine
7 Mnt. to Bishop Langton
8 Mediæval Sculpture
9 Mnt. to Bishop Sherburne
10 Mediæval Sculpture
11 Mnt. to Bishop Grove
12 „ „ „ King
13 „ „ „ Carlton
14 Tomb of Bishop Story
15 „ „ „ Day
16 Tombs of Seffred and Hildary
17 Mnt. to Thomas Bickley
18 „ „ Bishop Ralph
19 Bishop Waddington
20 Sir Jno. Miller's Vault
21 Stairs to Duke of Richmond's Vault
22 Tomb of Bishop Mouline

PLAN

barbarous as to be at once ignorant of the simplest arts, and furious against the incoming of foreigners. It was reserved for the great Wilfrid, of Hexham, Ripon, and

York, in one of his exiles (611)—caused originally by the high-handed partition of his overlarge diocese of York—to do what no one as yet had done for these poor rude heathen —what some Irish monks had tried to do and had failed. They were desperate with famine; he taught them to fish in the sea; for he was as ready in homely crafts of this kind as in adorning churches or educating young nobles; and as Bede says, "by this kind act he turned their hearts to love him; and they began the more willingly to hope for heavenly blessings under his preaching, when by his assistance they had received earthly good."

The first seat of the diocese was on the coast at Selsea; it was transferred to Chichester by Stigand in 1082, when other Norman prelates removed to fortified towns such as Lincoln, Exeter, and Norwich. In the south aisle of the choir are two sculptured slabs representing the meeting of Christ with Mary and Martha and the raising of Lazarus. The figures are the tall, emaciated, but dignified figures of archaic Byzantine art, their stature carefully proportionate to their importance. These slabs are usually said to have come from Selsea, and have therefore been supposed to be of Pre-Conquest date; more likely, like those in the west front of Lincoln, they are work of the twelfth century. Stigand was followed by Gosfried, who for some unknown sin sought and obtained absolution from the Pope. The original document in lead, with many other objects of great interest, may be seen in the library. "We, representing St. Peter, the chief of the Apostles, to whom God gave the power of binding and loosing, absolve thee, Bishop Godfrey, so far as thy accusation requests and the right of remission belongs to us. God the Redeemer be thy salvation and graciously forgive thee all thy sins. Amen." On the seventh of the Calends of April, on the festival of St. Firmin, bishop and martyr, died Godfrey, bishop of Chichester; it was then the fifth day of the moon.

I. NORMAN.—Godfrey was succeeded in 1091 by Ralph, whose stone coffin, marked "Radulphus," may be seen in the Lady chapel. Ralph is recorded to have built the present

Norman cathedral; the consecration took place in 1108. It was dedicated to St. Peter; the present dedication to the Holy Trinity dates from 1199. It is hardly likely that the whole cathedral was completed in seventeen years; and if the nave be examined, it will be found that its four western bays are rather later in date than the rest; they differ in the banding of the vaulting-shafts, in the diaper of the spandrels of the triforium arcade, which are of a different pattern in every bay; the masonry, too, is of superior character, as may be seen in the triforium chamber and clerestory; the pier-arches also are wider and the piers narrower. It is likely that the building of these four bays and that of the two western towers occupied the rest of the first quarter of the twelfth century. The lower part of the south-western tower survives. The Corinthianesque capital of eleventh-century Norman work, which appears also on the east side of Ely transept, occurs in the triforium of the choir.

THE PRESBYTERY

The church had the same type of ground plan as Norwich, commenced c. 1096, and Gloucester, commenced c. 1089; viz., an aisled nave, aisleless transept with eastern apses, aisled presbytery, encircled by a procession path, from which radiated three chapels, probably all apsidal. Externally, on the south wall of the choir, in the fourth bay from the west, may be seen traces of the curve of the wall of the ancient ambulatory, and also a triforium window which originally was in the centre of one of the narrow bays of the apse, but has now ceased to be central. (Below is a later consecration cross.) The apses of the transept were superposed, as at Gloucester; in the chamber above the Library, the curve of the upper apsidal chapel of the north transept is well seen. The pier-system is neither that of alternating piers, as at Jumièges and Ely, nor of cylinders, as in Gloucester nave, nor yet of alternating octagons and cylinders, as in Peterborough choir; as in the archaic abbey church of Bernay, the piers are merely lengths of wall with shafts attached. Similar piers occur at Christchurch in the adjoining county of Hampshire, which may be regarded as a sister church of Chichester cathedral. It is probable that the stalls were not placed in the crossing, but in the three eastern bays of the nave. It was just this part of the church which suffered most in the great fire of 1186; probably because here were placed the wooden stalls. The western bays suffered so little, being perhaps separated from the stalls by a stone screen, that it was unnecessary to reface with Caen stone the spandrels of the pier-arcade. (Nor did the presbytery suffer much; for some of its roof timbers were charred, but not consumed.) The presbytery must have been exceptionally long; occupying the apse and all three bays of the eastern limb as well as the crossing; at St. Alban's the presbytery contained four bays, but did not extend into the crossing. The three eastern bays and the western piers of the central tower have vaulting-shafts without rings, probably because rings would have been concealed by the stallwork which it was intended to replace after the fire. Whether Bishop Ralph's aisles were vaulted is doubtful. On the aisle side of the piers of the nave may be seen plinths designed for vaulting-shafts, shewing an undoubted intention to vault. But if groined vaults had been erected, it is very unlikely that they would have been removed in order to be replaced by the present aisle vaults, which were put up after the fire of 1186. In Rochester aisles are supports for a vault, but no vault was ever erected. Most of our churches are lopsided. Westminster is a brilliant exception—but perhaps only Romsey is so utterly out of the straight as Chichester. The axis of the nave changes no less than three times; the distortion is amazing as seen in the clerestory passage. The Lady chapel, too, swings over to the south, and there are many minor aberrations; arch differs in span from arch, and pier from pier in breadth. Finally the unsymmetrical church is backed up by the yet more unsymmetrical cloister. As for the western bays of the nave, they would probably be built from west to east; hence the twist at the junction with the older eastern bays. There is evidence also that the Lady chapel was built from east to west, which helps to account for its bad setting out.

INSIDE THE TRIFORIUM, LOOKING WEST

II. The walls of the three western bays of the Lady chapel are of the twelfth century; and their curious capitals of naturalistic foliage point to a date not earlier than 1175. We know that there was a second consecration in 1184. To the period c. 1175-1184 the work may therefore be referred; it probably meant the substitution of a long oblong chapel for an original apsidal one.

III. In 1186 there was a great fire. It did the more damage because the church had not only a roof, but a wooden ceiling beneath it, as at Peterborough. At the beginning of the conflagration the part first damaged would be the clerestory; at Chichester the Norman inner arcade of the clerestory windows seems to have been damaged beyond repair. After a time the burning timbers of roof and ceiling would fall down to the pavement, damaging in their fall the string-courses. The triforium arcade, however, would not be much damaged, except so far as it was affected by the burning roofs of the aisles. Below, however, especially if there was stallwork, the masonry of the piers and arches and their spandrels would be calcined and shattered by the heat of the mass of timber blazing on the pavement.

ENTRANCE TO THE LADY CHAPEL.

What therefore had to be done was to supply the clerestory with a new inner arcade, to insert new strings, and to reface the piers, arches, and spandrels of the pier-arcade. And, to save the church from risk of future damage by a fire in the roof, it was decided to vault the nave, choir, and transepts. All this was done. Bishop Ralph had used a shelly limestone from Quarr abbey in the Isle of Wight, with an admixture of Sussex sandstones, the green Eastbourne rock and brown Pulborough stone. Bishop Siegfried employed the white Caen stone and Purbeck marble;

THE NAVE, LOOKING EAST

for the cells of the vaults he used chalk, which was plastered internally, and at a later period covered with beautiful paintings (a fragment of one of which may be seen on the vault of the Lady chapel; others, also by the Bernardis, on the choir vault at Boxgrove Priory church); on the top of the vault was laid a thick bed of concrete. The addition of these vaults necessitated a new abutment-system. The original buttresses had been flat pilasters; to resist the thrusts of the vault it was necessary to give the new ones much bulk and great projection; two of them, one of work of 1091, the other of that of 1186, may be seen side by side on the west wall of the north transept. As at Canterbury, the small and narrow windows were replaced by larger ones set higher up, the heads of the old windows being sometimes re-used. Over the new buttresses an imitation of the eleventh-century billet string was continued. In the triforium chamber before the fire there had been transverse semicircular arches buttressing the nave walls; their springers may still be seen, and similar ones exist in the triforium chamber of Durham choir. Now that there were to be high vaults, these had to be removed in order to construct the present flying buttresses beneath the aisle roof, following the precedent of Durham nave. But these were judged not to be enough; so a second set of fliers was built above the aisle roof, *i.e.*, in the open air. Chichester therefore possesses a double set of flying buttresses. Both sets are very massive and plain; it is obvious that the buttressing system owes nothing to Canterbury choir, where the light fliers must be of French design. Similar heavy flying buttresses were employed a little later in the same county at New Shoreham and Boxgrove. All the refacing of the internal walls was done with great thoroughness, the blocks of Caen stone being carefully bonded in. In the profuse use of Purbeck marble in strings, shafts, bases, and annulets one sees the influence of Canterbury choir. It is probably at this time that for the semicircular apse in the north transept was substituted the double chapel with two altars, which is now used as a library: the zigzag ornament occurs on the ribs of its vault.

IV. But beside all these heavy repairs, a most important new work was carried out in the choir 1199-*c*. 1210. We have seen that there was a consecration in 1184, which probably included the new oblong Lady chapel. This may have been part of a scheme to make the whole of the eastern parts of the church rectangular. It may well be that when the repairs were finished in 1199, that the apse was shut off by a temporary wall, and the original scheme was proceeded with. This consisted in replacing the apse with its semicircular ambulatory, its north-east and south-east apsidal chapels by a rectangular retro-presbytery of two bays, with square-ended chapels flanking each side of the westernmost bay of the new Lady chapel. The needle-like pinnacles or spirelets of their turrets and the cusped rose windows in their gables should be noticed. This extension provided a procession path of two bays. At Canterbury a similar arrangement, but on a larger scale, was set out in 1175; the intention there being that the western part of the additional space gained should be ultimately utilised as a Saint's chapel; as a matter of fact it was not used till 1220. Chichester may have followed the Canterbury precedent in the expectation, which was realised in 1276, that she also would require such a chapel for a local canonised saint. Of the new work the general design and the detail, especially at the east end, is of superlative excellence; it is an Anglicised and improved version of Canterbury choir, though still retaining traces of French influence, as in the square abacus and the foliated capitals of piers and shafts. There is the same mixture of semicircular and pointed arches as in the Canterbury design, and with similar nonchalance the vaults of the aisles are distorted on plan in order to get the piers on either side central. The height of the ground story was fixed by the height of the new Lady chapel, and thus became greater than that of the Norman work to the west. The marble piers are unsurpassed anywhere; their design is reproduced at Boxgrove and St. Thomas, Portsmouth; it is imitated at West Wittering, near Selsea. When all these changes were completed, it is probable that the stalls were moved to the position they now occupy beneath the central tower. For the eastward movement of the choir Canterbury again afforded a precedent. It is possible that there was a special reason at Chichester for abandoning the nave. Nowadays there is a new parish church north of the cathedral on the other side of the road. This, the Sub-Deanery church, was from c. 1450 till 1853 located in the north transept with its double chapel for chancel. Originally, however, it occupied some part of the nave. The western bays of all the cathedrals were more or less open to the laity; and since in Chichester nave there was also a distinct parish church, the canons may well have thought it desirable to leave the whole of the nave free for parochial and general lay use. In Siegfried's work there are so many obligations to the Canterbury precedent, and the work of the masons is of such excellence, that there can be little doubt that many of them were the very men who had been trained under William of Sens and William the Englishman from 1175 to 1184, when Canterbury choir was consecrated and they would be thrown out of work.

JUNCTION OF SOUTH TRANSEPT AND CHOIR SHOWING CENTRAL TOWER

V. Documentary evidence makes it clear that building was still going on vigorously from c. 1210-c. 1253. In place of the apse of the south transept a square chapel and a watching chamber were built. A south porch, now inside the cloister, was built c. 1200; perhaps in place of a southern entrance through the south-western tower, where a small blocked Norman doorway, with zigzag ornament and voluted capitals, remains. At about the same time the sacristy was built, between the south porch and the south transept. Another porch was built (c. 1200) on the north side of the nave, probably for parochial use. It displays the nail-head ornament and good early foliage. Two towers are recorded to have fallen down in 1210; these would be the two western ones. Both were probably rebuilt in part at this period. The south-west tower retains its Norman basement; the north-west tower fell down again c. 1634, and was rebuilt by Mr Pearson in 1899-1900. The central tower, now rebuilt, may have been c. 1225-c. 1245.

VI. This period begins at the death of Richard of Wych. This energetic and saintly bishop died in 1253, and was buried in the north aisle of the nave. In 1261 he was canonised, and in 1276 his remains were translated to a shrine in the bay at the back of the High altar, which bay thus at length became a Saint's chapel. The platform on which his shrine stood remained till 1861; it occupied half the westernmost bay of the retro-choir. Offerings at his shrine increased the resources of the canons, and a second outburst of building commences. One result, which was destined to alter the whole character of the nave, was the building of additional chapels. In our parish churches it is common enough to find that pious and wealthy parishioners have been allowed to tack family chapels on to the aisles or nave. This was common enough, too, in the French cathedrals—*e.g.*, Laon and Amiens; but the naves of the English cathedrals were not as a rule altered in this way. At Chichester, however, there were now built three chapels—of St. George and St. Clement on the south of the south aisle, and of St. Thomas on the north of the north aisle at its eastern end. When the chapels were completed, the Norman aisle-walls were pierced, and arches were inserted where Norman windows had been; and Siegfried's buttresses, which had been added when the nave vault was erected, now found themselves inside the church, buttressing piers instead of walls. The new windows on the south side were built so high that the vaulting of the chapels had to be tilted up to allow room for their heads; externally they were originally crowned with gables, the weatherings of which may be seen outside. The buttresses were capped by beautiful pinnacles in the form of gabled spirelets, all now destroyed, and in connection with these a wonderful series of grotesques and

EXTERIOR OF THE NORTH SIDE OF NAVE

gargoyles should be studied. It is noteworthy that in St. Clement's chapel French masons must have been employed. Elsewhere, except in Westminster Abbey, France exercised little or no influence on the development of the Gothic architecture of England after the building of Canterbury choir. In St. Thomas' chapel is a charming example of a simple thirteenth-century reredos. The addition of these outer chapels makes Chichester unique among the English cathedrals, though it may be paralleled in Elgin cathedral and many a parish church. Artistically, the contrast of the gloomy and heavy Norman nave with the lightness and brightness of the chapels behind is most delightful; it looks infinitely larger and more spacious than it is; it is never all seen at a glance like the empty nave of York, and is full of changing vistas and delightful perspectives. Accidentally, the thirteenth-century builders had hit on a new source of picturesqueness.

VII. A little later, but still in the thirteenth century, two more double chapels were added on the north side of the nave, separated by a reredos, not by a wall, like those on the south side. The window tracery of the five chapels should be inspected in chronological order; it is an excellent object lesson of the development of bar out of plate tracery. But the great work of this period was the lengthening of the Lady chapel by two bays, and the remodelling of the three western bays. This was the work of Bishop Gilbert (1288-1305). The new work was done just when people had tired of conventional foliage, and hurried into naturalism. The capitals of the vaulting and window shafts are beautiful examples of naturalistic foliage. The window tracery, with long-lobed trefoils, occurs also in the beautiful chapel of the mediæval hospital of St. Mary, which should by all means be visited. To the earlier part of this period belongs the western or Galilee porch; in its arcading a later tomb has been inserted.

VIII. Then comes work ranging between c. 1315 and 1337. The canons set themselves to work to improve the lighting of the cathedral, which was bad; all the windows, except those in the new chapels, being small single lights. The south wall of the south transept was taken down and rebuilt, and in it was set a window of flowing tracery of admirable design (now filled with glass by Mr Kempe). Above the vault, and so only visible externally, is a circular window of flowing tracery. Bishop Langton (1305-1337), who gave money for the work, is buried in the canopied tomb below. The drainage of the roofs also was improved;

gutters and parapets being substituted for dripping eaves. Owing to the bends in the nave, it presents a concave curve on the north side, and a convex curve on the south. This is remedied on the north by constructing two corbel tables one above another; the upper one in a straight line; the lower one thick or thin as the curve requires. A somewhat different remedy is applied on the south. To this period also belong the stalls with ogee arches and compound cusping, and good misericords. At this period also the chapel of the Bishop's palace was remodelled. (The palace Dining-Room, with a fine panelled and painted ceiling, and kitchen, are also worth a visit.)

IX. In the time of Bishop William Rede (1369-1385), the tower at length was crowned with a spire, not quite so slender and graceful as those of Salisbury and Louth, which have an angle of ten degrees; that of the Chichester spire is of thirteen degrees.

X. The central tower seems to have shewn signs of weakness under the weight of the new spire; and so a detached Campanile was built, as at East Dereham: this work was in progress in 1411, 1428, and 1436. During this century, probably, was built at various dates the irregular three-sided cloister, in a quite abnormal position encircling the south transept. The object of it was to provide a covered way to the cathedral for the Canons, as well as for the Vicars, whose Close is hard by. Also the Canons' Gate was built. An upper story was added to the sacristy: it communicates by a secret door with a vaulted treasury over the south porch. The improvements in lighting were continued, the north wall of the north transept being treated in a similar way to that opposite. But settlements were the result, and a flying buttress had to be added to steady the north wall of the nave. This at last concluded the structural history of the cathedral. By Bishop Arundel (1459-1478) was erected a great stone screen between the western piers of the crossing; inside it were two vaulted recesses containing altars. After the Reformation it supported an organ of fine design, similar in character and position to those at Exeter and Gloucester, and greatly adding to the effectiveness of the interior. But screen and organ and return stalls were all swept away in 1859, with the vain idea of adapting a cathedral chancel for congregational services. The stones of the screen were numbered and stowed away in the campanile; but instead

FROM THE NORTH-EAST

of being replaced, a light wooden screen, designed by Mr Garner, has been put up. In 1829, moreover, the High altar was moved 6 ft. further eastward.

XI. From 1508-1536 the energetic Bishop Sherburne ruled. To him were due the admirable paintings on the vaults, in later days obliterated with yellow wash; also the paintings of the kings of England and bishops of Chichester. All this work was done by the Italian Lambert Bernardi and his sons. Sherburne is buried in the south aisle of the presbytery in a tomb which shews the influence of the Italian artists who did so much Renaissance work at Winchester cathedral, St. Cross, and Basing on their way from Southampton to London and Layer Marney.

Till 1829 the High altar stood 6 ft. further to the west than at present. At the back of it Sherburne erected a great reredos, somewhat of the character of those of Winchester and St Alban's, but of wood, and broader, because it contained a gallery. This gallery formed the Watching loft to the shrine of St. Richard, which was immediately below to the east. The gallery reached to the level of the triforium, and was removed in 1829, because the choir boys used to run races across it. An ugly stone reredos was subsequently substituted for the wooden one; this in its turn has recently been swept away, and fragments of the ancient oak reredos have been put together on the old site.

XII. In 1859 the central tower was found to be in danger; underpinning was resorted to, but matters got worse. "At noon, on February 21st, 1861, the workmen were ordered out of the building, and the people living in the neighbouring houses were warned of their danger; about an hour and a half later the spire was seen to incline slightly to the south-west and then to sink perpendicularly through the roof. Thus was fulfilled literally the old Sussex saying:—

> "If Chichester Church Steeple fall,
> In England there's no king at all."

In 1866 the tower and spire were rebuilt; the tower raised slightly so that the belfry windows might clear the roofs.

BIBLIOGRAPHY.—Professor Willis' *Chichester Cathedral.*
Gordon M. Hills in *British Archæological Association Journal*, xvii. 118, and xx. 155.
Prebendary Walcott's *Early Statutes of Chichester Cathedral.*
Dean Stephens's *History of the Diocese of Chichester.*

THE CATHEDRAL CHURCH OF CHRIST AND THE BLESSED VIRGIN MARY, DURHAM

BUILT FOR BENEDICTINE MONKS

THE bishopric of Durham has a long history, though there was no cathedral at Durham till 1018. The conversion of the Anglo-Saxon kingdoms north of the Thames had been brought about by the missionaries of the Irish and Scottish Church. Augustine's mission in Kent, and that of Paulinus in the north—both sent from Rome—had for their object, not so much the conversion of England, as to induce the English Christians to transfer their allegiance from the Celtic to the Roman Church. The success of Augustine's mission had been but short-lived. He landed in England A.D. 597; his death occurred in 605: and in 616 the Kentish kingdom relapsed into paganism. Paulinus landed in 601; proceeded to Northumbria in 625, but left it in 633, when, like Kent, most of Northumbria relapsed into paganism. The real "apostle of the north" was not Paulinus, but Aidan, who was sent at the request of King Oswald from Iona, and in the year 635 became the first bishop of the north of England.

(1) For thirty years the see was at Lindisfarne (Holy Island), but the jurisdiction of the bishop extended over all England north of the Humber, and over the south of Scotland (635-665). (2) In 678, Archbishop Theodore of Canterbury split up the vast Northumbrian diocese into the four bishoprics of York, Lindisfarne, Hexham, and Whitherne in Galloway. Twelve bishops ruled the now curtailed see from 678 to 900, the cathedral still remaining at Lindisfarne. The second of these was the famous St.

REFERENCES
A. CONSISTORY COURT
B. NORMAN PORCH
C. ENTRANCE TO GALILEE
D. SLYPE OR PARLOUR
E. CHAPTER HOUSE
F. CRYPT
G. KITCHEN
H. VESTRY
J. TREASURY

MONUMENTS
1. ST CUTHBERTS SHRINE
2. BISHOPS THRONE
3. BISHOP BARRINGTON
4. RALPH LORD NEVILLE
5. WOMENS BOUNDARY CROSS
6. FONT
7. ST BEDE'S ALTAR
8. CARDINAL LANGLEY
9. BISHOP SKIRLAW
10. BISHOP VAN MILDERT
11. BISHOP BEAUMONTS BRASS
12. REV. J BRITTON

PLAN

Cuthbert. (3) In 883 the monks, being apprehensive of a Danish inroad, removed the body of St. Cuthbert to Chester-le-Street, 7 miles north of Durham, and eight bishops had their cathedral at Chester-le-Street (900-995). (4) Once more, in fear of the Northmen, the see was removed—this for the last time—to Durham. Including Aldhun, the last bishop of Chester-le-Street and the first bishop of Durham, there have been, up to 1912, sixty-two bishops of Durham.

In the earliest days, we always read of monks as carrying about the relics of St. Cuthbert and serving the cathedral. Later on, but still in Anglo-Saxon days, the monks gave way to Secular Canons. These in turn were replaced by Benedictine monks by the Norman bishop, William of St. Carilef (1081-1096). In 1540 the monastic establishment was suppressed, and the cathedral was placed on the New Foundation, like the Benedictine cathedrals of Canterbury, Winchester, Ely, Norwich, Rochester, and Worcester, with an establishment once more of Secular Canons.

In Anglo-Saxon days, England was divided into provinces, whose earls exercised much the same power as the Viceroy exercises nowadays in India. These powerful and dangerous viceroyalties the Norman sovereigns abolished, with two exceptions. To guard the Marches against the Welsh, they left the old earldom or viceroyalty of Chester, putting it in the hands of a layman. To guard the Scottish border, they united with the bishopric of Durham the earldom of Northumberland. Between Tees and Tyne, and in some external districts, the bishop of Durham had palatine jurisdiction. Here the king's writ did not run; the writs were drawn in the name of the bishop. As feudal lord, his seat was Durham Castle ; as bishop, Durham Cathedral. Hence that wonderful group, castle and cathedral, which one sees from the Wear bridges towering overhead; unique in England, but not rare in the cities of the prince-bishops of the Holy Roman Empire: Lausanne, Chur, or Sitten. With the bishop of Durham rested the power of life and death in case of murder, or even of treason itself. The most magnificent of all these powerful prelates was Anthony Bek (1283-1310). His own personal followers, when he marched with Edward I. against the Scots, included 26 standard-bearers, 140 knights, 1,000 foot, and 500 horse. "Surrounded by his officers of state, or marching at the head of his troops, in peace or in war, he appeared as the military chief of a powerful and independent franchise. The court of Durham exhibited all the appendages of royalty; nobles addressed

THE WEST FRONT

the palatine sovereign kneeling; and instead of menial servants, knights waited in his presence-chamber and at his table, bareheaded and standing." But in 1536, Henry VIII. swept away the most important of the powers of the counts palatine. The ancient form of indictment, "contra pacem Episcopi," was altered to "against the King's peace," and the king's writ ran in Durham see. Still, the palatinate county of Durham was not fully an integral part of the realm, and up to 1675 did not send members to Parliament.

It was not till 1836 that the privileges of the county Palatine were fully and finally vested in the crown. Even now, the towers of Durham have a stern military air, such as no other English cathedral possesses; for a parallel to which we must go to the fortress-cathedrals of Albi, Narbonne, and the south-west of France. Durham cathedral is "half House of God, half castle 'gainst the Scot."

FIRST PERIOD.—Of the Anglo-Saxon cathedrals in wood or stone nothing remains. The architectural history of the present cathedral commences with the accession of the second Norman prelate, William of St. Carilef, or St. Calais on the southern border of Maine, who was bishop from 1081 to 1095, and is said to have laid the foundations of the Norman cathedral in 1093 on 11th August. By 1104 much of the eastern limb must have been finished; for in that year the shrine of St. Cuthbert was moved into it. In 1133, *i.e.*, in forty years, the whole church had been finished, including all the vaults. From architectural evidence it is pretty clear that the vaulting was executed in the following order: (1) the vaults of the aisles of the choir and transepts; (2) the high vault of the choir, now destroyed; (3) the vaults of the aisles of the nave; (4) the high vaults of the transepts and nave. The chronology of the high vaults is a very important question in the history of mediæval architecture, especially as affecting the reputation of English architects. If it is correct—and it is supported both by documentary and architectural evidence—it was the Durham architect who was the first to solve the great problem of mediæval architecture: how to construct and keep up a ribbed vault, oblong in plan, over a central aisle. The transverse arches of the high vault of the nave are pointed; so that it is in all respects a Gothic vault except as regards the moldings and enrichments of the ribs. It is a strange fact that when the Durham architect had thus solved the problem of problems of mediæval architecture—the construction of a high ribbed vault in oblong bays—most English builders went on putting up unworthy wooden ceilings for nearly another century. Durham was

THE NAVE FROM THE WEST

very slow in converting the twelfth-century builders of England to Gothic.

The bays of Durham are coupled, Lombard-fashion — *i.e.*, large and small piers alternate: with what object is uncertain. There were three parallel eastern apses. The central apse had no ambulatory. The lateral apses were square externally, as at Romsey.

Durham anticipates Gothic not only in vaulting its central aisles in oblongs with the aid of pointed arches, but in the employment of flying buttresses. These in the triforium of the choir appear in the form of semicircular arches, with a wall on them, which provided a support for the purlins of the aisle roof. But in the triforium of the nave they consist of segments of circles tilted up on end. Here they are genuine flying buttresses, which oppose resistance to any outward inclination of the clerestory wall. The only constructional difference between those of the nave and Gothic flying buttresses is that the former are placed underneath the roof of the triforium, sheltered from the weather, while the latter are usually placed outside and above the aisle roof, and are thus liable to disintegration by wind, rain, and frost. But even in Gothic, flying buttresses are not always displayed; they still remained concealed under the triforium in the early work at Salisbury; and even in the fourteenth-century work of Winchester nave.

THE CLOISTERS AND WESTERN TOWERS

Internally, the one fault of Durham is its shortness in proportion to its great breadth. Ely nave has twelve bays,

Peterborough ten, Norwich fourteen, Durham only eight But the architect could not build much further to the west, for close at hand is the precipice rising above the river; nor did he like to build further to the east, for the ground there is bad.

The internal elevation, however, is unsurpassed by that of any Romanesque church in Europe. At Winchester, Norwich, Peterborough, Ely, the three stories—pier-arcade, triforium, and clerestory—are about equal in height: a very unsatisfactory proportion. The architects of Gloucester and Tewkesbury rushed into the opposite extreme, and carried up their piers to such a vast height that the triforium and clerestory were dwarfed out of all proportion. But at Durham the proportions are absolutely right. The vault, too, is not so much later in date as to interfere with the solid monumental effect of the interior. Durham gives still the impression which it gave Dr. Johnson—one of "rocky solidity and indeterminate duration": the very reverse of the unsubstantial tenuity of Salisbury and Beauvais.

The doorway of the Chapter house is recorded to have been built by Bishop Galfrid Rufus (1133-1140). The north and south doorways of the nave (facing one another) are so similar to that of the Chapter house that they must also be his work.

SECOND PERIOD.—To Bishop Pudsey belongs the Galilee, *c.* 1175. He commenced to erect a Lady chapel in the usual position to the east of the choir. But St. Cuthbert, who had an ultra-monastic hatred of womankind, and would not brook to have the chapel even of Our Lady in the neighbourhood of his shrine, shewed his displeasure openly by the fissures and cracks and settlements which kept constantly occurring. In despair the bishop had to build in the cramped space between the west end and the precipice, thus blocking up the west doorway of the church. From the first this Lady chapel seems to have been called the Galilee; nobody knows why. In details it is not unlike the chapel in the keep of Newcastle. Built in the last quarter of the twelfth century, it is remarkable for the paucity of Gothic detail: the arches are all semicircular; they are not molded, but ornamented with bands of the old-fashioned zigzag. The bases, indeed, are transitional in character; and so is the voluted water-leaf of the capitals. But, spite of semicircular arch and Norman ornament, the spirit of the whole—its lightness, grace, and elegance—is Gothic. A building may have every arch pointed and molded, and yet in its heaviness be Romanesque at heart,

THE GALILEE

e.g., the Cistercian churches of Fountains and Kirkstall, the Augustinian church of Llanthony. In Durham Galilee, on the other hand, one feels that one is in a Gothic building, as truly as one does in presence of the semicircular arcades of Pisa or Lucca. Still more Gothic must have been the effect of the coupled shafts of Purbeck marble before Cardinal Langley added two more shafts of freestone. The cardinal is buried in front of the west door of the nave. Here also was the shrine of the remains of the Venerable Bede, stolen from the monks of Jarrow by the sacrist Elfred, one of the most successful of mediæval "body-snatchers."

THIRD PERIOD.—Early in the thirteenth century the western towers were carried up. At one time they had wooden spires. The present battlements were added about

1780. But the great work of this century was the noble eastern transept. Its position repeats that of Fountains Abbey, which was finished in 1247, and which also is known as the "Chapel of the Nine Altars." The object of the eastern extension at Durham was partly to provide nine more chapels, partly to make room for the shrine of St. Cuthbert, which, like those of St. Swithun and St. Birinus at Winchester, and that of St. Alban at St. Alban's, stood to the east of the high altar, and contained the body of St. Cuthbert and the head of St. Oswald.

The work was not commenced till 1242 (Bishop Farnham), and not completed till about 1280. When it was begun, lancet windows were still in fashion; when it was completed, they had given way to traceried windows with cusped circles in their heads. Later on, rectilinear tracery was inserted in the lancets: it is surprising that it has not been hacked out, as in Ripon façade, by architectural "purists." The circular window, 90 ft. across, was rebuilt by Wyatt. The architect was a layman, Richard Farnham, "architector novæ fabricæ Dunelm"; a mason "Thomas Moises posuit hanc petram." The foliated capitals, both here and in the eastern bay of the choir, are of unrivalled beauty. No less remarkable is the perfection of the masonry. The walls are nearly 8 ft. thick, with huge piers at the angles forming buttresses and weighted by pinnacles; they rise straight from the ground unaided by aisles or flying buttresses, "yet they have borne the lofty vault (80 ft. high) for more than three centuries without the slightest sign of settlement or flaw." The vaulting of the transept involved some rather difficult problems, which were solved somewhat awkwardly. Such was the reverence for St. Cuthbert that not a single person was buried in the cathedral till 1311, when that magnificent prelate Anthony Bek was brought into the Chapel of Nine Altars for interment, through a door on the north of the chapel (now blocked up), not through the cathedral; and even he has no monument. One sees why there is such a paucity of monuments in this cathedral.

THE CHAPEL OF THE NINE ALTARS

The next thing was to break the transition from Romanesque choir to Gothic transept by remodelling the eastern bays of the choir in the fashion of the day. Also a new Gothic vault was put over the choir in place of the eleventh-century vault, the marks of which may still be seen on the clerestory wall.

FOURTH PERIOD.—For a long time little was done at Durham; the cathedral was structurally complete. In the fourteenth century several large windows with flowing tracery were inserted, *e.g.*, the west window of the nave and the north window of the north transept; and four windows (restored) in the south aisle of the choir. The three westernmost windows in the north aisle of the choir were copied in 1848 from the fourteenth-century windows at Sleaford, Holbeach, and Boughton Aluph. To this period belongs the tomb of Bishop Hatfield, built in his lifetime (1345-1381), one of the best bits of design in England. The episcopal throne above it looks a little later, and seems to have been designed for some other position, as it does not fit the space between the piers. The altar reredos, or Neville screen, as it is called, was made in London between 1372 and 1380, and brought by sea to Durham: like that at St. Alban's, it is of clunch, a hard chalk. It is continued to right and left, forming sedilia on *both* sides of the sanctuary.

FIFTH PERIOD.—The great work of the fifteenth century was the central tower, which replaced a thirteenth-century tower, *c.* 1470. It is 218 ft. high; in spite of its vast weight, the Norman piers which support it shew no signs of strain. There are massive squinches at the angles, shewing that it was intended to be finished by a spire, as the western towers actually were finished. What an astounding spectacle Durham would have presented, capped with three spires! Imagine a Lichfield cathedral set on a hill 200 ft. high! In the nave is a series of Neville monuments. In the third bay from the west is the Women's Boundary Cross, beyond which women were not to venture, lest they should incur St. Cuthbert's wrath. The great window of the south transept was inserted about 1400.

SIXTH PERIOD. Between 1660 and 1672 Bishop Cousin did much to repair the damage done by the Scottish prisoners who had been confined in the cathedral after the battle of Dunbar in 1650. His stalls and font cover are of exceptional interest, as specimens of what is rare—seventeenth-century Gothic. It should be compared with the lovely work at Brancepeth, his old church, and the episcopal chapel at Bishop Auckland. Lord Crewe's fine classical choir-screen, with the organ in its normal and proper position upon it, has been destroyed at one of the many abominable "restorations" of which the authorities of this cathedral have been guilty. Now there is a pretentious marble and alabaster screen of mid-Victorian Gothic, and the ignorant and the tasteless have got that "unbroken vista" for which their hearts yearn.

EXTERIOR.—On the north doorway of the nave is the famous sanctuary knocker. Durham and Beverley, owing to the high reputation of the relics of St. Cuthbert and St. John of Beverley, both had large privileges of sanctuary. Beverley retains the Sanctuary chair, the Frithstool; Durham the knocker. It is thirteenth-century work. "Upon knocking at the ring affixed to the north door of Durham the culprit was admitted without delay; and after full confession, reduced to writing before witnesses, a bell in the Galilee tower ringing all the time to give notice to the town that some one had taken refuge in the church, there was put on him a black gown with a yellow cross on its right shoulder, as the badge of St. Cuthbert, whose peace he had claimed. When thirty-seven days had elapsed, if a pardon could not be obtained, the malefactor, after certain ceremonies before the shrine, solemnly abjured his native land for ever; and was straightway, by the agency of the intervening parish constables, conveyed to the coast, bearing in his hand a white wooden cross, and was sent out of the kingdom by the first ship which sailed after his arrival." During their stay in the church the culprits lived on the lower floors of the western towers. The atrocious setting of the doorway is modern; as also the pinnacles of the Chapel of the Nine Altars, where the famous Dun Cow is to be seen in a niche in the north-west turret. All the design of this side of the cathedral has been utterly ruined; having been pared away to the depth of 3 or 4 in. Originally each bay of the aisle had a transverse roof ending in a gable, as originally on the south side of Chichester nave.

THE CRYPT

The monastic buildings are numerous and important; the library contains precious MSS., touching relics of St. Cuthbert, and a wonderful collection of Pre-Conquest crosses and "hogbacks."

BIBLIOGRAPHY.—Durham cathedral is fortunate in its literature. There is an excellent guide-book by Canon Greenwell; and a descriptive account with numerous plates by R. W. Billings, 1843; while the *Rites of Durham* is a detailed account of the use and purpose of each part of the church and the monastic buildings. The *Rites* was written in 1593 and has recently been re-edited with valuable notes and appendices as vol. 107 of the publications of the Surtees Society by Rev. J. T. Fowler, D.C.L. To one who reads the *Rites* in Durham itself, the whole life of cathedral and abbey lives afresh.

FROM THE SOUTH-WEST

THE CATHEDRAL CHURCH OF THE HOLY AND UNDIVIDED TRINITY, ELY

BUILT FOR BENEDICTINE MONKS

"THE vast and magnificent cathedral of Ely," says Mrs Van Rensselaer, "looms up on the horizon, as we come westward from Norwich, like a great solitary ship at sea. As we draw nearer it preserves its isolated clearness of outline, lifted visibly above the plain, yet so little lifted that its bulk seems all the greater from being nearer the eye. As we enter the little town from the southwest we realise its enormous length, the grace of its octagon, and the stern majesty of the tall tower, which rises like a great cliff in a land where men might well build cliffs, since Nature had built none. But there is in truth no spot whence the great monarch of the fenlands may not be admirably seen, until we get so far off that it drops behind the horizon's rim. Wherever it may reveal itself it is always immense, imposing, majestic: only upon the plains

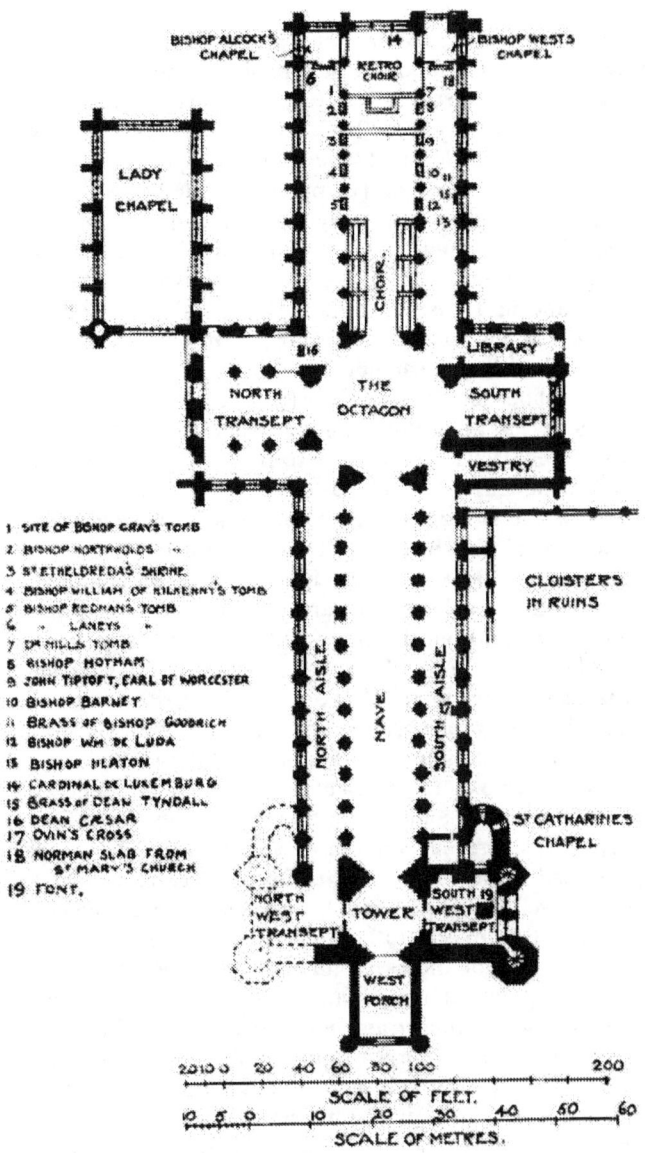

PLAN

of Egypt or Mesopotamia has Nature assisted the effect of man's work by such entire suppression of herself."

Ely, like Peterborough, Ramsey, Thorney, and Crowland, and like Glastonbury, goes back to early Anglo-Saxon days, when communities of monks and nuns sought solitude and safety in the recesses of far-spreading marshes and fens. In the beginning the monastery was founded as a nunnery, in 673, by Etheldreda, who became the first abbess and Ely's patron saint. From the nuns it passed to Secular Canons, and in Dunstan's time to Benedictine monks. In 1109 the abbot became a bishop, and the Benedictine church a Benedictine cathedral.

The bishop of Ely in his island, like the bishop of Durham in his hill-fortress, held powers such as no other English ecclesiastic was allowed to possess. His territorial powers included the whole Isle of Ely: and this, "the Liberty of the Bishops of Ely," was subject to the exclusive jurisdiction of the bishop. It is in these two facts—the possession of a local saint, St. Etheldreda or St. Audrey, of high repute through all England; and in the enormous revenues derived from the Isle of Ely—that the explanation lies of the vast scale on which the abbey-church was planned in the eleventh century, of the astonishing richness of its thirteenth-century presbytery, and of the enormous works undertaken and rapidly carried out in the fourteenth century.

FIRST PERIOD.—The present cathedral was commenced in 1083 by Abbot Simeon, brother of Bishop Walkelin of Winchester, where Simeon himself had been prior. Earlier still he had been a monk at St. Ouen, Rouen; so that he would be well acquainted with the contemporary architecture of Normandy. As was to be expected from the relationship of the founders of the two cathedrals, Ely and Winchester have many points of resemblance. Both are vast in scale, far surpassing the Abbaye-aux-hommes at Caen, or Lanfranc's copy of it at Canterbury. Both indulge in the luxury of aisles to the west as well as to the east of their transepts. Both had return aisles in the transepts—a feature borrowed from Cérisy-la-Forêt and the Abbaye-aux-hommes. Those of

FROM THE SOUTH-EAST

Winchester remain; those of Ely have been pushed back to the end-walls. The nave of Ely had no less than thirteen bays, its transepts four, its choir five. The choir aisles had square ends; the choir was intended to terminate in a semicircular apse, but was made square-ended between 1103 and 1106. The stalls were placed in the crossing and in the two eastern bays of the nave. There was a central tower; and, instead of two western towers, there was one tower with four flanking turrets. From the lower stories of the western transepts, of which only the southern one is left, apses projected eastward. Externally the western transept gave the church great breadth and dignity; and the plan of Bury and Ely was speedily copied at Peterborough, Lincoln, and Wells. Internally this south-western transept is the most picturesque bit of Norman work in the country. For western and central towers in a line parallels survive at Wymondham and Wimborne, and formerly at Bury and Hereford. Of Abbot Simeon's eleventh-century work little is left now except the vaulting shafts in front of his apse, to the east of the organ; the exterior of the west windows of the south transept, which alone have the nail-head molding; and the lower part of the eastern walls of the transepts, which have the Ionic capital. The masonry is rude and tooled with a large cross-stroke: the abaci and the soffits of the arches are square and unmolded. In 1106 the bodies of St. Etheldreda and her sisters were translated into the eastern limb, which was then probably complete. For a long time the work must have gone on very slowly; and the original design was so closely adhered to that it is difficult to recognise any substantial differences between the four eastern and the western bays of the nave. Throughout, regardless of the Durham improvements, the aisle-vaults are without ribs. Durham cathedral took only forty years to build, and as Abbot Simeon commenced Ely cathedral in 1083, it should have been possible to complete it c. 1133, allowing for the greater dimensions of Ely. But from the fact that the western transept was not finished till c. 1180, it is likely that the nave was not finished till well on in the century.

The lateness of the work is seen in the tall, slender, graceful shafts of the triforium and clerestory, and in the substitution of moldings for carved ornament in the orders of all the

THE NAVE

arches. The proportions are unusually good, both the pier-arches and clerestory being taller than usual in proportion to such a lofty triforium. Accordingly, the proportions of the Norman choir, then standing, were copied in the presbytery added east of the choir in the thirteenth century; and the proportions of the presbytery were reproduced in the fourteenth-century choir. It is this, doubtless, which gives such a feeling of unity in Ely, as at Worcester, in spite of the fact that the present cathedral consists of three blocks built in three different centuries in entirely different styles. At Canterbury, Rochester, Ripon, Gloucester, nave and choir quarrel; at Winchester and York, nave and transept; Ely has evolved harmony out of discord. The work seems to have been done in seven sections: first, the transepts; second, the eastern limb; third, the eastern bays of the nave; fourth, its western bays; fifth, the two doorways from the nave into the cloister; sixth, the lower part of the west transept; seventh, the upper stories of the western transept, the western turrets, and the upper arches of the crossing. To the last half of the twelfth century belongs also the Infirmary for superannuated, infirm or sick monks, east of the cloister, the remains of which are worth a visit. Between 1198 and 1215 the parish church of St. Mary was built; it has a lovely doorway, well worth a visit.

SECOND PERIOD.—Early in the thirteenth century the Galilee porch was added, in the same position as at Durham. Externally the design is commonplace; internally, "with its rich outer and inner portals, its capitals carved with delicate curling leafage, its side arcades in double rows of trefoiled arches, and the profuse dog-tooth enrichment of its moldings, it is one of the loveliest things ever built, and one of the most English in its loveliness." The early date of 1200 is assigned to this and to the equally beautiful western porches of St. Albans.

Then came the great reconstruction which every great English church went through to the east, in order to increase the length of the sanctuary, and to provide still further east a Saint's chapel, an ambulatory, and in most cases a Lady chapel. In 1235, to the east of the Norman choir, at the point where the Norman roof-shafts still remain, there was built in the days of Bishop Northwold, and mainly at his expense, a presbytery of six bays: a presbytery of inexpressible loveliness. "Nowhere," says Mr Freeman, "can we better study the boldly clustered marble pier with its detached shafts, the richly floriated capitals, the yet richer corbels which bear up the marble vaulting-shafts, the bold and deftly cut moldings of every arch, great and small. Lovelier detail was surely never wrought by the hand of man." The piers are closely spaced; and the arches, therefore, as at Beverley, are sharply pointed — in beautiful harmony with the lancet windows. On the other hand, the trefoiling of the triforium arches contrasts delightfully with the pointed arches of pier-arcade and clerestory. In contemporary work the beauty of Ely presbytery can only be paralleled at Beverley; but at Beverley the design owes everything to the architect; at Ely the sculptor may claim half the credit. Worcester choir may

INTERIOR OF GALILEE

be placed next in order; its proportions, indeed, are very similar to those of the Ely work. Westminster does not enter into comparison, being French in design. The presbytery was completed in seventeen years, and cost £5,040, which may be equivalent to about £90,720 of our money, or £15,120 per bay.

In this great work of Bishop Northwold is seen one of the earliest and most important examples of what was to be the accepted and final planning of the eastern limb of an English cathedral church; viz., an aisled parallelogram roofed full height to its east end, and with the ritual divisions separated only by screens. The work was finished in 1252. With this superb eastern extension the monks remained satisfied for nearly seventy years. Nothing was done in the cathedral except the insertion of larger windows with geometrical tracery to give more light to the chapels in the eastern aisle of the south transept.

THE EAST END

THIRD PERIOD.—But in the fourteenth century a most wonderful series of great works was carried out in Ely; the noblest works of that or perhaps of any period of mediæval building in England. First of all, it was resolved to give the Blessed Virgin the honour so long withheld from her at Ely. Her rightful position in the presbytery had been usurped by St. Etheldreda, as at Westminster by St. Edward.

Following the precedent of Bristol and Peterborough, a vast Lady chapel was begun in 1321, detached from, and on the north side of, the choir. It is a remarkable piece of mediæval engineering; the vault—a very flat one—being upheld by a minimum of wall and buttress. But it was more than engineering. It was the product of a time when "Catholic

WALL-ARCADE IN THE LADY CHAPEL

purity in the best natures was still allied to the tenderness of chivalry"—

> "When in reverence of the Heavene's Queene
> They came to worship alle women that beene."

It is said that when Pugin saw the ruins of its arcading, once so glorious in its beauty—wherein are carved, in the spandrels above each canopy, incidents in the scriptural and legendary history of the Blessed Virgin—he burst into tears. He estimated the cost of the restoration of the Lady chapel at £100,000, but said that no workmen could be found competent to do the work. The Lady chapel is said to have been finished in 1349; but the tracery of the east and west windows is evidently of later date. No doubt building was stopped by the Black Death of 1349, which wrought great havoc in the eastern counties. It was not till 1374 that these windows were inserted by Bishop Barnett. In the central lower light of the east window there was originally a stone niche, containing no doubt an image of Our Lady.

The year after the Lady chapel was commenced, the central tower fell; and falling eastward, ruined the western bays of the Norman choir. Nevertheless, though the monks had suddenly cast on them the vast task of rebuilding both tower and choir, they did not abandon or intermit their work in the Lady chapel. Side by side the different sets of works went on: the Lady chapel, the central octagon, and the choir. The octagon was finished in 1342, the choir probably not much later. How vast the resources of Ely must have been!

In 1322 Alan of Walsingham, then Sacrist at Ely and afterwards Prior, set to work to clear away the *débris* of the piers of the tower. It may well have occurred to him when he saw the great open space in the centre of the cathedral, what a pity it would be ever to close it up again in order to construct the usual circumscribed square central tower, the width only of the nave, under which one feels as if looking up from the bottom of a well. What was left, when he had cleared away the four tower-piers, was an area three times as large as that of the original crossing. This area was an octagon, with four long and four short sides: four long sides opening into nave, choir, and transepts; four short sides opening diagonally into the aisles. Why not throw four wide and four narrow arches over the piers of the octagon, and on these arches erect, not a small square tower, but a vast octagonal tower? Octagonal central towers were unknown in the English cathedrals; but there are plenty abroad, *e.g.*, magnificent examples at Coutances and Siena. The difficulty was how to roof a tower so vast. The noblest course would have been to cover it with a vault of stone.

But no English architect ever dared a vault 77 ft. wide. In Spain they might have done it: the vault of the nave of Gerona is 73 ft. in span. In England not so; the York people did not even venture to vault a nave 45 ft. broad.

Some sort of wooden roof, therefore, had to be adopted. That roof could not be a flat wooden ceiling; no beams of the length of 77 ft. could be had; and if put up they would have been unsafe. Instead, then, of a flat ceiling, Alan adopted much the same construction as is to be seen in the lower part of any normal spire of wood. In such a spire inclined beams resting on the tower at eight points support an octagonal collar of wood, on which upright posts are set, and to these the sloping timbers of the spire are affixed. In a spire the sides of the spire conceal from view the octagonal skeleton resting on the collar; at Ely there are no sloping sides, and the eight posts form a wooden lantern, with vertical sides, and the greater part of this lantern is visible in any external view. In this, or in some such way, Alan got his design, one of the most original and poetic conceptions of the Middle Ages; but arising, like all the best things in Gothic architecture, out of the exigencies of building construction.

The problem was solved on paper, but it proved immensely difficult in execution. Alan finished the stone piers and arches in six years, but the timber-work occupied twelve years more. He had to search all over England before he could find oaks big and straight and sound enough for the eight vertical angle-posts of his lantern. They are 63 ft. long, with a sapless scantling of 3 ft. 4 in. by 2 ft. 8 in. Oaks like those do not grow now in England. The eight angle-posts are tied together at top and bottom by collars of horizontal beams, and the whole skeleton lantern rests on the tips of inclined beams, whose lower ends are supported by corbels behind the capitals of the great piers below.

And as the inclined beams spread to right and left from the great piers below, it follows that the eight sides of the lantern are not placed above the eight arches below. This engineering necessity, also, is wrought into a new source of beauty. For advantage is taken of it to pierce the wall space above the low narrow arches with four tall windows, so that the central area, so gloomy at Winchester, Lincoln, and Wells, is irradiated with a flood of light from twelve vast windows; four below, eight above. There is not such a lantern in the world. Nor does any church in England present such dramatic contrasts of light and shadow in general; to the west, dark nave; to the east, darker choir; the centre all light and atmosphere. The views from the aisles of the nave across the octagon into the choir are veritable glimpses into fairyland. Externally, too, the octagonal lantern groups well with the great western tower; in height, in bulk, in shape they are in perfect ratio.

Side by side with the octagon went up the choir, as was necessary, that the octagon might have abutment to the east. The choir is "a little over-developed and attenuated in detail"; the windows are squat and ungraceful in proportion, and their flowing tracery wiry and unlovely. Window tracery is the one weak point in the Curvilinear work at Ely. Nevertheless, this choir is one of those works whose delicate loveliness disarms criticism. It even disarmed Mr Fergusson, who says that the proportions of the presbytery are reproduced in the choir, "with such exquisite taste that there is perhaps no single portion of any Gothic building in the world which can vie with it in poetry of design or beauty of detail."

But the monks had not finished even now. They were dissatisfied with the lighting of the older part of the cathedral. So they took out, now or a little later, lancets of the presbytery, not only those of the aisles but those of the outer wall of the triforium, and replaced them by broad windows of flowing tracery. Even this was insufficient, and so they substituted a flat roof for the steep lean-to roof of the two western bays of the presbytery aisles, and glazed the inner arcade of these two bays of the triforium. Thus more light was obtained for St. Etheldreda's shrine, which then stood between these two bays; its exact position is marked by the elaborate boss in the vault of the choir. Externally, the result is deplorable; a big gap being left in the choir aisles, where the lean-to roof formerly extended continuously. All this piercing of the walls with bigger windows tended to

THE OCTAGON FROM THE CHOIR

weaken the supports of the vaults, and the builders took the precaution to weight the buttresses with heavy pinnacles, and to rebuild the flying buttresses.

Beautiful stalls were then put up—the carved panels are modern—and for the ancient white marble tomb of St. Etheldreda a stone pedestal was erected. It is probably that which now stands between the north piers of the presbytery, in the third bay from the west; portions of its iron grilles may still be seen imbedded in the stone. On this was placed the Norman silver reliquary, "embossed with many figures, with a golden majesty blazing in its centre, with countless jewels of crystal and pearl, onyx and beryl, and amethyst and chalcedony."

Nor was this all. Alan designed for his friend Prior Crauden a little chapel which would be the cynosure of any other cathedral, but which passes almost unnoticed amid the glories of Ely: no one should fail to visit it.

FOURTH PERIOD.—These are the three great building periods at Ely. But between 1350 and the Dissolution much interesting work was done. The monks continued their improvements in the lighting of the cathedral, treating the Norman nave very much as they had treated the presbytery, i.e., putting bigger windows in the aisles, and also raising the aisle walls so as to get space for larger windows above, in the hope that more light might filter through across the triforium into the nave.

Moreover, they added another story to the great west tower, making it octagonal, perhaps in order to bring it more into harmony with Alan's lantern. The additional story threw more weight on the Norman arches below, under which new strengthening arches had to be built; this saved the tower. It is perhaps owing to pressure of the tower that the northern arm of the western transept collapsed.

To this period also belong the hammer-beam roofs of the transepts, and the Ely Porta or Walpole Gate, which was formerly the principal entrance into the precincts of the Abbey; it was built in 1396.

In 1488 was erected the chantry chapel of Bishop Alcock at the east end of the north aisle of the choir; and in 1534 that of Bishop West in a similar position in the south aisle. They are perhaps the two most superb chantry chapels in England, of marvellous richness and delicacy and vigour. That of Bishop West is of exceptional interest for the classical scrollwork above the doorway and on the vault; also the handsome iron gate; one rarely sees in an English cathedral the delicate art of the early Italian Renaissance. In Bishop Alcock's chapel notice the frequent passion-flower and the bishop's rebus—a cock on a globe; also the fan-vault with its big pendant.

FIFTH PERIOD; POST-REFORMATION WORK.—In 1539 the monks were expelled; the last Prior becoming the first Dean. In 1699 Sir Christopher Wren contributed a classical doorway to the north transept. The roofs of the nave and the lantern were painted c. 1862 by Mr Le Strange and Mr Gambier Parry. To Sir Gilbert Scott is due the gorgeous reredos, and he also removed the stalls from the presbytery; the plan in Browne Willis' *Survey* shews that they originally stood in the octagon.

MINOR WORK.—The cathedral abounds in interest; only some of the more important memorials can be enumerated here. (1) Starting from the extreme east end, between West and Alcock's chapels, in the easternmost arch on the south side is the monument of Cardinal Luxemburg, 1443. (2) In the easternmost bay of the *south aisle*, by the wall, is a Norman slab from St. Mary's church. (3) Opposite is what remains of the tomb of Bishop Hotham, 1337. (4) Beneath the next arch to the west is the tomb of John Tiptoft, Earl of Worcester, beheaded in 1470; beside him are effigies of his two wives. (5) Under the next arch is the base of the tomb of Bishop Barnett, 1373. (6) Under the next arch is the beautiful monument of Bishop William de Luda, 1298, resembling in style the Winchester stall work and the monuments of Edmund Crouchback and Aveline in Westminster Abbey. (7) In the centre of the aisle is the brass of Bishop Goodrich, 1554. (8) Next is the brass of Dean Tyndall, 1614. (9) Cross the presbytery to the *north aisle*, noticing the difference in the thirteenth and fourteenth century vaults of presbytery and choir On the left of the north doorway of the presbytery is the monument of Bishop Redman, 1505. (10) Now we proceed up the aisle eastward. First comes the effigy of Bishop Kilkenny, 1256. (11) Next is what is probably the pedestal of St. Etheldreda's shrine, now out of place, as are the High Altar, the stalls, and nearly everything else, as the result

WESTERN PROCESSIONAL DOORWAY

of divers restorations. (12) Next comes the beautiful effigy of Bishop Northwold, 1254; "si monumentum quæris, circumspice." (13) Then we retrace our steps; and leaving the north choir aisle, have immediately to the right the monument of Dean Caesar, 1636. (14) On the eight great corbels of the *octagon* are carved scenes from the life of St. Etheldreda. (15) Half-way down the *south*

ELY CATHEDRAL

aisle of the nave is the lower part of a seventh-century cross with an inscription to Ovin, the steward of St. Etheldreda:—

> LUCEM TUAM OVINO
> DA DEUS ET REQUIEM
> AMEN.

BIBLIOGRAPHY.—First stands the admirable *Architectural History of Ely Cathedral*, by Rev. D. J. Stewart, 1868. Bentham published in 1771 a valuable history of the cathedral. Archdeacon Chapman has recently edited specimens of the *Fabric Rolls* in two volumes. A good local handbook, revised by various Deans, and published by Mr G. H. Tyndall, Minster Place, Ely, gives a long list of books and documents relating to the cathedral.

A GLIMPSE OF THE CHOIR

THE CATHEDRAL CHURCH OF ST. PETER, EXETER

BUILT FOR SECULAR CANONS

IN the days of the so-called Heptarchy, the divisions of the Church followed those of the State. The diocese of Lichfield was conterminous with the kingdom of Mercia. In the same way the diocese of Winchester was coextensive with the kingdom of Wessex. Thus Devonshire, so far as it had been colonised by Anglo-Saxons before the eighth century, formed part of the diocese of Winchester. But these vast dioceses were too cumbrous to work. They had to be subdivided. So a western diocese was lopped off from Winchester, and a bishop of Sherborne was appointed as its head. Then, as the far west grew in population and importance, two more bishoprics were created—those of Crediton and Cornwall. These two, however, were soon amalgamated; and Cornwall has had no bishop of its own from the Conquest till the recent formation of the bishopric of Truro.

Just before the Norman Conquest, Bishop Leofric removed his see from the open town of Crediton to the walled city of Exeter, largely in consequence of attacks of Scandinavian pirates. At Exeter Leofric found a Benedictine monastery, dedicated to St. Mary and St. Peter. This conventual church he made his cathedral. "He was installed in the episcopal chair by Edward the Confessor, who supported his right arm, and Queen Eadgytha his left"; representations of which were inserted in the fourteenth-century sedilia. The Benedictine monks were removed by the Confessor to his new abbey at Westminster, and Leofric supplied their place by a body of Secular Canons, who lived together, however, and to some extent observed monastic discipline. Leofric was left undisturbed in his bishopric till his death, 1072. His successor, also, though a Norman,

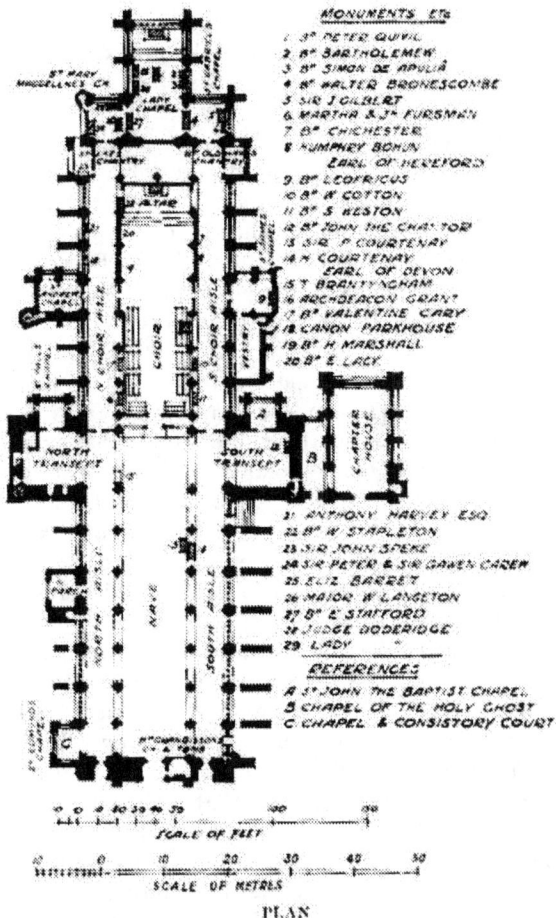

PLAN

was English and conservative by training; the venerable Anglo-Saxon church was good enough for him. But William Warelwast (1107-1128) was a great building prelate, and it was he who commenced the existing cathedral. Exeter cathedral, therefore, was commenced much later than most of the Norman cathedrals.

Up to 1551, the see of Exeter was one of the greatest prizes in the Church of England. And its bishops were in nearly all cases men of the highest ability, rank, and importance. It possessed thirty-two manors, fourteen palaces—two in Cornwall, nine in Devonshire, one in Surrey, one in London, of which Exeter Street, Strand, is a reminder. The present value of the income of the see would be at least £100,000. The first of the Protestant bishops was Miles Coverdale, who with Tyndale translated the Bible. Seth Ward (1662-1667) "cast out the buyers and sellers who had usurped the cathedral, and therein kept distinct shops to vend their wares." In the evil days of the Puritans the cathedral had been divided into two churches by a vast whitewashed wall, built on the choir-screen and separating choir from nave. The Independents worshipped in the nave, the Presbyterians in the choir. Here they had what they called "great quiet and comfort," till Seth Ward pulled the wall down. Seth Ward's restoration of the cathedral cost him £25,000—representing a far greater sum nowadays. He put the cathedral in substantial repair; and the restoration by Sir G. G. Scott, in 1870, did little damage.

FIRST PERIOD—BISHOP WARELWAST (1107-1136) AND BISHOP CHICHESTER (1138-1155).—Nothing remains of the church of the Anglo-Saxon monastery; nor is there any early Norman work, for, as we have seen, that church was allowed to remain standing till the year 1107. But early in the twelfth century a Norman cathedral was commenced by William Warelwast, nephew of the Conqueror. That cathedral included both the existing towers; it also included an aisled nave of the same dimensions as the present one. For the narrowed span of the westernmost arches of the pier-arcade is to be accounted for only on the supposition of the existence, to the west, of the wall of a pre-existing west front, and the immensely thick west wall of the nave has been found to have a Norman core; moreover the lower parts of Norman buttresses, pilasters, and plinths, and one base, have been found in the walls of the north and south aisles of the nave; while traces of an apse have been found at the end of the third bay of the northern choir aisle. So it is plain that the twelfth-century cathedral had west front, nave and aisles, transeptal towers, a choir of three bays, and probably an apse at the end of the choir, flanked by smaller apses; the towers also may have had eastern apses.

FROM THE SOUTH-EAST

Transeptal towers are rare abroad and unknown in England, except at Ottery St. Mary, where the church was made collegiate and rebuilt by Grandisson, bishop of Exeter, in the fourteenth century. From the advanced type of masonry and ornament it is likely that the towers are not earlier than the middle of the century. If the cathedral was built as rapidly as Durham, it might have been completed as early as 1150 by Bishop Chichester, who is recorded to have been "a liberal contributor to the buildings of his church." But as a matter of fact the works dragged on to the end of the century, till the time of Bishop Marshall (1194-1206). The probability is that the nave was his work; for on its south aisle-wall are three consecration crosses, two complete and one only blocked out, which may well belong to his period.

With regard to the work of Bishop Marshall enormous confusion has arisen. Hoker (1540-1583) says that Marshall "finished the building of his church according to the plat and foundation which his predecessors had laid." This plainly means that he finished the Norman cathedral of Warelwast and Chichester. Unfortunately, Archdeacon Freeman, in compiling his *Architectural History of Exeter Cathedral* from the Fabric Rolls, misunderstanding the architectural evidence, asserts that Marshall laid out and partially built all the eastern chapels, and that he also actually completed and vaulted the existing presbytery. This account was followed by the writer with considerable hesitation in the first edition of this volume; but a second visit to Exeter convinced him of its utter improbability, a condition which was changed to certainty on the publication of a paper on Exeter cathedral by Professor Lethaby in 1903. There is in reality no documentary and no architectural evidence for Freeman's hypothesis.

SECOND PERIOD—BISHOP BRUERE, 1224-1244.—It was this bishop who made over "to God and the Church of St. Mary and St. Peter sufficient ground to make a Chapter house," the lower part of which still remains. Bruere gave the cathedral body its present constitution : dean, precentor, chancellor, treasurer, and canons; it is natural that he should have constructed for them their Chapter house, with its fine arcading. Probably also when he built his Chapter house, he built the round-headed doorway at the north end of the east walk of the cloister, to give access to the Chapter house from the south aisle of the nave. It is possible that Bruere also commenced the stalls (now gone) with their beautiful misericords; but they cannot have been completed till after his death; for one of them has a lifelike carving of an elephant, a creature not seen in England till 1255.

THIRD PERIOD.—It was Bishop Bronescombe, and not Marshall, who, between c. 1270 and 1280, laid out the great eastern extensions and gave the cathedral the plan which we see now. The object here, as elsewhere, was to increase the length of the sanctuary, to get a dignified eastern Lady chapel as well as other chapels—he added chapels of St. Andrew and St. James, St. Mary Magdalene and St. Gabriel to the eastern limb, and St. Edmund's, north-west of the nave—to get a processional aisle or ambulatory all round the presbytery and choir, keeping it clear of the chapels, and arranging for all these parts to be thoroughly well lighted, and, finally, to transfer the stalls from the crossing to a choir in the western bays of the eastern limb. Moreover, tall pointed arches were substituted for low semicircular arches opening from the towers to the crossing. At this time also were built the rectangular eastern chapels of the towers; "in these chapels the plinth of the internal window-shafts, below the over-sailing member of the base, is *circular*, as it also is in the chapels of St. Mary Magdalene and St. Gabriel; while throughout the choir aisles west of the retro-choir, and in the first bay of the nave, the plinths are *octagonal*. In the choir chapels of St. Andrew and St. James they are circular too, but there is no over-sailing member above them." All this work was begun, but certainly not all finished by Bronescombe. It is known definitely that the opening up of the towers was going on in 1280; and that he arranged in 1280 to be buried in the new chapel of St. Gabriel, then nearly finished; "fere de novo constructa." As for the rest, the similarity of their details to that of St. Gabriel's chapel is evidence that they were planned and begun by Bronescombe. The plan of Exeter cathedral, therefore, as we see it now, one of the most admirable in the Middle Ages, is to be credited to Bishop Bronescombe.

The windows north and south of the retro-choir probably belong to his time. The lower lights of these windows are lancets; the circles in the head are cusped. The side windows of the chapels of St. Mary Magdalene and St.

THE EAST END AND LADY CHAPEL

Gabriel, on either side of the Lady chapel, also have geometrical tracery earlier than that of the Lady chapel, and may be attributed to Bronescombe.

FOURTH PERIOD.—So vast a work as that described above could not possibly be finished by Bronescombe; especially if, as is evident from the character of the window tracery, which is considerably more advanced than that of Westminster Chapter house (1255), it was not begun till the later years of his episcopate. Its completion and extension was handed over to his successor, Peter Quivil. This bishop finished the remodelling of the transepts, and no doubt the greater part of the work in various chapels begun by Bronescombe; then he went on to build a new presbytery, which, as the plan shews, could be done without disturbing as yet the eastern limb of the Norman church; hence he is styled "primus fundator novi operis"; *i.e.*, he was the first to set about the rebuilding of the main body of the church. As payments for marble columns to John of Corfe go on till 1299, it is probable that Quivil did not live long enough to finish even the ground story of the presbytery. Nevertheless the design of the whole interior and exterior must have been definitely decided upon in Quivil's time, and its general lines were adhered to till the very end. With the exception of the addition of a triforium arcade with a pierced balustrade above, and the introduction of flowing tracery in some of the western windows of the nave, the main features of the cathedral right up to the far west doors are as they were designed in the closing years of the thirteenth century. It is, of course, this exceptional unity and harmony of design that makes Exeter what it is —one of the most satisfactory mediæval interiors in this country. In cathedrals such as Rochester and Ely a Norman nave jars on a Gothic choir; or, as at Lincoln and York, two styles of Gothic mingle and conflict. But at Exeter, looking forward from west to east, hardly anything obtrudes on the original design. In no other cathedral, except Salisbury, do we find similar unity of design; but in the design of Salisbury simplicity becomes bareness and poverty. It cannot be compared for one moment with the richness of the interior of Exeter. Yet greater unity and harmony is gained by the way in which the battlements and pinnacles, flying buttresses, and cresting weld together the exterior, and the high vaults the interior, as at Norwich. The adherence, too, for so long a time to Bishop Quivil's design is interesting, because it shews that in the early years of the fourteenth century there was at Exeter, as at Beverley, Westminster, Ely, and St. Albans, a strong current in the direction of conservation of good design. Piers and vaulting and bosses and corbels and triforium and windows of the nave, built long after he was dead and gone, are all but reproductions of Quivil's early work. Most remarkable of all, perhaps, is the adherence to the early tracery patterns —the rose, the lily, and the wheel. Even the great west window, one of the last works, is but Quivil's straight-spoked wheel translated into flowing curves. Quivil was bishop from 1280-1291; he was buried in the centre of the Lady chapel, which even then was not finished, for its vaults were not painted till 1301. His successor completed Quivil's work in the presbytery.

It is worth while to turn aside for a moment and look at some of the piers hereabout; no church, here or abroad, possesses more noble arcades than Exeter. The piers of the Lady chapel looking into the side chapels are composed of four columns. The north-east and south-east piers of the choir have clusters of eight shafts instead of four; while in the pier between them the cluster of eight is developed into a cluster of sixteen columns. Finally, notice that these piers are set diamond-wise, with four flat faces, and the angles to the north, west, south, and east. The piers all consist of "vast horizontal slices of Purbeck marble, from nine to fifteen inches thick"; the arches of native sandstone. This profuse use of marble gives the interior of Exeter a magnificence rare in England; only surpassed by the churches of Italy. The colour contrast too between the blue-grey marble of the piers, the yellow sandstone of the arches, and the white Caen stone above, is delightful.

FIFTH PERIOD.—The next thing was to rebuild or remodel the choir. Hitherto the eastern work had all been done on clear ground. But west of the new presbytery there was standing a substantial Norman choir. At West-

THE CHOIR

minster Abbey the Norman work was demolished to make room for Gothic; but at Exeter, as so often elsewhere, it was as far as possible retained. The aisle-walls were retained; along the south side of the choir for three bays the Norman plinth may still be seen. Secondly, the clerestory wall of the choir is 12 in. thicker than that of the presbytery; it must be the old Norman clerestory wall cased over. Thirdly, the piers of the choir are 9 in. greater in diameter than those of the presbytery; this is because they have to support the thick Norman clerestory wall; the extra thickness, however, of these piers is thrown into the aisle and is not noticed from the choir. It would seem as if the builders took away both piers and arches from underneath the Norman clerestory wall, and put in new ones, without bringing the wall down—a kind of engineering feat which the mediæval builders undertook with a light heart. This work in the choir went on chiefly in the time of Bishop Bitton (1292-1307); the bosses of the vaults were carved and ready for erection in 1303. The glazing of the windows, however, was not completed, nor were the stalls removed into the new choir, till after his death.

It will be noticed that at the west end of the choir, on either side, there is an arch only 2½ ft. wide. It is likely that here stood the two great eastern piers of the crossing; in which case the remodelled choir would extend westward up to their eastern faces. The intention probably was to retain them as supports of a central tower. But when the rebuilding of the nave was begun, any such intention seems to have been abandoned. The result would be that for each Norman pier plus a Gothic respond, it would be necessary to substitute two Gothic piers bridged by a narrow arch. When, however, the rebuilding of the nave was commenced, the difficulty was got over more simply by making the new easternmost arch in the nave 15 in. broader than those to the west of it.

SIXTH PERIOD.—Much was still left to be done in the choir; and it was done by Bishop Stapledon (1308-1327). In the first place there was a complete break in the treatment of the intermediate stage or triforium of the choir and presbytery respectively. In the choir Bitton's triforium chamber had in front of it the little arcade which still exists. But in the presbytery Quivil's clerestory windows were splayed down till they rested on the summits of the pier-arches; to the same line were continued downward the shafts in the jambs of his windows, somewhat as may be seen at Pershore. This diversity of treatment of the two halves of the eastern limb must have had a very discordant effect; and Stapledon in 1318 corrected it by adding a triforium to the east, in such a way that though the eastern arcading is not so deep as the western, yet in perspective the difference is hardly noticed. Probably the next thing was to glaze the remainder of the sixty choir windows, only nineteen of which were filled with stained glass at Stapledon's accession. It seems likely that nearly all the stained glass for the choir and the transepts came from abroad—from Rouen. For the nave, later on, the place of the laity, English glass, cheaper and not so good, was thought sufficient. The glass was inserted by Walter le Verrouer (he has descendants still living in Exeter), at the moderate price of six shillings for a fortnight's work, of himself and "two boys," for one pair of clerestory windows. Hitherto the clergy had sat in the transept and the eastern bays of the nave; now, as in many other cathedrals, beginning with Canterbury, the stalls were moved into the western bays of the choir; this was in 1310. (The present canopies of these stalls are modern.) Next came the Bishop's throne (A.D. 1316), intended for his Lordship with a chaplain on either side; "a magnificent sheaf of carved oak, put together without a single nail, and rising to a height of 57 ft. The lightness of its ascending stages almost rivals the famous 'sheaf of fountains' of the Nuremberg tabernacle. The cost of this vast and exquisitely carved canopy (about twelve guineas) is surprisingly small, even for those days. The carved work consists chiefly of foliage, with finials of great beauty, surmounting tabernacled niches, with a sadly untenanted look, however, for lack of their statuettes. The pinnacle corners are enriched with heads of oxen, sheep, dogs, pigs, and monkeys." Next came what is perhaps the most exquisite work in stone in England, as the throne is unparalleled in woodwork—the sedilia, *c*. 1318; the seats of the priest to the east, and to the west of him, those of the Gospeller and Epistoler. These sedilia have been preferred even to the Percy tomb at Beverley and the arcading of the Lady chapel of Ely. "The canopy of the seat nearest the altar," says Mr Garland, "deserves particular attention. It is adorned with a wreath of vine leaves on each side, which meet at the point and there form a finial; and never did Greek sculptor, of the best age, trace a more exact portrait of the leaf of the vine, nor design a more graceful wreath, nor execute his design with a more masterly finish." The design of the sedilia passed on to the monuments of Edward II. at Gloucester, those of the Despensers at Tewkesbury, and even to far away Avignon, where the great monument of Pope Jean XXII., erected in 1345, is beyond doubt copied from these English examples. The tabernacled canopies of the later stalls, beginning with those of Lincoln, c. 1370, are but renderings in wood of the design of the Exeter sedilia. Then came the great work of all—the high altar, with its reredos, perhaps the most magnificent in Europe; the cost of it would amount now to about £4,800. Of this not a fragment remains. Finally, the choir was closed in with a great screen to the west (1317-1324), and on it was placed an organ; the ancient and best position for a cathedral organ. The accounts shew that 500 lbs. of iron bars were used to hold the screen together, and that the Rood, Mary and John, rested on an *iron* beam high above the choir screen. To Bishop Stapledon also may be attributed the crossing and the first bay of the nave. It is possible that they were begun by Bishop Bitton, but they were certainly not finished by him, for windows hereabout were being glazed in 1317 and 1318. The presbytery, choir, crossing, and first bay of the nave must have been nearly finished by 1327, the year of Bishop Stapledon's death, for there was a consecration by Bishop Grandisson in the following year. One other work is attributed to Stapledon, viz., the cloistered walk as far as the doorway of the Chapter house. "The cathedral of Exeter," as Stapledon's successor wrote to the Pope, "now finished up to the nave, is marvellous in beauty, and when completed, will surpass every Gothic church in England or in France."

SEVENTH PERIOD.—Bishop Grandisson (1327-1369) was

THE NAVE, LOOKING WEST

"the most magnificent prelate who ever filled the see of Exeter." He had been nuncio to the Pope at the courts of all the noblest princes of Christendom. He was even strong enough to bar the way to Archbishop Meopham, of Canterbury, when he attempted to enforce a visitation of the cathedral. Great as were his riches and magnificence, he was a good man of business. He lived forty years Bishop of Exeter; finished his cathedral, did many great works elsewhere, and yet died wealthy. Stapledon, we have seen, had finished one bay of the nave. It remained for Grandisson to complete the remaining seven bays. The piers of the nave were erected by 1334; the whole work was complete in 1345. Stapledon had commenced the Cloister; Grandisson built the north walk, running, in curious fashion, under a second and outer range of flying buttresses, as does the cloister of Westminster. The west front (except the west screen) was now built or remodelled, but not the fan-vaulting of the north entrance, which is later. And the curious chapel of St. Radegunde in the thickness of the west wall he remodelled, to form his mortuary chapel, expecting there ever to lie, looking towards the nave where his work had been done. But his tomb was destroyed by Elizabeth's Visitors, and his ashes were scattered to the winds.

As we stand near his empty grave, we see before us the whole of the great mediæval design, that was due in inception to Bronescombe, and was realised and consummated by Quivil, Bitton, Stapledon, and Grandisson, in the eighty years between 1270 and 1350. Professor Lethaby estimates that for these seventy five years the annual expenditure was £200; so that the whole cathedral cost £16,000, or about £240,000 of our money, which compares favourably with the expenditure on Ely presbytery, which cost £15,120 per bay, whereas the cost of each of the bays at Exeter was about £13,333. What strikes one first is that with revenues so immense, the bishops should have been satisfied with a cathedral so small—its area is less than half that of York. On the other hand, at York, owing to the vast dimensions of the new cathedral, commenced soon after the new work at Exeter, the builders were unable to vault it in stone.

Secondly, one wonders that they allowed their hands to be fettered, their design to be cramped, by the preservation not only of the aisle-walls, but of the clerestory of Warelwast's cathedral. But it is just in the subjugation of these limitations, in converting them into the special glory and distinction of the Exeter design, that the genius of Quivil's architect shines forth most vividly. He was limited by the area of the old cathedral to north, south, and west; not even the tiny transepts might be enlarged. But what was more serious, he was limited as to height. For instead of clearing away the clerestory of the Norman choir, as was done at Gloucester, it was determined to retain it, merely supplying it with a new arcade, triforium, and clerestory windows. The Gloucester clerestory, not being fettered, soared high into the air; that of Exeter had perforce to be low and squat. He set to work to make the best of the situation. It was not for him to emulate the lofty vaults of Salisbury and Westminster. It would seem, indeed, that the first intention of Quivil's architect was to give the presbytery an even lower vault than the present; for the springers, *i.e.*, the lower parts of the ribs, of the vault are of a different and flatter curve than the upper parts of the ribs, and if continued would produce a vault 4 or 5 ft. lower than the present one. While the work was going on, however, the builders sharpened the curve of the vault and built it as we see it now. Still, the church had to be low; the lowness of the choir had conditioned that of the presbytery; it was also to condition that of the nave.

The internal elevation, then, for a Gothic church of 1280, had to be exceptionally low. So it was determined—it was an intuition of genius—to see what could be done in design with lowness and breadth. Everything should be broad and low, outside as well as inside. Look at the east end of the choir—its two arches broad and low; above it, the great window—broad and low. Nowhere but at Exeter do you find these squat windows with their truncated jambs; here they are everywhere—in the aisles, in the clerestory, in choir, chapels, transepts, and nave; even in the great window of the western front: broad and low windows everywhere.

Still more original is the external realisation of the design; central tower and spire, western towers and spires, alike are absent. Long and low, massive and stable, stretches out uninterruptedly the long horizontal line of nave and choir. Breadth gives in itself the satisfactory feeling of massiveness, steadfastness, and solidity; and this is just what is wanting in the all-too aerial work of Gloucester and Beauvais; vaulted roofs at a dizzy height resting on unsubstantial supports and sheets of glass. But the Exeter architect has emphasised this satisfactory feeling of stability still further. The window tracery is heavy and strong; the vault is barred all over with massive ribs; in the piers there are no pretty, fragile, detached shafts; the massive clustered columns look as if they were designed, as they were, to carry the weight of a Norman wall.

But an interior may easily be made too massive; if it is not to be a Salisbury cathedral, it need not be a Newgate gaol. How was the prison-like appearance of an interior but 68 ft. high, with a stone vault of exceptionally heavy appearance weighing it down, to be avoided? How was oppressive heaviness to be counteracted? Triumphantly, by transparency. By stretching out the windows from buttress to buttress, aisle and clerestory became practically one continuous sheet of glass; the church was flooded with light and atmosphere; the heavy vault seemed to float in the air, borne up but by the lilies and roses and wheels of the window tracery and rows of painted saints in tabernacles of silver or of gold. There is no heaviness even now in the interior of Exeter; though the silvery panes of the choir, the golden glass of the nave, have perished long ago.

Another distinctive feature in Exeter, as in Salisbury, is that the architect produces his effect mainly by architectural means—is not driven to rely on sculpture. All the principal capitals have moldings, not foliage. Only in the great corbels of the vaulting-shafts and in the bosses of the vault does he permit himself foliage and sculpture. Wonderful carving it is; the finest work of the best period, when the naturalistic treatment of foliage was fresh and young. Very remarkable are the corbels with their lifelike treatment of vine and grape, oak and acorn, hazel leaf and nut, thorn and sycamore and fig, "as crisp and fresh," says a Devonshire man, "as if the dew were on them." Unfortunately the corbels, and still more the bosses, are so high up that their lovely detail is thrown away; and the corbels are out of scale.

And the patterns of the window tracery are wonderfully diverse. It is not, as in Lichfield nave or King's College Chapel, where every window is like its neighbour; so that when you have seen one, you have seen all. Here, all down each side of the church, almost every window differs. In dimensions, in general character, they agree; in details they differ; each window is a fresh delight; we have what even in Gothic architecture we rarely get—diversity within similarity.

Another striking feature of the design is its perfect bilateral symmetry. Gothic churches are, as a rule, most irregular, most unsymmetrical in outline; as a consequence, very picturesque. It is a mistake, however, to believe that they are intentionally unsymmetrical and picturesque. A Gothic architect no more aimed at irregularity than did the architect of the Parthenon. Only he was not a purist on the subject. If practical requirements—*e.g.*, the needs of ritual—made it necessary to break in on the lines of a symmetrical design, he broke in on them without the slightest hesitation; the building had to conform to its destination. But where a single design could be carried through from end to end, it was as symmetrical as a Classical temple. So it is at Salisbury; so it is at Exeter. Every window has its exact counterpart on the other side of nave and choir. Transept answers to transept, screen to screen, St. John the Baptist's chapel to St. Paul's, St. Andrew's chapel to St. James', St. George's chapel to St. Saviour's, St. Mary Magdalene's chapel to St. Gabriel's. But the architect was not so infatuated with the idea of symmetry as to place a porch on the south side because there was one on the north, or a chapter house on the north because there was one on the south; which is what academic professors of Classic architecture would have done.

We have seen how the design gained special distinction from the very limitations imposed by the lowness of the early choir, the upper parts of which it was desired to preserve. It was again to the early design that Exeter owes another distinction among English interiors. In the early design the towers were just those which we still see; there was no central tower. The very fact that it was ultimately decided not to build a central tower, and be like everybody else, shews what backbone and insight the men had. Cathedrals without central towers were as rare in mediæval England as cathedrals with central towers are rare in the Ile de France. Yet no central tower was built at Exeter. Central towers, standing as they do on four thin legs, are dangerous: many have fallen; others, like Salisbury, are always threatening to fall. But they are objectionable on another ground. The great piers on which they stand are an enormous block in the lengthened vista, which is the one great charm of an English cathedral, as compared with the lofty but short cathedrals of France. The fact that at Exeter there is no tower over the crossing, and no tower-piers in the way, produces the most open, uninterrupted, and impressive vista of any cathedral in England. The screen and organ being low, one sees the whole noble design in one glance from far west to far east. We have nothing like it: though it finds its counterpart in the great French cathedral of Bourges.

Another point should be noticed. Although the fourteenth-century nave is in nearly all important respects designed in the thirteenth-century manner—the exception being some windows with flowing tracery in the westernmost bays of the nave—yet the architects were not such purists as to carry out their minor work in anything but the style of their own day. Even in the thirteenth-century choir, all the minor work is of fourteenth-century design—*e.g.*, the great screen with its depressed ogee arches, the throne of the bishop, the sedilia.

EIGHTH PERIOD.—With the completion of the nave the great structural revolution came to an end. For convenience' sake we have divided it into periods; but the work seems to have gone on practically continuously from the days of Bishop Bronescombe, *c.* 1270, to those of Bishop Grandisson, *c.* 1350 and later. Indeed before the nave was finished,

THE WEST FRONT

Grandisson seems to have set to work on the west front. By the end of the century the whole of the west front, including the Image screen, was completed. To this period also may be assigned a south and probably a west walk of the cloister. The great east window was substituted by Bishop Brantyngham (1370-1394) for an earlier one, either because its tracery had decayed, or because it was unsuitable for stained glass. The so-called " Minstrels' Gallery" was put up as an afterthought, the earlier work being cut into to receive it. It is high up on the north side of the nave, and was probably intended to be used in the choral services on Palm Sunday, when the procession would pass beneath it if it entered the church by the north doorway of the nave.

In the fifteenth century the towers were crowned with battlements and turrets, as we see them now. The upper part of the Chapter house was rebuilt. Bishop Stafford erected canopies over monuments in the Lady chapel (1395-1419). The work includes a fan-vaulted entrance contrived in the northern part of the western screen, and later, two exquisite chapels, both built by Bishop Oldham—his own chantry (St. Saviour's) on the south side of the retro-choir, the Speke chantry (St. George's) on the north—and in addition, Prior Sylke's chantry in the north transept. All this work is admirable in design and execution. In Oldham's chantry is a charming series of owls, with the scroll DAM proceeding from the beak of each little owl. To Bishop Stafford and Bishop Oldham (1504-1519) is due the grand set of stone screens—one of the glories of the cathedral—no less than ten, which veil all the nine chapels and Prior Sylke's chantry, and add fresh beauty to the beautiful choir.

Whatever else, then, the student and lover of Gothic architecture omits, he must not fail to visit Exeter. He will find it fresh and different from anything he has seen before. Its unique plan, without central or western towers, the absence of obstructive piers at the crossing, the consequently uninterrupted vista, the singleness and unity of the whole design, the remarkable system of proportions, based on breadth rather than height, the satisfying massiveness and solidity of the building, inside and outside, the magnificence of its Purbeck piers, the delightful colour contrast of marble column and sandstone arch, the amazing diversity of the window tracery, the exquisite carving of the corbels and bosses, the wealth of admirable chantries, screens, and monuments, the superb sedilia, screen, and throne, the misericords, the vaults, the remarkable engineering feat from which its present form results, the originality of the west front and of the whole interior and exterior, place Exeter cathedral in the very forefront of the triumphs of the mediæval architecture of our country.

BIBLIOGRAPHY.—Archdeacon Freeman's *Architectural History of Exeter Cathedral*, Second Edition, Exeter, 1888.
Professor Lethaby in *Architectural Review*, 1903.

ARCADING IN THE LADY CHAPEL.

THE CATHEDRAL CHURCH OF ST. PETER, GLOUCESTER

BUILT FOR BENEDICTINE MONKS

The following is a convenient order for visiting the church. (1) The crypt. (2) The E. chapel of the S. transept. (3) The choir aisles or procession path, with the S.E. and N.E. chapels. (4) The E. chapel of the N. transept. (5) The E. bays and N. aisle of the nave. (6) The vault of the nave and the reliquary in the N. transept. (7) The S. aisle of the nave. (8) Edward II.'s tomb. (9) The S. transept. (10) The choir, with its stallwork and glass. (11) The N. transept. (12) The W. front, S. porch, and W. bays of the nave. (13) The Lady chapel. (14) The upper aisle of the presbytery. (15) The cloisters. (16) The exterior of the church.

THE foundation of Gloucester, like that of Ely, has gone through many changes. In 681 it was founded as a nunnery, and remained so till 769. In 821 it was refounded for secular priests; who, in the time of Canute, through the influence of Archbishop Dunstan, were replaced by Benedictine monks. It remained a Benedictine monastery from 1022 till 1541, when it was placed on the New Foundation, thus reverting to secular priests once more. The abbey church then became a cathedral, with a diocese carved out of that of Worcester.

FIRST PERIOD.—It is recorded that Aldred, Bishop of Worcester, "re-established the monks in 1058 and began to build a new church from the foundations." It is usually held that no part of his work remains; but in the crypt there is Norman work of two dates, the earlier part of which may be Aldred's. It consists of a large number of small shafts with capitals which are largely versions of the Corinthianesque capital common on the Continent in the middle of the eleventh century; the bases also are of classic outline. In the centre of the crypt these interesting shafts stand free in two rows; but three more rows on either side exist, cased up for greater strength in Norman masonry added later.

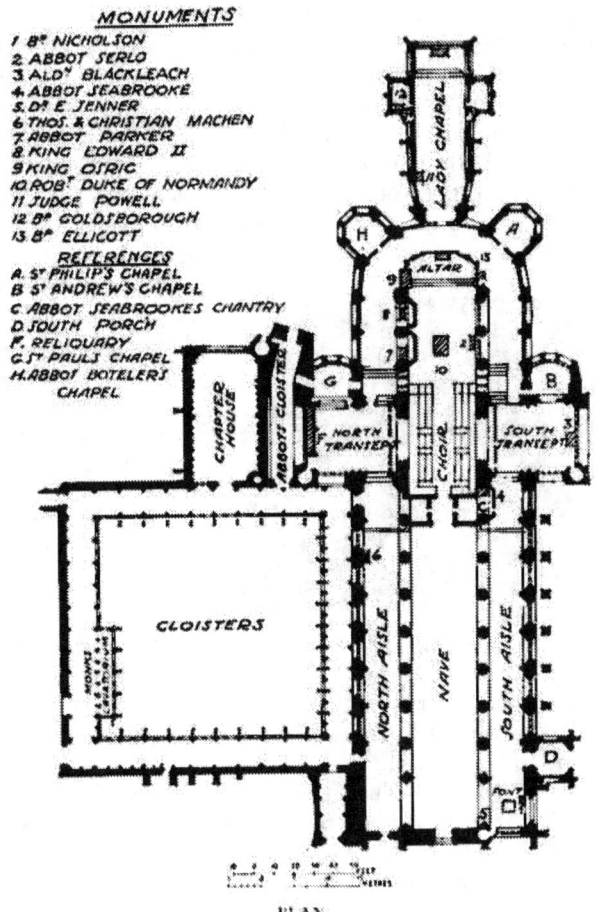

PLAN

when ribs also were built under the groins of the vault. Aldred was translated to York in 1060, but he may very well have set out the plan of the church and have built the crypt. It may be objected that the Gloucester plan with semicircular procession path and radiating chapels is too advanced for 1058; but there are reasons for believing that Westminster abbey, as set out in 1050 had this same periapsidal plan; as also certainly Battle abbey, founded in 1067; Winchester, begun in 1079; and Worcester, to whose diocese Gloucester belonged, begun in 1084; there is a marked resemblance between the crypts of Worcester and Gloucester; both are of an early type. Owing to the preservation of its crypt, the periapsidal plan can be studied better at Gloucester than anywhere else. Its great merit was that it provided a *via processionum* all round the sanctuary, which did not exist in such a plan as that of Durham, with three parallel eastern apses after the fashion of the abbeys of Normandy. Moreover, it provided three eastern chapels instead of two, and readier access to each of these chapels.

THE CRYPT

The other theory with regard to the crypt is that though the small shafts were got ready in Aldred's time, yet the crypt was not commenced till later.

SECOND PERIOD.—The great bulk of the work was undoubtedly done by Abbot Serlo, who began his rule with two monks, but before his death had a hundred. Work was started all afresh and a foundation stone was laid in 1089. In 1100 the church was dedicated. It is impossible, however, that the whole church was finished in eleven years; probably what was completed was the eastern limb with the lower stage of the central tower and its abutments. It is probable that in this work we see what formerly existed at

Westminster in that part of the Norman church there which was begun by Edward the Confessor in 1050 and dedicated in 1066. The documentary evidence points to the existence at Westminster of a sanctuary with a procession path, of upper as well as of lower chapels, and of an upper as well as a lower aisle encircling the sanctuary, and this upper aisle was probably vaulted, as at Gloucester, with a *demi-berceau* or half-barrel vault. A *demi-berceau* in the same position is to be seen in St. Stephen's, Caen, and the spring of one at Cérisy-la-Forêt. In one respect Gloucester surpasses in planning all the Romanesque churches of Normandy and England; in that, having a crypt, the three radiating apses are each three stories high, thus providing nine eastern chapels. And if to these be added the chapels in the eastern apses of the transepts, themselves also three stories high, we get the large total of fifteen chapels, an extraordinary number for such an early date.

THE TRIFORIUM OF APSE

In the provision of numerous chapels, which were essential in all the greater mediæval churches, Gloucester was exceptionally successful. It had, moreover, a procession path. The only thing which it did not have was a Saint's chapel at the back of the High altar. But as Gloucester never had a local saint, it never required such a chapel. The mother church, Worcester, had in St. Wulfstan and St. Oswald two local saints, and in Gothic days had to reconstruct its eastern limb in order to provide them with adequate local habitation. Gloucester therefore has remained to this day unaltered in plan; except that in order to provide room for a full monastic choir at the services of Our Lady, the easternmost chapel has been twice rebuilt on a larger scale.

By the construction of a crypt and by the utilisation of the triforium chamber as an upper aisle, the east limb of Gloucester practically consists of three churches: one underground, one on the ground floor, and one on the first floor; the two latter exist in the present Westminster abbey, though the upper church there has never been brought into use. In spite of its great popularity among English builders, in but few churches was the triforium chamber ever used; *e.g.*, in Beverley a solid wall is interposed in front of it, while at Lincoln it has no floor; frequently it has no windows; and it is usually approached only by narrow corkscrew staircases. Even when the triforium chamber was utilised, it was only that of the eastern limb and the transept, not that of the nave.

Gloucester chancel, as originally built, must have been excessively dark; that was the one defect in its planning; it had no direct light at all from the aisles; it was dependent for light on the clerestory windows, and on the small amount of light that filtered across the upper aisle. Consequently, when the nave was designed, a totally different and very logical design was adopted. A triforium chamber in the nave would have been of no ritualistic use; consequently the aisle roofs were flattened, and the chamber was made as low as possible. On the other hand, it was determined to get as much light as possible out of the windows of the aisle. These therefore were to be both lofty and broad. But there was a difficulty in the way. On the north side of the nave was set out the cloister. If the north aisle windows were inserted low down they would not have looked into the open air, but into the cloister. It was therefore necessary to set the windows so high up that their sills were above the cloister roof. This meant that the aisle-wall had to be exceedingly lofty. And of course the pier-arcade had to be exceedingly lofty also. If it had been built low, very little light would have succeeded in reaching the nave from the high set windows of the aisle. Hence the extraordinarily lofty piers of Gloucester nave; which are even loftier than they look, for the pavement has been raised above the original level. At Norwich the piers are 15 ft. high, at Gloucester they are 30 ft. At Norwich the piers have a diameter of 7 ft.; at Gloucester, though they are twice as lofty, of 6 ft. The result of this disposition was to give an internal elevation

THE NAVE, LOOKING EAST

very unusual in Norman days. In Norwich the ground story, triforium chamber, and clerestory are 25, 24, 25 ft. high respectively; in Gloucester nave they are 40, 10, 24; the ground story being actually taller than the other two stories put together. This is a peculiarly West of England arrangement; all the examples, the Benedictine abbey churches of Gloucester, Tewkesbury, and Pershore, are in the same district. Whence did this arrangement come?

there is nothing of the sort in Normandy. It is not impossible that this also derives from the Norman nave of Westminster, of whose design, however, nothing is known. Even on the Continent it is difficult to find a parallel, except in the case of the lofty cylinders of Tournus nave, to which the early date of 946-970 is assigned, and which in any case can hardly be later than the first half of the eleventh century. As to the date of the nave of Gloucester there is diversity of opinion. But it is known that the nave of Tewkesbury, which is ruder in detail and therefore earlier, was not consecrated till 1123; Gloucester nave therefore was probably not finished before c. 1130. It is only necessary to compare the moldings of the pier-arches in the choir and the groined vaults of the procession path with the moldings of the pier-arches in the nave and the ribbed vault of its north aisle, to be sure that a whole generation must have elapsed between the two designs. The period 1110 to c. 1130 may well have been spent in substituting for temporary sheds of wood permanent stone buildings in the way of cloister, chapter house, dormitory, refectory, cellarage, infirmary, guest houses, and other necessary appurtenances of a monastic establishment of the very first rank.

The nave was originally longer than now, perhaps by half a bay, and had two western towers or turrets. The shortness of the nave, as well its internal elevation, and the three-storied eastern limb, decisively mark off this church, with Tewkesbury and Pershore, from such examples as Bury, Ely, Peterborough, Norwich, and Christchurch. The three western churches form a distinct school of their own, the origin of which certainly is not to be found in Normandy.

THIRD PERIOD.—In the thirteenth century very much work was done, but much of it has disappeared. The northwestern tower had collapsed between 1163 and 1180, and was rebuilt in 1222. The south-western tower was rebuilt between 1228 and 1243. A central tower is recorded to have been built in 1222; this probably means that one or two stories were added to a low Norman central tower.

A rectangular Lady chapel was substituted for the easternmost chapel in 1227; the form of the latter in Norman days is determinable from its substructure in the crypt. At the end of the north transept stands what Mr A. W. Pugin was certain was a Reliquary. Others regard it as a lavatory, obtaining a parallel from the one in Lincoln Minster. It may have been the entrance to the thirteenth-century Lady chapel, removed when the present Lady chapel was built; but in those days there was no Society for the Preservation of Ancient Monuments, nor were the builders in the habit of removing and preserving ancient work merely for artistic reasons. In its vault is exquisite detail.

Gloucester was exceptionally unlucky in the way of fires, marks of which may be seen on the nave piers. There were great fires in 1088, 1101, 1122, 1179, and 1190. The monks made up their mind to fireproof the nave by inserting a vault under the roof; this was executed in two sections, as the work shews; one part is recorded to have been done by the monks themselves, probably the part in which is so much bungling. While the scaffolds were up, they took the opportunity to enlarge the clerestory windows, converting them into lancets, leaving, however, the Norman jambs, whose zigzag ornament may still be seen. The infirmary, of which the west end and an aisle arcade remain, belongs to this period; as also the north doorways of the cloister, the vaulted passage in its north-east corner, and the great gateway opposite to the memorial to Bishop Hooper. The church was rededicated in 1239, although the nave vault was not finished till 1242.

FOURTH PERIOD.—Between 1318 and 1329 the Norman south aisle of the nave had got into a very dangerous condition. The north aisle was safe, its wall being propped up by the cloister roof. But the vault of the south aisle had thrust the wall 11 in. out of the perpendicular. To save the vault, Abbot Thokey built on to the Norman pilasters the present beautiful buttresses. But the new buttresses also swung over 4 in., and the Norman vaulting had to be taken out; the aisle received a new vault, and its eastern bays were enriched with ball-flower. The beautiful windows are of late geometrical character, and are smothered in ball-flower. The profuse employment of ball-flower is quite a characteristic of the early fourteenth-century Gothic of the West country; it is equally remarkable in the grand windows of Leominster and Badgeworth, and at Ledbury and Hereford. "A horizontal line drawn just below the spring of the arch of each window at Gloucester cuts through thirty-two bands of ball-flower." There are no less than 1,400 ball-flowers in each window.

FIFTH PERIOD.—In 1327 Abbot Thokey made the fortune of Gloucester abbey. The fly in the ointment in this great abbey was the lack of a pilgrimage shrine with all its consequent spiritual and material advantages. Abbot Thokey made up for it by welcoming to his church the body of a murdered king. On 21st September Edward II. had been murdered at Berkeley castle. Bristol, Kingswood, and Malmesbury monasteries were appealed to, but none dared receive his body for interment, fearing the anger of the Queen and her party. Abbot Thokey brought the body to Gloucester in his own carriage, and caused it to be solemnly buried in the presbytery. Soon miracles were wrought at the tomb, pilgrimages set in, immense sums were contributed in offerings; Gloucester, like Hereford, became a pilgrim-church, and, like Hereford, used the vast income that accrued—enough, the monks said, to have erected a brand-new church—in improvements in the church and abbey. The tomb of the murdered king, erected by his son, Edward III., still exists, and the leaden coffin below, in which, when opened in 1855, the body was found "in a wonderful state of preservation." (We wonder what would be said if our antiquaries exhumed the bodies of George III. and Archbishop Benson, and stole their rings and vestments to put them in a show-case in the vestry.) On one side of the monument, facing the aisle, is the bracket on which offerings were laid; above is one of the loveliest canopies in existence, but much restored; it was modelled probably on the sedilia of Exeter. Hard by, in the north aisle, is a stone

GLOUCESTER CATHEDRAL

FROM THE SOUTH-EAST

lectern, from which it is said the monks told the pilgrims standing in the transept the story of the king's death and the miracles wrought at his tomb. This is unlikely, for it does not face the transept. Perhaps the monks' attendance in choir was checked off by a "scrutator" from a list on this desk, just as undergraduates' names are or were on entering college chapel. To the same period belong various windows inserted in the aisles and chapels and in the triforium chamber.

SIXTH PERIOD.—The monks, with the rich revenues now at their disposal, would perhaps have liked to rebuild the presbytery *de novo*. But the cultus of Edward II. was just now at its height, and the surroundings of the shrine were crowded every day and all day with the pilgrims from whom the money came. They therefore confined themselves to such improvements as could be effected without interfering with the flow of pilgrims and of offerings. The first thing needful was to provide more light : above all, in the presbytery, where the centre of attraction was ; and in the crossing, where their daily services were held. Secondly, the church had suffered severely from fire again and again. The nave had already been safeguarded against fire by vaulting ; it was desirable to extend the same protection to the transepts and presbytery by covering these also with stone vaults.

First, there was the lighting problem. Abbot Thokey had done a good deal in improving the lighting of the south aisle of the nave, and the aisles and chapels and triforium of the presbytery. Abbot Wygmore commenced operations in the south transept. The north transept was in daily use, as the cloister was on the north side of the nave, and the monks passed through the north transept to their daily services in the crossing. The improvements in the presbytery were postponed for a time, so as not to interfere with the pilgrims. In six years, before 1337, Wygmore is recorded by Froucester (who was himself Abbot from 1381 to 1412) to have cased, lighted, and vaulted the south transept.

If Froucester is correct—and his evidence is almost that of a contemporary—we have in the south transept of Gloucester one of the greatest puzzles in the history of mediæval architecture. The whole of this work in the south transept is in the style which elsewhere did not come into use till late in the century. We have to believe that it is contemporaneous with the utterly different work that was being done everywhere else in England; that it was contemporaneous with the monument of Edward II. in Gloucester itself; with the Percy shrine at Beverley; with the Lady chapel, octagon, and choir of Ely. It seems incredible. But Gloucester presbytery was not taken in hand till after the south transept, and it was finished not later than 1350. No other work like that of the south transept occurs in the kingdom till Edington church (1352-1361), and the western part of Winchester nave. So that, if we accept Froucester's statement, we have to believe that while the rest of the world was working in one fashion, the Gloucester masons, not later than 1330, were working on new and totally different lines.

We have to believe, also, that though this style ultimately became universally popular in England, overspread the whole country, and maintained its hold on English architecture for three centuries, at the outset it smouldered at Gloucester, unnoticed, unappreciated by anybody, till Edington took it up twenty years later in rebuilding the church of his native village. All the other improvements in mediæval building were caught up instantaneously—passing from one end of the kingdom to the other with the rapidity of the fashion of a Paris bonnet or mantle. England hesitated long before it could consent to exchange the richness of Ely design for the simplicity of that of Gloucester. However, the new choir of Gloucester, eulogised everywhere as it must have been by admiring pilgrims, showed the capacities of the new style. Then it came in with a rush. So,

"Si parva licet componere magnis,"

the Royal and Ancient game of golf smouldered on for centuries at Blackheath, till the psychological moment came, and it passed on to Westward Ho, and then swept like wildfire over all England.

The first question the monks had to decide was that of lighting. Their answer was a momentous one. They decided to get additional light by pulling down the low Norman clerestory and substituting a tall Gothic one, inserting in it big windows which form almost a continuous sheet of glass. The nave was internally 67½ ft. high. To get a big clerestory, they raised the south transept and presbytery

THE CHOIR

to the height of 86 ft. Similar tall clerestory windows were being built, but with an earlier type of tracery, in the choirs of Lichfield and Wells. But as yet clerestory windows were, as a rule, rather small; and some big churches of this period, such as Grantham and Patrington, had no clerestory at all. For what was to be the glory of the closing days of English Gothic architecture—the Lantern type of church—we must give the credit to the masons of Gloucester. And also for the new type of window. The new big window, occupying the whole breadth and nearly the whole height of the end wall of the south transept, had to be strengthened by cross-bars or transoms; and the tracery of the head had to be strengthened by the substitution of vertical straight lines, as far as possible, for curves. Here, then, we have the genesis of rectilinear tracery.

GLOUCESTER CATHEDRAL   149

Then there was the question of the vault. If we can believe Abbot Froucester, so early as 1337 the monks put over the south transept not only one of the earliest lierne vaults of the kingdom, but one so accurately worked that the junctions of the ribs did not require to be masked by bosses: they mortised the ribs together with as much precision as if they were dealing with joints in cabinet work. And over the choir and under the tower they put up the most amazingly complicated lierne vault that was ever constructed: this, too, not later than 1351. Not having reached yet the development that the pendant was to receive in later days, they got the necessary supports for the vault of the crossing by throwing skeleton arches across from east to west.

Thirdly, they appear to have intended to separate the presbytery from its aisles by the usual stone screens—designed to correspond with the tracery of the clerestory windows. This would have left an ugly cavernous arch—that of the eleventh-century triforium—in each bay, between the screen below and the clerestory above. The pattern of the tracery of the clerestory window had been repeated once in the screen below: what more natural than to repeat it a second time in the shape of a screen set in front of the open arch of the triforium? It remained merely to join up the mullions of all three—lower screen, triforium screen, and clerestory window—and the three members were welded together into one composition; harmony and unity reigned from pavement to vault. Here again we have at Gloucester not only the commencement, but the full development of what became the leading principle in later English Gothic—the determination to impose unity on the elevations of their churches by repeats of window tracery.

Most successful of all is the treatment of the vaulting shafts; they rise sheer in unbroken flow from the pavement to the vault above. Thus the lofty choir becomes to all intents and purposes a one-story design; it consists essentially of nothing but lofty vault supported by lofty pillars. Elsewhere and often the builders had been groping in this direction. At St. David's and Pershore the internal elevation had been reduced to two stories; at Exeter and York the triforium had been almost attenuated out of existence. Nowhere, however, had any one dared to conceive the possibility of bringing out the organic unity of an interior by reducing it to a single story. This was done first at Gloucester; and, moreover, at Gloucester only was it ever worked out successfully. Imitations there were, again and again, of the Gloucester design—indeed, nearly all later design is in essentials modelled on Gloucester—at Winchester, Christchurch, Malvern, Norwich, Sherborne, Canterbury—but no one succeeded in reproducing the organic unity of Gloucester's one-story choir.

One question still remained unsolved: how to treat the east end of the church. At Norwich, where the Gloucester precedent was largely followed a century later, the central apse and procession path and radiating chapels were all retained—with most beautiful effect. At Gloucester they pulled down the central apse; and on the wall of the three eastern bays of the ambulatory they erected three gigantic windows, so welded together as to compose one window. And, to bring the whole into view, they made the new easternmost bays of the presbytery, which had now to be rebuilt, wider to the east than the west. Thus they got one of the biggest windows in the world, and one of the ugliest. However, no one looks at the tracery of the window, but at the painted glass which it still retains. This glass is decidedly late in character, but the armorial bearings in it show that it was completed by 1350. All the characteristics of late Gothic glass are there. Thus the canopies and the figures alike are silvery white, and yellow stain is introduced here and there. The drawing, however, is shockingly bad; and the colour is got in a very artless way by inserting alternating backgrounds of vertical stripes of red and blue.

At the same time—between 1337 and 1377—the monks were provided with new choir-stalls. But while stone-work and glass alike are rectilinear in character, the stalls have bowing ogee canopies of the Ely type.

Next the north transept was remodelled (1360-1374). It is very much like its brother, but is 8 ft. higher, and the vault has bosses.

SEVENTH PERIOD.—The next work was the rebuilding of the cloister. This was built in two sections; as far as the doorway of the Chapter house in 1351-1377; the rest in 1381-1412. It is covered with a fan-vault, the earliest

THE CLOISTER

example of the kind, except those of two monuments in the neighbouring Abbey Church of Tewkesbury.

EIGHTH PERIOD.—The west front with its towers or turrets seems to have been giving trouble, and Abbot Morwent (1421-1437) pulled it down, and built the present west front; also the south porch. He also found it necessary to rebuild the western bays of the nave. The two bays he built are quite different in height and span and general design. With his big west window, and with the insertion of rectilinear tracery in the north aisle and in the clerestories of the nave, the improvement of the lighting of the church may be said to have been effectually completed.

NINTH PERIOD.—The monks now turned their attention to the central tower. The tower was of no use as a lantern, for the lierne vault of the choir had been carried beneath it. So it long remained unaltered. But in the days of Abbot Seabrooke the thirteenth-century tower was taken down, and the present magnificent tower was built under the superintendence of a monk named Tully, to be in character with the new exterior of choir and transepts (1450-1460). A very imposing tower it is; fully able, from its massiveness as well as from its height, to gather together the masses of the building—all the more so because the transepts are so short. It succeeds where the central towers of Worcester and Hereford fail; in fact, it is as effective in its way as Salisbury spire. The pinnacles, again, bear witness to the love of these later artists for harmony and unity: each pinnacle, with its two ranges of windows, is a repeat of the two stages of the tower below.

TENTH PERIOD.—Then—after the tower had been erected —it was decided to rebuild the thirteenth-century Lady chapel. So an immense detached building was constructed to the east of the great window of the presbytery; without aisles, but with little transepts; almost one continuous sheet of glass, and with a superb vault. The upper stories of the little transepts have book-desks, and probably were meant for the singers of prick song or harmonised music, which at this date was just coming into fashion, but was not as yet allowed in monastic choirs. This Lady chapel had to be joined up to the presbytery, but the great east window was in the way. However, the difficulty was got over by a series of ingenious shifts and dodges, which must be seen to be appreciated (1470-1490). It contains the remains of a beautiful reredos, and in the east window much of the old glass; also remarkable modern glass by Mr C. Whall, ruined by juxtaposition with a window containing glass of the most commonplace commercial type, for the insertion of which it

GLOUCESTER CATHEDRAL 153

is difficult to conceive an excuse. With the Lady chapel ends the great building-period at Gloucester (1330-1499), which turned the course of English architecture; so that the style of 1315 to 1350 was to find its natural development on the Continent in Flamboyant, but in England was switched off to a wholly different type of design.

THE CLOISTER.—(1) Leaving the north transept for the cloister, immediately on the right is seen a passage called

THE LADY CHAPEL

the Slype, the first part of which is Early Norman work. (2) Next comes the Chapter house, which with its pointed barrel vault is also Norman, except the eastern part, which was rebuilt in the fifteenth century. (3) At the end of the east walk of the cloister is a vaulted passage leading to the ruined arcade of the infirmary, and to a picturesque little cloister of uncertain use, as well as to the chief gateway of the abbey precincts. (4) Returning to the north walk of the cloister, we see on its south side the finest monastic lavatory in England. On the opposite wall of the cloister walk is a recess for towels; this wall was the southern wall of the refectory. Near the towel recess is the doorway of the refectory. The north alley was screened off, and formed the monastic school; on the stone bench at the foot of the wall are diagrams composed of holes for "fox and geese," and other boys' games. (5) At the end of the west walk of the cloister on the right hand is another Norman passage or slype; this, as at Westminster, was the outer parlour by which the cloister was reached from the outer court, and in which the monks were able to meet their relatives. (6) We return to the church by the south walk, having on the left the twenty little studies or "carrels," where the monks, each at his own little table, wrote, copied, and illuminated manuscripts. Notice the line in the floor for bookcases, which is not seen in the other walks of the cloister.

MINOR WORK.—(1) Behind the High altar, as at Winchester, is a narrow space called the Feretory, once roofed in overhead. On the one hand it formed a procession path for the priest, when he had to pass round, asperge, and cense the High altar in the course of the Sunday procession; on the other hand it provided space for cupboards for the keeping of treasures as well as two recesses for relics beneath the High altar. (2) In Abbot Boteler's chapel, the north-east chapel of the ambulatory, are good tiles and the remains of a fine reredos, *c.* 1450. (3) To the centre of the presbytery, its original position, has been restored the wooden effigy of Robert Courthose, Duke of Normandy, son of William the Conqueror, who died in 1134; from the coat of mail and long surcote it would seem to be twelfth-century work, but the wooden chest on which it rests is not earlier than the fifteenth century. The tomb of King John occupies a similar position at Worcester, as did that of Edward Confessor at Westminster up to 1245. Nor is there any reason why it should not have been placed once more in its original and proper position. (4) At the entrance to the crypt is a bracket to support a light; it rests on two figures supposed to represent a mason and his prentice. (5) In the upper aisle are several beautiful windows and piscinas; at the extreme east of it is an original stone altar inscribed with consecration crosses. From this point the superb lierne vault of the Lady chapel is best seen, with its exquisite foliated bosses. This chapel is approached by the well known Whispering Gallery. To the upper aisle also has been transferred an important picture of the Doom, not earlier than the reign of Henry VIII. (6) The cathedral possesses very fine tiles. Tiles of the time of Abbot Parker (1515-1541) remain in his chantry chapel, which is in the next bay west of the tomb of Edward II.; and there is a large collection of tiles of various dates in the presbytery and the altar platform. (7) In the eastern chapel of the south transept is glass of the period when the transept was remodelled (1330-1337).

Space fails to speak of the artistic charm of this great church. Internally it abounds above all others in ever varying vistas and perspectives and dramatic contrasts of light and shadow. Externally it is magnificently impressive by sunlight and by moonlight, seen near at hand or far away. It is one of the greatest glories of England and the English race. It has been well cared for of late years by Mr Waller and his masons.

BIBLIOGRAPHY.—Professor Willis in the *Gentleman's Magazine* for September 1860.

F. S. Waller, *Notes and Sketches of Gloucester Cathedral*, Gloucester, 1890.

W. H. St John Hope, *Notes on Gloucester Abbey*, page 90.

Rev. W. Bazeley, "Notes on the Thirteenth-Century Lady Chapel," page 12, and "Notes on the East Window," page 10. These three papers appeared in the third volume of the *Records of Gloucester Cathedral*.

T. Gambier Parry, "On the Builders of Gloucester Abbey," in the first volume of the *Records of Gloucester Cathedral*.

C. Winston, "On the East Window," in the *Archaeological Journal*, xx. 238.

FROM THE SOUTH-WEST

THE CATHEDRAL CHURCH OF ST. MARY AND ST. ETHELBERT, HEREFORD

BUILT FOR SECULAR CANONS

HEREFORD boasts a cathedral which, though one of the smallest, is, both externally and internally, one of the most picturesque in the country. As at Salisbury, Lincoln and Chester, a noble view of the exterior is to be had from the north-east. To the archæologist and the architectural student, its *mélange* of styles makes it a perfect treasure-house of mediæval design: early and late Norman, Transitional work of the early, middle, and late thirteenth century, and work of the fourteenth, fifteenth, and sixteenth centuries are all represented in the structure, to say nothing of the Gothic of Wyatt, Cottingham, and Scott.

Hereford is one of the oldest of all the sees, going back, at any rate, to the year 601, when St. Augustine had a conference with the Welsh bishops. It owed its riches and reputation mainly to two saints, King Ethelbert and Bishop Thomas Cantilupe. In the year 792 the great King of Mercia, Offa, inveigled Ethelbert, King of East Anglia, to

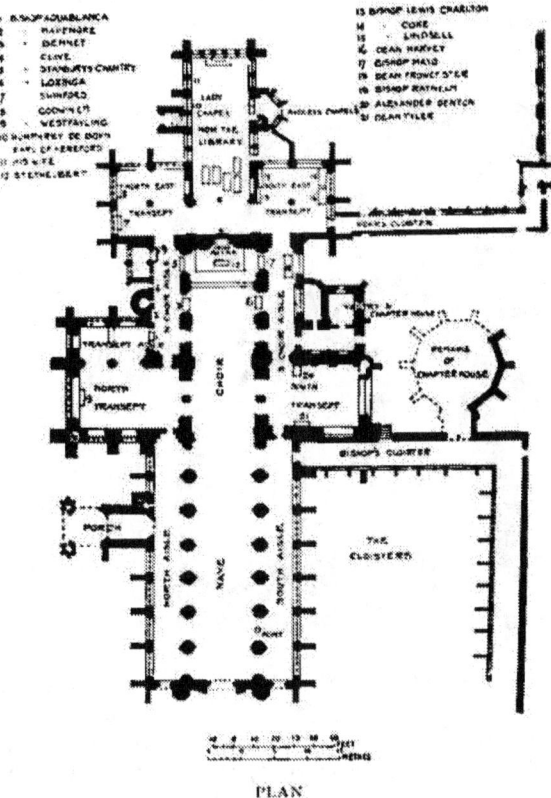

PLAN

the west of England, where he was treacherously murdered. "On the night of his burial, a column of light, brighter than the sun, rose to heaven;" three days later his ghost appeared and gave directions for the removal of his body. He was interred at Hereford; and in 825 "a noble church of stone" was erected over his remains. Of this or any subsequent Anglo-Saxon cathedral nothing survives.

FIRST PERIOD (1079-1110).—In 1079 the present cathedral was commenced by Robert de Losinga. He held the see till 1095. It is asserted by Sir Gilbert Scott that none of his work remains. But it seems certain that the east wall of the south transept, the east end and pier arcade of the choir, and perhaps the triforium also, are eleventh-century work.

THE SOUTH TRANSEPT

The design of the transept is curiously artless and archaic. The tall arches of its wall arcade have reminiscences of many a church in Lombardy; the squat little balustraded triforium is just what one finds in the eleventh-century transepts of St. Albans and Chester and Pershore. Proceeding into the choir aisles, probability rises into certainty. The masonry is of the roughest, and coursed in the most casual way; the strings and the bases have the rudest caricatures of moldings. The piers, too, are just the heavy masses of wall which one finds at St. Albans and Chichester: it is impossible that these piers and the light cylinders of the nave can both have been erected in the twelfth century. What has deceived archæologists is that, though the skeleton of the choir is of the eleventh century, it was smartened up immensely in the following century. In fact, it has gone through a similar process to that which took place at Porchester and Romsey, where the early Norman caps have been recarved by a late Norman sculptor; only at Hereford the renovation has been much more drastic. Looking at the east wall of the south transept, it is impossible to believe that the noble bay of the triforium above the arch of the aisle is of the same date as the balustrated triforium to the right of it. Although so early, the Norman church was in its plan the most advanced in England. The great fault of churches planned, like Durham, with three parallel eastern apses was that there was no processional aisle or ambulatory round the presbytery. This fault was remedied at Hereford by making the presbytery rectangular, and placing the high altar between the easternmost bay and the next bay to the west; the easternmost bay thus providing the ambulatory desired. To the east of the ambulatory were three apses; of these the two lateral apses were entered from the side aisles, but the central one from the ambulatory. And this central apse was not the broad and lofty central apse which may still be seen at Peterborough and Norwich, containing the eastern part of the presbytery, but was quite low and narrow, little broader indeed than the Norman arch by which it was entered and which still remains. So that we must not think of the old Norman east end of Hereford as consisting of one vast central apse as tall as the rest of the church or nearly so, flanked by low minor apses, but as consisting of three parallel eastern apses, all of about the same size and all low, and the central of them forming merely a little eastern chapel. The three little apses were independent buildings, each with its own separate roof; being separated by the flat Norman buttresses which still remain on the east side of the east wall of the presbytery. What the appearance of the church would be within may be gathered from the sketch by Sir Gilbert Scott in the *Building News* of 9th August 1878, where, however, the altar steps are wrongly placed in the easternmost bay.

Another portion of the early work remaining is the building projecting eastward from the south transept; it forms a rectangular sacristy, with rude, unribbed vault; it was enlarged to the east in the fifteenth century. In 1110 the cathedral was dedicated; which means, no doubt, the part then completed; viz., the eastern limb with its three small external chapels, the north and south transepts, the eastern limb, and that part which contained the stalls of the choir, viz., the crossing and the first bay of the nave. Of the eastern limb, two bays would be presbytery and one bay ambulatory. On his monument Bishop Reynelm is styled founder of the church, "fundator ecclesie"; the same phase occurs in an old Obit, but in this "hospitii" is substituted for "ecclesie" in a later hand, which would mean that he built a guest house. Reynelm certainly can have done very little in the church between 1107 when he became bishop, and in 1110, when the dedication took place; but having consecrated it, he has been wrongly given the credit of the whole work.

THE REREDOS

SECOND PERIOD (1110 to *c.* 1145).—To this period

belong the nave and the renovation of the choir. The capitals of the nave, greatly restored, are richly carved, and like all pre-Gothic carving, are full of classical survivals, acanthus, honeysuckle, &c. The Norman work is far richer than that of Ely, Peterborough, Durham, Gloucester, or Tewkesbury. The design of the nave, and still more of the choir, was probably the most solid and satisfactory in the country, not even excepting Durham. The triforium is especially magnificent; a copy of it was executed in the transept of Romsey. The bays of the choir are separated by broad pilasters, apparently to carry broad transverse arches. But whether these arches were intended to carry some form of wooden roof (their spandrels being built up), or a vault, cannot be determined. Sir Gilbert Scott's sketch shews a groined vault. The nave was completed "with great expense and solicitude, and dedicated by Bishop Robert de Bethune" (1131-1148).

THE EASTERN TRANSEPT, FROM SOUTH

THIRD PERIOD.—The next alteration appears to belong to the time of Bishop William Vere de Vere (1186-1199). The puzzling character of this work is probably due to a change of intention. Evidently what was wanted, and all that was planned at first was (1) an ambulatory of four bays in place of the three little eastern apses; and (2) east of that, a Lady chapel; this is precisely the plan of the east end of Norman Romsey. This would set free the easternmost bay of the architectural choir, which could then be used as Saint's chapel for St. Ethelbert. This first work would naturally be commenced at the east; and to it belongs (1) the external doorway leading to the crypt of the Lady chapel, and (2) the northern and southern walls now serving as vestibule to the Lady chapel, and containing windows which were at first intended to look into the open air. But while the work was going on it seems to have occurred to the builders that the opportunity might be seized for building in addition four eastern chapels. This was done; and in order to get access to each end-chapel the ambulatory was extended another bay northward and another bay southward. Thus the builders got not only the originally intended ambulatory and Lady chapel, but a low eastern transept in addition, as later on at Southwell, Exeter, and Wells, plus four chapels. Much of this work remains. In the jambs of the unglazed windows are shafts with conventional stalky foliage; while the arch of the window-head is enriched with the Norman diamond ornament. The vaulting ribs are enriched with zigzag. The central piers have, one conventional foliage, the other a scalloped capital. In the south-east transept there are remains of the doorway, and of a plinth which seems to have supported a pier between the two eastern chapels. The piers of the processional aisle are so arranged that two of them are in a line with the centre of the semicircular arch which led from the choir into the former Norman central apse. The intention of the builder perhaps was to reconstruct the east end of the choir, or it may be to rebuild the whole choir, substituting for the single semicircular arch a pair of pointed arches, as at Exeter. This was never done, however; and so, quite fortuitously, Hereford gets most charming vistas from the choir across to the eastern transept and the Lady chapel. Possibly the whole of the lower part of the Lady chapel was built in this period. The crypt-worship of the eleventh century had gone out of fashion; and the Hereford crypt, like that at Norwich, was probably built as a golgotha or charnel-house.

FOURTH PERIOD.—About 1220 the upper and eastern

parts of the Lady chapel were completed. It is a work of great beauty, especially in the rich clustering of shafts in the window-jambs and in the fine composition of the east end, with its quintet of lancets. The chapel is curiously low internally. The builder was an exceptionally cautious person. He not only provided for the thrusts of the vault by heavy buttresses and pinnacles, but, to get the thrusts as low down as possible, he made the vault spring below the window-heads. Moreover, down below he constructed a lofty

FROM THE NORTH-EAST

crypt, thus raising considerably the floor of the Lady chapel. Thus encroached on from below and from above, the interior of the Lady chapel contrasts remarkably with its lofty and imposing exterior. Externally, moreover, as the window-heads could not rise high, owing to the low spring of the vault, a large amount of wall-surface was left, and had to be decorated. This was done in a remarkable way; the arcade which runs round it being the old-fashioned Norman arcade of intersecting semicircular arches—probably the last appearance of this design on the stage.

FIFTH PERIOD. The history of the cathedral now resolved itself for the next hundred years into a series of attempts to get rid of the "dim, religious light," so dear to the modern, so abhorrent to the mediæval ecclesiastic. Hereford presbytery was even worse lighted than Norman churches generally, being blocked to the east by a transept, and having enormously bulky piers. So the Norman clerestory, if it existed, was taken down, and a Gothic clerestory with an inner arcade—an early and interesting example of plate-tracery—was erected. It is possible, however, that the Norman clerestory had never been built, but that the chancel was roofed at the triforium level like the nave of Christchurch, Hampshire. Moreover, the presbytery was made fireproof by being vaulted in stone, c. 1250.

SIXTH PERIOD.—About 1260 more drastic measures were taken with the Norman north transept. It was pulled down bodily, and rebuilt on a design which is perhaps the most original, as it certainly is one of the most beautiful, in the history of English Gothic architecture. To the north and west were built enormous windows, with tracery of cusped circles, quite exceptional in their elongation, more like late German than English work. On the east side the elevation is exceedingly interesting. Its arches, almost straight-sided —its triforium windows—a ring of cusped circles set under a semicircular arch—its clerestory windows, spherical triangles enclosing a cusped circular window—the composition of the triforium—the north and west windows—make up an exceptional design and were copied in later work in the city and neighbourhood. At the south end of the aisle is the exquisite tomb of Bishop Peter Aquablanca (*d.* 1268); no doubt built in his lifetime. The tomb is as unique as the transept, and closely resembles it in design. The inference is that Bishop Aquablanca built the transept. The credit of it, however, is constantly given to his successors, apparently on account of his private vices. But sinners as well as saints have liked to leave memorials behind them in stone; and, moreover, Aquablanca had his good points. To this day four thousand loaves are distributed every year out of funds which he bequeathed. It is recorded, too, that, of a fine which was imposed on the citizens for encroachments on his episcopal rights, he remitted one half, and handed over the other for works on the cathedral. Moreover, he was a foreigner, from Chambery; and has probably received no more favourable judgment from the English chroniclers than they were wont to give to foreign favourites of the king who at this time were swallowing up the best things in the English Church.

SEVENTH PERIOD.—Then came a turning-point in the history of Hereford. The reputation of King Ethelbert as a miracle-worker may well by this time have worn a little thin. In 1287 Hereford found that it had obtained a new saint. This was Bishop Thomas Cantilupe, a man of saintly life, and one of the greatest churchmen of the day.

ST. THOMAS' SHRINE

"He was a pluralist of the first dimension—Chancellor of England and of the University of Oxford, Provincial Grand Master of the Knights Templars in England, Canon of York, Archdeacon and Canon of Lichfield and Coventry, Archdeacon of Stafford, Canon and Bishop of Hereford." In 1282, with his chaplain, Swinfield, he visited Rome, and died on the journey home. Swinfield, following a not uncommon mediæval practice, had the flesh of the body separated from the bones by boiling. The flesh was buried in the church of St. Severus, near Orvieto; the heart and bones he conveyed to England.

The heart was interred at Ashridge, the bones in Hereford cathedral. Five years afterwards miracles commenced: "There were raised from death to life threescore several persons, one-and-twenty lepers healed, and three-and-twenty blind and dumb men received their sight and speech. Twice King Edward I. sent sick falcons to be cured at his tomb." In 1320, by the expenditure of vast sums of money, his canonisation was procured; ever since, the see of Hereford has borne the arms of Cantilupe. He was the last English saint; and, being the newest, was for a considerable time the most fashionable. The fame of St. Wulfstan of Worcester and St. Swithun of Winchester paled before that of St. Thomas of Hereford. Till Gloucester secured in 1327 still fresher relics in the murdered body of King Edward II., Hereford held the greatest attraction for pilgrims in all the west country. For some forty years—from 1287 to 1327—the pilgrims resorted to the new shrine in vast numbers. Swinfield's foresight was justified by the huge sums which poured into the cathedral treasury.

Swinfield succeeded Cantilupe as bishop in 1283, and occupied the see till 1316. With the vast resources now at his disposal he set about a series of great works. His first pious act was to construct for his benefactor and predecessor a noble shrine, the pedestal of which now stands once more, after many vicissitudes, in the aisle of the north transept. It is a work of the rarest beauty, executed just at a time (1287) when, tired of conventional foliage, the mediæval carver, with ever fresh delight, was making the most exquisite transcripts in stone of the leaves of the trees and the flowers of the field.

Secondly, he constructed a north porch—the present inner porch—the design of which is plainly by the same hand as the pedestal of the shrine.

Thirdly, he went on with the improvement of the lighting of the cathedral. Beginning probably at the north-east transept, which was rebuilt, together with its eastern aisle, and working along the choir and nave to the west end, and then *vice versa* on the south side of the cathedral, he took

down all but the lower part of the walls of the Norman
aisles, rebuilt the upper part higher, and inserted very large
windows. This lighted the nave, at any rate, very satisfac-
torily. The design of these windows is unusual and effective,
owing to the largeness of the trefoils employed in the tracery.
It is noticeable externally that the curious ground-course of
the north transept is continued all round the cathedral, except
the south transept, south-east transept, and Lady chapel.

FROM THE NORTH-WEST

EIGHTH PERIOD (1316-1360).—The work seems to have
gone on without intermission from the accession of Bishop
Orleton in 1316. The greatest task, which may have been
begun a little earlier, was to rebuild the central tower on
the Norman piers and arches. To lessen the weight as much
as possible it was built in two skins, the inner skin consisting
of a framework of upright stone girders, as in the towers of
Wells and Lincoln. Externally it is smothered in ball-
flower. At one time it carried a tall timber spire; the

loss of which greatly injures the external elevation of the cathedral.

To the same period belong the stalls and the beautiful Chapter house, now in ruins. The lead of its roof was cast into bullets in the Civil War; sacrilegious bishops used its stones as a quarry for their palace.

FROM THE SOUTH-EAST

There are monuments of Bishop Swinfield (*d.* 1316) and Bishop Charleton (*d.* 1343).

Finally the lighting scheme was continued by the rebuilding of the south-east transept with its eastern aisle. This was executed in a cheap and inferior way, even the clumsy twelfth-century plinth being retained for the new central column of the transept. The windows have flowing tracery of poor design. It may be that the revenue from pilgrims had fallen off; or this work may have been done after the first outbreak of the Black Death at Hereford in 1350 or after the still more serious outbreak in 1360.

NINTH PERIOD.—The lighting scheme was at last completed by the insertion of two huge windows, with the now fashionable rectilinear tracery, in the south transept, of which the eastern has been recently filled with magnificent stained glass by Mr Kempe. Its south wall was rebuilt and it was vaulted. All this was the work of Bishop Travenant (1389-1404) whose monument is below.

On the north side of the choir Bishop Stanbury (1453-1474) built for himself a pretty little chantry-chapel, like those at Lincoln; it has fan-vaulting. It was he probably who built the cloister from the cathedral to the Chapter house; the rest of it may be later. He gave nearly half of the episcopal garden to the Vicars' Choral as a site for their College to the south-east of the cathedral; so we may probably also attribute to him the charming Vicars' Cloister with magnificent roof (which should be visited), together with the fan-vault over the entrance to the College.

BISHOP BOOTH'S PORCH

Bishop Audley (1492-1502) built himself a pentagonal chantry-chapel, two stories high, like the Islip chapel at Westminster, projecting from the south side of the Lady chapel. But, as he was translated to Salisbury, he had built another chantry-chapel there, in which he is buried. Bishop Booth (1516-1535) built the outer north porch—an admirable specimen of late Gothic design.

TENTH PERIOD.—In 1786 the western tower, which, as at Ely, was in the centre of the façade, collapsed, and Wyatt pulled down the westernmost bay of the nave and the whole of the triforium and clerestory, the sound as well as the damaged, and rebuilt both, together with the west front, in

THE NAVE

the Gothic of his day. About 1843 Cottingham did much work; rebuilding the east end of the Lady chapel and the upper part of that of the choir, and also securing the central tower. He found that the Norman piers which support it consisted of a thin ashlar casing, the interior of which was filled with a rubble core, composed of broken stones, loam and lime grouting. The ashlar facing and the engaged columns on the face of the pier, not being well bonded and deeply headed into the rubble cores, had split and bulged, and the cores, for want of a proper proportion of lime, had diminished and crushed to pieces. The gaudy choir-screen and coronal were executed by Skidmore of Coventry, from the designs of Sir Gilbert Scott, who also jammed the stalls into the presbytery. Recently a handsome west front, in the style of the fourteenth century, from the design of Mr J. Oldrid Scott, has replaced that of Wyatt.

BIBLIOGRAPHY.—Gordon M. Hills in *British Archæological Association Journal*, 1871; xxvii. 61 and 497.

Sir Gilbert Scott in *Archæological Journal*, December 1877.

M. H. Bloxam, "On certain Sepulchral Effigies in Hereford Cathedral," in *Archæological Journal*, xl. 406.

THE CATHEDRAL CHURCH OF ST. MARY, LICHFIELD

BUILT FOR SECULAR CANONS

THIS is how Lichfield presented itself to Mrs Van Renselaer. "Approaching it from one street or another, we see it suddenly across the silver stretches of its Pool, and it is hard to determine whether the shining water at Lichfield or the green lake of turf at Salisbury makes the lovelier foreground. Standing on the causeway which leads towards the western entrance of the Close, it is not merely a fine view that we have before us; it is a picture so perfect that no artist would ask a change in one detail. Perhaps accident has had more to do than design with the planting of the trees and shrubs which border the lake, and above which spring the daring spires. But a landscape gardener might study this planting to his profit; and when we see or think of Lichfield from this point of view, we wish that the tall poplar may be as long-lived as the tree Yggdrasil—so pretty a measure does it give of the loftiness of the spires, so exquisite is the completing accent which it brings into the scene. If we come from the south-east, we cross another causeway, on either side of which the lake spreads out widely; and we see not only the spires, but the apse and the long stretch of the southern side. Enormously long it looks—longer almost, owing to its peculiar lowness, than those cathedrals which are actually greater. To the north of the church the ground rises quickly into a broad, terrace-like walk flanked by rows of large and ancient, yet graceful lindens; and beyond the trees, behind low walls and verdurous gardens, lies a range of canons' dwellings. And in any and every aspect, but more especially when foliage comes near it, Lichfield's colour assists its other beauties. Red stone is warm and mellow in itself; and Lichfield is red with a beautiful soft ruddiness that could hardly be matched by any sandstone of any land."

The ancient kingdom of Mercia was converted to Christianity, like the rest of England north of the Thames, by missionaries of the Celtic church of Northumberland, c. 653. Of the early bishops, by far the most famous was St. Chad (669-672). St. Chad, or Ceadda, was a good and saintly man. He is first heard of as Abbot of Lastingham, a sequestered abbey hidden away in a fold of the Cleveland moors. Then Abbot Chad became Bishop of York, and set to work on a visitation of his vast, wild diocese—not in a

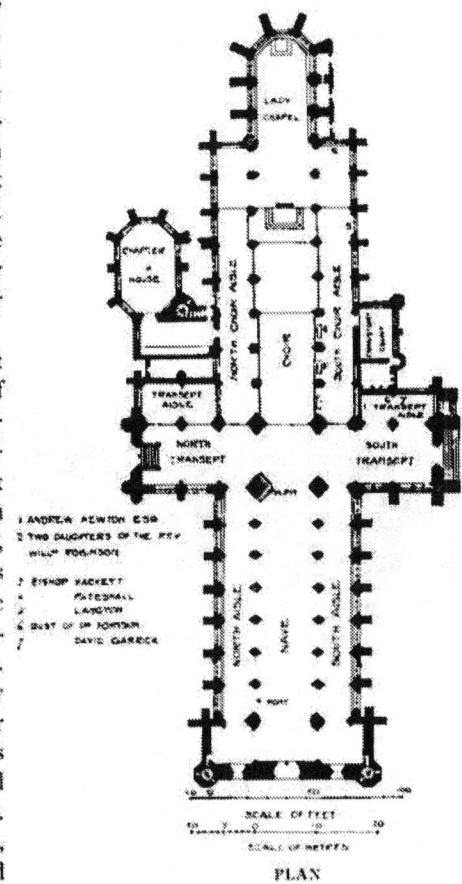

PLAN

carriage and pair, but on foot. Plainly these early bishops were what we should now call Missionary Bishops, such as that Missionary of the Southern Seas whose effigy lies in Lichfield's Lady chapel, the face irradiated by the southern light. Bishop Chad visited town and country, village and hamlet, cottage and castle; and preached everywhere. It was another Journey of St. Paul. But in 669 the famous Greek Archbishop of Canterbury, Theodore, pronounced his consecration faulty, and deposed him from

THE SOUTH SIDE FROM THE POOL

York. Soon afterwards, however, finding him a saintly man and an excellent preacher, he appointed him to the bishopric of Mercia, to the see of Lichfield. What was York's loss was Lichfield's gain. At Lichfield he lived, tradition says, in a cell with his missionaries, at the upper end of the Pool, where now stands St. Chad's church. It behoves all who come to Lichfield to visit St. Chad's church and to drink the water of St. Chad's Well. Two years and a half only Bishop Chad had left of life; but that was enough for him to win the reverence of his own and many successive generations. Beautiful stories are told of him by Bede. One of the eight monks who lived with him heard one day a joyful melody of some persons sweetly singing, which descended from heaven into the bishop's oratory, and filled the same for about half an hour, and then rose again to heaven; and on the seventh day thereafter, having received the Body and Blood of Our Lord, he departed unto Bliss, to which he was invited by the happy soul of his brother, St. Cedd, and a company of angels with heavenly music. In the statutes of Bishop Lonsdale (1863) the cathedral is described as "our cathedral church of St. Peter, St. Mary and St. Chad in our City of Lichfield."

Thus the diocese of Lichfield preserves the memory of the bygone kingdom of Mercia; and its cathedral is largely built of the offerings at St. Chad's shrine. How big the ancient diocese was is seen from the fact that the following dioceses have been carved out of it: Hereford in 676, Lindsey in 678, Leicester in 680, Worcester in 680 (and out of Worcester, Gloucester in 1541), Chester in 1537 (and out of Chester, Manchester in 1848, Liverpool in 1880), Southwell (the Derbyshire portion) in 1884. For a time even greater honour came to Lichfield. From 758 to 796 a great and mighty king reigned in Mercia: this was Offa. In one direction he defeated Kent; in the other he drove back the Welsh. It was Offa who settled once for all the Welsh frontier: Shrewsbury became an English town. Offa's Dyke, which still exists, from the mouth of the Wye to the mouth of the Dee, became the effectual bulwark of England to the West. A king so mighty disdained to owe allegiance to an archbishop of defeated Kentishmen, and got from the Pope Adrian I. an archbishop of his own, to be head-bishop of all Mercia and East Anglia. But Offa died, and this was the only archbishop Lichfield ever had. Lichfield was never so important again. Indeed, she had a narrow escape of losing her bishop altogether, just after the Norman conquest. The new Norman prelates did not feel safe, and probably were not safe, in open towns amidst an alien and disaffected population. The Bishop of Dorchester set up his pastoral staff under the shadow of the new Norman castle at Lincoln; Exeter castle attracted the Bishop of Crediton; in similar fashion the Norman Bishop of Lichfield transferred himself to Chester, where also was a castle of strength. The next bishop migrated again—this time to Coventry, which possessed a famous monastery, founded by famous people, Earl Leofric and Lady Godiva, the church whereof was so wealthy that "its walls were all too strait for the treasures that were therein." Finally the bishops returned once more to Lichfield, retaining, however, their hold on Coventry; and from 1129 to 1840 they styled themselves "Bishops of Lichfield and Coventry." Lichfield, however, was and is a cathedral of the old foundation; it had no monks, but secular canons. It may well be imagined, therefore, that there was not much peace and good will between the canons of Lichfield and the monks of Coventry. They quarrelled scandalously; above all when they had to meet for joint election of a bishop. There was a desperate free fight in 1190, when Bishop Hugh ejected the monks from Coventry cathedral; the bishop himself was wounded at the altar.

In the thirteenth century there must have been a series of great building bishops; but not much is known of them. Bishop Langton, however, was a very great personage, Keeper of the Great Seal, Treasurer of England, and executor to Edward I. (1296-1321). He built a new episcopal palace at Lichfield, and other castles and manor-houses elsewhere, also a magnificent new shrine for the relics of St. Chad; and he surrounded the cathedral with a wall and foss, thus making of it a moated fortress, such as one sees to this day in the palace at Wells. Robert Stretton (1360-1385) had the distinction of not being able to read. Then we pass on to the great Civil War, when Bishop Langton's fortifications proved a heritage of woe. Being fortified, and being held by loyalists, Lichfield cathedral was besieged by the Parliamentary forces under Lord Brooke, who prayed aloud that God would by some special token manifest unto them His approbation. The special token came on St. Chad's Day, 2nd March, and is commemorated by a tablet on a house in Dam Street, which the visitor should look for: "March 2nd, 1643.—Lord Brooke, a general of the Parliament forces, preparing to besiege the Close of Lichfield, then garrisoned for King Charles the First, received his death-wound on the spot beneath this inscription, by a shot in the forehead, from Mr Dyott," a deaf and dumb man, "who had placed himself on the battlements of the great steeple to annoy the besiegers." It may interest some to know that the distance of the shot was 185 yds. 1 ft. 3 in. In the end the garrison was starved out. A month later Lichfield Close was recaptured by Prince Rupert. In 1646 it was retaken by the Parliamentarians. In the first siege the Parliamentary cannon brought down the central tower and most of the vault of the choir. This was not all. The Puritans smashed the stained windows, battered down the statues, stripped the lead from the roof and the brasses from the tombs, burned the registers, and broke up the bells and organs. They are said each day to have hunted a cat down the aisles, and to have draped a calf and given it a mock baptism at the font. "I confess," says an apologist for her Puritan ancestors, "there were moments in my English journey when I hated the Puritan with a godly hatred, and wished that he had never shown his surly face to the world: a rude destroyer of things ancient, and therefore to be respected; a vandal devastator of things rare and beautiful, and too precious ever to be replaced, a brutal scoffer, drinking at the altar, firing his musket at the figure of Christ, parading in priest's vestments through the market-place, stabling his horses in the house of God." Then came the Restoration, and with the Restoration Bishop Hacket, best of good bishops. The very next morning after his arrival he set his coach horses to work at clearing away the ruins of the fallen spire and roof. For nine years he gave himself and his substance to the work; his contributions in money amounted to £10,000; the King gave "one hundred fair timber trees"; the prebendaries and canons subscribed half their income; every town, every village in the diocese aided the good work; the central tower was re-erected; most of the clerestory of the choir was rebuilt; his last task was to put in a peal of bells. "He went out of his bedchamber to hear the tenor bell, the only one as yet hung, and blessed God who had favoured him with life to hear it, but that it was his own passing-bell; whereupon he retired to his chamber and never left it till he was carried to his grave." Next to St. Chad, one likes to think of good Bishop Hacket in connexion with Lichfield. In 1788 James Wyatt arrived, but did less mischief than at Salisbury, Hereford, and Durham. Even more terrible vandals followed Wyatt, with a mania for Roman cement, in which beautiful material they reconstructed the statuary of the west front. All this is now swept away, and this fairest of façades is seen in something like its pristine beauty.

At Lichfield there was as usual a Norman cathedral; and as usual the authorities set to work to improve it. Elsewhere the improvements were of a very conservative character. At Lichfield, Wells, and York, they were drastic: the Norman cathedral was improved by being swept off the face of the earth, not a scrap of it being left above ground. Beginning at the east end, it was pulled down and rebuilt, the work occupying more than a century. The most astounding thing about Lichfield is that when the new thirteenth-century cathedral was finished, the canons set to work once more at rebuilding, and in the first half of the fourteenth century remodelled the whole of the eastern limb of the cathedral; the cathedral was never out of the builders' hands from $c.$ 1190 to $c.$ 1350.

FIRST PERIOD. Of the Norman church nothing is known except by excavations. These shewed that the presbytery was of the periapsidal plan we see at Gloucester; it had consisted of an apse preceded by three rectangular bays, and was encircled by a procession path. No doubt there were three radiating chapels opening out of the procession path; some indications were found of the easternmost of these. Late in the twelfth century, a long oblong chapel was built projecting eastward.

SECOND PERIOD.—Section by section the whole of the

THE CHOIR, LOOKING WEST

Norman church was rebuilt. As usual, the presbytery was rebuilt first. Excavations shewed that the new presbytery consisted of five aisled bays opening, as at Exeter and Southwark, by two arches into two low rectangular bays, of which the western would be employed as procession path, while the eastern would contain four altars, as again at Southwark. The three western bays of this new presbytery remain, but have lost both triforium and clerestory. The date 1200 is usually assigned to them. But the entrance arch of the north choir aisle has the diamond pattern enclosing a roll, as in the west transept of Peterborough, which is known to have been built between 1195 and 1200; the square alternates with the rounded abacus; the piers are heavy, the arches low, the moldings large and vigorous, and the foliated capitals at the west end of both aisles are so archaic in character that it may have been commenced some years earlier. The work should be compared with the early Gothic work in Chester cathedral, which was originally in Lichfield diocese. The peculiar plan of the piers, encircled by shafts of freestone arranged in triplets, stamps the work decisively as part of that great school of Western Gothic which arose at Wells, Worcester, and Glastonbury, and, which, uncontaminated by any foreign influence, wrought out an individual style of its own and extended its outposts as far as Chester, Lichfield, and Dublin. At about the same time as the new presbytery was built the sacristy and the adjoining treasury, which originally was accessible only from the sacristy. St. Chad's chapel above the sacristy, from the form of its windows and the character of its capitals, also belongs to this work; but it must be a trifle later, for its doorway is the central light of an aisle window. The new vault and other detail by Sir Gilbert Scott completely distort the history of the chapel.

This West of England work at Lichfield has never received the careful study it deserves. There is much more of it than there appears to be at first sight. In the choir it includes the three western bays of the ground story; as these no doubt were intended to have a high vault, as in the work at Worcester, c. 1175, and as there were to be no flying buttresses, the walls had to be very thick in order to abut the high vault, and therefore required as supports massive columns and arches. For additional safety, these were kept very low, as at Wells. The piers are surrounded by eight groups of shafts arranged in triplets, as in Wells nave; several of these are filleted, and the fillets pass down through the bases and plinths. The arch-molds have large rolls, which are largely repeats of one another. Of the capitals some are elongated, as at Llandaff, and have simple, conventional foliage with very long stalks; some have the pollarded willow design with enrichments; a few have the plantain leaf; a few have the reflexed trefoil leaf, which appears in Dore retro-choir; but the great majority, especially in the arcading, have solid, knobby capitals of foliage, of little projection and but slightly undercut. On the internal walls of the aisles is arcading consisting of trefoiled arches. The aisle-vaults have been rebuilt and filled in with ashlar; the ribs are original, and seem rather later than the pier-arches, as do the two or three foliated bosses which remain in the south aisle. A curious feature in this west country Gothic is the continuous bowtell without capitals or bases; it is well seen in the wall arches and in the arch leading into the south aisle of the nave. In the triforium chamber there are gutters at the foot of the clerestory buttresses; which looks as if the chamber originally had a span roof, and not a lean-to. The piers of the crossing have been thickened to carry the present tower; inside, however, they must be the piers of c. 1190; for a bay of the clerestory of that date remains adjoining each tower-pier; the bay has been narrowed by the thickening of this pier and its form altered; the best preserved is that on the east side of the north transept. The greater part of the transepts also belong to this work; as may be seen by examining the capitals of the vaulting-shafts and the remains of the windows. In one respect the work differs not only from that of the Northern and South-eastern school, but also from that of the West; viz., in the design of the windows, which is unique. Elsewhere single windows are employed, except one graduated triplet in the north aisle of Pershore. But at Lichfield all the lower windows seem to have been triplets; they are singularly squat and ugly: they are well seen in the unglazed windows at the inner ends of the transept aisles; and one of them has been restored and glazed in the southern bay of the aisle of the south transept.

It is to be added that the nave also is but a later and advanced development of West of England design; as appears from the shafting of the piers, the character of the arch-molds, and the non-use of marble shafting.

THIRD PERIOD.—About 1220 the south transept was commenced. The builders of the choir had planned it for an aisleless transept. When, therefore, the transept was built with an eastern aisle, the westernmost window of the choir aisle looked into the transept aisle and no longer into the open air. Moreover, owing to the presence of the western wall of the treasury, the last aisle of the south transept could not be made so broad as that of the north transept.

About twenty years later the north transept seems to have been taken in hand; the original group of five lancet lights has recently been restored on the evidence of fragments found in the wall. The doorways of both transepts are of rich and lovely design.

About the same date as the north transept, a Chapter house and vestibule were built on the north side of the choir, as at Lincoln, York, and Southwell. This had not been contemplated by the builders of the choir; consequently the doorway of the vestibule had to be placed where before was a lancet window. The vestibule is a bold and vigorous piece of design, with a remarkable range of thirteen arcaded seats on its western side. The Chapter house is unique in plan, being an octagon with two long and six short sides. The doorway has bold tooth ornament; the wall is surrounded by a trefoiled arcade. Above the vestibule is a room which was once the chapel of St. Peter; above the Chapter house is the present library. Among the treasures of the cathedral is the priceless copy of "St. Chad's Gospels," written by an Irish scribe probably about the end of the seventh century; it is now placed in a glass case behind the reredos of the altar.

LICHFIELD CATHEDRAL.

FOURTH PERIOD.—About 1260 the present nave seems to have been commenced. Its remarkable clerestory windows—spherical triangles enclosing cusped circles—occur in the Westminster triforium, and, rather later, in the clere-

THE NAVE

story of Hereford north transept. The spherical triangles fit perfectly into the wall arches of the vaulting, and, as Mr Fergusson says, "give a stability and propriety to the whole arrangement which has never been surpassed." In fact, taken in conjunction with the uninterrupted flow of the vaulting-shafts to the pavement, they afford a glimpse of a design which was not to be fully realised till Gloucester choir was built as a single-storied interior. The weak point is the want of organic connexion between the triforium and the clerestory stages. They might well have been fused into a single composition, by flattening the aisle roofs and glazing the triforium arcade, as was done at Troyes cathedral, c. 1250. The proportions of the nave are singularly beautiful. Though it is inconsiderable in height, yet each separate bay is so lofty in proportion to its width, that the lowness of the vault does not strike one. The numerous vertical lines arising from the large number of shafts attached to the piers, and the great height of the unbanded vaulting-shafts still further increase the appearance of loftiness. The foliated capitals are of marvellous beauty and interest, running the whole gamut from conventional to naturalistic sculpture; and are almost untouched by the restorer, having been preserved by thick coats of whitewash. The vault, too, of which, however, the five eastern bays had to be removed in 1760 when they were rebuilt in plaster, is most satisfactory—not simple to bareness, like that of Beverley and so many French cathedrals, nor over-elaborated, like those of the naves of Winchester and Norwich; a curious feature of it is the omission of the transverse ribs, so as to reduce the number of ribs for which room had to be found on the abacus of the vaulting-shafts. The design of the interior of Lichfield nave is one of the loveliest in Christendom. It derives great impressiveness from the fact that the vault ranges the whole length of the cathedral in almost undiminished height; and from the fact that the church is not cut up, as at Canterbury, into two distinct buildings. Indeed, small as the cathedral is, the vista from west to east is one of the longest of all the English cathedrals. And its termination in the beautiful polygon of the Lady chapel, so unusual to English eyes, glimmering in the distance "like some great casket of jewels at the end of the long dusk perspective," makes an impression never to be forgotten. By this one remembers the interior of Lichfield, as its exterior by the glorious coronal of spires. Nave, transept, and choir are all of the same length. The same scheme of proportions was adopted a little later in planning York Minster.

Externally, the nave is well seen from the north, about the only part of the exterior which has not been rebuilt; notice the curious system of drainage of the high roofs, resembling that of Chichester nave, by which the water was conveyed along the channelled backs of the flying buttresses; here and on the Chapter house the buttresses are still crowned with gablets; except at Westminster, pinnacles had hardly come into use yet, to weight the buttresses of the flanks of churches.

FIFTH PERIOD.—The nave finished, the west front was taken in hand. The first stage, up to and including the row of kings, may be *c.* 1280; the second stage *c.* 1300, the upper part, including the belfry windows, *c.* 1320; in this stage and on the spires is much ball-flower, an ornament which was in vogue most between 1307 and 1327. The central doorway retains much of its original ironwork.

Great works were going on simultaneously to the east of the cathedral. In two respects it was defective in plan; viz., that it gave little honour either to Our Lady or to St. Chad. What was wanted was a grand Lady chapel and a Feretory. Walter Langton, who was bishop from 1296 to 1321, set to work to provide both. Starting to the east of the existing church, a vast Lady chapel was commenced; at first entirely detached so as not to interfere with the services. Being exceedingly lofty and without aisles, it was possible to have exceptionally lofty windows. These elongated windows, the absence of pinnacles, and the polygonal plan, give the exterior a curiously foreign appearance. The window tracery is geometrical, being composed of groups of trefoils. But the ogee-dripstones of the windows shew that the work overlaps into the fourteenth century; indeed, it was unfinished at Bishop Langton's death in 1321. Inside the southern wall are chapels, the central of which contains the monument of Bishop Selwyn, of New Zealand and Lichfield. But the glory of the Lady chapel and the cathedral is the magnificent painted glass of the sixteenth century—similar in character to that of Margaret of Austria's church at Brou-en-Bresse, Burgundy. The first window on each side was inserted recently. The remaining seven windows are also Flemish glass, of the date 1530 to 1540, bought by Sir Brooke Boothby in 1803, from the Cistercian nunnery of Herckenrode, near Liège, for £200. The second window on the north is particularly interesting, as it contains portraits of patrons and benefactors of Herckenrode, kneeling at altars, with their patron saints behind them. The third window also has portraits of great nobles of the Netherlands. The remaining five windows contain Scriptural subjects.

SIXTH PERIOD.—The next stage of the work, which was left for Bishop Norbury, 1325-1359, was to join up the Lady chapel to the church by the insertion of an additional bay. About the same time would be erected a stone pedestal for the shrine of St. Chad; the foundations of this have been laid bare. It did not stand in the usual position at the back of the High altar, but occupied the western half of the bay adjoining the Lady chapel. Thus the new procession path would pass to the west of it, and not as usual to the east. This done, the cathedral was complete and as we see it now. It contained (1) nave, (2) transepts, each with two eastern chapels, (3) choir of three bays, (4) presbytery of three bays with High altar in its present position, (5) procession path, (6) Feretory with two lateral chapels at the east ends of the choir aisles, (8) Lady chapel, (9) sacristy and treasury. But even the last great extension was not enough for the canons. They were seized with the mania for floods of light and acres of stained glass which raged like an epidemic through the fourteenth and fifteenth and sixteenth centuries. They pulled down all the choir except the piers and arches of the three westernmost bays—these would not be visible owing to the stallwork in front of them; besides, to remove them might have endangered the central tower—they built new piers and arches in the eastern bays, and a new clerestory along the whole length of the choir with huge windows of flowing tracery, two only of which are left. The result of the new design was to convert the chancel into a two-story interior as opposed to the three-story interior of the nave. The original triforium may have been similar to that of the transept. At the same time they replaced all the lancets of the aisles by big windows with similar tracery. The jambs of the clerestory windows they enriched with bands of quatrefoils; one of the windows of the south aisle of the choir, opposite to which the tomb of Bishop Langton formerly stood, and beneath which good Bishop Hacket's tomb is now placed, has big crumpled leaves running up the jambs. The junction of the early piers and capitals with those of the fourteenth century is well seen in the third pier from the central tower. Between the bays were placed statued niches, as in the contemporary church of St. Mary's, Beverley, from which rose the vaulting-shaft. The whole design should be compared with the presbyteries of Wells and Chester, which were in course of "restoration" at the same time and in the same ruthless fashion. In the choir aisles is a delightful arcade of bowing ogee arches. The development of the Gothic foliated capital may be studied most delightfully by inspecting successively the capitals of the choir, transepts, Chapter house and vestibule, nave and presbytery. About the same time, or a little later, were built the central gable of the west front and the south-western spire.

SEVENTH PERIOD.—The equipment of the presbytery was completed about the middle of the fifteenth century by the erection of a magnificent altar-screen after the fashion of those at Winchester and St. Albans. Six of its canopies are reused in the present sedilia. In a line with the reredos there were gates across the aisles; thus the procession path, Saint's chapel and Lady chapel were entirely shut off from the chancel. The shrine of St. Chad is recorded to have

188 LICHFIELD CATHEDRAL

been completed by Bishop Stretton c. 1386. At the Dissolution the bones of St. Chad were conveyed away by Prebendary Dudley; they passed through various hands, and are now shewn in St. Chad's cathedral, Birmingham, deposited in a reliquary placed above the High altar. As with St. Hugh at Lincoln, there was a separate shrine for

THE WEST FRONT

the head of the saint, which was probably kept in the existing aumbry of St. Chad's chapel. From its gallery the head shrine could be shewn to pilgrims passing below. The head shrine of St. Chad is mentioned in an inventory of 1345 or 1346. From "St. Chad's pennies" collected in the many churches of this large diocese and from the offerings of pilgrims at the two shrines the cathedral drew a very large revenue. Even at the Dissolution, when the relics of St. Chad were ordered to be destroyed, the precious metals and jewels of the shrine were by exception allowed to be retained by the Chapter.

In the fifteenth century also the northern spire was copied from the southern one. More big windows were inserted in the transepts and the west end of the nave. The latter has been replaced by a modern window with geometrical tracery; that of the north transept by a quintet of lancets. Finally, the whole cathedral was rendered fireproof by the erection of vaults over both transepts and under the central tower. The south transept, however, would seem to have had a vault previously—but it may have been of wood—for a little lower than the abacus of the vaulting-shaft is one of the thirteenth century. In 1512 Dean Yotton was buried in the north aisle of the nave, near the chantry chapel which he had built projecting from the second bay west of the transept; fragments of its doorway are still visible externally.

EIGHTH PERIOD.—In the two sieges the clerestory and aisle windows and the vault of the choir suffered greatly, and the central spire was destroyed. The latter was rebuilt, it is said, but without warrant, by Sir Christopher Wren, and rectilinear tracery replaced the fourteenth-century tracery which had been destroyed in the windows of the Lady chapel and the clerestory of the choir. In 1813 the fronts of the choir arches, being decayed, were cut away and replaced in stucco; now they are once more rebuilt in stone.

The poor, thin metal screen is by Skidmore of Coventry, and replaces a massive stone screen made up of the fragments of the ancient reredos, and carrying a noble organ. The metal pulpit, the font, the lectern, the litany desk, the stalls, the bishop's throne, and the reredos are all modern. The cathedral is rich in good examples of the glass of Mr Kempe and Messrs Burliton and Grylls; to Mr Kempe also is to be credited admirable minor work in St. Chad's chapel and the fine altar rails of alabaster (with the Blessed Virgin's vase of lilies) in the Lady chapel. Over a grand effigy of Bishop Lonsdale by Mr Watts, on the north side of the presbytery, is an atrocious canopy in carpenter's Gothic; not much better is the monument of Hodson of "Hodson's Horse" in the south aisle of the presbytery. In this aisle are several interesting monuments; in the first bay from the east Chantrey's "Sleeping Children"; in the third bay the monument of Bishop Hacket; in the fourth bay that of a tired man, Archdeacon Moore, by Armstead; in the sixth and seventh bays fine effigies of thirteenth-century bishops.

BIBLIOGRAPHY.—Professor Willis' paper in the *Archæological Journal*, vol. xviii., 1861.
Sketch of the Restorations in Lichfield Cathedral, Lichfield, 1861.
Woodhouse's *Short Account of Lichfield Cathedral*, Lichfield, 1811.
History of St. Chad's, Birmingham, Birmingham, 1904.

THE CATHEDRAL CHURCH OF ST. MARY, LINCOLN

BUILT FOR SECULAR CANONS

"Beautiful for situation, the joy of the whole earth."

THE cathedrals of Lincoln, York, and Southwell were ever served by secular canons and not by monks; but each cathedral has been styled a minster from time immemorial, as if it were or had been a monastic church (*monasterium*).

FIRST PERIOD.—The history of the cathedral only commences in 1074, when the first Norman bishop, Remi or Remigius, made Lincoln the seat of the see instead of Dorchester on the Thames. As Canon Venables puts it: "He refused the tabernacle of Birinus, and chose not the tribe of the South Angles; but chose the tribe of Lindsey, even the hill of Lindum which he loved; and there he built his temple on high, and laid the foundation of it like the ground which hath been established for ever." The blank wall with its curious apsidal recesses, which forms the centre of the west front, is Remi's work. So are the Corinthian capitals, square-edged arches, and wide-jointed masonry in the ground story of the western towers.

If we pass within beneath the north-western tower, the semicircular arches, though blocked up, of the Norman triforium may still be recognised; and the clerestory

192   LINCOLN CATHEDRAL

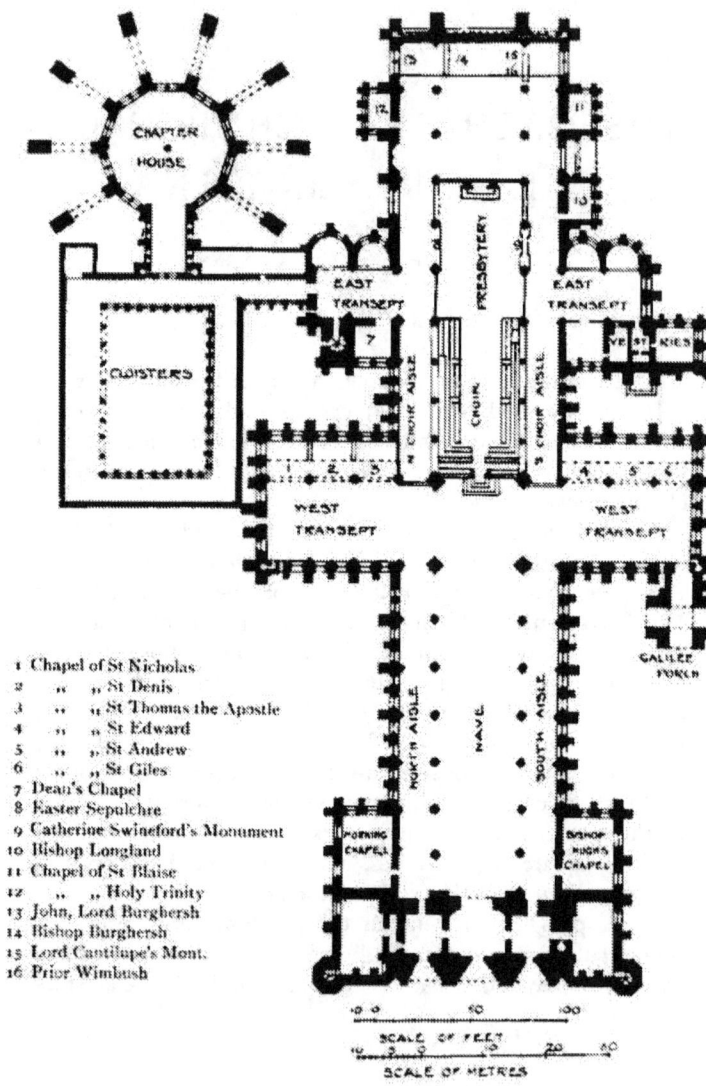

1 Chapel of St Nicholas
2   ,,   ,, St Denis
3   ,,   ,, St Thomas the Apostle
4   ,,   ,, St Edward
5   ,,   ,, St Andrew
6   ,,   ,, St Giles
7 Dean's Chapel
8 Easter Sepulchre
9 Catherine Swineford's Monument
10 Bishop Longland
11 Chapel of St Blaise
12   ,,   ,, Holy Trinity
13 John, Lord Burghersh
14 Bishop Burghersh
15 Lord Cantilupe's Mont.
16 Prior Wimbush

PLAN

windows retain their angle-rolls with the original caps; ground story, triforium, and clerestory were about equal in height. The nave was 5 ft. 6 in. narrower on each side than at present from aisle wall to aisle wall; the arches between the nave and aisles were separated by piers which were 17 ft. 2 in. from centre to centre; there were ten bays in the nave. There was a transept, narrower than the present one by about 4 feet on one side; and a

THE WEST FRONT

short-aisled presbytery, ending in three parallel eastern apses.

SECOND PERIOD.—The archaic façade was improved c. 1160 by the insertion of a more ornamental central door way. Also curious plaques, in rather high relief, were stuck along the wall, as at St. Michael, Pavia. They are not in chronological sequence, and so may have been transferred from elsewhere. Moreover, two low western towers were carried up, with rich and beautiful gables; of which those to the north and south survive. The south-western tower should be ascended to see Remi's eleventh-century work, the twelfth-century gables, the "elastic beam," and the superb view of the interior of nave, choir, and presbytery. The font in the south aisle of the nave, like that of Winchester, is one of a series brought from Tournai; there is another at Thornton Curtis, near the Humber. The north and south doorways of the west front were probably inserted c. 1170. Their capitals have faint reminiscences of Byzantine design. They should be contrasted with the archaic capitals in Remi's work.

THIRD PERIOD.—We now walk up the nave and enter the choir. In 1190 a Carthusian monk, Hugh of Avalon, near Grenoble, who for ten years had been prior of Witham, Somerset, became bishop. Like Fitz-Jocelyn of Wells, and like the Lichfield builders, he determined to sweep away the Norman cathedral and build a new one. He probably had no choice, for Hoveden relates that in 1185 a great earthquake was heard almost throughout the whole of England, such as had not been heard in that land from the beginning of the world. Rocks were split, stone-built houses fell into ruin, and the church of Lincoln was torn asunder from top to bottom.

Bishop Hugh commenced work in 1192; commencing no doubt some considerable distance east of the short Norman choir, and completing his presbytery before the latter was removed. Excavations, marked by lines incised in the pavement, shew that the presbytery was of Continental type, but with special peculiarities of its own. It terminated in a semi-hexagon, and was encircled by a procession aisle; from the latter radiated seven chapels. Of all this nothing is left above ground except a fragment of arcading on the exterior of the north wall of St. Paul's chapel (kept locked up). Next would come the building of the choir transepts; it is a strange fact that the end bay of each was only one story high. The end wall of the southern choir transept has been removed; that of the northern one still remains, but its windows no longer look into the open air,

LINCOLN CATHEDRAL 195

and are unglazed. To this period belong also the chapels on both sides of the choirtransepts. Of the four chapels on the east side of the transepts three only were apsidal. The fourth, the northernmost, is as we see it now, apsidal, having been shortened and narrowed and remodelled generally by Essex in 1772; originally it was a long oblong building; the foundations of its eastern bays may be seen outside in the turf; the doorway in its north wall is not *in situ*; it is a composite one, put together no doubt by Essex from various sources. This oblong building was probably the original Chapter house.

In the choir transepts and the choir there is nothing of Continental design; they are to be compared with such work as that of Ripon nave (before aisles were added), and the choirs of Fountains Abbey and Beverley Minster. It is only in a few minor details that the influence of the French choir of Canterbury appears. The chapels of St. Hugh's apse and choir transepts were probably vaulted as we see them now. As to the aisles of the choir it is not so easy to determine. It was very rare in a cathedral church, whether Romanesque or Gothic, not to vault the

ARCADING IN BOYS' VESTRY

aisles; but originally the aisle-walls of the Lincoln choir were too thin to support a vault. It was only when it was decided to vault these aisles that they were thickened by adding in front of them the tall trefoiled arcade now seen. (The pointed arcade at the back has its moldings and tooth ornament fully worked, even where masked by the trefoiled arcade; and the latter is built independently of the former; plainly it is an afterthought. The construction of this double arcade is best seen in the end bays of the south choir aisle and the adjacent central transept.) The change of intention must have occurred very shortly after the beginning of the choir works, for at the cills of the aisle-windows the wall is solid throughout. As for the high vaults of the choir transepts and the choir, there certainly were none in St. Hugh's time; for the whole abutment system by which their thrusts are stopped is of a later period. It seems probable that the triforium and clerestory also, as we see them now, depart very widely from St. Hugh's design. As for the latter, if we search the pockets of the high vaults, we find a number of blocked lancets between each pair of clerestory windows; when there were no high vaults, these would be visible from below. They must be part of St. Hugh's clerestory; which, judging from these indications, had either another lancet window, or an unpierced pointed recess, between each triplet of lancet windows. If now we pass into one of the choir transepts and look up at the clerestory passage of the choir, we shall see in each bay three dark pointed openings; these look into the triforium chamber. But if we pass into the latter, we shall find a fourth and larger opening at the back of the springers of the present high vault. These four pointed openings are probably the upper part of a triforium arcade of St. Hugh's time, much loftier than the present one. All four may have looked into his triforium chamber; or only the three narrower arches, the fourth being an unpierced pointed recess.

To St. Hugh's time we may probably refer the commencement of the central transept; inside, a stoppage of

LINCOLN CATHEDRAL. 197

the works is indicated by a change of the design of the wall arcade in the bays next the choir; externally there are equally well marked differences.

St. Hugh's work is of exceptional interest both from its early date and from the extraordinary transformation which it has undergone. Special attention should be paid to the two chapels on the west sides of the choir transepts. That in the north transept goes by the name of the Dean's chapel; in the thirteenth century it was walled off, floors were put in, and doors and windows were inserted in the ground story (notice the original ironwork on the doors and shutters). The chapel in the south transept was screened off in the fourteenth century as a sacristy; it is now the boys' vestry; its southern doorway passes through a thick wall which was originally part of the end wall of St. Hugh's south choir transept.

CENTRAL TOWER AND TRIFORIUM OF CHOIR

Everywhere the foliated capitals are of great beauty and interest, as are the moldings; the figure sculpture in the Dean's chapel merits special attention. At the junction of the choir aisles with the choir transepts are remarkable piers with hollow-chamfered marble shafts and vertical bands of crockets of early type.

FOURTH PERIOD.—St. Hugh died in 1200, and the work seems to have been carried on by the same architect, Geoffry de Noiers. This included the remainder of the central transept and a central tower. This transept also was designed not to have a vault; as is shewn by the fact that the top of the northern circular window is masked by the present vault. This window and those below contain admirable contemporary glass; there is none finer in England; of fine design, too, externally, is the northern doorway into the Dean's garden.

FIFTH PERIOD.—The next work was the building of the nave, which from the first was designed for a vault. Whoever the architect was, it was not Geoffry de Noiers, but some one who was a good engineer—so good an engineer that in the interior he somewhat sacrificed art to engineering. The piers he set as far apart as possible, and made them as thin as possible; but they are beautifully built, and rest on foundations which are continuous underground from pier to pier, and in addition are kept from shifting by transverse foundations extending from each pier to the aisle-wall. The

THE NAVE AND NORTH TRANSEPT

object of making the bays so broad was to get plenty of room for a high vault without obstructing the clerestory windows. The obtuse arches, however, of the pier-arcade and the attenuated piers are not satisfactory to the eye. On the other hand, the exterior of the nave, with its knife-edge buttresses and tall gablets and strong base-courses, is one of the best designs in all Gothic; it is of almost Greek severity. The height of the nave, when vaulted, was 82 ft., as compared with the 74 ft. of the vaulted choir. A Frenchman would have given a nave so broad (42 ft.) a height of some 120 ft.

The original design had been, probably, to make the nave much longer than it is now, and then to build a brand-new west front, as at Wells and Lichfield. Ultimately, however, it was decided not to sweep away, but to utilise the Norman west front and western towers as far as possible, and to curtail the nave accordingly. Unfortunately, the new cathedral had not been built at right angles to the Norman façade. The axis, therefore, of the western bays of the nave had to deviate so as to strike the façade as centrally as possible. Moreover, the vault of the nave was too lofty for the façade, so it was suddenly dropped two feet at the end of the five eastern bays; and the distance between the completed bays and the façade being insufficient for two arches of the span of the eastern ones, the two western bays had to be built narrower than the rest.

All this is regrettable: but though the nave is shorter than it should be, the vast spaces of the interior, dimly lighted with scanty beams filtering through narrow lancets, are wonderfully impressive; the distances, yet further enhanced by the interposition of organ and screen, seem really infinite. It is not, like Ely, a study in contrasts, but in harmonies. The design of the nave leads without a break to that of the transepts; the design of the transepts to that of the choir; the design of the choir, aided by the rich stalls and screens, to the splendour of the presbytery, where the light breaks forth at length to irradiate all loveliness of molding and foliage and sculptured imagery.

Though the length of the nave was now curtailed in the altered design, compensation was found in throwing out a flanking chapel on either side of the two westernmost bays. The position of these chapels may be founded on those of

THE NAVE

Ely; it was repeated by Wren in St. Paul's. In all three cathedrals it gives a noble air of spaciousness on entering by the western doors. The vault of the northern chapel is supported by a beautiful central pier consisting of eight shafts of Purbeck marble, very acutely pointed, and once so highly polished, like the rest of the Purbeck shafts, says a mediæval versifier, that they positively dazzled the eyes.

Then came the west front. We may not like it; but given the conditions—the retention of an enormous oblong area of Norman wall with two Norman towers behind—it is not easy to see how anything better could have been done. Its vast height and breadth are astonishingly impressive from the narrow courtyard which coops it in.

To the same period belongs the Chapter house, the first polygonal Chapter house after those of Margam and Abbey Dore. "The strong flying buttresses, like colossal arms stretched out to bear up the huge fabric," were added later.

All the work of this period is attributed to Bishop Hugh of Wells (1209-1235); but the completion of it was due to his successor.

SIXTH PERIOD.—Hugh of Wells was followed by a great and masterful prelate, Robert Grostéte (1235-1253). So far as is known, the church up to now had nowhere any high vaults. Grostéte's great task was to put up high vaults everywhere. He had also to complete the upper part of the west front, where notice his characteristic trellis work; it is probable also that he finished the two western chapels of the nave. These works may well have been put in hand at once. But in 1237 a great catastrophe occurred—the fall of the central tower—killing three people who were listening to a sermon. However it fell vertically, damaging only the bays immediately adjacent in the choir and central transept. The old piers of the tower were strengthened and recased, and new arches put on them; and on the arches a low central tower, inside which notice Grostéte's trellis work. The ruined bays were rebuilt hastily and carelessly. The choir piers were strengthened by ugly freestone columns without capitals, and were stiffened by building stone screens between them. The new moldings on the westernmost side of the westernmost arches of the ground story of the choir do not fit the old, and a ring of stone was worked to hide the awkward junction; in the clerestory freestone is substituted for marble. The reconstructed pier-arches may be recognised by having hood-molds.

Then the choir, choir transepts, and central transepts, had to be prepared for vaulting. In the clerestory every fourth window or recess, whichever it was, was blocked up with masonry. As for the triforium, every fourth opening was blocked up with masonry to receive the springers of the high vault; and the old triforium arcade was taken out and a new one put in its place—and that without taking down the roof or clerestory or the upper courses of the old triforium arcade. Inside and outside the triforium chambers clerestory buttresses were built, for the heads of flying buttresses to rest on; and transverse arches were thrown across the chamber to stiffen the new triforium arcade. Outside, the main buttresses were built higher, and flying buttresses were thrown across from the tops of these buttresses to the new clerestory buttresses. Then, the supports and the walls having been adequately strengthened, high vaults were put up.

Where there were two windows in a bay, sexpartite vaulting was employed; viz., in the choir transepts and the central transepts and the westernmost bay of the choir. (In the aisles where there was no support for one of the six ribs, quinquepartite had been employed instead of sexpartite vaulting by St. Hugh.) In the choir, except in the westernmost bay, there were three windows in each bay, and sexpartite vaulting could not be used. Nor again, owing to the narrowness of the bays of the choir, was there room for such a vault as that now existing in the nave; however, as much of a vault of this type as could be put up without obstructing the clerestory windows was built; a very queer vault it is, fortunately unique. The vaulting of the Chapter house, with its beautiful ridge-rib system, also belongs to this period. Richest of all in its moldings, and quite perfect in its articulation, is the vault of the nave; when built, it must have been by far the finest vault to be found here or abroad. The vault of the eastern bays of the nave of Westminster Abbey is almost identical with it; as it was put up between c. 1254 and 1270, it may well have been modelled on that of Lincoln nave. To Grostête also may be assigned the remarkable vaults of the two western chapels of the nave. The vault of the northern chapel is cleverly designed as if it were an oblong chapter house with a central stalk; the southern chapel, more cleverly still, stands safe without a central stalk.

In addition to all this Grostête made important extensions. To him we may attribute the beautiful Galilee porch (in it the tooth ornament is repeated 5,355 times; notice also the base ornaments); it was designed as a state entrance from the episcopal palace, which is opposite. Moreover, a new Chapter house having been built by the preceding bishop, the old Chapter house would be converted into a chapel, perhaps that of St. Mary Magdalene. In the south choir transept Grostête took down St. Hugh's end-wall from top to bottom, and built two additional stories to the end bay. A vast amount of work is here attributed to the eighteen years between 1235 and 1253; but to a bishop and chapter so wealthy, and with aid from a diocese then extending to the Thames, and with, in addition, the rich offerings

INTERIOR OF THE CHAPTER HOUSE

at St. Hugh's shrine, funds were not likely to be lacking; and if at times they did run short, there were always Jews at Lincoln to apply to for loans.

SEVENTH PERIOD.—The cathedral was at last finished;

THE ANGEL CHOIR

but hardly was it finished than building recommenced (*c.* 1255). St. Hugh had been buried in the north-eastern chapel of his apse, in what is the place of greatest honour in every church at the right hand of the High altar. Great crowds of pilgrims resorted to his tomb in their anxiety to have benefit from the miracles wrought thereat, but the tomb was placed in a most inconvenient situation for that purpose. So it was resolved to pull down St. Hugh's apsidal presbytery and its procession path and chapels, and in lieu to build five new bays. Of these two were assigned to the presbytery, and in the easternmost of the two was placed the High altar, where it stands now. In the next bay, *i.e.*, at the back of the High altar, just as at St. Albans and Westminster, was placed the shrine of St. Hugh, to which his remains were solemnly translated in 1280. The bay after that provided a procession aisle. In most churches the easternmost bay has an altar dedicated to Our Lady, but this was not necessary at Lincoln, where the High altar was dedicated to her. This altar, therefore, under the great east window, was dedicated to St. John Baptist, the patron saint of St. Hugh. Nevertheless the special services to Our Lady were not held in the choir, but in this eastern chapel, so that it was practically a Lady chapel except that its altar was dedicated to St. John Baptist. This great eastern extension goes by the name of the Angel choir, apparently from the angels carved in the spandrels of the triforium; it is of course ritualistically not a choir at all, but a combination of presbytery, Saint's chapel, processional aisle, and eastern chapel. A little too crowded with ornament, perhaps, and a little too squat in its proportions, it is yet the most lovely work of the age—one of the masterpieces of English Gothic. To the same period or rather earlier belong the superb arches inserted at the west end of the choir aisles; also the eastern screen of the presbytery, parts of which are old, the rest built by Essex in 1769.

About 1290 were built the Easter Sepulchre and so-called tomb of Remigius, on the north side of the choir, with naturalistic foliage of oak, fig, and vine. Here the consecrated Host was watched from Maundy Thursday to Easter Sunday. Still finer Easter sepulchres may be seen at Hawton and Heckington. The upper stage of the central tower was erected in 1307. The tower is 271 ft. high;

and anxious, as usual, for external effect, the canons actually added a timber spire, raising it to the vast height of 525 ft., a height which exceeds even that of the new spires of Cologne cathedral. The effective cut battlements are by Essex. The tower is not built solid, but, to save weight, is "constructed of two thin walls, tied at intervals, with a vacuum between them" (*cf.* Hereford and Wells). It is gathered in 2½ in. near the top, so as not to look topheavy. The remains of the shrine of Little St. Hugh (in

THE EAST END

the south choir aisle) seem to be *c.* 1310. In the cloisters built *c.* 1296, is a great curiosity—an incised slab with a portrait of a Gothic architect, Richard of Gainsborough, the builder of the central tower. Replicas have been made of it.

EIGHTH PERIOD.—In 1320 died good Bishop Dalderby. He was venerated as a saint, though Rome refused his canonisation. His remains were placed in a silver shrine on the west side of the south transept: some pedestals belonging to it may be seen there still. Miracles were wrought at his shrine; and from the offerings the gable of this transept was in all probability reconstructed, including the "Bishop's Eye," which is as strong constructionally as it is beautiful; it is filled with fragments of ancient glass; the moldings of the circle are those of the earlier window. The lovely pierced parapet of this transept should be noticed, and the fine window in the gable above the vault. The parapet was carried westward all along the south side of the nave and across the west front; and handsome pinnacles were erected, with niches once peopled with statues. Now also was erected the choir screen, of charming design, very similar to that of the west side of Southwell screen. A little later are the screen of the choir boys' vestry in the south choir aisle, diapered with lilies; and in the north-east of the Angel choir, the Burghersh monuments. These formerly had canopies; the choir boys used to jump on them, so the dean and chapter thoughtfully had them destroyed, lest there should be an accident. There was a separate shrine for the head of St. Hugh; what may have been the pedestal of it remains at the west end of a Burghersh monument, where the stone is worn by the scraping of the feet of pilgrims kneeling at the shrine.

NINTH PERIOD.—To the latter half of the fourteenth century belong the famous choir stalls with excellent misericords; also the ogee arcading beneath the central tower.

TENTH PERIOD.—To the fifteenth century belong the west windows of the nave; also the miserable statues of English kings over the west door. The western towers were also raised to their present height, and all three towers were vaulted.

The west front now consists of an oblong area of early Norman work, which is decorated above by a late Norman arcade of semicircular intersecting arches, and midway by a row of late Norman sculptured plaques, and by the late Gothic niches with the kings: the windows are late Gothic; but the central doorway and the side doorways are twelfth century. The central arch of the early Norman work has

FROM THE NORTH-EAST

been replaced by a pointed one; and the whole of the early Norman work is surrounded by thirteenth-century work, which in turn is crested with a fourteenth-century parapet. The lower stages of the towers are late in the twelfth century, the upper stages belong to the fourteenth and fifteenth. The west front has been constantly censured for hiding the western towers, "like prisoners looking over the bars of their cage." But anyone who has seen the western towers of St. Stephen's, Caen, will recognise that, but for the west front, the Lincoln towers would look top-heavy.

To this century belong also the battlemented parapet of the Galilee porch; Bishop Fleming's chantry; the screens of the chapels in the north and south transepts; and Bishop Russell's chantry.

In TUDOR days was built Bishop Longland's chantry (1521-1547), the niches of which have Renaissance detail; it was never completed. The three chantries are so low that they do not interfere externally with the main lines of the cathedral; and, being low, give scale to it.

It may interest land surveyors to know that the minster covers 2 acres 2 roods and 6 perches, as measured by Schoolmaster Espin of Louth.

ELEVENTH PERIOD.—The date of the brass Eagle lectern is 1667. In 1674 Wren built the Library in the Cloister. The brass chandelier in the choir is of 1698. The supporting arches of the western towers were inserted in 1727.

BIBLIOGRAPHY.—Precentor Venables in *Archæological Journal*, xl. 159 and 377.

"Notes on the Architectural History of Lincoln Minster from 1192 to 1255," by Francis Bond and William Watkins, in the *Journal of the Royal Institute of British Architects*, 26th Nov. and 10th Dec. 1910, which contains a bibliography.

THE CATHEDRAL CHURCH OF ST. PAUL, LONDON

BUILT FOR SECULAR CANONS

FROM Lincoln and Lichfield to St. Paul's, the transition is vast and abrupt. It is a transition from the archaic, mediæval, feudal world to modern England. Mediæval religion, mediæval art is dead—killed by the printed book. Mediæval architecture also succumbs before the printed book. The master-masons of the old cathedrals, whose very names for the most part are unknown, give place to architects of European fame—men who read books, write books, and work to book. The mediæval architect was a builder and nothing else. The Renaissance architect was first of all a scholar, and secondly an artist; and only incidentally an architect. He learnt the art of design, not in the builder's yard, but at the goldsmith's bench. From jewellery he turned with equal facility to painting and sculpture, to civil engineering or the art of fortification, to water-colours, stage mechanism, landscape gardening, poetry, politics or diplomacy. Among men of this versatile genius Christopher Wren holds a worthy place. He proceeded to Oxford at the early age of fourteen, and obtained a fellowship at All Souls'. Physical science and astronomy were his first love. At the age of twenty-five "he was known in scientific circles all over Europe," and was Professor of Astronomy. He wrote on comets, and gnomonicks, and diplographic pens. In his twenty-ninth year he was honoured with the degrees of D.C.L. and LL.D. at Oxford and Cambridge. He helped to found the Royal Society,

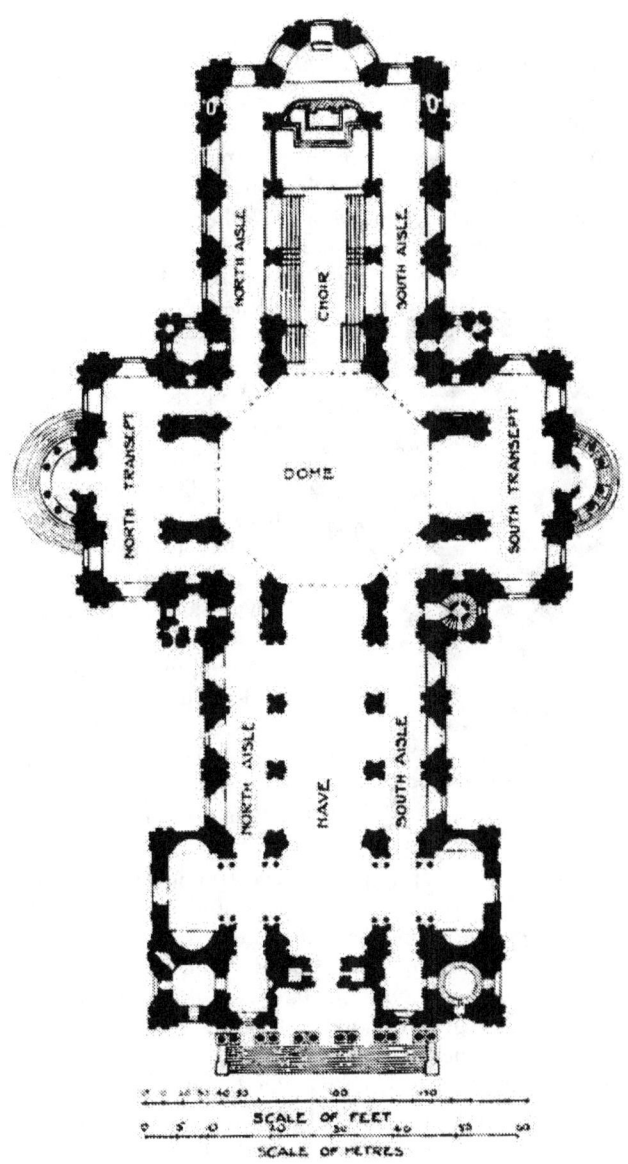

PLAN

and was twice its President. He was a Member of the House of Commons in two Parliaments. In his thirty-first year he turned his attention to architecture—attracted, no doubt, largely by the physical and mathematical problems involved. Two years later he set out to the Continent to see for himself the great works of the Revival of Classical Architecture. Unfortunately he went no farther than Paris: those masterpieces of the Renaissance, Brunelleschi's dome at Florence, Michael Angelo's dome at Rome, he was fated never to see. For the rest of a life unusually prolonged he was to be occupied in imitating models which he had never seen. The result is perhaps not to be regretted. He left behind him not the close copy of Italian Renaissance work which we might have had, in less troubled times, from Inigo Jones, but an English Renaissance style of marked individuality and originality, and of great interest. He had to think out all his problems—problems of construction and problems of planning—for himself.

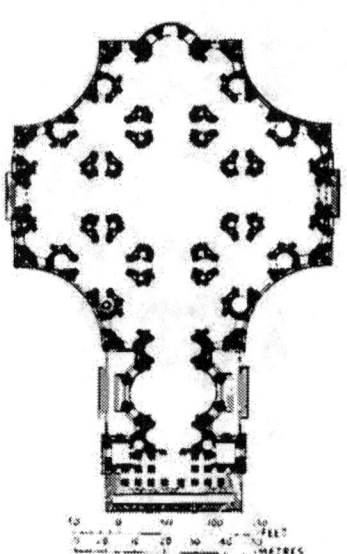

PLAN OF WREN'S ORIGINAL DESIGN
(⅔ Scale of other Plans)

Wren, like his employers, the citizens of the City of London, was a sound Protestant; and when he was commissioned to rebuild St. Paul's after the Great Fire, his wish was to give London a Protestant cathedral. He was less concerned to provide processional aisles and altared chapels than a vast unencumbered central area for preaching. The new cathedral was to be a gigantic preaching-house. To provide the vast central area demanded, the narrow crossing beneath the central tower of a Gothic cathedral was abandoned. Instead of a central tower he resolved to employ a dome—the only form of roof which would cover so vast a span. One mediæval cathedral in England, and one only, had such a crossing. It was the superb cathedral of Ely, where Wren's uncle was bishop. But it was no doubt of St. Peter's, Rome, that Wren was thinking, rather than of Ely. Just as St. Peter's, Rome, had been built to rival and surpass the Florence Duomo, so Wren designed that his own cathedral

THE ORIGINAL DESIGN, FROM SCHYNVOET'S ENGRAVING

should be an improvement on St. Peter's, Rome. In the supports of his dome he chose to follow the unhappy precedents of Florence and Ely rather than the nobler type of St. Peter's and Santa Sophia; he blocked up his central area with eight piers, instead of poising his dome on four supports, as in the metropolitan cathedrals of the East and West.

In Wren's favourite design, as shewn in the model still preserved in the cathedral, the dome was to be abutted to the west by an aisleless vestibule or nave, itself crowned by a minor dome; while to the north, east, and south it was intended to give it the support of a surrounding ring of domical chapels, opening into the central area by a series of fairy-like vistas and ever-changing contrasts of light and shadow. But the Anglican clergy rose in revolt at the position assigned to them in the cathedral—a position contrary to any precedent of the Anglican Church; and refused to sit in a ring all round the central area beneath the dome. And the Court party, almost openly expecting, and with good reason, the restoration of the old religion, wanted an aisled nave with room for the pageantry of processions and with provision of chapels for the veneration of the saints soon to be restored. Romanisers and Anglicans alike united in condemning a plan which failed to provide for the ritualistic needs of either. Wren had to start again; and London had to put up with a Renaissance cathedral which in plan is as mediæval as that of Ely, with aisled nave, aisled choir, aisled transepts, and even with a western transept, as again at Ely. St. Paul's, then, is primarily an aisled (*i.e.*, a basilican) church, with, incidentally, a dome thrown in. And therein lies the fault of the design. Internally, the church predominates over the dome. Unless you stand beneath or near the dome, you can hardly see that a dome is there at all. Narrow nave, narrower aisles, the multiplied obstructive masses of the various piers, hide the dome away from view. Rightly designed, a great central dome ought to be all in all; everything should lead up to it; everything should be suppressed that does not lend it strength or grace. Its thrusts are great, and cannot be resisted by the piers of aisles, unless the piers are positive mountains of masonry; aisles, then, should be omitted. The dome should rest on four arches, and their thrusts should be resisted by the solid walls of an unaisled nave and choir and transepts. And these four great limbs of the church should be kept short, to give the dome full value.

Again, just as the central dome should dictate the plan of the church, so it should dictate the form of the vaulted

ST. PAUL'S 215

roof. There were three types of vault at Wren's disposal. One was the intersecting vault, a second the dome, a third the waggon or tunnel vault. The first is altogether out of harmony with a central dome, though Wren has employed it in some of his City churches. What he adopted was the second: he vaulted the nave with a row of four saucer-shaped domes, the choir with a row of three. Thus, it might be thought, with seven domes leading up to a central

THE NAVE

dome, Wren had secured harmony and success. It is not so. Nothing can be more distressing to the eye than to follow the up and down line of the little domes till it suddenly plunges into the central abyss. The only tolerable form of vault in connection with a central dome is the tunnel vault, as it is employed in St. Peter's, Rome; or, still better, in S. Annunziata, Genoa. Such a tunnel vault, however, should start direct from the cornice, and not, as

THE CHOIR AND REREDOS

at St. Paul's, from a meaningless attic interposed between cornice and vault.

As it stands, in the internal elevation of the cathedral Wren has given us a hybrid design. It reminds one of Gothic, for there is a travesty of a clerestory; it is Classic, for beneath is a gigantic Order. Wren has hesitated between two opinions. He might have given us a three-storied interior—pier-arcade, triforium, and clerestory—of course with Classical detail, as is done with charming effect in the noble cathedral of Pavia; or a one-storied interior, as at St. Peter's. As his patrons insisted on having aisles, he might well have adopted the former alternative, and have presented us with what might have been very beautiful—a Classic triforium. If he wanted the majesty of the single gigantic Order of St. Peter's, he should have omitted the attic, run up the Order 20 ft. higher, and lighted the nave by lunettes cut through a tunnel vault. As it is, the attic is of no value in itself, while it diminishes the importance of the pier-arcade. However, as we have seen, Wren is not responsible at all for the plan, and only partially for the proportions of the interior of St. Paul's. He has not given us of his best, because the world of his day would not have it. Most of the defects that one laments are absent from his earlier and favourite design: *e.g.*, the ugly subsidiary arches under the oblique arches of the octagon of the dome, and the bad lighting of the dome itself.

Externally everything is different. No ritual, Anglican or other, interfered. Wren had free play: all his success and any faults are his own. What it fails to do internally the great dome does externally with colossal success: it dominates everything—not only the church, but London. Every part of the vast building gathers up into the all-compelling unity of the central dome. Inside, St. Paul's is all church; outside, it is all dome. Into this exterior has grown in concrete embodiment all Wren's aspirations: his aspirations for grandeur, massiveness, and power; for monumental stability, for unity, for harmony, for symmetry and proportion, for beauty of curve and line. St. Paul's has none of

the airy lightness of Salisbury and Lincoln; it possesses in
compensation the rock-hewn solidity and majesty of Durham.
In Lincoln and Salisbury, and in Exeter and York, the
windows are counted by hundreds; along the flanks of St.
Paul's windows are few and far apart, and they are confined
to the aisles; the great screen wall above rises sheer like a
precipice, almost unbroken by an opening. Simple and
grand, too, is the handling of the masses. At the re-entering
angles of the transepts square masses project to form a

FROM THE SOUTH-WEST

stable platform for the mighty dome; towers project to the
flanks of the western bays of the nave, giving breadth and
dignity to the main façade. Otherwise the design is
symmetry itself. Everything is in the "grand manner."
Perhaps the side elevation is a little monotonous, and the
western chapels block off the towers at their spring, but
they were forced on Wren against his better judgment:
internally the nave gains greatly by them; externally they
are a mistake. One would perhaps have liked also that the

screen wall of the side aisles of the choir and transepts, instead of ending square, should have circled round in one vast majestic sweep, in harmony with the curving dome above, after the fashion of the fine cathedral of Como. The flatness, moreover, of the side elevations gives but little room for play of light and shade. There are none of the pits of shadow that lurk between the buttresses and transepts of Salisbury and Lincoln. Only in the recessed west front and behind the colonnade of the dome the shadows brood. Nature, however, or rather London smoke, has given St. Paul's a chiaroscuro of its own—not to be washed off, as has been foolishly proposed, by fire engines. Where the rain lashes the building, especially its angles and projections, the good Portland stone is white and clean; where sheltered by projecting cornices, it is black as Erebus.

Externally, it is a building of two stories. Wren designed it originally for one story, but was unable to get big enough blocks of stone to carry a single gigantic Order, as at St. Peter's, up to the cornice; for which perhaps we may be thankful. The façade also is composed of two Orders of columns, and they are necessarily comparatively small columns. But all appearance of weakness is admirably removed by arranging them in couples; indeed, one would be sorry to have instead of this noble design Wren's own one-story façade as shewn in his model,—still more to have that of Inigo Jones.

The harmony, too, of the noble design is delightful. The two stories of the columns of the façade become two stories of pilasters on the flanks of the nave; at the ends of the transepts they sweep round into lovely semicircular colonnades; colonnades form the central stages of the western steeples; the drum of the dome is encircled by a superb colonnade; the dome itself culminates in a colonnaded lantern. See, too, how the lantern, domical above and colonnaded below, sums up the composition of the dome beneath; and how the western steeples prepare the eye for the transition from the rectilinear colonnades of the great façade to the swelling curve of the dome, itself reproduced in the north and south circular porches and in the apsidal choir. St. Paul's is "a house at one with itself."

It is true that the dead wall from aisle windows to cornice

THE WEST FRONT

is perhaps the "most unmitigated building sham upon the face of the earth." It has absolutely nothing to do at all except to hide away some flying buttresses—the very ugliest eye ever saw—which Sir Christopher might well be reluctant to expose to the jeers of the man in the street. It is true, too, that there is built up in this dead wall enough good stone to construct half a dozen parish churches. It has been urged that it was built to weight the foot of each flying buttress after the manner of a Gothic pinnacle. But not even a Gothic baby would have provided continuous abutment for intermittent thrusts. The dead wall may perhaps be defended on artistic, but certainly not on constructional grounds.

In the dome, Wren had three conflicting ideals to realise: (1) To make the dome so lofty that it should be visible externally from base to summit; (2) to make it so low internally that it should range with the vaulting of nave, choir, and transepts; (3) to finish it with a stone lantern as heavy as an ordinary church spire. At St. Peter's, Rome, the dome externally squats down so low that from most directions one must walk a mile away to get a complete view of it,

THE FLYING BUTTRESSES AND SCREEN WALL.

while the internal dome is so lofty as to be invisible from most parts of the church; the lantern is much smaller and lighter than is required by so mighty a dome; and yet is in a condition of very unstable equilibrium, badly supported, cracked, and tied together in all directions. All these difficulties Wren triumphantly disposed of; nevertheless, for his triumph he has received little but censure and abuse. He made two domes; and brought the inner dome, which is of brick (see diagram), far lower than the outer one—though not low enough. Secondly, he mounted the outer dome, which is of wood covered with lead, on a lofty colonnaded drum visible of all men even from the narrow street below. Thirdly, between the two domes (see diagram) he built a cone of brick, and on this cone he poised the lantern—which is of stone and 50 ft. high—in perfect security. If

THE INNER AND OUTER DOMES AND THE BRICK CONE

the outer dome were removed—*e.g.*, if it were burnt, as it may be some day, as it is of wood—the lantern would still stand perfectly safe on its conical support. In the dome of St. Paul's Wren's engineering capacities culminate. But it is more than a piece of engineering. No tower, no spire, no group of towers or spires, impresses itself on the imagination like the dome of St. Paul's. Lincoln and Salisbury, Lichfield and Durham, retire before the claims of this overwhelming younger pile,

> "whose sky-like dome
> Hath typified by reach of daring art
> Infinity's embrace."

BIBLIOGRAPHY.—Mr W. Longman's *St. Paul's Cathedral*, London, 1873.
Canon Benham's *Old Paul's*, 1902.
Mr W. Dunn, on the construction of the lantern, in *R.I.B.A. Journal*, 23rd November 1907.

THE ORGAN AND PULPIT

THE CATHEDRAL CHURCH OF ST. MARY, MANCHESTER

FORMERLY PAROCHIAL AND COLLEGIATE

THE see was founded in 1848. Externally and internally the cathedral is but a magnified parish church. The absence of a central tower, the extraordinary breadth of the interior, the absence of a triforium, the wooden roofs, all stamp it with parochialism. Indeed,

FROM THE SOUTH

the nave and aisles are still the parish church of Manchester. Looked at as a parish church and a collegiate church—for from 1422 it was both—it is a magnificent specimen of late English Gothic, dating from 1422-1522, when the ambition of architects was to make of their churches "stone-lanterns." In the same accidental way as Chichester cathedral it has become possessed of picturesque double aisles, by the incorporation on either side of sets of chantry chapels. It has been so thoroughly "renovated" that it is practically a modern church. But it is very impressive. There is no jarring of styles. And the colour effects, externally and internally, are superb. Its woodwork, too—rood screen, parclose screens, tabernacled stalls, misericords, and roofs—is of great richness and fine design. The whole church in its fortuitous picturesqueness appeals to one much more than the icy regularity of such churches as St. Mary Redcliffe, or Bath abbey.

(1) In 1422-1458 the choir and its aisles and the Chapter house were built. (2) The nave is said to have been finished between 1465 and 1481. (3) The chapel of the Holy Trinity was founded in 1498. (4) In 1506 the Jesus chapel was founded; it is now the vestry and library. (5) In 1507 the Ducie chapel or St. James' chapel was built, (6) St. George's chapel was built, and the choir stalls were put up in 1508. (7) The Derby chapel was begun between 1485 and 1509. (8) The Ely chapel was built in 1515. (9) The Lady chapel was remodelled in 1518. (10) The tower was built in 1868.

BIBLIOGRAPHY.—Mr J. S. Crowther's *Manchester Cathedral*.
Rev. Thomas Perkins' *Manchester Cathedral and See*, 1901.

THE CATHEDRAL CHURCH OF ST. NICHOLAS, NEWCASTLE

FORMERLY PAROCHIAL

THE see was founded in 1882. The church is work of the fourteenth century, to which a tower and spire, east window and font were added about 1470.

FROM THE NORTH-WEST

The spire, with its pinnacle supported on converging flying buttresses, is a bold and effective composition. Spires of similar construction occur in the Cross Steeple, Glasgow, and King's College, Aberdeen, and formerly existed at Linlithgow and Haddington. London has a fine example by Sir Christopher Wren in St. Dunstan's-in-the-East. There is a fine Jacobean monument, pulpit-shaped, to Henry Maddison, and another to William Hall.

BIBLIOGRAPHY.—Mr W. H. Wood's "Tower and Spire of Newcastle Cathedral" in *Journal of Royal Institute of British Architects*, 30th September 1905.

THE CATHEDRAL CHURCH OF THE HOLY TRINITY, NORWICH

BUILT FOR BENEDICTINE MONKS

THE ancient kingdom of East Anglia, after more than one relapse into paganism, finally accepted Christianity at the hands of a Burgundian monk, Felix, who became the first bishop of East Anglia—the diocese, as usual, being co-extensive with the kingdom—and fixed his see at Dunwich, in 630. The see was subdivided by Archbishop Theodore in 660, and there were bishops intermittently both at Dunwich and Elmham, Suffolk, till *c.* 950, when the diocese was again reunited, and the cathedral was at Elmham, till the bishop migrated in 1075 to Thetford, and in 1094 to Norwich.

The present cathedral was commenced in 1096 by Herbert Losinga, who is usually described as a Lorrainer, but who seems to have been of Norman blood and of good family, born at Hoxne, Suffolk. He is recorded to have finished the whole cathedral before his death in 1119 as far as the altar of the Holy Cross. His successor finished the nave and west front, and carried up the central tower (1121-1145). In 1171 there was a great fire; the damage would be greatest where there was most woodwork, *i.e.*, where the stalls and screens stood, especially if the latter were of wood. It has been recently found that inside the *third pier from the north* is cased up an earlier cylindrical pier; evidently one of those which suffered from the fire and had to be recased.

In front of the cathedral is an open space with the curious name of Tombland. Evidently Bishop Herbert appropriated for his precinct a large slice of the old town "Tombland"

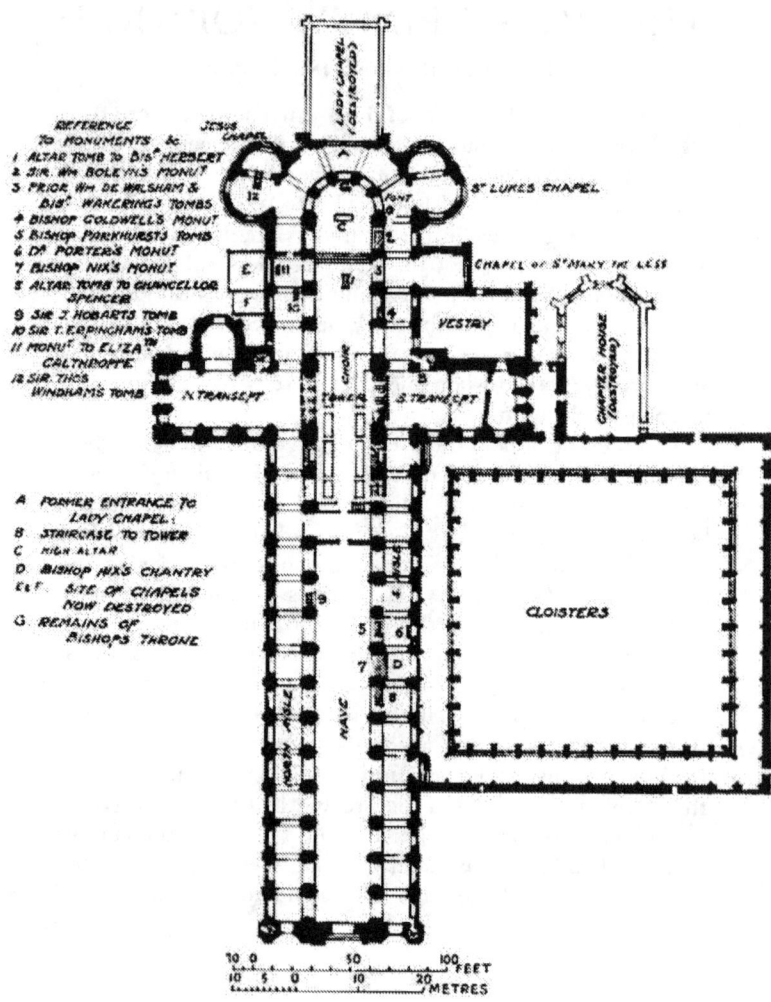

PLAN

or meeting place, which is now triangular instead of oblong. Also the road from the bridge was diverted from its original track. The Tombland was the converging point of the three ancient roads, and the rallying ground of the two communities of Conesford and Westwick, Saxon and Danish respectively. At the Conquest the Norman settlers formed a third community and occupied the Mancroft (great croft), and henceforward Tombland was no longer important and Losinga would have no difficulty in appropriating as much as he wanted of it, together with the rich town meadows or "Cowholme."

The plan of the Norman church is that of Gloucester (1089) and probably Norman Westminster (1050); this peri-apsidal plan occurs between 997 and 1014 in the great pilgrim church of St. Martin, Tours; between 990 and 1007 at Notre Dame de la Coûture, Le Mans; and at St. Rémi, Reims, c. 1005. In

ACROSS THE NAVE

Normandy it is very rare, but it occurs at Fécamp in 1082: and as Bishop Herbert had been prior of Fécamp abbey till 1087, it is probably from Fécamp that the Norwich plan of 1096 immediately derives. The nave contains fourteen bays, of which the nine western ones were more or less accessible to the laity. When this vast nave was completed, the monks seemed to have come to the end of their resources, for no western towers were ever built. The nave being so long, there was no need to crowd the stalls into the eastern limb, as at Canterbury; they were placed, as at present, under the central tower and in the two eastern bays of the nave; in this part of the nave the vaulting-shafts do not descend to the pavement, but are stopped at corbels in order to leave headway for the stalls. The choir screen occupied the whole of the third bay, as at present, and at some period an altar to Our Lady of Pity was placed in it. The fourth bay was occupied by two altars enclosed in screens. At the end of the fourth bay was the rood screen, which, as at Durham, was no more than a

THE CHOIR AND APSE

wall. The whole of the fifth bay was screened off, and against the centre of the rood screen was placed the altar of the Holy Cross. On either side of this altar (Holy Cross) was a door leading into the space between rood screen and choir screen, and before the altar was a light screen or trellis, *i.e.*, between the two circular piers. It was in front of this latter that the returning procession divided, to reunite at the single door in the centre of the choir screen. Each transept consists of four bays, and from each an apse projected eastward; the southern apse has perished, the northern one has been rebuilt. The whole eastern limb is occupied by a presbytery of four bays terminating in an apse. A procession path runs all round the presbytery. From it radiated three chapels; that to the east has perished; it was apsidal; between 1146 and 1174 it was replaced by a long and lofty Lady chapel, the doorway of which remains; the Lady chapel was pulled down c. 1580. The Jesus chapel to the north-east and St. Luke's chapel to the south-east are curiously composed of two segments of circles of different size; the object of this unusual plan was probably to get the altars as far as possible north and south, so that the celebrant should face due east. In the east wall of the apse the throne of the bishop has been found. The inappropriateness of such an arrangement as that at Norwich ultimately led to bishops' thrones being removed into the choir, as at Exeter.

The history of Norwich cathedral differs *toto cælo* from that of every other English cathedral, except that of Gloucester. With the exception that both Gloucester and Norwich ultimately increased the dimensions of their eastern Lady chapels, few eastward extensions of any moment took place; the chief exception at Norwich is the chapels built out from the north and south aisles of the presbytery at a later period. This was not because the Norfolk people were more conservative than other folk, or, in a remote corner of England, were behind the times; but because the plan of the Norwich cathedral was convenient for mediæval ritual, and the plan of the other cathedrals was not. Other cathedrals had a diminutive presbytery and a short nave; at Norwich there was a spacious presbytery and the nave was of vast length. Other cathedrals had to build a procession aisle at the back of the High altar; at Norwich it was there already. Other cathedrals had to throw out eastern transepts to provide chapels for the great saints of the Church,

St. James, St. John, St. Peter and the rest; Norwich cathedral from the first had five apsidal chapels. In most tangential chapels, even in Westminster abbey so late as 1245, the altar was placed in a wrong position; at Norwich the celebrant could face due east. Other cathedrals had a local saint of the first rank, and had to build a special saint's chapel or feretory for his shrine: Canterbury for St. Thomas, Chester for St. Werburgh, Durham for St. Cuthbert, Ely for St. Audrey, Hereford for St. Ethelbert, Lichfield for St. Chad, Lincoln for St. Hugh, Oxford for St. Frideswide, Rochester for St. William, St. Albans for St. Alban, Winchester for St. Swithun, Worcester for St. Wolfstan. Norwich had no local saint of repute, except a poor little boy who was alleged to have been crucified by the Jews.

The very fact that Norwich is practically unchanged in plan makes it the best object lesson in the country for the study of Anglo-Norman architecture. The long nave from end to end, the transepts, much of the presbytery, and nearly the whole of the aisles remain as they were built between 1096 and 1145. The aisles have groined vaults; in this respect falling short of Durham, Peterborough, Southwell and Gloucester naves. The piers of the ground story alternate in form, as at Jumièges, the Abbaye-aux-Hommes, Durham, Selby, Ely, Waltham, Lindisfarne. The ground story is kept low, because it was not intended to rely on the aisle windows for light. The triforium chamber is lofty, to allow windows to be inserted in its back wall. The triforium arcade consists of a single arch, as in the Abbaye-aux-Hommes, Wymondham and Binham abbeys, so as to obstruct the light as little as possible. For the same reason the shafts which support the inner order of the arch of the triforium chamber are set back in triplets flat against the jambs; the same arrangement occurs in alternate piers of the ground story. The alternation in height of the Norman vaulting-shafts shews that the church was intended to have a high vault throughout of sexpartite form, such as those erected in later days at Canterbury and Lincoln.

NORWICH CATHEDRAL. 233

In the triforium of the nave, presbytery and apse are supports for flying buttresses, intended, like those of Durham nave, to be built beneath the triforium roof. In the triforium of the presbytery the flying buttresses seem

THE NAVE

to have been actually built; probably they were removed when the present vault of the presbytery was erected with external flying buttresses. The clerestory has a wall passage, and each window was flanked by a blank arch, both internally and externally. The architect had a great fondness for multiplicity of stories, and obtains five on the external wall of the aisle by the use of four string-courses. The moldings of the arches, *e.g.*, in the triforium of the presbytery, are numerous, small and refined. Corinthianesque capitals, but without acanthus, abound, as in the eastern parts of Chichester and Ely, and throughout Christchurch, Hampshire; a capital with acanthus occurs at the back of the triforium of the apse. The façade of the north transept is quite the finest Norman composition in existence: by means of six string-courses it is divided into seven stories. The architect has a great liking for arcading; on the external walls of the aisles an arcade is inserted below the Norman windows (now blocked) of the triforium; in the transept façade three tiers of arcading are introduced. The Norman arcading on the west wall of the south transept is unequalled. Taking it as a whole, the work at Norwich is in advance of anything of the period in England, with the one exception of the vaulting; if the contemplated high vault had been erected, it would even have surpassed Durham.

THE CENTRAL TOWER

The rest of the history of the cathedral reduces itself in the main to three sets of building operations: first, repairs necessitated by fire or storm; secondly, attempts to improve the lighting of the building; thirdly, the erection of vaults to make it fireproof.

Taking these works in the above order, we first have to

note the mischief done by fire and storm. In 1297 the tower seems to have had a wooden spire. This was blown down in 1361; and, falling eastward, damaged the clerestory of the Norman presbytery. Both the spire and clerestory had to be rebuilt; and in rebuilding the clerestory the monks took the opportunity to remedy what was the gravest defect in all the Norman cathedrals — their extreme darkness. Now, it happened that, only some ten years before, the magnificent clerestory of Gloucester presbytery had been completed; and the report of the brilliant illumination and translucent glass of this grand work was bruited, no doubt, all over England by pilgrims returning from the shrine of the murdered Edward II. at Gloucester. Therefore, just as at Gloucester, the monks determined to raise the new presbytery higher than the nave—they raised it 11 ft.—and to make the clerestory practically a continuous sheet of glass. In one thing, fortunately, they did not copy Gloucester, as Edington did in Winchester nave—which is of the same date as the Norwich work—they did not think it necessary to discard altogether the beautiful flowing tracery of the curvilinear period; and so here, as in many Norfolk churches, we find inserted, side by side, at the same time, flowing and rectilinear traceried windows. Another charming feature of fourteenth-century design was the ogee niche, such as those of the arcade of Ely Lady chapel. These niches at Norwich were inserted between each pair of clerestory windows: probably they were intended to receive statues, as at Shepton Mallet. In the same century a determined attempt was made to get rid of the darkness of the nave by inserting large windows with flowing tracery all along the aisles. Nor was this all. As at Ely, the monks raised the aisle-walls still further, closed the Norman windows of the triforium, flattened the roof of the triforium, and thus managed to get high up a range of tall windows, each of four lights, that the light from them might find its way into the nave across the triforium. The result is extraordinary, as seen from the cloister garth. The south side of the cathedral, instead of the usual three or four stories, seems six stories high. First there are the openings of the cloister; then its upper story; then the blind arcade of the triforium; then the Norman triforium windows; then the Gothic windows; then the Norman clerestory. Large square-headed windows were inserted in the triforium of the presbytery also: even this was insufficient. The eastern bays of the nave, where the stalls were placed, and where, most of all, light was needed, were the darkest of all, being obstructed by the stalls and by the cloister roof. So in the two easternmost bays of the nave the triforium roof was sloped up instead of down, and large windows were inserted still higher up than those to the west, to give as much light as possible to the stalls below. For the same reason large Gothic windows were inserted in the transepts. Several of these, however, have recently been replaced by Norman windows: "genuine Gothic by sham Norman." In the middle of the south aisle of the nave Bishop Nix (1501-1536) built himself a gorgeous chantry, to light which he inserted two large windows, high up so as to clear the cloister roof.

FROM THE SOUTH-WEST CORNER OF THE CLOISTER COURT

In the fourteenth century was built the Bauchun chapel, projecting from the south aisle of the presbytery; its vault is a century later; the bosses of the vault illustrate the Life, Death and Assumption of the Blessed Virgin. At some period a chapel was built bridging the north aisle of the presbytery; it communicated with another chapel to the north, now destroyed, said to have been the Reliquary chapel; it may have been used for the exposition of relics to pilgrims passing below, like St. Chad's gallery at Lichfield; it is of late date, and may have carried an organ, like Islip's upper chapel at Westminster, to accompany the Jesus anthems which would be sung on Friday evenings in the neighbouring Jesus chapel. To the early years of the fifteenth century probably belong the stalls; notice the arches crocketed with hawks, the arms of Bishop Wakering (1416-1425). The misericords are very fine; those below polygonal seats appear to be late fourteenth-century work; the rest are of the time of Bishop Wakering. To the earlier work belongs the pelican lectern; to which three statuettes were added in 1845.

Now we come to the measures taken to make the building fireproof. These took the form of costly stone vaults, and they seem to have been undertaken by the monks most reluctantly. All the high vaults are the outcome of some great fire, and but for the fire evidently would not have been undertaken. There was a great conflagration in 1171, and in the fearful riots of 1272 the cathedral was set on fire by the citizens. Still, when the presbytery was remodelled in 1362, it was again roofed in wood. In 1463 the wooden spire was struck by lightning, and did more damage. At last the monks had to bestir themselves. To secure the spire against fire they rebuilt it in stone instead of wood; and, to make the nave and presbytery fireproof, they made up their minds to vault both in stone. Between 1463 and 1472 Bishop Walter Lyhart put up over the nave the present magnificent lierne vault, and at his death bequeathed two thousand marks to his successor to continue the work. His rebus, a *hart lying in water*, occurs as a corbel on alternate vaulting-shafts. The subjects of the nave bosses form a pictorial scripture-history, beginning at the tower with the Creation, and ending with the Last Judgment. In the centre of the fifth bay from the tower this vault has a large hole instead of a boss. A Sacrist's Roll has charges "for letting a man down from the roof, habited as an angel, to cense the rood." The roof timbers blazing on the pavement had damaged the bases of the Norman shafts; new bases were inserted facing the nave, the other shafts were scraped down in very perfunctory fashion.

Bishop Goldwell vaulted the presbytery between 1472 and 1499. It seems to have been difficult to get the funds for this costly work. Bishop Goldwell, however, was a personal friend of the Pope, who had consecrated him with his own hands; and was able to persuade the Pope to grant a perpetual indulgence in the terms that "all who came to the cathedral on Trinity Sunday and Lady Day, and made an offering towards the fabric, should be entitled to an indulgence of twelve years and forty days." The superposition of a heavy stone vault on a lofty clerestory containing so large a surface of glass made it necessary to erect flying buttresses outside; the buttresses on which these rest are weighted by pinnacles placed in "false bearing," *i.e.*, not on the buttresses so much as on the haunches of the flying buttresses; they carry seated figures in good preservation, as in the eastern chapels of Peterborough and the cloister of Magdalen College, Oxford. The clerestory of the nave is 11 ft. lower than that of the presbytery, and is much more solid, and the vault springs low down in the clerestory; therefore, as in the naves of Gloucester, Tewkesbury, Sherborne (which has flying buttresses to the presbytery), flying buttresses were not added there. In the clerestory of the presbytery the damage done by the fire of 1463 is very visible. When the blazing timbers fell down, they seem to have calcined the piers of the presbytery, which accordingly were recased in Gothic fashion. Beneath one of the southern arches Bishop Goldwell lies buried: the effigy affords a fine example of pontifical vestments. The remodelled piers contain a bull's head, the device of Sir Thomas Boleyn, who died in 1505, and whose monument is under the first arch on the south side; probably he erected between the arches the stone screens which were removed in 1875. The present stone spire is probably also the work of Bishop Goldwell.

The transepts still had wooden roofs. It required another fire, in 1509, in which these roofs were consumed, to compel the monks to complete the vaulting of the cathedral. This was done in the time of Bishop Nix, between 1509 and 1536. The bosses of the vault illustrate the life of Christ. At the end of four hundred years Norwich cathedral was at length fireproof. The vaulting lowered the level and cut off some earlier stonework.

The great fire of 1272 had also destroyed the cloister, which had probably wooden roofs; it was rebuilt with vaults, the bosses of which are of exceptional interest. This work was executed very slowly, the window tracery ranging from geometrical, through curvilinear, to rectilinear design. On entering the cloister by the eastern door of the south aisle of the nave, and commencing at the easternmost window of the north walk, the windows will all be seen in chronological order, if the east, south, west, and north walks are visited successively. The work ranges from 1297 to 1430. In the *east* walk the first doorway is that of the slype; the next three openings were those of the Chapter house; further on is the doorway of the day stairs leading down from the monks' dormitory, which occupied the first floor of the buildings east of the cloister and adjoining the south transept. In the northern half of the east walk notice on the wall-bench the numerous sets of "holes" for the novices' games; also the cupboards for books, here and in the south walk. The *south* side of the cloister was occupied by the refectory, the doorway of which is at the west end of the south walk. In the *west* walk, close at hand, is the lavatory; two bays further on a doorway led into the cellarage and to a Guesten hall; the doorway in the last bay leads into the choir school, which has a ribbed barrel vault, and is partly of twelfth, partly of thirteenth century date; it was the outer parlour of the monks. In the *north* walk the eastern doorway is that by which the Sunday procession left the church; the western doorway is that by which it re-entered the church after making the circuit of the cloister.

Between the south transept and the presbytery aisle is a fine screen; on the lock are the initials R. C., P. N., *i.e.*, Robert Catton, Prior of Norwich, 1504-1529. In the south aisle of the presbytery is a fine, but mutilated font with representations of the Seven Sacraments, and the Crucifixion. In the Jesus chapel is a truncated altar slab of Barnack stone which was found beneath the pavement of the chapel; in it is inlaid a small slab of Purbeck marble; on both slabs are incised five consecration crosses. In the few ancient tiles of the chapel pavement which remain there are five dents or punctures; this may refer to the Mass of the Five Wounds, which the Sarum Missal directed to be celebrated on Fridays, and which would be sung in the Jesus chapel. The painted altar-piece which formed the retable of the Jesus chapel is now placed in the choir aisle; it is probably English work, and has been assigned to the end of the fourteenth century.

The doorway of the West Front was built by Bishop Alnwick, *c.* 1440; in its spandrels is the inscription, "Orate pro animo Domini Wilhelmi Alnwyk Epi." The window above was built soon after 1449. A little to the west, on the right, is a crypt which formed the charnel-house, and, above, the chapel of St. John Evangelist, built *c.* 1316; in the crypt were two altars; the porch was added between 1446 and 1472. The Erpingham gateway, facing the west front of the cathedral, was built after 1411 by Sir Thomas Erpingham who fought at Agincourt; "a knight grown grey with age and honour." At the south end of the close is St. Ethelbert's gateway, built by the citizens as part of the penance inflicted on them for the great fire of 1272.

One word about the superb interior of the cathedral. It is hardly too much to say that of Norman interiors, that of Norwich is unequalled in all England. One reason is that it is vaulted throughout. Ely, Peterborough, St. Albans, Rochester, Romsey, Waltham, Southwell—with their paltry wooden ceilings—are not to be compared for a moment with Norwich. Gloucester and Chichester naves are vaulted, but the vaults are too slight and flimsy for the stern and massive work below. Durham vault is strong and satisfactory. But the lierne vault of Norwich is a far more glorious crown and finish than the rude work of Durham. It might be thought that the richness and magnificence of the lierne vault of Norwich would be out of harmony with the simplicity and heaviness of Norman piers and triforium and clerestory. It is not so. A tower, like that of Magdalen College, Oxford, may be ever so plain below, and yet terminate fitly with a glorious coronal of battlements, parapet, and pinnacles. So it is with this interior.

Its rivals are to be found in Winchester and Tewkesbury. But at Winchester the vaults of nave and presbytery are cut in two by the unvaulted transept, and the presbytery vault is of wood. Norwich and Tewkesbury are vaulted everywhere—from east to west and from north to south. And in both, the vaults being uniform in character, and not changing character half-way as at Gloucester, weld together the spreading limbs of the church into a marvellous unity. But while the Tewkesbury vault is low and squat, that of Norwich soars aloft, rising to supreme height in the far east.

There is another fine feature about the interior of Norwich, as in that of Gloucester: it is the striking contrast of light and shade, of shadowy nave and brilliant choir. Ely and Hereford present us with the reverse effect—bright nave and gloomy choir. Both effects are dramatic; both, doubtless, are unintentional. If they had known how, or could have afforded it, Ely and Hereford would have flooded their choirs with sunshine, Norwich and Gloucester their naves. The mediæval builders wanted none of these dramatic contrasts of light and shade; they were always working to get rid of the dim religious light that nowadays we venerate; they would have liked their churches lighted thoroughly well throughout. What they wanted was the light, uniformly good, of Lichfield, or of Salisbury, bright and gay as a ball-room.

But the most subtle and most important element in the

beauty of the interior of Norwich is to be found in its proportions. The nave is of an immense length, but it is very narrow. York, Canterbury, Gloucester, Durham, all have naves too short for their breadth. And what is more important still is the ratio of the height of the Norwich interior to its span. In most English cathedrals it is not much more than 2 to 1; but in Norwich nave the ratio rises to nearly 2.6, and in the presbytery it is nearly 3 to 1. In Norwich presbytery, then, we have just those proportions which we find in the great Gothic cathedrals of France, but in England hardly anywhere except at Beverley, Ripon, and Westminster.

One thing more remains to be said in praise of Norwich, as of Gloucester. It is that the greatest splendour of the church is concentrated at one spot, and that the most important spot in the church. It is in approaching the High altar that vaults and clerestory soar aloft, that loveliest vistas open out into ambulatory and chapels, while the noble windows above fill all with light and atmosphere. "I would back it," says Dean Goulburn, "against any similar effect in almost any cathedral in Christendom."

BIBLIOGRAPHY.—Professor Willis and Rev. D. J. Stewart's papers on the cathedral in *Archæological Journal*, xxxii. 16, and on the cloisters in xxxii. 155.

Harrod's *Gleanings from Churches and Convents of Norfolk*.

Dean Goulburn's *Ancient Sculptures and History of Norwich Cathedral* gives photographs of the bosses.

W. T. Bensly and W. H. St. John Hope's paper on Norwich cathedral in the *Transactions of the Norfolk and Norwich Arch. Society*, xiv. 105.

Dr Jessop and Dr Montague James' *Life and Miracles of St. William of Norwich*, 1896.

Britton's *Architectural Antiquities*, iii. 86.

FROM THE NORTH

THE CATHEDRAL CHURCH OF CHRIST, OXFORD

BUILT FOR AUGUSTINIAN CANONS

"ABOUT the year of Our Lord 727, there lived in Oxford a Saxon prince named Didan, who had an only child, Frideswide ('bond of peace'). Seeing that he had large possessions and inheritances, and that she was likely to enjoy most of them after his decease, Frideswide told her father that he could not do better than bestow them upon some religious fabric where she and her spiritual sisters might spend their days in prayer and in singing psalms and hymns to God. Wherefore the good old man built a church, and committed it wholly to the use of his daughter, purposely to exercise her devotion therein; and other edifices adjoining to the church, to serve as lodging-rooms for Frideswide and twelve virgins of noble extraction.

There she became famous for her piety and for those excellent parts that nature had endowed her withal; and Algar, King of Leicester, became her adorer by way of marriage. Finding that he could not prevail with her by all the entreaties and gifts imaginable, he departed home, but sent to her ambassadors with this special and sovereign caution, that if she did not concede, to watch their opportunity and carry her away by force. Frideswide was inexorable. Wherefore at the dawning of the day the ambassadors clambered the fences of the house, and by

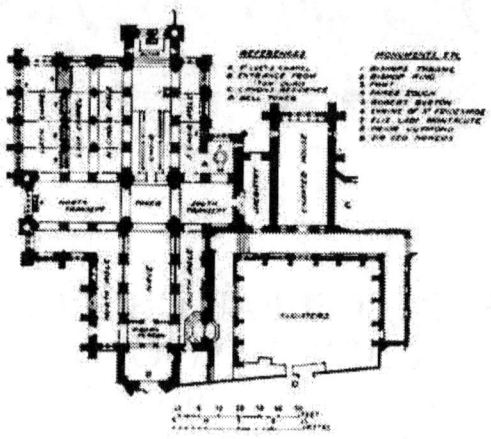

PLAN

degrees approaching her private lodging, promised to themselves nothing but surety of their prize. But she, awakening suddenly and discovering them, and finding it vain to make an escape, being so closely besieged, fervently prayed to the Almighty that He would preserve her from the violence of those wicked persons, and that He would shew some special token of revenge upon them for this their bold attempt. Wherefore the ambassadors were miraculously struck blind, and like madmen ran headlong yelling about the city. But Algar was filled with rage, and intended for Oxford, breathing out nothing but fire and sword. Which thing being told to Frideswide in a dream, with her sisters the nuns Katherine and Cicely, she fled to the river side, where there awaited her a young man with a beautiful countenance and clothed in white, who, mitigating their fear with pleasant speech, rowed them up the river to a wood ten miles distant. There the nuns sheltered in a hut, which ivy and other sprouts quickly overgrew, hiding them from sight of man. Three years Frideswide lived in Benton wood, when she came back to Binsey and afterwards to Oxford, in which place this maiden, having gained the triumph of her virginity, worked many miracles; and when her days were over and her Spouse called her, she there died." Such is the account of her which Anthony-a-Wood drew from William of Malmesbury and Prior Philip of Oxford, both of whom unfortunately lived long after the events which they narrate.

FIRST PERIOD.—In the east walls of the north choir aisle and the Lady chapel three small rude arches have recently been found, and outside, in the gardens, the foundations of the walls of three apses. Hence it has been concluded that we have here the eastern termination of Frideswide's eighth-century church. It may be so, but the central arch seems very small for the chancel-arch of an aisled church. It is indeed a foot wider than the chancel-arch of the Saxon church at Bradford-on-Avon, but that tiny church has no aisles. Moreover, if the side arches led into aisles, they would be likely to be of the same height, whereas the southern arch is considerably the higher of the two. A more serious objection is that the plan with three parallel eastern apses is not known to occur in Western Christendom before the ninth century.

SECOND PERIOD.—The establishment went through many vicissitudes, passing from nuns to secular canons, and finally in 1111 to regular canons—*i.e.*, canons living in monastic fashion under the rule (*regula*) of St. Augustine, as at Bristol and Carlisle.

The first business, probably, of the regular canons was to house themselves—*i.e.*, to build themselves the usual cloister, with its appanages of chapter house, refectory, dormitory, &c. Of the chapter house which they built, c. 1125, the doorway still remains; the slype also is their work.

In 1004 King Ethelred had rebuilt the Saxon church; and probably it was found possible to put this church into such repair as would allow the services to be held in it for the time being. At any rate, it was not till after 1158 that they commenced the present church, first pulling down Ethelred's church; the present church was probably finished by 1180; for in that year it was ready for the translation of the relics of St. Frideswide. It has been urged that the present church is in the main the one built in 1004; which is as who should say that *Paradise Lost* was written by Chaucer.

This late twelfth-century church was very remarkable in plan. Not only had it an aisled nave and an aisled choir, but it had the architectural luxury, unparalleled in our Norman architecture except in the vast churches of Winchester and Ely, of eastern and western aisles to its transepts. Both the transepts were three bays long, as were their aisles; the aisled nave had eight bays according to Browne Willis' plan; the choir aisles had four bays, the choir had five, thus getting good light in its easternmost bay for the High altar. Through lack of room, however, the ground story of the end bay of the south transept had to be given to the slype or passage which provided access from the cloister to the infirmary and other buildings; the same arrangement is found at Hexham, another church of Austin Canons.

But the canons wanted also a Lady chapel, especially as the church seems to have been dedicated originally to the Holy Trinity, St. Mary, and St. Frideswide. The normal position of a Lady chapel is to the east of the sanctuary. But here also the canons were cramped; for quite close to the east end of the church ran the city wall. To get in a Lady chapel, therefore, they had to build an additional aisle north of the north aisle of the choir. It was four bays ong. Its westernmost bay was the central bay of the east aisle of the transept; the second bay had a semicircular arch on the north and no doubt another on the south; as for the two eastern bays, it is possible that they were simply the north aisle of the Anglo-Saxon church. There was yet another chapel, north of the Lady chapel, probably of two bays; the westernmost bay being the end bay of the eastern aisle of the transept, and the next bay communicating with the Lady chapel by a semi-circular arch, traces of which may be seen above the present pointed arch.

The east end of the sanctuary is square. The present east end is a fine composition by Scott, more or less conjectural. The work commenced, as usual, at the east, as is shewn by the gradual improvement westward in the design of the capitals.

ST. FRIDESWIDE'S CHAPEL.

The evidence of the vaulting, too, points in the same direction. In the choir aisle the ribs are massive and heavy; in the western aisle of the north transept they are lighter; in the south aisle of the nave they are pointed and filleted.

The transepts are narrower than the nave and choir; the crossing, therefore, is oblong, and, as at Bolton Priory, its narrow sides have pointed arches: semicircular arches would have been too low. The faces of the piers of the towers are flat, because the stalls of the canons were placed against them, leaving the whole eastern limb as sanctuary.

The clerestory walls are only 41½ ft. high; therefore, to have adopted the usual Norman design—viz., three stories more or less equal in length, each only about 14 ft. high—

THE NAVE

would have given an insignificant pier-arcade and a dwarfed clerestory, and the interior would have been seen to be miserably low and squat. But it looks quite lofty; for though the real pier-arcade (the arches of which are corbelled into the piers low down) is very humble indeed, yet in front of it there rises a sham pier-arcade with lofty columns, and with arches that run up to the string-course of the clerestory.

The design is not original; for it was tried at Romsey and there abandoned; it was worked out more successfully at Dunstable Priory and Jedburgh, both churches of Austin Canons, and in grand fashion at Benedictine Glastonbury. The clerestory windows of the nave would be built not much before 1180; naturally, therefore, they are pointed, while in choir and transepts they are semicircular. The capitals are of extraordinary interest; we have nothing like them in the country. All the old Romanesque motifs are tried with

JUNCTION OF NORTH TRANSEPT AND CHOIR

variations, and as the work advances, the capitals more and more approach to Gothic. The most interesting are those which are got by the decomposition of the Corinthian capital of ancient Greece and Rome. Those in Canterbury choir may be finer, but they are the work of French carvers; for the third quarter of the twelfth century, the capitals at St. Frideswide's are unparalleled; for the last quarter they find rivals at New Shoreham, Reigate, and Abbey Dore.

This twelfth-century church is exceedingly interesting. There is not yet the lightness and grace of Ripon; still less the charm of Canterbury choir, Chichester presbytery, Glastonbury, and Abbey Dore—Gothic in all but name. In spite of its foliated capitals, in spite of a pointed arch here and there, it is Romanesque to the core; it was built by old-fashioned people; though Durham had had high vaults for half a century, there are none here, nor any preparation for them. Except in the foliation of the capitals, there is not a sign that Gothic was close at hand, nay,

THE NORTH SIDE, WITH LATIN CHAPEL

already in existence by 1180 at Worcester, Glastonbury, and Wells. Oxford, then as ever, was the refuge of "lost causes and mistaken beliefs and impossible loyalties."

THIRD PERIOD.—In the first half of the thirteenth century the works went on apace. An upper stage was added to the tower, and on that the spire was built—the first large stone spire in England. To some extent it is designed like a broach spire; for the cardinal sides of the spire are built right out to the eaves, so that there is no parapet. On the other hand, instead of having broaches at the angle, it has pinnacles. Moreover, to bring down the thrusts more vertically, heavy dormer-windows are inserted at the foot of each of the cardinal sides of the spire: altogether a very logical and scientific piece of engineering, of a type very rare in England, but normal in Normandy, *e.g.*, the spires of the Abbaye-aux-Hommes at Caen, of which it is probably a variant.

The Chapter house also was rebuilt (*c.* 1240); rectangular, to fit the cloister. Also, the canons rebuilt the Lady chapel, replacing the Anglo-Saxon arcade on the south, if such there was, by an arcade with light piers and pointed arches also the pointed arch into the chapel adjoining on the north was at this time inserted. The cult of the Virgin, much fostered by the Pope, Innocent III., was at its height in the thirteenth century. The Lady chapels of Bristol, Hereford, Salisbury, Winchester, and Norwich were contemporaries of that of Oxford.

In the year 1289 the relics of St. Frideswide were translated to a new shrine. Fragments of the pedestal of this have been recently put together; it contains beautiful naturalistic foliage like that of the contemporary shrine-pedestal of St. Thomas of Hereford.

FOURTH PERIOD.—A great deal of work was done in the fourteenth century, especially in improving the lighting of the church by substituting large traceried windows for the original small Norman lights. Of these new windows a very fine example remains in St. Lucy's chapel, opening out of the south transept; with tracery starting below the spring of the arch; it contains early fourteenth-century glass, in which is a representation of the martyrdom of St. Thomas of Canterbury. Another fine window, restored, is seen high up in the end wall of the south transept. In the second quarter of the century the little northern chapel east of the north transept was pulled down, and in its place was built a chapel of four bays, with four side windows of singularly beautiful tracery, and all different. They contain late fourteenth-century glass, which should be compared with that in St. Lucy's chapel and in Merton College chapel. The bosses are very beautiful: one of them has a representation of the waterlilies of the adjacent Cherwell. Hard by, in the second arch from the east, is the tomb of Lady Montacute, who died in 1353 and gave the canons about half the Christ Church meadows to found a chantry; from its style the tomb would seem to have been built in her lifetime. In the third arch from the east is the canopied tomb of a prior; perhaps Prior Sutton, who died in 1316. The chapel is dedicated to St. Catherine, perhaps in part reminiscence of Frideswide's sister Catherine, who retired with her to Binsey wood. In modern days it was fitted up for Divinity lectures, and was called the Divinity chapel or the Latin chapel. It contains rich woodwork; in some of the poppy-heads of the stalls a cardinal's hat and tassels are carved; the stalls may have been made for the vast collegiate chapel which Cardinal Wolsey had commenced, but which was soon to be abandoned.

FIFTH PERIOD.—For a century or more nothing else was done or needed doing, except further improvement of the lighting by the insertion of large windows with rectilinear tracery, and the erection of the so-called "Watching-chamber," the lower part of which is the tomb of a merchant and his wife, the upper part probably the chapel belonging to it, c. 1480; it is probable that the merchant was only allowed to have a tomb in this sacred spot on condition that it was designed for its upper story to be used, like the upper story of the Watching Loft at St. Albans, to watch the treasures of St. Frideswide's shrine, which was but a few feet away. It is probable that the upper chapel of Henry V. at Westminster similarly served a double purpose. It may be added that it was quite common in parish churches to secure burial near the High altar by putting up in the north wall of the chancel a recessed tomb which could be used as Easter Sepulchre.

The one remaining great undertaking, which, as at Norwich, had been postponed as long as possible, was the ceiling of choir, transepts, and nave with high vaults. The

OXFORD CATHEDRAL 253

choir vault and clerestory were taken in hand first, in the last quarter of the fifteenth century. For its design is based on that of the Divinity School at Oxford, which seems to have

THE CHOIR

been built between 1481 and 1483, and it is earlier than the vault commenced in the north transept for which Canon Zouch left money; he is buried below beneath the great north window. As Mr Fergusson well says, "the vault of the choir, except in size, is one of the best and most remarkable in Christendom." In the clerestory of the nave also corbels were inserted to support a stone vault; but the resources of the canons seem to have failed, and the rest of the church received roofs of wood; that of the nave is probably Wolsey's work. Another considerable work was the rebuilding of the cloister. In order to get room for the northeast corner of the new cloister the two southern bays of the west aisle of the south transept were swept away. Nor was this all the demolition; for when the whole establishment was granted in 1524 to Cardinal Wolsey, he pulled down the three western bays of the nave, as obstructing the quadrangle of his new college; one bay has been recently rebuilt.

THE CHOIR VAULT.

SIXTH PERIOD.—In 1542 Henry VIII. founded the new diocese of Oxford. Till 1546 the seat of the bishopric was at Osney abbey. On the suppression of the abbey it was transferred to Wolsey's confiscated foundation; and the ancient priory church became a cathedral, while at the same time it is the chapel of the college of Christ Church. There is an interesting window in the south choir aisle, the only Norman window left in the church; the glass in it has a portrait of the first bishop of Oxford, King, with Osney abbey on one side. The "merry, merry, Christ Church bells" came from the tower shewn in this window. At the entrance to the Great Hall is the last bit of genuine Gothic done in England, a sort of chapter house in fan tracery, ceiling the staircase.

OXFORD CATHEDRAL 255

The cathedral possesses a charming Jacobean pulpit, and a large amount of fine Flemish glass of the seventeenth century—all of it taken out and stowed away in some lumber room at a recent restoration, except one window at the west end of the north aisle of the nave, in order to insert some sham mediæval windows. There are also five windows from designs by Sir Edward Burne Jones— three of them of great beauty so far as the drawing is concerned; good windows by Clayton and Bell in the end walls of the transepts; and a reredos by Mr Bodley, who also has the credit of the bell tower.

The following are the more important dates of the cathedral and the college:—740 + *The First Church*; St. Frideswide. 1002. *The Second Church*; Ethelred. 1065. Burnt and restored. 1158-80. *The Third (present) Church*. 1190. Damaged by fire (?) 1250 (?). Chapter house and Lady chapel. 1289. St. Frideswide's new Shrine dedicated. 1359. The Latin chapel completed: one bay having been begun in thirteenth century. 1450 + Restorations: Choir clerestory side windows. 1480. Restorations: Watching chamber. 1500 + Restorations: N. transept window: roof of tower and transepts: roof of the Choir: Cloister. 1524-9. Wolsey's "Cardinal College"; Kitchen, Hall, E., S., W. sides of Tom Quad (W. side not complete): Chapel begun on N. side: three bays of the Church nave destroyed. 1532. Henry VIII.'s Foundation. 1546. Seat of Bishopric of Oxford moved from Osney to Christ Church. Bp. King: Abbot of Osney 1542-1546, Bishop of Oxford 1546-1557. 1640. Staircase of the Hall. 1630. Restorations in the Cathedral: brasses destroyed: "Jonah" window. 1648. Deanery archway into Peckwater (*Samuel Fell, Dean*). 1668. North side of Tom Quad. 1680. "Tom" recast; the original bell came from Osney abbey. 1682. Tom Tower, upper part (*Sir Chr. Wren*). 1705. Peckwater Quad (*Dean Aldrich*). 1716. Library begun. 1720. Fire: S.W. angle of Tom Quad destroyed; Roof of Hall injured. 1761. Library finished. 1778. Canterbury Gate (*Wyatt*). 1862-6. Meadow Buildings. 1871. East End of Cathedral "restored'

(*Sir G. G. Scott*). 1879. Belfry Tower over Hall Staircase.

BIBLIOGRAPHY.—Sir Gilbert Scott's "Report" in Murray's *Eastern Cathedrals*, p. 45. Pamphlet by J. Park Harrison on the Saxon arches in the east end of the church.

Bloxam, M. H., "Sepulchral Monuments in Oxford Cathedral,' *Royal Archæol. Institute*; Oxford volume, 1860.

THE TOWER AND SPIRE FROM THE CLOISTER

THE CATHEDRAL CHURCH OF ST. PETER, PETERBOROUGH

BUILT FOR BENEDICTINE MONKS

ABOUT the middle of the seventh century Peada and Wulfere, successive kings of Mercia, are said to have founded a monastery at Peterborough, then called Medeshamstead ("the homestead in the meadow"), and to have consecrated the church in the names of St. Peter, St. Paul, and St. Andrew. Then said King Wulfere with a loud voice: "This day do I freely give to St. Peter and to the abbot and to the monks of this monastery these lands and waters and meres and fens and weirs; neither shall tribute or tax be taken therefrom. Moreover I do make this monastery free, that it be subject to Rome alone; and I will that all who may not be able to journey to Rome should repair hither to St. Peter." This consecration took place in 664 or 665. In 870 this, the first church, was destroyed by the Danes, and Abbot Hedda and all his monks were murdered. It was not fully rebuilt till 963 or 966. Abbot Elsinus (1006-1055) collected many relics: pieces of the swaddling clothes, of the manger, of the cross, and of the sepulchre of Christ; of the garments of the Virgin, of Aaron's rod, a bone of one of the Innocents, portions of the bodies of St. John the Baptist, St. Peter, and St. Paul, the body of St. Florentinus, for which he gave 100 lbs. of silver, and, most precious of all, the incorruptible arm of the Northumbrian king, Oswald, believed by half the population of England to be an effectual cure for diseases which defied the material power of drugs. Here is Bede's account of it: "When Oswald was once sitting at dinner with Bishop Aidan, on the holy day of Easter, and a silver

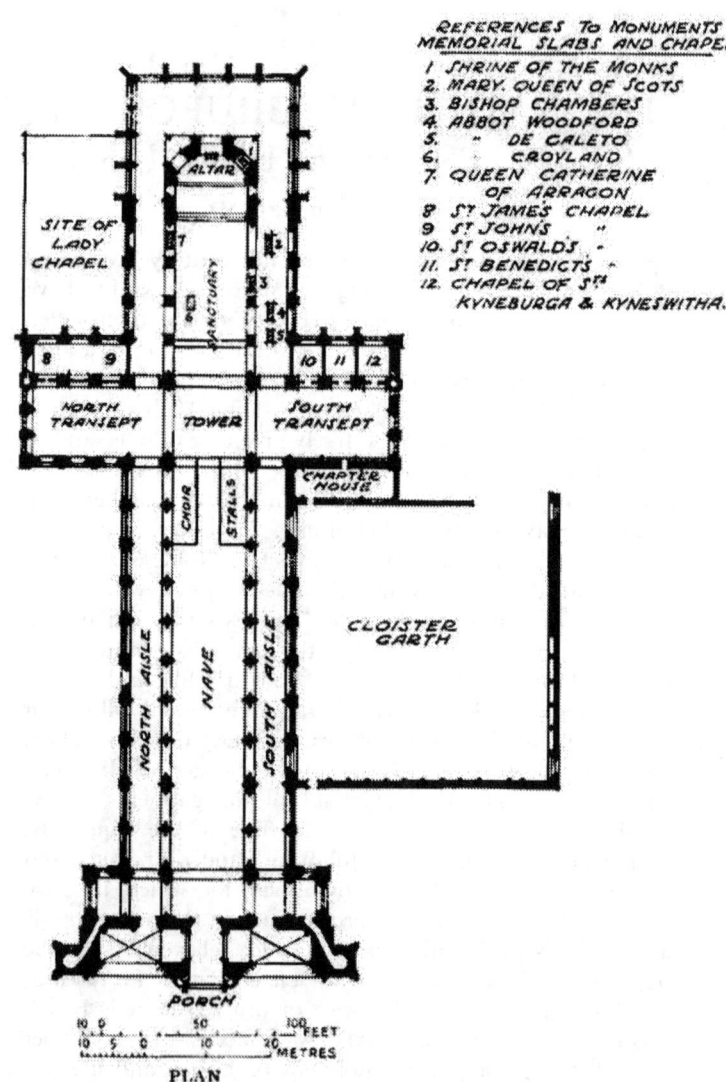

dish of dainties was before him, the servant, whom he had appointed to relieve the poor, came in on a sudden, and told the king that a great multitude of needy persons were sitting in the streets begging alms of the king. He immediately ordered the meat set before him to be carried to the poor, and the dish also to be cut in pieces and divided among them. At which sight the Bishop laid hold of the King's right hand, and said, 'May this hand never perish,' which fell out according to his prayer; for his arm and hand being cut off from his body, when he was slain in battle, remain entire and incorrupted to this day, and are kept in a silver case as revered relics in St. Peter's church in the royal city." Even King Stephen came to see it; and, what is more, remitted to the monks forty marks which they owed him. Benedict was a monk at Canterbury when Becket was murdered; and when he became abbot of Peterborough in 1177, he brought with him the slabs of the pavement which were stained with the blood of the martyr, fragments of his shirt and surplice, and two vases of his blood. So that the monastery was called "Peterborough the Proud," and waxed rich and mighty, and church and close were holy ground, and all pilgrims, even though of royal blood, put off their shoes before passing through the western gateway of the close.

FIRST PERIOD.—The second Saxon church of 966-972 seems to have lasted till 1116, when it was destroyed by fire, and the present church, the third, was commenced. The foundations of part of this Saxon church have been recently disinterred beneath the present south transept. It was cruciform, with perhaps a square east end, and was without aisles. The east limb was 23 ft. each way; the transept was 88 ft. long. Its walls were under 3 ft. thick, so that it cannot have been intended for a vault. It is uncertain how far it extended westward.

On the inside of the east wall of the north transept a part of the stone seating can be seen. It was in this church that Hereward the Wake was knighted by his uncle, Abbot Brando. Saxon monuments were found *in situ* under the floor of the transept of the present church in 1887. A subway has been constructed so that the eastern foundations may be viewed.

SECOND PERIOD.—In 1116 the Saxon cathedral was seriously injured by a great fire, and in 1117 or 1118 Abbot John de Sais (Séez) commenced the present Norman church. He died in 1125. His successor did nothing. Abbot Martin de Bec (1133-1155) completed sufficient to allow the monks to hold their services in the eastern limb. (Probably the monks had been able to patch up the damaged

FROM THE SOUTH

Anglo-Saxon church, and held their services in that till 1140 or 1143.) The work done by Abbots John and Martin includes the whole of the eastern limb, full height, and the aisles and the two lower stories of the eastern sides of the central transept; in the north transept the west wall was built up to the string-course of the ground story; the south transept adjoined the monastic buildings, and so more work was done in it; this included the south wall with the windows of the ground story, and on the eastern side the three northern bays of the triforium (the fourth bay has a plain tympanum). Of the central tower the eastern piers were built full height, and the western piers about half way up: it follows that the first choir was confined to the eastern limb. A start was made with the nave; this included on the north side the arch from the transept into the north aisle, and the first bay of that aisle up to the string-course over the wall arcade, where the moldings change. Also he built the two eastern bays of the ground story on each side of the nave. Hitherto the north wall of the Saxon nave had probably been retained to shut in the cloister on the north; now it was pulled down and replaced by the wall of the present south aisle of the nave, as far as the east side of the bay containing the western procession doorway.

THE PRESBYTERY

THIRD PERIOD.—Then came in 1155 another great builder, William de Waterville; unfortunately, he got the convent into debt, was unpopular with the monks, and was deposed by them in 1175; so the monastic chroniclers give the credit of a great deal of Waterville's work to their favourite, Benedict, who had enriched the monastery with the relics from Canterbury, and who is said by them to have built the whole of the nave, which he certainly did not. Waterville's work falls into two parts; first, he completed both transepts, the piers and arches of the crossing, and a central tower of three stories; he also built the vestry on the west side of the south transept. Secondly, he did a great deal of work in the nave. The two easternmost bays of the nave he completed on both sides up to the top of the triforium; the tympana of these triforium bays have similar decoration to those in the choir triforium. No doubt he put up a temporary roof at the triforium level, and western boarding; and this done, he transferred the stalls in 1175 to the two eastern bays of the nave and the crossing, where they are at present. On the north side of the nave Waterville only built as much as was necessary to buttress the new central tower to the west; viz., four bays of the ground story, two of the triforium (which have rude ornament not found elsewhere in the nave), and one bay of the clerestory; also he finished the first two eastern bays of the north aisle, which were in a line with the new choir, and built the third, fourth, and fifth bays of the aisle up to the string-course above the wall arcade. Most of his work was done on the south side—partly because the south aisle-wall was already standing, having been built by Abbot Martin, partly because the south aisle, being adjacent to the cloister, was wanted more urgently than the north aisle. On the south side he built all the eight eastern bays of the ground story (the eighth is that which is opposite to the western procession doorway). No doubt he roofed in the corresponding bays of the aisle to enable it to be used; and he may have vaulted several bays of it. Of the south triforium he erected the first two bays, of the south clerestory only the easternmost bay. A curious proof that the south side of the nave was completed and left in the open air for a considerable time before the completion of the north side is that when the whitewash was taken off at one of the restorations, the putlog holes on the south side were found to be full of remains of birds' nests, of which there were none on the north side. It will be noticed that the eighth piers from the east are exceptionally massive and strong, and that in this bay the aisle-walls are thickened. This, together with the position of the western processional doorway, shews that the original intention was that the nave should end at this point in two western towers in an axis with the aisles; of these the southern tower was carried up for some distance.

THE SOUTH AISLE

All this Norman work of c. 1117 to c. 1175 is of sternly simple character; nevertheless both artistically and constructionally it ranks very high. There are few internal elevations in Europe finer than that of the north transept; and few vistas so picturesque as that of the presbytery from the south transept. The builders, too, understood perfectly the independence of the load and the support; in the choir the abacus, in the nave the shafts of the piers are in exact co-ordination with the orders of the pier-arch and the vault. To get level ridges for the aisle-vaults, the builders stilted the transverse arches of the aisles and the pier-arches, while they built each diagonal arch in rather less than a semicircle. In the spandrels of two triforium bays in the choir are anticipations of plate tracery.

FOURTH PERIOD.—Then came Abbot Benedict (1177-1193), who, thinking the nave too short, abandoned the western towers commenced by Waterville, and added two more bays to the west. The nave now had ten bays, and Benedict completed these ten bays from pavement to roof, and the aisles as well, including their vaults, with the exception that he left undone the tenth bay of the clerestory. The present ceiling of the nave is probably that put up by Benedict;* but, strange to say, there are signs of an intention to vault the nave; for round the clerestory windows are wall-arches; there is a springer of a vault in the westernmost bay of the clerestory; and the clerestory passage is blocked with masses of masonry to give a solid backing to the springers of a high vault; moreover, to carry the diagonal ribs, corbels were inserted just below the clerestory spring-course, as in Durham nave; these corbels were chiselled off, when it was decided to have a ceiling and not a vault. With the exception of the last bay of the clerestory on either side and the west front, the church, begun about 1117, was finished by 1193. It had, therefore, occupied some seventy-six years. During that long period the original design, as at Ely, was steadily adhered to. Regardless of the vast changes in style which were to be seen elsewhere, the builders went on using the selfsame templates for the moldings, and the self-same archaic capitals and abaci. The chief exceptions are that from Waterville's time the waterholding molding occurs in the bases of the piers; that the wall-arches in the clerestory are pointed; and, strange to say, about the centre of the southern triforium some Corinthianesque capitals, which may have been carved by a mason who had been working in Canterbury choir; perhaps he was on his way to a job at Oakham hall, where alone is to be found a complete set of

* The roofs of the great transept also are probably original. That of the nave was flat at first; but when the pointed arches were inserted in the central tower, the ceiling was tilted up to clear the new eastern arch. At the same time a new roof was put up over the presbytery.

foliated capitals copied from those of the work of William of Sens at Canterbury, begun in 1175.

Having destroyed the western towers begun by Waterville, Benedict commenced a new west transept at the end of the tenth bay of the nave. It has towers in the axis of the aisles, and lofty flanking chapels crowned by gables. Thus the transept consists of chapel, tower bay, the eleventh bay of the nave, tower bay, chapel. Of this Benedict built the east walls about as high as the cill of the clerestory windows, abandoning the precedents of 1117 and designing the work with noble pointed arches, overlaid, however, by a profusion of Norman zigzag.

FIFTH PERIOD.— Benedict was followed by Abbot Andrew (1195-1200), who built the westernmost bay of the clerestory and finished the western transept. His northern tower still remains; in 1730 it had a wooden spire. Andrew also commenced a spacious

VAULTING UNDER THE WEST TOWER

porch to lead into his central doorway, after the manner of the Galilee porch of Ely (1198-1215). Of this he finished only "the side walls from the springing of the wall arcades at the east to a few courses above the bases to the west; and the lower parts of the central opening and the two narrow side openings."

SIXTH PERIOD.—Then came Abbot Acharius (1200-1210) from St. Albans, where he was Prior, and where a lovely west front was building or on the point of being built. Even Benedict and Andrew's west front was not good enough for Acharius, and he decided to build yet another façade in front of theirs, finishing and absorbing into it Andrew's western porch. (Something similar occurred rather later at Lincoln, where a new Gothic west front was built up around the old Norman façade and towers.) It was the retention of this porch which gave the central opening of the façade the peculiarity of being narrower than the side openings. (The side openings could not be narrowed, because they had to span the space from Andrew's central

THE WEST FRONT

porch to the ends of his western transept.) In addition to the three great openings, flanking towers were built, which were constructed solid (except for staircases) to resist the thrusts of the broad and lofty side openings. It is probable that the three gables of the façade were meant originally to be loftier, for their wheel windows are too large for their present position. It may be that they had been already carved at Barnack quarry when it was decided to put up lower gables (nearly all the moldings, &c., seem to have been carved at the quarry). Built, like the whole cathedral, even the western chapels, practically without foundations, the north and south gables had to be taken down in 1896; foundations were put in, and each stone was returned to its original position; only 170 out of about 2,000 stones needed to be renewed—a thoroughly sound and conservative piece of work. After Acharius came an interval of three years, when King John appropriated the revenues of the abbey; then came Robert de Lindsay, who was abbot from 1214 to 1222, and who probably completed the west front.

The west front of Peterborough has been severely criticised, especially by Mr Pugin. To many it will seem to be at once the most original and most successful façade in English or in Continental Gothic. Yet, magnificent and poetic as it is, we have not the full effect contemplated by the mediæval builders. They meant to have four towers, not three. The north-west tower was once crowned by a wooden spire; we may

A GABLE CROSS

be sure that there would have been a spire also on a south-west tower. Add, too, in the background, a tall spire on the central tower, and you have a group before which even Lichfield and Lincoln would pale into insignificance. Even curtailed as it is, the design attains the sublime. When first its Titanic arches rose into the blue sky, its builders may well have repeated the psalmist's words: "Lift up your heads, O ye gates; and be ye lift up, ye everlasting doors; and the King of Glory shall come in." They had built a worthy portal to the House of the Almighty. In 1238 the church was at last dedicated; of the stalls then put up two remain in the morning chapel, with Jacobean backs. The font is thirteenth-century work; its beautiful bowl was found in a prebendal garden; the supports are modern.

SEVENTH PERIOD.—Little more was done till 1272-1286, when the east bay of each aisle of the presbytery, which was square externally, semicircular internally, was converted into a square-ended chapel; and the present parapet was added to the apse. Also large windows, with geometrical tracery, were inserted to give better light to the eastern aisle of each arm of the central transept. In this period, c. 1270, the bell tower was carried up; and a magnificent Lady chapel was built as at Bristol, to the north of the choir. On the west it was joined on to the north transept, but between it and the presbytery was a space, in which afterwards a small chapel was inserted. It could not be built east of the choir, as a high road passed near the apse. This Lady chapel was pulled down in the seventeenth century for the sake of its materials.

EIGHTH PERIOD.—In the fourteenth century the weight of the Norman tower, which had of course very thick walls, and was three stories high, was found to be too much for the exceptionally weak piers on which it stood. Warned, perhaps, by the fate of the central towers of Ely and Wells, both of which collapsed about this time, they took down the Norman tower, and built a new one (which has recently been rebuilt), much lighter and much lower; first strengthening the northern and southern arches by building pointed arches above them, and substituting pointed for semicircular eastern and western arches. The south-west spire was also built—a design of exquisite beauty.

Much attention was now paid to improving the lighting of the church and the drainage of the roofs. The process of substituting large traceried windows for small Norman windows commenced in the aisles of the nave and the south presbytery at the beginning of the century. As at Norwich, the triforium roof was raised to give headway to larger windows in the upper part of the aisle-wall, throwing light through the triforium chamber into the nave. Windows of charming flowing tracery were inserted in the apse of the presbytery, c. 1340. Gutters and parapets with flowing patterns were put up at the foot of the high roofs; the builders, however, with their wonted conservatism retained the Norman corbel table, which, as at Southwell, has the nebule ornament. A porch was inserted, c. 1370, in the central arch of the west front; where it was constructionally useful in keeping the two central piers from bulging inwardly; it was occupied by a semi-choir on Palm Sunday.

THE SOUTH TRANSEPT AND CENTRAL TOWER

NINTH PERIOD.—In the fifteenth century more Norman windows were taken out and replaced by larger windows with rectilinear tracery; altogether some seventy-five windows were treated in this way; and the builders in the end accomplished their object, for the cathedral is thoroughly well lighted; we may be thankful that they did not insert big windows in the end walls of the central transept. The eagle lectern was given to the abbey some few years before 1471.

TENTH PERIOD.—Till the last years of the fifteenth century the cathedral remained unchanged in plan. But it had no procession path, and only two eastern chapels; between 1438 and 1528 therefore the apse of the presbytery was encircled by a low square-ended aisle broad enough to contain a procession path and three chapels. This was the work of Abbot Ashton (1438-1471) and Abbot Robert Kirton (1496-1528), whose rebuses occur repeatedly. It is ceiled with a fan vault; if this be examined, it will be found that most of the joints occur about half-way between the ribs: really therefore, constructionally, it is not a ribbed vault at all; but consists of panels accurately fitted together, with decorative ribs carved on their inner surfaces. Outside, the buttresses have seated figures instead of pinnacles.

THE RETRO-CHOIR

As completed, the ritualistic divisions of the church, commencing at the east, were as follows: (1) Three eastern chapels and procession path; (2) aisled presbytery, consisting of four bays and an apse; with the High altar to the east and probably the choir altar in the centre; (3) choir occupying the crossing and the two eastern bays of the nave, as at present; at the west of it, between the second piers from the tower, was the Choir screen, on which an altar was placed; (4) the Rood screen was between the next pair of piers; some traces of its loft may be seen in the triforium; (5) the ritualistic nave containing eight bays, including the central bay of the western transept; on the north is the doorway which led to the lay cemetery; on the south the two procession doorways which communicated with the cloister.

ELEVENTH PERIOD.—In 1541 the church was made a cathedral on the New Foundation. Henry VIII. is said to have preserved it as a mausoleum to his first wife, Catharine of Arragon, who is buried in the choir.

In 1643 Peterborough was occupied for a fortnight by two regiments of Cromwell's troops, and the cathedral was atrociously maltreated; hence the bareness of its interior. Recently stalls have been re-erected, and the mistake has been made of paving the presbytery with marble, making the venerable freestone around look mean and common. Over the altar Mr Pearson has erected a baldachino of Italian design. The ritualistic arrangements have been sadly muddled; the eastern part of the church is too large for the daily services and too small for great diocesan gatherings, as also is the nave. What was wanted was to screen off the daily services in the presbytery, as in Abbot Martin's time, and from 1830 to 1883; leaving the whole of the rest of the area of the church for congregational purposes, and providing it with an altar and stalls of its own.

BIBLIOGRAPHY.—Gunton's *History of Peterborough*, with Dean Patrick's *Supplement*, 1686.

John Bridge's *Northamptonshire*, 1793.

G. A. Poole's "Peterborough Cathedral"; in the *Associated Architectural Societies Reports*, 1855, p. 199.

F. A. Paley's *Peterborough Cathedral*, 1859.

Canon Davys' *Guide to Peterborough Cathedral*, 1860.

Thomas Craddock, *History of Peterborough Cathedral*, 1864.

J. P. Irvine in *Archæological Journal*, vol. 50, and in *Builder*, 5th May 1894.

The most complete and most accurate account of the cathedral is that given by Mr C. R. Peers in *The Victoria County History of Northamptonshire*, 1909.

For manuscript and other sources see the bibliography in Craddock's *Peterborough Cathedral*, p. 227.

THE CATHEDRAL CHURCH OF ST. PETER AND ST. WILFRID, RIPON

BUILT FOR SECULAR CANONS

RIPON minster has passed through strange vicissitudes. It was founded c. 657, but on a different site, for Scottish monks attached to the Celtic Church. In 661 it was taken away from them and granted to the famous St. Wilfrid. In 681 the church became a cathedral, but only till 686. At some period before the Norman Conquest it became the church of a college of secular canons. It was dissolved with the other collegiate establishments by Edward VI., but was made collegiate once more by James I. In 1836, for the second time, it became a cathedral.

FIRST PERIOD.—Both the minsters built by St. Wilfrid—Ripon and Hexham—retain their crypts. He was a Romaniser in architecture as in ritual, and well acquainted with Italy. So his seventh-century church at Ripon was modelled after the early Christian basilicas which he had seen at Rome. Like them, it had a confessionary or crypt, which still exists beneath the central tower; like them, it was orientated to the west. He seems even to have brought over Italian masons to direct or to execute the work, for the crypt is vaulted, and the vaulting is of excellent construction; the masonry is smooth, and is covered "with a fine and very hard plaster which takes a polish." At present the altar is at the east end, but it may originally have been at the west end; at its east end an aperture through which a glimpse of the interior might be obtained from the Saxon nave. Round the walls are little niches in which lights were placed. "St. Wilfrid's Needle" is merely a niche with the back knocked through. Similar Saxon crypts remain at Hexham and Wing, and a Norman crypt at St. Peter-in-the-East, Oxford. They usually consisted of a small central chamber, with a passage all round it. There were two staircases descending from either side of the nave; pilgrims went down one flight of steps, proceeded along the passage, getting a glimpse of the relics through openings in the wall of the central chamber, and then returned up the other flight of steps into the nave. Both staircases survive in the Hexham crypt.

SECOND PERIOD.—Early in the twelfth century a Norman church seems to have been built, wholly or in part, by Archbishop Thomas or Archbishop Thurstan. Of this there remains only an apsidal building, with undercroft beneath, on the south side of the south aisle of the present choir. An eleventh-century chapel formerly existed, with crypt beneath it, in precisely the same situation at Worcester; and there is a twelfth-century chapel in the same position in Oxford cathedral; in Oxford this chapel was the Lady chapel. It may be that the Ripon chapel also may have been a Lady chapel. If the Norman church extended as far eastward as at present, it would have been impossible to build a Lady chapel to the east of the choir; the ground falls far too steeply eastward. On the other hand it may have been an apsidal sacristy with undercroft. In the upper chamber, the present vestry, on the south side of the apse are piscina and aumbries, pointing

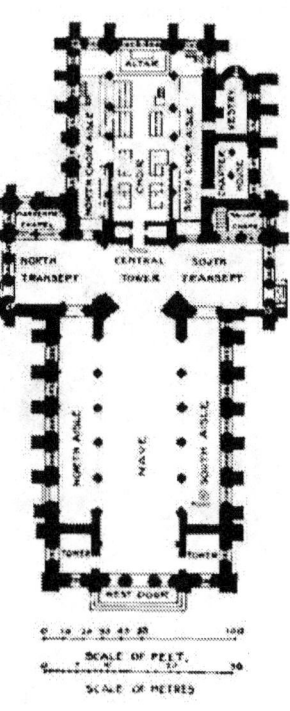

PLAN

to the existence of an altar. Now at Westminster the Revestiary forms at its east end the chapel of St. Faith. It may be then at Ripon that the upper apse held an altar of Our Lady, but that the rest of the upper chamber together with the undercroft formed the sacristy and treasury of the church, and were retained by Archbishop Roger when he built his choir. In the south-eastern buttress is a curious chamber which, like the feretory at Gloucester, may have provided a treasury for small objects of exceptional value.

THE SOUTH TRANSEPT

THIRD PERIOD.—From 1154-1181 there ruled at York a man of great energy and power—Archbishop Roger. He condemned his two Norman churches at York and Ripon; made no attempt, as at Peterborough and Ely, to improve them; simply pulled them down, and started again *de novo*. The two new Yorkshire minsters seem to have been somewhat similar: both had square east ends, both had exceptionally broad naves. But Ripon minster was merely a collegiate church; therefore it was not planned in cathedral fashion. Its eastern limb was probably of the same dimensions as at present. The original ritualistic arrangements have been swept away by the restorers, and the levels altered—so that the eastern limb might be used for congregational purposes, for which it was never intended, and for which it will always be inadequate. Originally both the High altar and the sedilia were in the second bay from the east, and the easternmost bay formed the procession path; it seems also to have contained the Head Shrine of St. Wilfrid, whose body was buried, first on the south side, but afterwards on the north side of the presbytery. The Saint's chapel with the shrine of St. Wilfrid was not east of the High altar, but beneath the easternmost arch of the north aisle of the choir. The minster was and is still parochial as well as collegiate; and for its parishioners a big nave was built. It was built, as parish churches originally were as a rule built—without aisles. This was the great feature of the minster, a 40-ft. nave without aisles. The combination of unaisled nave and aisled choir must have produced a very remarkable interior; quite unlike anything now existing in England, but to be paralleled by such cathedrals as Gerona and Toulouse.

Of this remarkable nave nothing is now left except two fragments, one at the east, and one at the west end on either side. All the rest has been replaced by sixteenth-century piers, arches, and clerestory. But if in imagination the two ends of the nave are joined together—it is well to do so in an actual drawing—the design of the whole of the original nave can be recovered with exactitude. A very remarkable design it was. It consisted of three stories; the lower story was simply a blank wall. The second contained a passage in the thickness of the wall, which was divided into bays alternately broad and narrow; the broad bays having semicircular, the narrow bays pointed arches; which again were respectively subdivided into four and two minor arches, all pointed and with the spandrels pierced. A similar wall passage occurs in the pretty nave of the nuns' church at Nun Monkton, near York. In the clerestory the narrow bays had a blank arcade of three pointed arches; the broad bays a round-headed window flanked on either side by a blank pointed arch. Neither in the ground story nor in the middle story were there any windows. Everywhere else people were trying to get all the windows possible into their churches; here alone a "dim, religious light" was preferred. And filtering in, as it did, through small lancet windows at a great height, as in Pugin's cathedral at Killarney, the effect must have been most dramatic. The destruction of this unique nave is one of the heaviest losses that English architecture has sustained.

Of the central tower, the south-east pier has been rebuilt; the north-east and south-west piers have been cased. The north and west arches of the tower survive; the south and east arches have been rebuilt. The nave was considerably wider than the central aisle of the choir; the tower was therefore not built square; the northern arch being set obliquely, and not parallel to the southern one. Outside, however, the north side of the tower is corbelled out till the tower becomes square.

The design of the choir is similar to that of the north transept, which retains the original round-headed windows. The design of transept and choir is almost Cistercian in its severity. Very effective is the contrast of broad wall-surface and plain splayed window with the light and slender shafted arcades of triforium and clerestory. In proportions, too, it is superior to most later designs. The pier-arches are tall and narrow, and the triforium thoroughly subordinated to the tall clerestory; the proportions approximate to those of Westminster abbey and Beverley minster. It is remarkable, too, for the studied absence of foliated ornament. Not that the builders could not design a foliated capital; they have left one or two, in unnoticed corners of the north transept, to shew their powers. All the capitals of the choir are molded capitals; as at Byland, Furness, Holme Cultram, Roche, Old Malton, Darlington, and Hartlepool; these hollow-necked capitals are evidently due to the influence of the Yorkshire Cistercians; like them, the builders chose to rely on architectural effects pure and simple. Equally remarkable is the abolition of Norman ornament. The billet, the zigzag, the whole barbaric congeries of Norman ornament is contemptuously cast aside. In this respect, indeed,

RIPON CATHEDRAL

Ripon is much more advanced than Canterbury choir, which was not commenced till 1175. The clerestory, however, is of a familiar Norman type, being an adaptation of

THE NAVE, LOOKING EAST

that of Romsey and Waltham abbey, and Peterborough and Oxford cathedrals; another version of it was produced a little later in Hexham choir.

The aisle of the north transept is vaulted in square bays,

each quadripartite, with wall-ribs and also with ridge-ribs, both longitudinal and transverse. The ridge-ribs consist only of a single roll and are merely decorative. The diagonal ribs have a triple roll. The cells are filled in, French fashion, with courses parallel to the ridges. The bays are separated by broad, square-edged arches. It is a most extraordinary vault for the period; for such a combination of longitudinal and transverse ridge-ribs does not occur elsewhere till the vault of Lincoln nave was set out c. 1240.

The vaulting-shafts of the choir rest on the abaci, French fashion, and occur in groups of five, which in the clerestory are reduced to a single shaft; shewing that, as in the western bays of the nave of St. Albans, it was originally contemplated to vault the choir, but that the intention was abandoned when the triforium was completed. It is probably because it was meant to vault the choir, that it was set out so much narrower than the nave, in spite of the awkward plan which resulted in the central tower. In the transept there are three vaulting-shafts in each group, pointing to an intention to build a quadripartite vault, similar to that of the choir aisles. But in the choir there are five vaulting-shafts in a group. These are difficult to explain. It may be that the central shaft was to carry the transverse rib of the vault, while its flanking shafts carried the diagonals; and that the outer shafts were merely to support the wall-ribs; in that case it would be a simple quadripartite vault.

The façades of the north transept present a rare example of a complete façade of the period; the doorways of both transepts are of much interest.

In spite of round-headed windows and round-headed arches here and there, the whole design of the interior was light and graceful, thoroughly Gothic. Externally it was just the reverse; but for a pointed arcade in the clerestory one might imagine one was back again in the early days of the twelfth century. It is when one compares the interior with that of Oxford cathedral, which is precisely contemporary, and with St. David's, which is later still, that one realises what a long step forward in the evolution of our Gothic architecture was taken at Ripon. It may well be that Archbishop Roger's choir at York, pulled down c. 1380, was a sister design to his Ripon minster. With Ripon should be compared Holy Trinity church, York; and for the later development of the design the choir and eastern transept of the neighbouring abbey of Fountains and the thirteenth-century portion of Beverley minster. To get at the genesis of the Ripon design it would be necessary first

FROM THE SOUTH-EAST

to study the contemporary examples, and those a little earlier, of Cistercian architecture in Yorkshire, such as Roche and Byland; and secondly, to look for analogies and precedents in the district from which Cistercian design hailed, viz., Burgundy and the neighbouring districts, e.g., the resemblances in design between Ripon minster and Notre Dame, Chalons-sur-Marne, are numerous and striking. The whole subject of the Early Gothic school of the North of England remains practically unexplored.

FOURTH PERIOD.—To the thirteenth century belong the vaulting and piers of the present Chapter house; and the west front, which, like York transept and Southwell choir, is attributed to Archbishop Gray. Indulgences for its completion were issued in 1233 and 1258. The west front is flat; deficient in play of light and shade; correct and uninteresting. It is ruined by the loss of its wooden spires, removed in 1664; and by the miserable little pinnacles put up in 1797. Before the aisles were built, these towers projected clear of the nave, and their inner walls formed the western bay of Archbishop Roger's nave, with fine arches cut into them in the thirteenth century to throw them open to the nave.

FIFTH PERIOD.—About 1290 the east end of the choir seems to have collapsed—partly, perhaps, in consequence of the steep fall of the ground eastwards. It was rebuilt, with the damaged portions of the choir, with exceptional strength in consequence. The east end is a vigorous, massive design, something like that of Guisborough or Selby. Only the eastern portion of the choir has flying buttresses. The clerestory windows have an inner arcade. Ripon choir alone, of English cathedrals, possesses a complete "transparent" triforium, the lean-to roof of the aisles having been replaced by a flat roof.

Inside the south-eastern buttress is a staircase at the top of which is a cell, probably for an anchorite.

SIXTH PERIOD.—To the first half of the fourteenth century belong the Sedilia and the Lady Loft. The shafts of the sedilia have been clumsily renewed at some later period. It has been suggested that the original altar of Our Lady was in the apse of the sacristy. In the fourteenth century a separate Lady chapel was built above it. The lower row of lancets in the west front once had charming tracery, inserted 1379-1380. This was removed by Scott; an abominable example of "restoration." A good illustration of the windows before the "restoration" will be found in Murray's "Northern Cathedrals," i. 151.

SEVENTH PERIOD.—In 1458 the southern and eastern

sides of the central tower collapsed, greatly damaging the adjacent parts of the choir and south transept. The eastern aisle of the south transept and much of the south side of the choir, as well as part of the tower, had to be rebuilt. In the choir both in the work of 1290 and in that of 1458, the builders preserved all they could of the twelfth-century work, retaining in the triforium the semicircular arch of the older design. The result is a curious blend of styles. Of the piers, those on the south which are lozenge-shaped

THE NORTH SIDE OF THE NAVE

belong to the fifteenth-century work; the rest of the work of the choir is of the twelfth century where the material is gritstone; in some cases, however, the twelfth-century gritstone may have been reused in the work of 1290. To give more support to the tower, the north-east and south-west piers were cased; the south-east pier was rebuilt, as well as the southern and eastern arches. To strengthen the eastern piers of the tower, the two western bays of the arcade of the choir were blocked up, and a massive choir-screen was inserted *c.* 1480. To this period belong the magnificent stalls with tabernacled canopies, bench ends, elbow rests, and misericords unsurpassed in England.

EIGHTH PERIOD.—In the next century, 1503-1521, the canons unhappily determined to give their unique church more of the look of a cathedral by adding processional aisles to the nave. It is pleasant to add that they were unsuccessful. The nave is low in proportion to its exceptional span; and being, moreover, unprovided with a triforium, does not look in the least like a cathedral, but like an ordinary parish church. Externally, the buttresses are of fine composition, and if the pinnacles were completed, the nave would be very handsome externally. Indeed all the details of the work are exceptionally good. It will be noticed that all the three west doorways opened into the old unaisled nave. The window above the font has a collection of fragments of fine early fourteenth-century glass.

NINTH PERIOD.—In 1593 the central spire—of timber and lead—was struck by lightning, and in 1660 it was removed. It was 120 ft. high. In 1664, for fear of a similar catastrophe, the western spires also were removed. The result is that, seen from a distance, *minus* spires and *minus* pinnacles, Ripon minster is somewhat stunted and squat. Nevertheless, seen from the railway the masses compose well; and seen at a distance the cathedral holds its own and is a dominating feature in the landscape.

BIBLIOGRAPHY.—*Chapter Acts and Memorials of Ripon Minster*, edited by Rev. J. T. Fowler, D.C.L., for the Surtees Society; vols. 64, 74, 78, 81.
  Sir Gilbert Scott in *Archæological Journal*, vol. xxxi.
  Sir Gilbert Scott's *Recollections*.
  J. R. Walbran's *Guide Book*.

THE CATHEDRAL CHURCH OF ST. ANDREW, ROCHESTER

Built for Benedictine Monks

ROCHESTER and London, next to Canterbury, are the oldest of all the English bishoprics, unless we are prepared to accept a pre-Augustine bishopric of Hereford. St. Augustine, soon after his landing in 597, came to preach at Rochester. His reception was not encouraging; the rude people hung fish-tails to his coat. Wherefore in anger the saint prayed "that the Lord would smite them *in posteriora* to their everlasting ignominy. So that not only on their own but on their successors' persons similar tails grew ever after." The worst of it was that the story spread, and not only Rochester people but all English folk were believed on the Continent to be *caudati* (tailed). So that even in the sixteenth century "an Englishman now cannot travel in another land by way of merchandise or any other honest occupying, but it is most contumeliously thrown in his teeth that all Englishmen have tails."

Among St. Augustine's Italian missioners were St. Justus and St. Paulinus. St. Justus became first bishop of Rochester in 604. St. Paulinus, after eight years of mission work in Northumbria, became bishop of Rochester in 633. The first English bishop was Ythamar (644-655). Paulinus, Justus and Ythamar were the chief local saints of Rochester in early days.

St. Augustine and his missioners had come from the monastery of St. Andrew, Rome. To St. Andrew, therefore, they dedicated the first Saxon cathedral. In 1542 the cathedral was re-dedicated to Christ and the Blessed Virgin

Mary of Rochester. Till 1082 the cathedral was served by secular canons; Archbishop Lanfranc replaced them by Benedictine monks.

FIRST PERIOD.—In 1888 the foundations of an early church were found running towards the south-west; its apse was beneath the north-west corner of the nave. It had neither aisles nor transepts; the walls were only 2 ft. 4 in. thick; it was 42 ft. long, 28 ft. broad. From the resemblance of its plan to that of St. Pancras, Canterbury, and Reculvers, especially in the possession of a chancel arch composed of a triple arcade, it would seem to be of seventh-century date; in which case it is the identical church recorded to have been built by King Ethelbert of Kent.

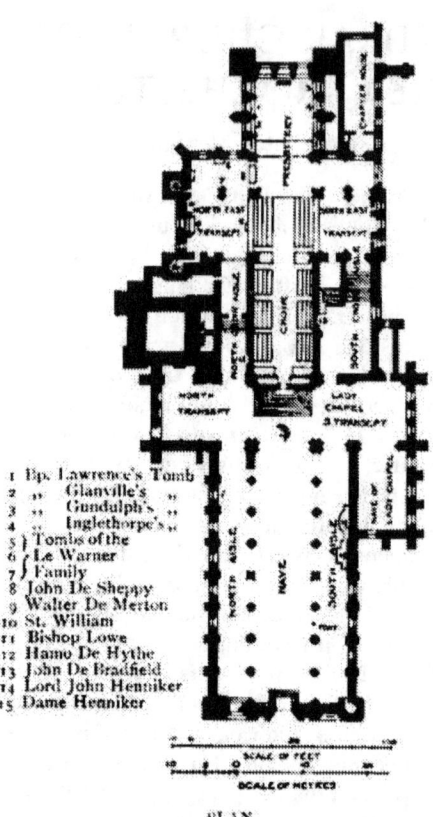

1 Bp. Lawrence's Tomb
2 ,, Glanville's ,,
3 ,, Gundulph's ,,
4 ,, Inglethorpe's ,,
5 } Tombs of the
6 } Le Warner
7 } Family
8 John De Sheppy
9 Walter De Merton
10 St. William
11 Bishop Lowe
12 Hamo De Hythe
13 John De Bradfield
14 Lord John Henniker
15 Dame Henniker

PLAN

SECOND PERIOD.— Soon after 1082 a Norman cathedral was begun; in this Gundulf received much aid from Lanfranc. Gundulf first built to the north a detached tower, the lower part of which remains. Being detached, and having walls 6 ft. thick, it was probably a military keep. Gundulf was fond of building keeps; those of the Tower of

London and Malling still exist. Rochester had suffered from attacks of the Danes, sailing up the Medway, in 840, 884, and 999. There was a striking memento of them on the great west doors of the cathedral, which Pepys, as late as 1661, found "covered with the skins of Danes." We may conjecture that it was as a refuge against similar attacks that Gundulf built the northern keep. But the tower was also used as a campanile as early as 1154. Of Gundulf's church there remain portions in the keep, the nave, the choir, and the crypt. The original monastery was built in the normal position, south of the nave. To enclose the cloister, therefore, on the north, the south side of the nave would be proceeded with first. The south aisle-wall is very thin and not intended to support a vault; it extended west from the transept to about 9 ft. from the present west front. The six piers adjacent to what remains of the aisle-wall, are, like it, of tufa, but were afterwards cased up. The pier-arches are also Gundulf's, but the outer order on the side of the nave was replaced a little later by richer work. On the north side of the nave he seems to have built only the three bays westward of the transept; these are marked by a rich string-course and two shafted pilasters on the aisle-wall. His presbytery, the present choir, was separated from the aisles by solid walls, as at St. Albans. There were transepts, but they had no eastern apses; for to the east of the north transept is Gundulf's keep, and east of the south transept was a smaller engaged tower; a fragment of tufa quoins remains in the south wall of the south choir aisle, west of the cloister doorway. Excavations in the crypt have shewn that the presbytery was square-ended, and that there projected centrally from it a small square eastern chapel. This plan is utterly different from either of the Anglo-Norman normal plans; it is neither periapsidal, like Gloucester and Norwich, nor has three parallel eastern apses, like Durham; one suspects that it was a church— the only large Norman church in England—which followed Anglo-Saxon traditions of planning. The western part of the present crypt is Gundulf's. It has a groined vault, which retains the Norman plaster and the board-marks of the centering. There remain two detached shafts which are monoliths, and circular and rectangular responds of coursed tufa; they have rude cushion capitals.

THE NAVE, FROM THE EAST

THIRD PERIOD.—The works on the church were now probably suspended for a considerable time, while the monks, as at Gloucester, replaced the temporary buildings of the monastery by permanent ones. These temporary wooden buildings seem to have been situated in the usual position—viz., south of the nave. It was perhaps not to interfere with these that the permanent monastic buildings were placed in an abnormal position, south of the choir. Much of this work was done by Bishop Ernulph (1114-1124), who had been a great builder at Canterbury, while prior, and afterwards at Peterborough, as abbot. Parts of his cloister, refectory, and chapter house remain at Rochester.

When at length the builders returned to the nave of the cathedral (*c.* 1120), fashions had changed. Gundulph's eleventh-century design and his rough tufa masonry must have seemed archaic and barbaric. His tufa was therefore cased on the side of the nave with good Caen stone, as was done later in the century at Chichester; his piers and capitals were remodelled, and on the side of the nave the outer square order of the pier-arch was covered with zigzag ornament. Then the north arcade of the nave was completed, the form of each pier being copied from the corresponding one in the south aisle; the new piers were not built in tufa, but in ashlar; the western bases have a "spur" of leafage, a sign of late date. The aisles, as at Hereford, where a precisely similar transformation of eleventh into twelfth century work was taking place at the same time, were left unaltered. Gundulph had placed shafted pilasters along the inner face of his north aisle-wall; perhaps intending that the aisles should be vaulted; but his successors apparently thought the walls too thin, as at Carlisle, to support a vault; so, instead of vaulting the aisles and obtaining thus a continuous chamber the whole length of the church, they constructed a passage in the thickness of the wall of the triforium. Thus Rochester has the distinction of possessing a sham triforium. Waltham abbey also has a triforium arcade, but no triforium floor; but that is because the vaults which originally covered the aisles were subsequently taken down. In the triforium passage of Rochester the arches are slightly pointed to get more head-room.

Still later about the middle of the twelfth century—is the west front, with its magnificent doorway, and the diaper of the triforium. Originally the spandrils of the triforium arcade were open, as at Romsey; afterwards they were filled up solid with diapered blocks, which, where they did not fit the containing arch, may be seen to have been hacked to shape. Foundations for small western towers have been found, but, as at St. Albans, they were never carried up. In the south-west angle of the nave is a staircase-doorway with voluted caps. The west windows of the aisles have true tooth ornament. Taking the tooth ornament and the "spurs" of the western pier-bases into account, it is probable that the nave was completed not before but after the dedication of 1130. In this case what was dedicated would be the monastic part of the church westward up to the rood-screen, leaving the western bays of the nave unfinished. These bays were parochial and had the parochial altar of St. Nicholas backing on to the rood-screen. (In 1423 a church of St. Nicholas was built for the parishioners to the north of the cathedral, cf. Chester cathedral.)

FOURTH PERIOD.—In 1179 the cathedral was greatly damaged by fire; partly because of this, and, as at Canterbury, partly because the eastern half of the cathedral had been planned inconveniently, the monks set to work to rebuild the eastern limb. First, they built to the east a new presbytery, and as they did not wish it to be at a low level like the eastern extension at Worcester, they had to extend the crypt eastward. In the centre of the presbytery, more to the west than its present position, they placed the High altar; the supports of its reredos may be seen in the crypt. Most of the vault is sexpartite, following the precedent of Canterbury choir. The presbytery is admirably lighted, having no less than twenty-two windows. On the other hand, it is the only English cathedral destitute of a procession aisle round the High altar. Moreover, the presbytery has occupied the position usually filled by an eastern chapel. The loss of the chapel, however, was remedied by throwing out an eastern transept, with eastern aisles, each containing two altars. The aisles are vaulted; and above the vaults are chambers with external windows, so that there is no triforium arcade or clerestory. Nor is there a triforium chamber anywhere in the church. Another defect in the plan is the absence of provision for a feretory. The result was that St. William's shrine had to be placed in the

THE CHOIR

northern arm of the eastern transept. (It was approached from the north choir aisle, the steps in the middle of which, now covered with wood to protect them, are deeply worn by the footsteps of pilgrims.) The presbytery, however, was spacious, and there was both a choir or matins altar in the crossing of the eastern transept and the High altar farther eastward. The presbytery was finished in 1214 or earlier, for in that year Bishop Granville was interred in it. His mutilated tomb is on the north of the presbytery in the third bay from the east.

FIFTH PERIOD.—The next task was to convert the western part of Gundulph's presbytery into a choir; its internal walls were convenient as a backing for stalls, and so were retained. The supports of the desks of these stalls remain. The northern thrusts of the sexpartite vault of the choir were provided for by a flying buttress; but owing to the great width of the southern aisle and the presence of the cloister south of the aisle, all that could be done was to build a huge buttress inside the choir aisle: it is close to the steps leading down to the crypt. The wall paintings in the choir, including the Wheel of Fortune, are *c.* 1345. The monks entered their new choir in 1227; but the eastern works cannot then have been finished, for the new eastern limb was not dedicated till 1240.

SIXTH PERIOD.—Next, the north arm of the central transept was built between 1240 and 1255, but not yet vaulted. On the east wall of its eastern recess was a Rood; the corbels which supported it are still there.

SEVENTH PERIOD.—Hitherto there had been no central tower. It was now determined to build one, and first the eastern and then the western piers of the crossing were carried up. At the same time, two bays of the ground story were rebuilt to some height; a solid buttress, still existent, being set against the north-west pier of the crossing. Springers also for a vault were put up in the adjacent bays of the aisle.

EIGHTH PERIOD.—The south transept was next built, and the piers and arches of the crossing were completed. The north transept was then vaulted.

NINTH PERIOD.—Next, Gundulf's southern tower was removed, the space gained being thrown into the south choir aisle. The tower being removed, it was now possible to build the clerestory of the east wall of the south transept, and to vault the transept in wood. This practically brings to an end the *Novum Opus* which, begun after the fire of 1179, must have occupied a whole century. The development of the window tracery in the sixth, eighth, and ninth periods is particularly worth study.

What enabled the monks to undertake such a great work as the rebuilding of the cathedral, and why, after doing so much, they suddenly stopped, has now to be explained. What had brought wealth to Rochester was that in 1201 the monks acquired a new saint, St. William. "He was by birth a Scot, of Perth; by trade, a baker; in charity so abundant that he gave to the poor the tenth loaf of his workmanship; in zeal so fervent that in vow he promised, and in deed attempted, to visit the places where Christ was conversant on earth; in which journey he made Rochester his way, where, after that he had rested two or three days, he departed toward Canterbury. But ere he had gone far from the city, his servant—a foundling who had been brought up by him out of charity—led him of purpose out of the highway, and spoiled him both of his money and his life. The servant escaped, but his master (because he died in so holy a purpose of mind) was by the monks conveyed to St. Andrews and laid in the choir. And soon he wrought miracles plentifully." It was, then, from offerings at the shrine of St. William of Perth, left by countless pilgrims on their way to the shrine of a yet greater saint at Canterbury, that the expenses of the *Novum Opus* were paid. And it was probably because in the course of time the repute of the murdered baker paled and waned before the ever-growing fame of the martyred archbishop, that the monks had to renounce their ambitious project of rebuilding the whole of the nave. It seems, however, that for a considerable time they were unwilling to give up hope; for one bay of the Norman triforium was pulled down, leaving a gap, which was not filled up till the fourteenth century; when it was rebuilt in the same Norman style as before, but in greensand —a rare mediæval example of "architectural forgery."

TENTH PERIOD.—But though the rebuilding of the nave was definitely abandoned, a good deal of other work was done in the first half of the fourteenth century. Another story was added to the central tower, and in 1343 this was capped by a wooden spire. A solid stone screen was inserted between the piers; a grand doorway to the Chapter house was built; its two principal figures represent the Christian

FROM THE SOUTH-WEST

and Jewish dispensations; to the same work belong the windows on either side of it with flowing tracery. Then the north aisle of the choir was raised and vaulted : and traceried windows were substituted for lancets on either side of the presbytery. Later in the century come the sedilia (1373-1389).

ELEVENTH PERIOD.—The next step was to improve the lighting of the nave. Larger windows, with rectilinear tracery, were inserted in the aisles, and the clerestory was rebuilt and heightened, and consequently a new roof nearly flat, the present open timber roof, had to be put up; also the great west window of the nave was built. And a nine-light window was inserted in the east wall of the presbytery; this was restored away by Sir Gilbert Scott.

TWELFTH PERIOD.—In the sixteenth century the monks set to work to enlarge their Lady chapel. This was in the south transept, where the previous double bay had already been thrown into one bay to hold a central altar of Our Lady. Now the transept was prolonged three bays to the west. The extension was planned to have two central columns carrying a fan vault; but the monks did not dare to erect it, because of the lack of abutment on the north side.

THIRTEENTH PERIOD.—In 1664 much of the south aisle of the nave was recased; in 1670 it was found necessary to rebuild three bays of the north aisle; viz., the third, fourth, and fifth from the west front. In 1749 the upper part of the tower and the spire were rebuilt; in 1830 they were taken down by Mr Cottingham, who built a new tower. A wooden spire has recently been put up from a design of Mr C. Hodgson Fowler, based on seventeenth-century prints.

BIBLIOGRAPHY.—The history of this cathedral is too complicated and perplexing to be more than summarised here: it is set forth in detail in Mr W. H. St. John Hope's *Cathedral Church and Monastery of St. Andrew, at Rochester.* Mr Livett's papers in recent volumes of the *Archæologia Cantiana* should also be consulted.

THE CATHEDRAL CHURCH OF ST. ALBAN

Built for Benedictine Monks

OF all our cathedrals none is so composite and heterogeneous as the ancient church of the Benedictine abbey of St. Alban. It is mainly built—even the fourteenth-century Lady chapel—of Roman tiles. Saxon balusters appear in the triforium of the transepts. In the nave and transepts and tower is Early Norman work, unequalled in extent and scale; in the south transept are built up the fragments of a Late Norman doorway, to which period, 1151-1166, belongs the interlacing arcade now placed above it. In the west front and the western bays of the nave is early thirteenth-century work of two periods. In the sanctuary, ante-chapel, and Lady chapel the work went on almost uninterruptedly from c. 1250 to c. 1320. To the style of the first half of the fourteenth century belong the five eastern bays on the south side of the nave, the remains of the cloisters, the shrines of St. Alban and St. Amphibalus, and the Rood screen. This practically completed the abbey church structurally; but much important minor work was added in later days up to the Dissolution. It included the alterations to the cloisters, the abbey gatehouse, the triforium windows on the north side of the nave and choir, inserted when the aisle roofs were lowered, the watching loft, the chantries of the Duke of Gloucester and Abbot Wheathampstead, and the reredos and painted ceiling. Tudor work appears in the chapel of the Transfiguration, and in the admirable chantry of Abbot Ramryge; while the "Gothic revival" is stamped on every feature of Lord Grimthorpe's façades to the west, north, and south. There is not a single hiatus in the series. St.

ST. ALBANS CATHEDRAL

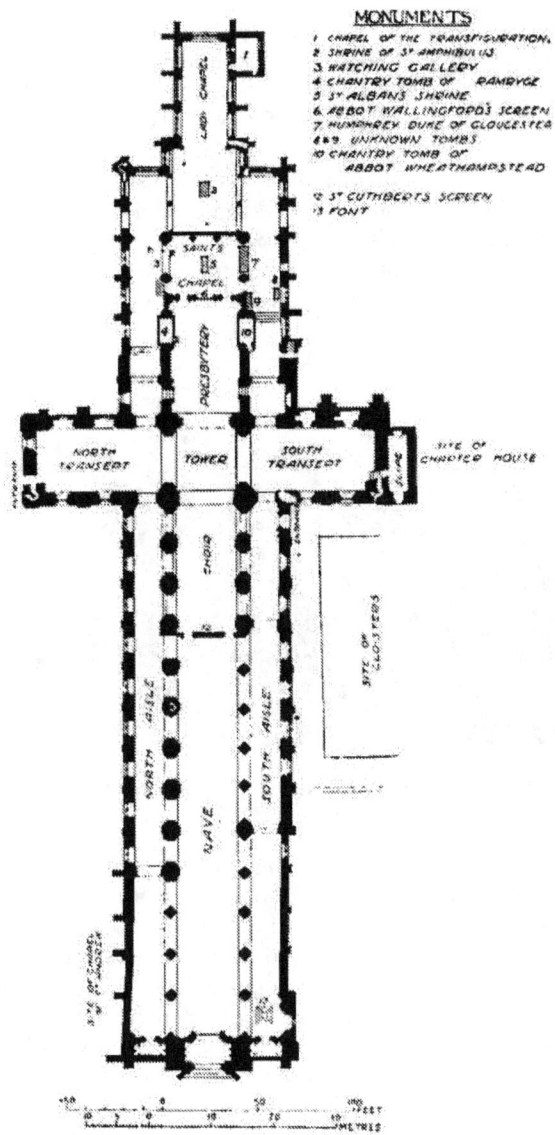

PLAN

Albans is a veritable architectural handbook, written in brick and stone. The student should remember, however, that at St. Albans there is a good deal of what is called assimilation. The two groups of Gothic bays in the nave are not typical and characteristic of their respective periods. The architects of these bays had not a free hand. They were not able to compose the design simply to suit the fashion of the day. The design was to be brought up to date only so far as might be without ruining the general appearance and proportions of the nave as a whole. With

FROM THE NORTH-WEST, SHOWING THE WEST FRONT BEFORE RESTORATION

these reservations, the tyro in architecture is recommended to select St. Albans as his "Introduction to Mediæval Architecture." If he comes from London, he should choose the longer route, by the London and North-Western Railway: he will have less distance to walk on arriving, and will see the cathedral from the most picturesque point of view. If time permits, he may proceed direct from the railway station to Verulamium, and see the Roman walls and fosse, and the interesting church of St. Michael's, with the famous monument of Lord Bacon, before visiting the cathedral.

ST. ALBANS CATHEDRAL.

In Roman times the city was on the other side of the little river, the Ver, a tributary of the Colne, and hence was called Verulamium. In the revolt of Boadicea it was burnt, but was soon rebuilt. In the year 303, "there was gret persecution of Christen pepell by the tyrant Diocletian"; and Alban, a citizen of Verulamium, who had given shelter to a Welsh priest, Amphibalus, was scourged, and then dragged along the ancient British causeway, which still exists, across the Ver, and up the lane to the top of the hill afterwards called Holmhurst, and there put to death.

FROM THE SOUTH-WEST, SHOWING THE NEW WEST FRONT

Amphibalus suffered the same fate. On the west wall of the north transept of the cathedral, just under a round-headed window, is a small black cross cut in stone. "This marks the traditional site of the martyrdom of St. Alban, when there was neither town nor abbey in this place, but only a flowery slope planted with trees." In the fifth century the English conquered the district. They abandoned Verulamium, perhaps because it was not on the main road, and built the present town on the hill of Holmhurst, calling it Watlingceaster, as Watling Street ran through it. In the year 793, Offa, King of Mercia, treacherously murdered

Ethelbert, King of East Anglia. It was revealed to him in a vision that, by way of penance, he should seek out the body of St. Alban, and there erect a monastery. King, archbishop, bishops, priests, and a great multitude of common people searched the hill of Holmhurst, and found the relics of the martyr. A church was built, and richly endowed, and was entrusted to Benedictine monks. It remained a Benedictine abbey church till the Dissolution, in 1539. Then it became a parish church, and in 1875 a cathedral.

The relics of St. Alban had an eventful history. First they were carried off by pirates to Denmark, but were afterwards restored. Then, in expectation of another Danish raid, they were sent for safety to Ely. When the Danes had gone, the monks of Ely, being desirous to keep the precious bones in their possession, palmed on the monks of St. Albans some supposititious relics. Whereupon the monks of St. Albans asserted that neither had they sent to Ely the genuine relics, but only sham ones, to draw attention away from the fact that they had hidden the authentic bones of the martyr in a hole in the wall of their own church! "*Credat Judæus Apelles.*"

Towards the end of the eleventh century Nicholas Breakspear was born at Abbots Langley, in Hertfordshire. He applied to the abbey of St. Alban to be admitted a monk, but was scornfully rejected, and rebuked for his impudence, being, as he was, son of one of the menials of the convent. This same man became Pope in 1154—the only Englishman who ever became Pope. And when he became Pope, under the title of Adrian IV., he forgot not the monks of St. Albans, but forgave them, and made their monastery free of episcopal jurisdiction for ever, and subject only to the see of Rome. And to the abbot he gave precedence over all other English abbots; which precedency, after much dispute with Westminster, St. Albans retained till the Dissolution.

In 1455 was fought the first battle of St. Albans, when Henry VI. was wounded in the neck by an arrow, and made prisoner by the Yorkists under the Earl of Warwick.

The forces met in Holywell Street between the Key and Chequer. In the second battle, 1461, the Earl of Warwick was defeated by Queen Margaret.

St. Albans was an exceedingly wealthy abbey; it had estates in almost every county in England, and at the present value of money its income would amount to at least a million. Its conventual buildings must have been immense. One of the guest halls, in addition to parlours and bedrooms, had stables for three hundred horses. Of all these vast structures nothing remains but one of the gatehouses, built *c.* 1380. In it were detained the French prisoners in the Napoleonic wars; afterwards it became a common gaol; now it houses the Grammar School.

In visiting the church, the first thing to be done is to walk the whole length of it from west to east, inspecting successively the seven divisions now to be described.

Internally, it is divided from west to east, in ancient monastic fashion, into (1) nave, (2) choir, (3) sanctuary, (4) Chapel of St. Alban, (5) Chapel of St. Amphibalus, (6) processional path or ambulatory, (7) Lady chapel. Only at Winchester can the ritualistic arrangements of a monastic or cathedral church be studied so easily and clearly. (1) The ritual *nave* occupies the ten western bays only of the architectural nave, and terminates at the Rood screen. (2) The ritual *choir* is not placed in the eastern limb; but, following a more ancient precedent, in the three eastern bays of the architectural nave, and in the crossing (that part of the transept which is beneath the central tower). This was the place of the choir in the primitive basilicas, and in the early monastic churches. The "Coro" of the Spanish cathedrals is still placed in the nave. The same arrangement survives in this country in Westminster abbey and Norwich, and has lately been restored at Peterborough. Of this space the stalls occupied the eastern part, extending up to the eastern arch of the tower; in the western part of it there was a choir screen, against which the stalls were returned, *i.e.*, backed. Between this choir screen and the existing rood screen there would be room for a couple of altars, one on either side of the central doorway of the choir screen. (3) The *sanctuary* extends from the tower to the great reredos, and provided a free space in front of the High altar. It is so long that it probably also contained, as at Westminster, a "matins" or "choir altar" placed about the centre of it. The sanctuary, with its two altars, seems to have been separated from the choir, as at St. David's, by a light wooden screen; the end of the upper portion of this screen remains imbedded in the centre of the southern pier of the tower. (4) The *Saint's Chapel* proper, that of the patron saint, was occupied, as at Westminster, by a shrine resting upon a stone pedestal (lately replaced); at Westminster the shrine or coffer contains to this day the body of St. Edward Confessor, here it contained that of St. Alban. Till the great reredos of the High altar was erected, the shrine of St. Alban would be seen all the way down the sanctuary and choir, towering up above the High altar. (5) In the next bay to the east—that on the other side of the three eastern arches of St. Alban's chapel—the shrine of St. Amphibalus was placed by Abbot de la Mare (1349-1396). (6) The next bay eastward provided a processional path, or *ambulatory*, or eastern choir aisle at the back of the shrines. (7) The Lady chapel possesses the unusual feature of a small vestibule, for two small lateral altars. At St. Albans it occupies the normal portion of a Lady chapel, viz., the extreme east. Where there was no room for further eastward extension of the cathedral, the Lady chapel may be found on the north or south side of the choir, as at Bristol and Oxford. Here, as at Salisbury and Winchester, the high roofs do not extend over the easternmost of the ritualistic divisions of the church; at York, Lincoln, and Ely the church retains its full height uninterruptedly to the extreme east end; the ritualistic divisions of the church were there marked by screens only.

In Norman times the church did not extend so far eastward. The sanctuary ended in three semicircular apses, of which those of the aisles were semicircular inside but square outside, as at Romsey. And, in lieu of eastern aisles, the transepts had each a pair of semicircular chapels, the arches leading into which may still be seen in their eastern walls; excavations shew that the inner of each pair was much longer than the other.

FIRST PERIOD.—We now retrace our steps to the *choir* and examine the Norman masonry above the new stalls. "In 1077, Paul, a monk of St. Stephen's, Caen (the Abbaye-aux-Hommes), was elected Abbot, through the influence of Archbishop Lanfranc, whose kinsman he was." In these words we have the origin of St. Albans cathedral; and not of St. Albans only, but of all the mediæval architecture of our land, whether Romanesque or Gothic. Before the Norman conquest we had a native style of our own; a kind of primitive Romanesque, of which remains survive at Jarrow, Wing, Worth, Deerhurst, and elsewhere, as well as in the crypts of Ripon, Hexham, and Repton. But the invasion of the Normans changed all this. The primitive indigenous

THE SOUTH TRANSEPT, EAST WALL.

Romanesque of England was thrown aside in favour of the far more advanced Romanesque of Normandy. From the great monastery of St. Stephen, Caen, came Lanfranc, the first, and Anselm, the second Norman Archbishop of Canterbury. When Lanfranc set to work to rebuild Canterbury cathedral, he made it in length and breadth and height an exact copy of the church of St. Stephen, Caen. What Lanfranc did at Canterbury, the Walkelins did at Winchester and Ely, and Abbot Paul at St. Albans. They set to work to rebuild the English minsters after the manner of the abbey churches of Normandy, especially St. Stephen's, Caen, and Cérisy-la-Forêt; these churches are the chief links between the eleventh-century architecture of Normandy and the eleventh and twelfth-century architecture of England.

But though in origin Winchester, Ely, St. Albans, and the rest hail from Normandy, they all far surpass their models in vastness of scale. Winchester and Ely even committed the magnificent extravagance of having a western as well as an eastern aisle to the transepts; and though St. Albans, like Canterbury, had an aisleless transept, yet its nave was set out on the same gigantic scale as the naves of the Norman churches of Winchester, Old St. Paul's, Bury St. Edmund's, Peterborough, Ely, and Norwich. In the thirteenth century three more bays were added to the nave, making the nave 292 ft. long and the whole church about 430 ft. long, while the transepts had a length of 177 ft. In the fourteenth century, owing to the eastward extensions, St. Albans became longer still—520 ft. inside, 550 ft. outside. (Winchester is even longer still: 2 yds. longer than St. Albans; 3 yds. longer than Ely; 4 yds. longer than Canterbury.)

Of the work of Paul of Caen (1077-1093), we have the central tower and transept practically complete, and large portions of the nave and sanctuary. The design is strictly conditioned by the material, Roman tiles; in consequence of the employment of which the architect was driven to rely for his effects, not on ornament or detail, but on what is nobler far, vastness of scale. It is worth while to compare the tile transept of St. Albans with the contemporary transept of Winchester, where the design is conditioned by the use of stone. The masonry consists mainly of tiles, with a large amount of flint and some stone brought from Verulamium; nearly all the tiles are 16 by 12 in., and 1½ in. thick; the joints are nearly as thick as the tiles, and cement rather than mortar was employed. All wall surfaces, both internal and external, including those of the tower, were cemented over, and no doubt the cement was whitewashed: when finished, the whole church would be white as snow, both within and without; the flint and tile work was not intended to be visible. Simple decorations were painted on the surfaces of the internal piers and arches, and have recently been restored. On the nave piers are remains of reredoses painted above altars which must have stood against the west side of the piers; those on the west faces of the piers are of the thirteenth century, those on the south are of the fourteenth. Internally the Norman church was

THE TRIFORIUM OF SOUTH TRANSEPT

divided into three stories nearly equal in height; in each bay of the triforium was a single open arch, and another in the clerestory, rather taller. The piers are compound, and the arches are semicircular and have three narrow recessed orders or sub-arches; instead of capitals, they rest on plain imposts. This rude work extends far down the nave on the north.

If now we pass from the choir into the *south aisle*, we see overhead some of the original groined, *i.e.*, unribbed, vaulting, of rubble. In the triforium of the *south transept*, hard by, the balusters are Anglo-Saxon, provided with additional Norman capitals. Below the balustered stage are seen blocked arches, which led to two apses now gone. The Norman church is said to have been finished in 1088, but it was not consecrated till 1110; what was finished in 1088

THE SOUTH ARCADE, LOOKING WEST

probably was the eastern part of the church as far west as the Norman Choir screen.

SECOND PERIOD.—To the second half of the twelfth century belongs the fine arcade and doorway removed from the slype, *i.e.*, the passage on the other side of the doorway, to the *south wall of the south transept* by Lord Grimthorpe. He is good enough to tell us that the new work which he has interpolated in it is so artful that no archæologist in future shall be able to ascertain which portions are old and which are new.

THIRD PERIOD.—We now walk down the nave and out into the open air by one of the *western doorways*. Vast as was the Norman nave, it was still not enough in the eyes of the thirteenth-century builders. It was resolved to add three bays to it, and to put up a fine west front, which, after the manner of Bury, Peterborough, Lincoln, and Wells, was to have flanking towers. They began at the west end of

THE CHOIR TRIFORIUM, SOUTH SIDE

the nave. First, John de Cella in 1198 proceeded to build a new *west front* on a lovely design, and with a wealth of costly marble and carving. Of this work there remain portions in the north-west and central porches of the façade.

FOURTH PERIOD.—We now return into the church and look at the westernmost bays on each side of the *nave*. John de Cella's successor, William de Trumpington, was more economical, and produced more work. He completed the porches, and built in the *western end of the nave* four bays on the north and five bays on the south side. It can still be seen how he economised, not only on John de Cella's design, in the arch that was to have led into a south-western tower, but on the design of his own bases, piers, and vaulting-shafts, leaving places for marble shafts which he never put in; he even renounced the idea of vaulting his work at all —a very ungothic procedure.

FIFTH PERIOD. —We now pass up the nave to the *sanctuary*, where the next work was done. The nave was now completed, but it is recorded that the eastern part of the church had become ruinous. It is difficult to see how that could be considering the enormous massiveness of the walls, unless, indeed, the sanctuary had a high vault against whose thrusts adequate abutment had not been provided. Anyhow, the Norman apse was demolished, and all of the side walls of the sanctuary except the ground story; if these had been removed the tower might have collapsed. Note the coloured altar-piece in high relief by Mr Alfred Gilbert; in which is represented the Resurrection in a highly original way.

ST. ALBAN'S SHRINE

Soon after, the lower parts of the *Saint's chapel* and the eastern chapels were built; these were not completely finished till *c.* 1315. There, too, "vaulting ambition had o'erleapt itself": the monks made preparations for a stone vault—inside, the springers of vault ribs are to be seen, outside, the places where the flying buttresses were to have been inserted in the wall—but in the end they put up a flat wooden ceiling, recently repainted.

SIXTH PERIOD.—Passing on into the *Lady chapel*, we see the last of the eastern extensions. Begun *c.* 1300, it was ready for glazing in 1308. Notice the tracery of the windows and the trails of ball-flower in their jambs; also the admirable leaf-carving, designed and executed by Mr John Baker, an epitome of local botany.

THE WATCHING LOFT

SEVENTH PERIOD. —The monks had now done all they meant to do. The eastern limb was rebuilt. They meant to do no more in the nave. But their hands were forced. In 1323 five Norman bays collapsed on the south side of the nave, and the monks had perforce to rebuild them. And as the walls fell on the cloister, that had to be rebuilt also, as may be seen outside. The design of the new bays of the nave is closely assimilated to that of the thirteenth-century bays to the west; the clerestory actually having lancet windows without tracery; but the tooth ornament is replaced by the ball-flower.

EIGHTH PERIOD.—The rest consists of minor work, but of the greatest importance and interest. Pass once more eastwards towards the Lady chapel, and turn to the left into the north choir aisle. (1) Here have been put together fragments of the shrine pedestal of *St. Amphibalus, c.* 1350. (2) A little further west, on the left, is the back of the Watching Loft, with delicate carving of the "Months." (3) Passing into the Saint's chapel, in the centre is the shrine pedestal of *St. Alban, c.* 1308. (4) Its treasures

THE REREDOS

were watched by monks stationed in the upper floor of the oak Watching Loft, in the lower part of which are cupboards for relics (1420). (5) Opposite is the monument of *Duke Humphrey of Gloucester*, with the original palisades (1447). Returning to the *south aisle*, a few steps to the right is the immense brass, not *in situ*, executed in Flanders, of *Abbot de la Mare* (1396). Then entering the *sanctuary* again, on the south is the chantry chapel, which, from the presence of wheat ears in a shield, has usually been attributed to Abbot Wheathamstead; it is, however, that of Abbot William of Wallingford, who erected the great reredos, where also a shield with wheat ears occurs; on the north is that of *Abbot Ramryge*—rams with RYGE on the collar.

The great *reredos* to the east was put up between 1476 and 1484. The fine stalls in the *choir* are by Mr J. O. Scott. The visit ends with the pretty seventeenth-century bread cupboards affixed to the west wall of the *south transept*.

In recent times vast sums have been spent in underpinning and securing the walls and tower; and we have had a commonplace west front and atrocious transept ends designed by Lord Grimthorpe.

BIBLIOGRAPHY.—Messrs Buckler, *History of the Architecture of Saint Albans*.

Neale's *St. Albans*.

Guide Book by Sir Edmund Beckett.

Paper by Mr John Chapple, Clerk of the Works, in *St. Alban Archit. and Archæol. Society*, January 1874.

Victoria County History of Hertfordshire, vol. ii. p. 483.

FROM THE RIVER

THE CATHEDRAL CHURCH OF ST. MARY, SALISBURY

BUILT FOR SECULAR CANONS

TWO English cathedrals surpass all others in external effect: Lincoln and Salisbury; each of them at its best as seen from the north-east. But Lincoln lacks "the quiet tranquillity of the close of Salisbury, the half-hidden houses, covered with vine and creepers, that nestle among the trees, the sense of being shut off from the work-a-day world. If Durham seems the petrified interpretation of the Church militant, Salisbury is the very type and picture of the Church of the Prince of Peace. Unworldliness and peace brood over church and close."

The ancient Norman cathedral stood within the fortifications of Old Sarum. The site was cramped, and extension was impossible; there was too much wind and too little water; moreover, the soldiers who garrisoned the castle were objectionable neighbours. So, by permission of the

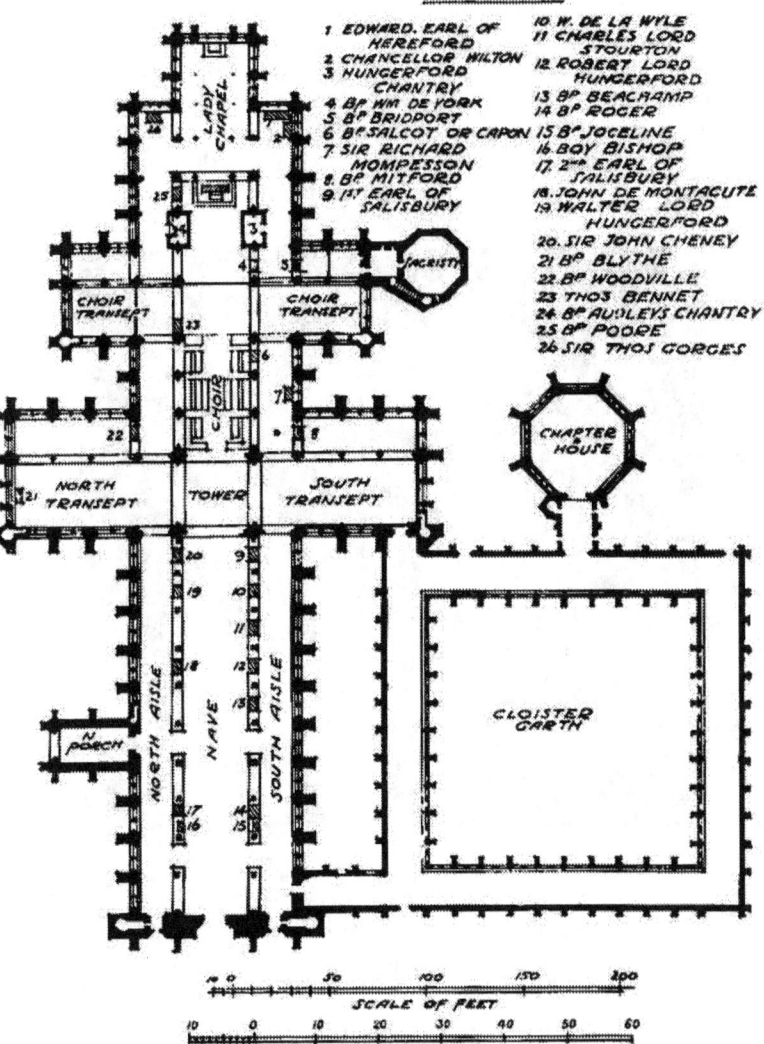

PLAN

Pope, Bishop Richard Poore in 1220 commenced a new cathedral on the present site.

It was a virgin site: and from this fact resulted a cathedral different from any other in England, and as a study in design more important than any other we possess. In other cathedrals we study the mediæval architect designing under difficulties; what we see in

THE NAVE, LOOKING WEST

such a composite cathedral as Hereford or Chichester or Rochester is not one design, but half a dozen designs trying to blend into one design; sometimes, as at Canterbury and Rochester, rather ineffectually, sometimes, as at Beverley and Westminster, with remarkable success. At Salisbury it is not so: the design is one design; all sprang from a single brain, except the west front and the upper part of tower and spire. We have no such homogeneous design in our mediæval cathedrals. The French were less conservative; their Gothic architects were iconoclasts; no French architect could have allowed such solecisms to remain as disfigure the English cathedrals to the purist eye, and endear them to the artist.

THE CHOIR, LOOKING EAST

Bishop Poore's architect had—what no other of our Gothic architects had—a free hand. Salisbury, then, tells us what no other cathedral does—what an English architect thought a cathedral ought to be like, when not hampered by having to preserve or assimilate pre-existing work or to build on pre-existing foundations. Canterbury nave is not the best the architect could do: it is the best he could do subject to the restriction that his nave must be neither longer nor broader than Lanfranc's ancient nave. Here there were no such restrictions; the cathedral was to be built in the green pastures, and there was plenty of room. It has the distinction among our cathedrals of having a design which is practically uniform. It is said, indeed, and with perfect truth, that the homogeneity and uniformity of the design of Salisbury makes it less interesting than the usual composite cathedral of England, with its design changing, as in Binham and Selby naves, almost in every bay. When we have seen one bay of Salisbury nave, we have seen the other nine, and we know that we shall find practically the same design in the choir. Yet we can afford very well, in England, to have one great design, the product not of a dozen minds, but of one mind; a work completed in less than half a century, and not spread out, like Canterbury, over four centuries, or like Hereford, over seven.

Again, building on a virgin site, the architect did what all great builders have always wished to do—he made his building symmetrical. It is the fashion to contrast the symmetry of Greek with the picturesqueness of Gothic architecture. The comparison may be carried too far. The Erechtheum is as unsymmetrical and picturesque as any Gothic building. The great cathedrals of northern France, and Salisbury and Exeter, are quite classical in their symmetry. But they are not pedantic in their symmetry. Because nave balances choir, the north transept the south transept, and the north-east transept the south-east transept, the builder was not so foolish as to construct on the south a big porch to balance that on the north side of the nave. Instead of that, he built to the south an octagonal Chapter house, and this he placed unsymmetrically—*i.e.*, picturesquely—because, so placed, it was more to the convenience of those who would have to use it. In other words, he did not purposefully aim at the picturesque and the irregular. Gothic cathedrals are picturesque, either of accident, as at Canterbury, owing to the casual collocation of work of different

FROM THE NORTH-EAST

design in the course of several centuries, or because the different parts of the cathedral, being intended for different functions, have been designed different in plan, in dimensions, and in details. The latter is the case with Salisbury.

Two chief types of cathedral plan were at the architect's disposal: what we may call the York type, and the Wells type. In the latter, the cathedral continues at full height from the western doors to the far east of the presbytery; then the retro-presbytery (sometimes divided into Saint's chapel and procession path or ambulatory) is roofed at a lower level, and east of it is a Lady chapel, similarly on a low level. And, of course, as the upper wall of the east end of the sanctuary requires to be supported, arches have to be built beneath it opening from the sanctuary into the retro-presbytery. The plan is a beautiful one—it is our English equivalent for the "chevets" of northern France. Externally, the different portions of the eastern limb tell distinctly the purposes for which they are built: standing to the east of Winchester, or Wells, or Hereford, you say at once, "This building is the Lady chapel; there is the procession path and probably the shrine of the local saint, there is the east end of the sanctuary, and the light from that east window at the early morning services streams down on the High altar below." Internally, too, the effect is delightful; the upper story of the cathedral is, of course, really greatly curtailed in length, but the interior is not shortened to the eye: the mysterious vistas through the east arches of the presbytery more than restore the height lost above; the glimpses of Lady chapel behind ambulatory, and ambulatory behind Saint's chapel, as seen from far west in the nave, make the termination of the Lady chapel, invisible from many points of view, seem infinitely distant. Of these mysterious distances, shadowy recesses and changing vistas, there is nothing in such an interior as that of York; the whole eastern limb is seen at a single glance, and, unfortunately, is foreshortened by the eye. Salisbury internally looks longer than it is, York much shorter. In mediæval days, however, the ritualistic divisions of churches were marked off by a series of screens, each adding apparent length to the interior. So many of these screens, however, have been swept away by Wyatt, Scott, and the like, or replaced by paltry open work, as at Lichfield and Durham, that many cathedrals are now mere open barns; all sense of mystery, all sense of magnitude gone. Externally, York, Lincoln, and Ely have the best of it. The sweep of a skyline, 500 ft. in length, at a height so vast, is sublimely impressive. The cost of an exterior kept at an unbroken height for such a distance is very great, but it is worth the cost.

Cathedrals of the latter type are quite presentable with a central tower of moderate height, provided that it is reinforced by more important towers to the west. An exterior of the former type, that of Wells and Salisbury, demands an important central tower. Accordingly, every cathedral of this type has a big central tower, viz., Gloucester, St. Albans, St. David's, Wells; Exeter has two central towers; Chichester and Hereford had both central tower and spire. (Winchester is an exception which proves how much a lofty central tower is needed.) In such exteriors, looked at from the east, hills rise beyond hills, alps beyond alps, and the eye instinctively looks up to see the highest ranges aspire into the pyramidal outline of a Matterhorn. And this is what is given us at Salisbury.

It is not, however, what the original architect meant. No spire, or even upper tower, says Sir Christopher Wren, was originally contemplated, any more than at Westminster. The slenderness of the piers of the crossing is certain evidence of that. The diameter of the piers on which the central tower of Canterbury rests is 12 ft.; those at York, Norwich, and Winchester have a diameter of 10 ft.; those at Worcester 9 ft.; those of Peterborough tower (which collapsed) and of Salisbury, 7 ft. only. It is almost terrible to stand between these four slight piers of Salisbury and think how many hundred tons of stone in tower and spire above they have been made to bear. They were never meant to bear any such weight, especially planted as they are, like the whole cathedral, on the insecure foundation of a spongy bog. Indeed, not merely the tower and spire, but the whole cathedral, ought never to have been built where they are. Recklessness is by no means a strong enough word to use of the mediæval builders' wanton carelessness about foundations. Peterborough cathedral was built practically without foundations on water-logged peat; beneath the central tower of Carlisle cathedral were two running springs; Wells is reared on the boggy shores of a ring of pools. "Salisbury," a local saying goes, "is the sink of Wiltshire, and the cathedral close is the sink of Salisbury." In the cathedral continuous bases are built from pier to pier.

XVTH CENTURY STONE GIRDERS IN TRANSEPT

The original design, no doubt, was to give us an exterior something like that of Beverley minster or Westminster abbey. The whole elevation of the cathedral, however, clamoured for a tall tower and spire. The first design was abandoned, and the foolhardy enterprise was taken in hand (c. 1320) of adding to the existing tower, which only just rose above the roofs, two more stages, and on these a spire, and that not of wood, but of stone. To abut the tower as much as possible, great flying buttresses were added, some external, others running through the clerestory and triforium of the interior of the church. Moreover, to lessen the weight, the tower walls were built in thin shells; while the spire, which for 20 ft. is 24 in. thick, is reduced thenceforth to 9 in. That the builders left their timber scaffolding in the spire, where it still is, to give its sides a little additional support against wind pressure, shews that they were alive themselves to the fragility and insecurity of their work. Later on, in the fifteenth century, stone girders were put across the piers of the central and eastern transepts, as at Canterbury and Wells, by way of struts, to keep the piers from bulging inwardly, though, as a matter of fact, ties were wanted quite as much to keep them from bulging outwardly.

Externally, however, the madness of this engineering feat does not trouble one. The addition of the tower and spire gives to the whole composition that pyramidal outline which always presents such a satisfactory appearance of stability to the eye. In Wren's masterpiece, St. Paul's, one has the same central pyramidal outline of all the masses, but in a still higher degree. In both cases, in St. Paul's and in Salisbury, unity is secured. Salisbury spire is tall enough, St. Paul's dome is tall and broad enough, to impose unity on all the diverging masses of the building. The low towers of Worcester and Hereford have no such supreme dominance.

Next to the abiding presence of the spire, unity is secured by scoring strong, horizontal lines round the building, welding its masses into one composition. Most cathedrals are contented, like Wells, with one strong horizontal line— a broad parapet. But at Salisbury there is not only a horizontal parapet, but a horizontal corbel table as well; and there are no less than three horizontal strings—one running round the base of the walls, a second running along beneath the windows, and a third running round the buttresses; moreover, each of these horizontal lines is scored far more heavily than anywhere else. Especially remarkable is it to find the upper flow of the buttresses stopped by a heavy string. Equally strong is the determination to keep in check the vertical lines of the interior. Bold string-courses, above and beneath the triforium, emphasise the horizontal lines of the whole church, from west to east, from north to south; nor are the vaulting-shafts allowed to descend to the floor story; so that the pier-arcade of the nave is tied by the string courses to the west front of the tower, and not to the vault above. How gladly would he have tied together the bays of his vault by a horizontal ridge-rib; but this the Lincoln folk had not invented when Salisbury was set out. Usually, in Gothic, if a horizontal meets a vertical line, the former gives way; here, as in Greek architecture, the vertical gives way to the horizontal line. This architect saw, what few others of his day saw, that you may make too much of the "aspiring principle" of Gothic; that if you suppress the horizontal lines, you weaken the unity of the building, by failing to tie all its parts together.

As we have seen, the appearance of stability was enhanced by the pyramidal outline which the whole building ultimately assumed. But the eye instinctively looks downwards also to see that the pyramidal outline is continued there; it instinctively demands an emphatic spreading base. It likes to see a rock-like foundation. At Salisbury all below is but greensward. All the more carefully, therefore, has the builder spread out and broadened and emphasised his base-courses, till art gives the appearance of stability which nature had denied.

Stable, therefore, below and above, the exterior of Salisbury has much of that "monumental appearance, stability, and indeterminate duration" which is the attribute of a great architecture, which one desiderates in a building "built not for time, but for eternity, whose walls will long be washed by the passing waves of humanity." Such a building gravity and simplicity befit; its design should be solid and monumental, sober and restrained; it is not a field for the frippery of ornament; its best decoration is the stain of time. Built for eternity, it should suggest infinity—

an infinite length which the eye cannot measure, an infinite height which the eye cannot estimate, a vastness of area that overpowers the imagination. Bigness counts for much in the painter's work and the sculptor's; it counts for yet more in architecture. A building in the grand style has to be big, and if it is a Gothic building it has to look bigger still. Salisbury is really big: it is 473 ft. long, its spire is 404 ft. high, its vaulted roof, 84 ft. high, is the highest of any English cathedral. But the eye does not measure in feet. Salisbury spire and Louth spire, acute and slender, look hundreds of feet above their real height; Oxford and Chichester spires look lower than they really are. As for length, follow the wall of Salisbury from east to west. As you pass round cape and headland and promontory, you forget the point from which you started, or the goal for which you are bound. How foreshortened in comparison is the long façade of Pitti Palace! As for area, in all honesty Mr Whittington gravely declared that Salisbury was "a much larger church altogether than Amiens." The error was natural. Amiens has fewer parts than Salisbury, and necessarily seems smaller. Going round Salisbury we pass no less than seven façades, at Amiens only three. There are thirty-nine bays in Amiens; in Salisbury there are sixty. As usual, multiplicity of parts produces apparent increase of magnitude.

Much of the impressiveness of the exterior is due, not only to its grandeur of scale, both real and apparent, but to the lovely hue of the stone of which it is built, and the perfection of the masonry. At first sight the appearance of the masonry of Salisbury is almost uncanny. Salisbury is not mouldered or corroded with age. "Time prints no wrinkles on its brow." Its antiquity is that of a goddess ever young. The masonry, too, is that of a Greek temple; the precision that of the builders of the Parthenon; the joints fine; the blocks squared with mathematical precision; pass round the building from south transept eastward to north transept, and you will find that the stones in each course preserve their height with utmost exactness all these hundreds of feet. And so the building has the feeling of Greece in it. Gothic is a "small-stone" style, with joints openly displayed. Here, as in a Parthenon, the joints are practically invisible; the whole building seems one solid block —a monumental effect indeed. The crumbling masonry of Ely might belong to the ancient days of Saturn; Salisbury seems the work of a younger race of gods. Only when we scan its colour—the lovely colour of the Salisbury stone, that is seen nowhere else —"a pale, ashy grey, stained below with broad patches of red and yellow lichens"—do we realise that this is no temple of yesterday, but one that has faced the stress of storm for more than six centuries. Her perpetual juvenility is at once the charm and the disappointment of Salisbury.

Very noteworthy, also, are the sobriety and restraint and repose of the whole design: very ungothic, too. At first it passes unnoticed; after a time it is noticed—and noticed with astonishment—that the beauty of a design of consummate loveliness is gained in some mysterious way with hardly any use of ornament. One realises at Salisbury —perhaps for the first time—that ornament is non-essential even in Gothic design. What ornament there is is of the slightest—a floriated finial to a buttress, a trefoiled corbel-table, a few foliated capitals round the High altar; the design would be little the worse if even this trifling amount of decoration were omitted.

The success of the exterior of Salisbury depends, not on the littlenesses of architectural design, but on the great leading factors of every great style—vastness of scale, yet further enhanced to the eye by multiplicity of parts; bold handling of the masses, combined nevertheless into a symmetrical whole: unity, harmony, proportion, shadow-effects. Beside these elemental factors, sculptured ornament is but "mint and cummin."

Straighten out Salisbury cathedral in imagination, till Lady chapel and retro-choir and eastern transepts and choir and central transepts and nave are all in one long straight line. Then let it resume its shape, and you will see what is meant by "bold handling of the masses," and the difference it makes. Nevertheless, don't go away with the idea that the lines of Salisbury cathedral were pulled about in this way for picturesqueness' sake—for the sake of effect. The Gothic architects—*pace* Peterborough west front—did not design for effect. All the parts of the building are there either for some constructional or for some ritualistic reason. A central tower weights the piers of the crossing in the same fashion as pinnacles do buttresses; a big central tower will not stand without abutment to the north and south; therefore there has to be a central transept. The long stretch of clerestory wall—which in the church as first built had no external flying buttresses—will be all the better for the support of two transepts and a lofty porch: they are added. Transepts, moreover, were useful in providing chapel-room for various great saints of Christendom, as well as for the local saints of the cathedral, and they provided altars where each of the forty-two canons should say his daily Mass. The porch is useful as providing neutral ground for various functions—half religious, half secular; the porch is added. And so with the Chapter house. Every one of the appanages which make a Gothic exterior so picturesque was built, not because it would be picturesque, but because it would be useful. The one exception is the spire.

And see what pits and abysses of shadow lurk behind each projecting buttress, and still more in each deep sound that runs inland, like some Norwegian fiord, between towering precipices on either side. But these grand shadow-effects—varying from minute to minute as the sun moves round—varying from day to day as summer treads on spring, autumn on summer—were not in the designer's first intent. The projecting masses had to be there; the play of light and shadow which ensued, he did not plan; he only welcomed it. He had little control over it; in the windows, indeed, which were within his control, he made the jambs so shallow that the windows are externally almost shadowless; almost the whole depth of the window he gave to the interior, preferring to enrich the interior of each window with an inner arcade—feeling, doubtless, that he need do nothing externally to add to the shadow-effects of the projecting buttresses.

But the life-blood of an architectural design is proportion. Unfortunately one never notices its presence. Only when a building is out of proportion does one recognise that such a thing as proportion exists. And as it is the most subtle, so it is the most important factor in design—design small or large—Salisbury cathedral, the Pandolphini Palace, a Chippendale chair, or a Wedgewood vase. Alter the shape of the vase, and see the difference. In the same way, see if you can lengthen or shorten Salisbury nave for the better, or the transepts, or the porch, or the Lady chapel; or if you could heighten the Lady chapel or retro-choir to advantage; or if you could make the roofs an inch more acute or more flat. The proportions of this, as of every really great building, are subtle in the extreme and interlock in every direction. Each part is in proportion to the whole; each part is in proportion to contiguous parts; and each individual bit of each part is in proportion to the rest of it. More than that —the proportions of the nave, choir, transepts, &c., are those which are suitable to a church 473 ft. long and 404 ft. high. If you built a church with a nave, choir, and transepts exactly twice as large as those of Salisbury, it would not be in proportion, but out of proportion. The same lack of proportion would ensue if you copied the design of Salisbury in a parish church of exactly half its dimensions. Salisbury cathedral, like the Parthenon, cannot be copied with impunity, unless you preserve not the dimensions but the ratios. Modern designers, not recognising this, have too often wrought themselves disappointment by unintelligent imitations of ancient work.

To the north and south another charming effect is seen in the gradual growth of the ornament upward. This is to the credit of Time, and not of the architect. From 1220 to 1330 window-tracery was ever growing richer day by day, and Salisbury cathedral was ever growing upward. And so the ornament culminates most rightly, yet most accidentally, in the higher stories of the transepts, in the tower and spire.

Finally, nature has come to the aid of art. In France the cathedral is a town church; it rises precipitous from the narrow lane or the huxtering of the "place," its flanks hemmed in by squalid shops, in front a sahara of dust. Here great elms branch up from emerald turf, each giving scale to cathedral and spire; while all around are the creepers and flowers, and warm brick and mouldering stone

THE LADY CHAPEL, LOOKING WEST

of canons' houses. Surely there is no more lovely environment upon earth.

Only one criticism suggests itself before we leave Salisbury cathedral as seen from the north-east. Are not the voids in excess—two windows in the aisles and three in the clerestory, where one would produce a more monumental and solid effect? Such single windows, filled with the opaque grisaille glass of the period, would have subdued the glare of the interior. But I have not the slightest doubt that the critics of the day infinitely preferred the uniform good lighting of Salisbury to the "dim, religious light" of Lincoln and its darksome corners and recesses. In Salisbury there is not a quiet spot anywhere where you can pray in peace; the blinding light pursues you everywhere. But good people in those days liked a cheerful church—full of light, sparkling with stained glass, brilliant with gilding and paint: religious gloom had not yet become fashionable; it did not come in till the time of the Puritans. In every other respect in Salisbury, as in Lincoln minster, internal seems to have been subordinated to external effect.

JUNCTION OF CHOIR AND NORTH TRANSEPT (UNDER THE CENTRAL TOWER).

The interior is, indeed, very fine. It could hardly help being fine; a nave so spacious and so proportioned could under no circumstances be a failure. It is immensely high, and is long in proportion. The proportion of height to span ($2\frac{1}{2}$ to 1) is better than in most English churches. The harmony of the design — practically the same from east to west, and from north to south—is unique in England, and is most impressive. The Lady chapel is a miniature church, with nave and aisles duly adjusted for three eastern altars. But, as in

Lincoln nave, to the eye every support is alarmingly insufficient for the work it has to do; the piers are too tall and slender, the walls too thin, and pierced with too many openings. The triforium is an unfortunate design. In West-

THE WEST FRONT

minster and Lincoln presbyteries and Lichfield nave, two arches are placed in each bay of the triforium arcade. If both these be set under a common containing arch, as in York transept and Bayeux choir, the triforium arcade has to be heightened so much that it has to be given height which ought to form part of the clerestory. This the Salisbury architect saw; and he got out of the difficulty by flattening his containing arch, producing a form utterly out of harmony with every arch of the cathedral. In his arcade, moreover, he makes great use of Purbeck marble shafts; yet it was not to be expected that its dark marble shafts would tell against a dark background—black on black. Add to this the dreadfully new look of everything—partly due to the very perfection

THE CLOISTERS

of the masonry, partly because Scott has been here—and the overpowering glare: one almost feels as if one were in the Crystal Palace. But this will be remedied as more of the windows receive good modern grisaille glass. Begun in 1220, the whole cathedral, except west front, tower, and spire, was complete in 1258, having cost what is equivalent to nearly half a million of our money.

As this was not a church of Regulars, the whole of the nave and probably the central transept were accessible to the laity. The choir screen stood under the eastern arch of the tower and had two altars west of it. The choir occupied three bays, as did the presbytery; the High altar, dedicated in honour of the Assumption of the Blessed Mary, was placed one bay further to the west than at present, as may be seen from the foliation of the capitals and from the representation of "Our Lord in Glory" painted on the vault. In the bay now occupied by the High altar was probably the altar of St. Osmund, whose tomb, however, was in the Lady chapel, where also his shrine was erected on his canonisation in 1456. East of the three eastern arches was the procession aisle. Then came the Lady chapel, three bays long, flanked by chapels. In the Lady chapel there were three altars; that is why it has three aisles and three gables. There was room in the transepts for ten altars. The cathedral therefore was planned for a minimum of eighteen altars, all placed due north and south. There were ultimately at least twenty-seven altars. The plan is typically English, and satisfies every single requirement of ritual.

INTERIOR OF THE CHAPTER HOUSE

To this superb cathedral was tacked on quite the worst façade in England; replacing the twin towers which originally no doubt were intended. The cloister was not at first contemplated; when therefore it was erected, it could not be built up to the south aisle of the nave, but had to be built detached; its date may be c. 1270. The Chapter house is a little later; beneath the pavement were found several pennies of Edward I., who came to the throne in 1272; the sculptures of its doorway are particularly fine.

BIBLIOGRAPHY. Francis Price's *Observations on Salisbury Cathedral*, 1774.

W. H. Jones, *Fasti Ecclesiae Sarisberiensis*, 1879.

Dayman and Jones' *Statutes and Ordinances of Salisbury Cathedral*. Privately printed in 1883.

Canon Wordsworth's *Ceremonies and Processions of the Cathedral Church of Salisbury*, 1901.

THROUGH THE CLOISTERS

THE CATHEDRAL CHURCH OF ST. SAVIOUR, SOUTHWARK

BUILT FOR AUGUSTINIAN CANONS

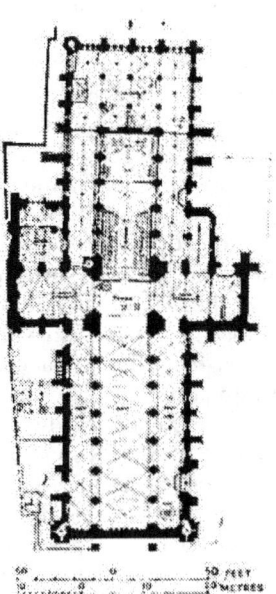

THE original dedication of the church was to St. Mary Overie. Like many other churches, it received a sound Protestant dedication *temp*. Henry VIII. It is probable that St. Mary-over-the-Rie merely means St. Mary-over-the-river; just as in Norfolk Burnham Overy is a village separated by a small stream from the other Burnhams. Stow tells a story that the first church was founded by Mary Overy, whose father, John Overy, possessed the tolls of the ferry across the river, where now is London Bridge; and that with the wealth inherited from him she built a house of sisters here. Probably, however, the whole story was elaborated to account for the etymology. Stow goes on to say that St. Swithun, Bishop of Winchester from 852 to 862, refounded the nunnery as a college of priests, *i.e.*, Secular Canons. Up to the Reformation the diocese of Winchester extended east to the south of London, and included St. Mary Overie; moreover the great palace of the Bishop of Winchester was next door to the church. From the first great interest was taken in St. Mary Overie by bishops of Winchester, St. Swithun, Peter de Rupibus, Cardinal Beaufort, Richard Fox, and Lancelot Andrewes.

In 1106 its constitution was once more changed, and it was handed over to Regular Canons of the Augustinian order as a Priory, and was served by these Austin Canons up to 1540, when the house was dissolved, and under the new name of St. Saviour, the collegiate church became parochial. In 1897 it was made collegiate once more, and became a cathedral in 1905.

FIRST PERIOD.—Of the church built soon after 1106 some portions remain. They include the wall of the north aisle of the nave, in which, towards the west, is a tomb recess with a Norman segmental arch; and to the east, the eastern of the two processional doorways. The banded shafts and bases with the "spur" ornament and the Corinthianesque capitals point to a date early in the twelfth century for this doorway. The four piers of the central tower are enormously massive, and no doubt contain a Norman core of rubble cased over with Gothic ashlar. The thick north wall of the transept, in which may be seen a fragment of a sculptured Norman string, appears to be of still earlier date. Norman also is the double chapel, that of St. John the Divine, east of the transept. But while the scalloped capitals of this double entrance point to a twelfth-century date, the fragmentary shafts and string in the north-eastern corner of the chapel are just as clearly Norman work of the eleventh century. Putting these data together, it results that the Norman nave was probably of the same dimensions as the present one, as was its narrow northern aisle. But as the present southern aisle is wider than the northern one, it is possible that it was added at some later period; it may be, indeed, that, as originally built, the Norman church had an aisle on the north side only. It had a crossing and central tower, and a northern transept of the same dimensions as at present; and no doubt a corresponding southern transept. An eastern limb of some sort it must have had; doubtless this would be but short, containing merely the presbytery.

The puzzle of the church is that the foundations of an apse have been found, set centrally in the eastern chapel of the north transept, and occupying the whole breadth of it. Since the rectangular chapel is eleventh-century work, the apse must belong to a still earlier period. Two explanations may be offered. (1) It has been assumed that it is the eastern apse of a Pre-Conquest transept. The objection is that this is to assume a type of plan which is common enough in Norman work, but which is not known to have been in use in any Anglo-Saxon example. (2) That being so, it seems likely that it is the apse of the Pre-Conquest church of the Secular Canons; its nave would extend west across and beyond the transept. This apse was superseded by a large rectangular presbytery built by the Secular Canons in the latter half of the eleventh century, which may itself have had an apse east of the present east wall of the chapel. In 1106 came the Austin Canons, who retained the chapel; but, as they wished to build a lofty north transept, substituted a double arch for the previous single arch of entrance, which would have been unable to carry the weight of the east wall of the transept.

SECOND PERIOD.—The next event was the rebuilding both of the eastern and western limbs by Bishop Peter de Rupibus (1205-1238); this was partly brought about by the damage done by a fire in 1213; as regards the eastern limb it was also due no doubt to the desire to increase the length of the presbytery and to provide it with a procession path, and in addition to erect four eastern chapels. As at Gloucester, there was no local saint, and therefore no need to provide a saints' chapel. The High altar stood where it stands now, or perhaps a little more to the west, and the whole of the space up to the central tower formed the presbytery. The choir was in the crossing; which is one step higher than the nave; the piers of the central tower are flat-faced so that stalls might be placed against them. The choir screen was beneath the western arch of the tower; and the rood screen was one bay further to the west. Both the Norman transepts, with their chapels, seem to have been left untouched. The retro-choir, which really is a retro-presbytery, contains a procession path and four chapels, each of which is two bays deep. Underneath each of the four eastern windows would be an altar; the piscina of the northernmost of the four remains; another has been found, and blocked up. From the presbytery there opened into the retro-choir two

THE CHOIR LOOKING WEST

open arches now closed. The plan is a reduced version of that of the mother church at Winchester. A similar plan, on a still smaller scale, is seen in the church of the Cistercian abbey at Dore, Herefordshire. Of this admirably planned church all that was east of the crossing remains, but largely restored by Mr Groilt (1821-1832), the exterior being wholly new. The design of the presbytery is a remarkable one. Though not commenced till after the fire of 1213, it altogether lacks the lightness and grace of

Lincoln choir and Winchester retro-choir, still more that of its contemporaries, Salisbury cathedral and the Temple choir, London. It is kept as low as possible; and the piers, though short, are exceedingly thick, as are the arches and walling which they support. The triforium arcade is reinforced by a solid wall behind. Evidently no confidence was felt by this architect in the new-fangled system of relying for stability on buttresses and flying buttresses: at Southwark he relies on thickness of wall, and that wall kept as low as possible. Nor is there any of that profuse use of Purbeck marble which, even before the twelfth century was ended, Canterbury choir had taught Durham and Chichester and Lincoln. Remove all the pointed arches and substitute semicircular ones, and the church would be seen to be what it is—almost as Romanesque in construction and in feeling as Malmesbury.

The nave has been rebuilt by Sir Arthur Blomfield from very careful drawings of the thirteenth-century nave made by Mr Dollman; the historic value of the reproduction is, however, gravely diminished by wholesale deviations from the drawings. It is said that the nave was originally vaulted, and that its flying buttresses were removed *temp.* Richard II. occasioning the fall of the vault. Then it was roofed in wood, and this roof remained till 1831, when the nave was demolished. (A new nave was built in 1838, which in turn was pulled down in 1890.) The surviving bosses of the old roof are piled up in the north transept; one of them has the rebus of Prior Burton (1462-1486), "three burs or thistles on a barrel." Between the south-west doorway of the nave and the west end of the interior of the church there remains part of the original arcading of the aisle walls: at one place a corbel has been substituted at some later period for a shaft; this has been repeated in the new arcading of the west wall. The south-west porch is one of the finest we possess, and bears comparison even with the western porches of Ely and St. Albans; authority for it is to be found in an old print of Hollar. The second piers from the west were originally very big and massive, and they carried a very broad arch;

evidently the church was planned to receive a large square tower as broad as the nave, and engaged in the aisles. Whether any such tower was ever carried up is not known. The presbytery and retro-choir have simple quadripartite vaulting; it should be noted that the wall-ribs die away into the web, and that the spring of the vaulting cells is of pronounced "plough-share" form, in order to block the light from the windows as little as possible.

THIRD PERIOD.—At some date later than 1273 the Archbishop of York is recorded to have promised thirty days' indulgence to all who helped in the good work at St. Mary Overie. We assign, therefore, to the last quarter of the thirteenth century certain large windows with geometrical tracery, as well as the greater task of remodelling the Norman north transept. The three walls of the transept were cased over with lofty pointed arcading. On the east side, as now, there was a central pier between two Norman arches. This fixed the position of the two northern arches of the arcading. But the space left for the southern arch was too narrow; hence its present truncated form. On the south side of the transept are bases greatly stilted; evidently a solid wall of considerable height blocked off this transept from the crossing. It looks as if on this side of the church of St. Mary there was what was practically a distinct church of St. John the Divine, of which the north transept formed the choir, and the Harvard chapel the sanctuary. At the same time there may have been in the transept other altars, the position of one of which is indicated by the aumbrey in the north wall.

Not much later may be placed the work in the lower half of the west wall of the south transept; two examples survive of naturalistic foliage, greatly undercut; this work can hardly be later than *c.* 1310. Then there seems to have been a stoppage of the works for some time; and when they were resumed, the remainder of the transept and ground story was completed in a simpler style without marble shafts.

FOURTH PERIOD.—A good deal of work was done in the second quarter of the fourteenth century. Tracery of that date is seen on the west wall of the retro-chancel above the tomb of Bishop Andrewes. This must mean that at this time a low reredos such as the contemporary one in Beverley minster was now erected; what we now see is the back of it; the west side of it must have been removed to make room for Bishop Fox's reredos. In the north-east corner of the retro-choir is a window with reticulated tracery, inserted to give more light to the northernmost of the four altars of the retro-choir. In the third bay from the north two straight joints in the eastern wall of the retro-chancel fix the position of a projecting Lady chapel now built out. Old prints shew that its side windows had reticulated tracery; it is therefore part of the work of this period. Where the High altar of a church was dedicated, as here and in Lincoln minster, in honour of Our Lady, it had been unusual to provide a special Lady chapel; at Lincoln the Lady Mass was held at the altar of St. John Baptist. But in later days it became common in such churches to build, as at Southwark, a separate Lady chapel. In this chapel, which had two bays, originally stood the canopied tomb of the saintly Bishop Andrewes (*ob.* 1626), after which date it was known as the "Bishop's Chapel." The Lady chapel was pulled down in 1830, as interfering with the approach to London Bridge, which it did not. At this time the bishop's tomb, minus its canopy, was transferred to its present position: converting, unintentionally, this bay of the retro-choir into a saint's chapel in the normal position of those of Winchester and St. Albans.

FIFTH PERIOD.—The eastern and western windows of the south transept somewhat resemble those of Abbot Litlington at Westminster in the cloisters and the abbot's hall; in both the Westminster windows of 1349-1362, and in the Southwark ones the supermullion is just beginning to find its way into the tracery. But the Southwark tracery is much more complicated in character; and is more likely to be early fifteenth-century work, done by Cardinal Beaufort, who was Bishop of Winchester from 1405 to 1447. It was he probably who at last completed the remodelling of the church, which had occupied some two hundred years. On the east wall of the transept is carved a cardinal's hat and tasselled strings, enclosing his arms: as son of John of Gaunt he quarters the fleur-de-lis of France with the lions of England. Similar tracery, both in the aisle windows and in those of the clerestory, replaced the lancet lights of the nave, with two or three exceptions; the only one replaced by Sir Arthur Blomfield is that above Gower's tomb. He also substituted his own design for that shewn in the drawings of the great south window of the south transept. The arch now occupied by the organ once was the western entrance of the church of St. Mary Magdalene, which adjoined the south aisle of the presbytery.

SIXTH PERIOD.—By Bishop Fox the great reredos was put up in 1520; on it appears his crest, the pelican, and his rebus, a man chasing a fox. Here again the influence of Winchester is apparent. The great reredos of Winchester probably came from the same shop as that of St. Albans, which was put up between 1476 and 1484. About 1520 the poor upper portion of the tower is thought to have been erected. A new western façade was also built; not reproduced in the new nave; drawings appear in Mr Dollman's folio.

MINOR DETAILS.—No church in England possesses such an interesting collection of modern glass; it deserves special attention. The following is a convenient route round the church. (1) Proceed up the *north aisle of the choir*. On the wall is a bust of John Trehearne, Gentleman Porter to James I.; with an amusing inscription. (2) Nearly opposite are three charming kneeling figures of Richard Humble and his two wives, erected in 1616; the pretty verses are worth copying. (3) On the wall are two tomb recesses, in style resembling the doorways of the reredos, and therefore *c.* 1520. In the eastern recess has been placed an oak effigy, quite admirable sculpture, of a knight in mail armour and surcoat, *c.* 1300. (4) At present there lies in the north-east corner of the *retro-choir* a stone skeleton, originally placed beneath some effigy in rich costume or armour, as a monition of the vanity of riches and power. (5) Mr Kempe's window in the north-east corner represents three martyrs, King Charles the martyr, Saint Thomas of Canterbury, and Archbishop Laud; by way of counterblast apparently to the commemoration of Protestant martyrs in the other windows. In 1555 the trial for heresy took place in this chapel of Rev. L. Saunders, Bishop Ferrar of St. David's, Rev. Rowland Taylor, Rev. John Rogers, Bishop Hooper of Gloucester, and Rev. John Bradford, whose portraits appear in eastern windows successively from north to south. All were found guilty and burnt; with them was burnt Archdeacon Philpot, who is commemorated in the central window on the south side. (6) Proceeding down the *south aisle*, just before we reach the transept, are some ancient tesseræ, removed here from the graveyard to the south-east, where more remain; they are said to be of Roman date. (7) In the *south transept*, on the left, is Cardinal Beaufort's hat and arms; and on the wall opposite a small tablet to William Emerson, 1575, "who lived and died an honest man"; from him has been claimed descent of Ralph Waldo Emerson. There is fine glass by Kempe in the great south window; and in the eastern wall has been inserted in his memory perhaps the best glass of that character yet produced. (8) From the centre of the *central tower* hangs in its original position a magnificent chandelier presented in 1680. (9) We now proceed down the *south aisle of the nave*; passing a series of windows by Kempe. (10) The large window probably indicates the site of a screened chapel with altar; there is known to have been in the north aisle, nearly opposite, a chantry chapel to St. John Baptist. In the central light is a figure of Poesy, with Shakespeare and Spenser on either side. Shakespeare's brother, Edmund, is buried in the church; a modern gravestone commemorating the fact may be seen in the choir. (11) In commemoration of Massinger's play of the "Virgin Martyr" St. Dorothy is represented below; and above she is shewn bringing a basket of flowers from heaven to convince a sceptic.

Massinger is buried somewhere in the church. (12) In commemoration of the "Knight of Malta" by Fletcher, who also lies in an unknown grave in the church, the ceremony of the investiture of a knight of Malta is shewn; below is St. John Baptist, the patron of the knights (13) The next window, with a representation of David and Jonathan, commemorates Fletcher's fellow-dramatist, Beaumont. (14) Then comes a window to Edward Alleyn. Below is a figure of Charity. Above, Alleyn is reading the charter of his foundation at Dulwich to Lord Chancellor Bacon, Inigo Jones, and others. (15) Then comes a font by Mr Bodley, which badly wants an elaborate cover. (16) Behind it is a window to St. Paulinus, shewing one of his famous baptisms in the Swale or the Medway. He died bishop of Rochester. St. Mary Overie was first in the diocese of Winchester, then in that of Rochester, now in that of Southwark, which extends south through Surrey up to the Sussex border. (17) Then comes a window to St. Swithun, who introduced the Secular Canons. (18) Overhead is a flaming window by Mr Henry Holiday, overcrowded with subjects, which include the Six Days of Creation and the canticle "Benedicite omnia opera." (19) We pass now into the *north aisle*. The western window is to St. Augustine, in memory of the Austin Canons who served the church from 1106 to 1539. (20) The window in the first bay is intended for Oliver Goldsmith. Below is a late Norman recess. (21) The next window is to Samuel Johnson. Below were found the foundations of the western procession doorway. (22) Next is a window to Dr Sacheverell, chaplain here from 1705-1709. (23) Next is a window to the writer of Cruden's "Concordance," buried in this parish. (24) Next comes the tomb of John Gower, "father of English prose," who died in 1408 and is buried below. (25) The next window is to Geoffrey Chaucer. Below, on the other side of the door, is the fragment of the Norman eastern procession doorway. Near it is a big, rude holy-water stoup, also very ancient. (26) Passing into the *crossing*, we see high up to the east, above the reredos, an impressive window by Kempe. (27) In the *chapel of the north transept* is a window presented by Mr J. H. Choate, the American ambassador, to commemorate the founder of Harvard University, John Harvard, of Emmanuel College, Cambridge, who was baptized in St. Saviour's in 1607. The lower panels, very beautiful in colouring, exhibit a pretty if unconventional treatment of the Baptism of Christ; the effect is somewhat marred by the insertion of a square of ancient glass between the arms of Emmanuel College and Harvard University. (28) *In the north transept* have been placed (*a*) an inlaid oak chest, one of the grandest specimens of furniture in England; it was presented by Hugh Offley, sheriff of London in 1588. (*b*) Above it is the highly allegorical monument to William Austin, who died in 1663. (*c*) By the north wall is a coffin of Purbeck marble, incised with a floriated cross; perhaps of the thirteenth century. (*d*) Near it is the simpering effigy of a successful seventeenth-century druggist, patentee of a pill extracted from sunshine, and efficacious against most mortal ills. (29) Outside, near the west front, is some herring-bone brickwork, found beneath the vestry.

BIBLIOGRAPHY.—F. T. Dollman, *Priory of St. Mary Overie, Southwark*, 1881; W. Thompson, D.D., *Guide to Southwark Cathedral*, second (enlarged) edition, 1906.

THE CATHEDRAL CHURCH OF THE BLESSED MARY THE VIRGIN OF SOUTHWELL

BUILT FOR SECULAR CANONS

SOUTHWELL MINSTER, as it is usually but incorrectly styled, was originally what is called a collegiate church.

It is as if, in any parish church of unusual importance or with an exceptionally large population, there should be not one rector, as nowadays, but a dozen or so, this dozen being formed into a corporation, with a dean, precentor, chancellor, and treasurer (the two first officials did not exist at Southwell). All the cathedrals of the old foundation had from the earliest time such a collegiate constitution as the above: viz., Chichester, Exeter, Hereford, Lichfield, Lincoln, London, Salisbury, Wells, York, and the four Welsh cathedrals. But all these were also cathedrals: *i.e.*, they possessed a bishop's chair (*cathedra*); Southwell did not become a cathedral—there was no bishop of Southwell—till 1884.

Like the other ecclesiastical colleges—those of cathedrals excepted—that of Southwell was suppressed by Edward VI.; but under Queen Mary it had the good fortune to be reconstituted and re-endowed. Its sister church, Beverley minster, also a college of Secular Canons—*i.e.*, priests not living under a monastic rule—became and has remained a parish church. The only collegiate churches remaining with their original constitution are Windsor, Westminster, Heytesbury, Middleham, and St. Katherine's Hospital, London—omitting, of course, the cathedrals of the old foundation.

SOUTHWELL CATHEDRAL. 343

Though, however, there was till recently no bishop of Southwell, yet the church up to the Reformation was practically a cathedral. Just as the bishop of Wells had at different times other cathedrals besides that of Wells—at one time at Bath, at another time at Glastonbury; and as the bishop of the Mercian diocese had at one time three chairs—viz., at Lichfield, Chester, and Coventry—so the archbishop of the immense northern kingdom of Northumbria required and possessed four cathedrals: viz., at York, Ripon, Beverley, and Southwell. The latter was especially the cathedral of Nottinghamshire. The archbishops had a palace at Southwell which has recently been restored; and several of the archbishops of York are buried in the minster.

FIRST PERIOD.—In the seventh century St. Paulinus was engaged in mission work in or near Southwell, baptizing great numbers in the Trent, and according to Camden, who gives Bede as his authority, he founded the minster. But long before his time—in the third century, or thereabouts—the Romans were at Southwell. There actually survives *in situ* a tesselated pavement beneath the floor of the south transept, which may well have belonged to a Romano-British basilica.

SECOND PERIOD.—The tympanum of an early Norman

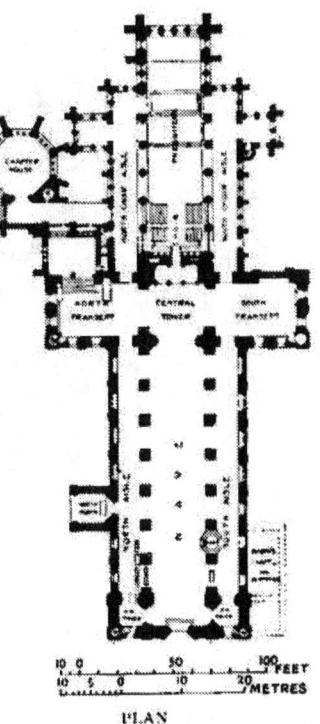

PLAN

doorway remains in the north transept. It is not *in situ*, for the head of one of the principal figures has been cut off to make the slab fit its present position. On the left is a lion which is being throttled by David or Samson; on the right is St. Michael slaying the dragon; in either case the symbolism is the victory of the Church over the powers of evil.

THE NAVE, LOOKING EAST

THIRD PERIOD.— Between 1109 and 1114 the present Norman church was begun. Of this the presbytery has disappeared. As this would be built first, 1120 is given as an approximate date for the transept and central tower and for the nave. The cable-moldings, however, of the crossing and transepts, and the carving of the nave-capitals, are so rich and effective that the work may be somewhat later. Indeed, the whole of the ornamentation is far ahead of that at Ely, Norwich and Peterborough, Tewkesbury or Gloucester. The carved capitals may be compared with those of the nave of Hereford. The interior of the nave is low, but has been improved by Mr Christian's semicircular ceiling. The piers are stumpy cylinders; the elevation is that of Malvern or St. Bartholomew's, Smithfield; here there are none of the tall compound piers of Peterborough or Ely, still less the Brobdingnagian cylinders of Tewkesbury or Gloucester. Each bay of the triforium was to have had the same kind of arcade as that of Romsey choir: viz., two minor arches, with a small shaft rising from their point of intersection. (Projecting stones, intended for the arches and the shaft, may be seen in each bay.) The Romsey design was not a success even in the eyes of the Romsey people, for they tried five other designs in the triforium of their transept; and the Southwell canons very sensibly omitted this inner arcade. The whole design is illogical; the great arches were left open, as at Norwich, so that a flood of light might pour into the nave from the windows in the upper part of the aisle-wall; but these windows are so small that very little light at all can have been obtained from them; a similar mistake is made at Romsey. The clerestory, with its circular windows, is remarkable; a similar design was worked out very beautifully, later on, in the north transept of Hereford. From each transept projected eastward a two-storied apse, as at Norwich; the arch into the lower chapel remains, and also the noble arcades which opened into the upper chapels. The curve of the apse of the northern transept is marked on the pavement of the present vestry. It is noteworthy that the aisles are vaulted, as at Kirkstall, in oblong compartments; the mason is also feeling his way towards the execution of bosses to take the intersection of the diagonal ribs; both indications of late date. The tall square spires of the west front—which, as well as the conical roof of the Chapter house, were

THE SOUTH AISLE

FROM THE NORTH-WEST

restored by Mr Christian on the authority of a drawing attributed to Turner, give the church quite a Rhenish appearance. The two lower west windows of the towers are modern shams; they replace excellent windows inserted in the fourteenth century; originally the bottom stages of the towers were probably solid. The north-west tower has a pointed arcade, and is therefore a little later than its neighbour, which has an intersecting arcade of semicircular arches. Originally the façade would be such a one as that which remains in St. Stephen's, Caen.

THE SOUTH TRANSEPT DOOR

A fine string-course of zigzag ornament runs along the nave and round the transepts. In places it has been taken out, reinserted in a different place or copied, when larger windows were inserted in the aisles of the nave; only one of the original Norman windows is left; viz., in the north aisle next to its western tower. In the south transept the string-course takes the unusual form of a segmental arch over the archbishop's doorway. The great emphasis given to the horizontal lines of the Norman building is as remarkable here as at Norwich. There are good examples of the "nebule" corbel table with a later parapet, and of Norman pinnacles; one of these, over the north porch, is hollow, and served as a chimney for the sacristan or sexton, who, it was enacted, "should lie within the church, to be at hand to ring the bells at the right time." Inside his chamber above the north porch are a fireplace, chimney, and cupboards constructed in the thickness of the walls. The gables of the transept have very effective zigzag, with interesting differences of treatment; the pinnacles of the transepts seem to have been removed at some time or other to the central tower, for which they are too small. Norman sculptured capitals of great interest remain on the eastern piers of the tower, but are now unfortunately covered up to make room for more organ pipes. (A mania for big organs appears to be raging in our cathedrals : nothing short of the roar and rumble of an earthquake will bring people nowadays into a devotional frame of mind.) Photographs of the capitals have been taken by Mr A. J. Loughton. Among the subjects represented are the Last Supper, the Presentation in the Temple, Christ washing the disciples' feet, the Paschal Lamb, and Palm Sunday. In plan, the Norman church had a presbytery of four bays; its aisles ended in apses, but the presbytery was square-ended, which is remarkable. A still more advanced type of plan was, however, in existence at Hereford and Romsey.

FOURTH PERIOD.—The Norman presbytery barely existed for a century. The new eastern limb is much influenced by the design of Lincoln nave and central transept, which were well on the way in 1220; there are the same sexpartite and quinquepartite vaults, the same doming of the vaults, the same longitudinal ridge-rib, the same choir transepts, the same chamfered buttresses with the same gablet-heads, the same strong ground course. In plan and internal elevation the work resembles Pershore, which seems to have been built in the early years of the thirteenth century. In 1233 Archbishop Gray of York issued an indulgence for "the completion of the fabric begun some time ago." Also in 1241 a chantry was founded in the new work (*in novo opere*). We may therefore assume that the work was begun c. 1230 and finished c. 1250. Externally, the eastern limb of Southwell is a singularly fine composition, and before its mutilation, must have been one of the best mediæval designs in Europe. Unfortunately the roofs have been lowered, and in the flattened battlemented eastern gable a misshapen late window now appears. Originally the roof of the eastern transepts rose nearly to the top of the clerestory walls, as is shewn by the weatherings remaining. But being built without flying buttresses, the clerestory wall began to bulge out, and in the fourteenth century flying buttresses and big pinnacles were built; (one of the flying buttresses used to have a channel on its back to carry down the drainage from the gutter of the upper roof). Take these away in imagination, raise roofs and gables to as sharp a pitch as those of Beverley and Lincoln, and you have a design as noble as it was simple. The alternation of aisled choir and unaisled presbytery with the projecting masses of the eastern transepts provided charming contrasts of light and shadow; the base-courses are almost as strong and emphatic as at Salisbury; the sharply chamfered buttresses, with their acute pyramidal gablets, are particularly effective: contrary to Salisbury fashion, the windows are deeply recessed externally. The whole design is vigorous and effective.

The interior of the choir is equally original and interesting. Its design is conditioned by the fact that the architect had made up his mind to vault the chancel, but refused to employ flying buttresses. This made it necessary that the vault should spring low down; not in the clerestory, as at Beverley, but in the triforium story, as at Salisbury. Moreover, the diagonal arches of the vault were slightly pointed, to bring the thrusts down more vertically. To make things safer still, he kept his ground story low; instead of the lofty piers of Lincoln nave and Salisbury, his clustered columns are comparatively low, and are connected by a continuous bench-course. Moreover, to make these low piers yet more secure, he dispensed with the beautiful but unconstructional shafts of Purbeck marble which were put up by hundreds at Lincoln; in the plan of his piers he followed the Yorkshire use, which is to be seen at Ripon and Beverley. In his refusal to employ flying buttresses, he was no doubt also influenced by Ripon precedent. In Lincoln nave the method adopted was to employ external flying buttresses, thus enabling greater height to be given to the nave; at Southwell no flying buttresses were employed, and great height was therefore unattainable. The Southwell interior then being necessarily low, the next thing to do was to make it look high. A similar problem had confronted the builders of St. Frideswide's, Oxford; they solved it by framing the triforium arcade in what looks like the arcade

THE CHOIR, LOOKING WEST

of the ground story. At Southwell and Pershore it was solved by eliminating the triforium arcade. The triforium chamber is there with a blank wall in front of it; but this wall is set back, and pretends to be nothing but the cill of the clerestory window, whose jambs are brought down to the cill of the triforium. The result is that instead of having two low upper stories, the interior seems to have a single tall story; it appears to have an elevation, not of three, but of two stories; and, as two tall stories look taller than three low ones, the architect manages to some extent to disguise the real lowness of his interior. Nevertheless, in spite of all the trouble he has taken, the interior certainly lacks the aspiring verticality one expects to find in early Gothic.

The planning of the new work is difficult to understand. It has always been assumed that the High altar stood as at present near the eastern wall. The ground for this is that churches dedicated to St. Mary needed no Lady chapel, and that Lincoln minster has none. But it is only necessary to turn to the cathedral of St. Mary of Salisbury to find a church of this dedication with an important eastern Lady chapel. Nor is it a difficulty that there were altars to Our Lady elsewhere in the Southwell church; for in the Lady chapel at Salisbury none of the three altars was dedicated to Our Lady. It is probable, therefore, that the two unaisled eastern bays of Southwell formed a Lady chapel. In that case the next bay would form the Procession path. There would be no Feretory, as there was no pre-eminent local saint. This would leave six bays east of the central tower. The westernmost of these was filled with a wooden screen, for which the present stone screen was substituted in the following century. The prebendaries were only sixteen in number, and were seldom in residence: the stalls are known to have been placed, as at present, in the two next bays, which furnished room enough for the canons or their vicars choral. This would leave to the east a dignified presbytery of three bays, in the easternmost of which—the fourth from the east wall—the High altar would be placed; it would thus be in a line with the eastern transepts, precisely as at Worcester, Salisbury, Beverley, and Pershore. It is true that the sedilia are not now in this bay, but in the second bay from the east. But they are known not to have been removed to their present position till some years before 1839. It will be seen that all the upper parts, with the finials and pinnacles, have at some time been cut away, so as to leave a horizontal upper edge. This was probably to support a gallery when the sedilia stood beneath one of the southern arches of the presbytery. It is also on record that the sedilia replaced a screen. As is clear from the marks in the northern and southern walls of the western bay, a very lofty oak screen formerly stood in front of the Lady chapel, like the stone screen still existing in front of the Lady chapel of Ottery St. Mary. As for the *altars* of Our Lady, one was the High altar, the other stood "in the north part of the church," whatever that may mean. As at Beverley, eastern transepts were thrown out to north and south, each to hold an altar. This would have left the eastern bays free to serve as part of the procession path; but strange to say, they contain piscinas and aumbries, and that of the south aisle has sedilia as well; each therefore contained an altar, which must to a large extent have blocked the procession path. It is remarkable that the church does not lie due east, but is orientated some points south of east.

To interfere with the services as little as possible, the eastern half was built first. If the foliage of the capitals and corbels and bosses be examined, it will be found to be somewhat stiff and formal in the eastern bays, and to be worked with more crispness and freedom towards the west. Moreover the bases of the eastern piers have the water-holding molding; those of the western ones a triple roll. The next thing was to pull down the Norman presbytery, the material of which is found to be largely built up in the western, but not in the eastern bays. In rebuilding the western bays, the first consideration was not to endanger the Norman tower. So the work was not continued from the east, but was started afresh from the tower. The two portions met in the fourth bay; when it was found that, owing to inaccurate setting-out, the arch on the south side of the choir and the string-course on the north side were at a different level to that of the older work to the east. The awkward junction of the arches was masked by a curious medallion, while the string-course takes a sudden jump upward. The vault of the aisles and transepts is quinquepartite, as in St. Hugh's aisles and transept at Lincoln; the high vault is quadripartite; and both vaults have the wobbling longitudinal rib of the great transept of Lincoln. If the east wall had had the usual group of five lancets, this rib would have dropped down on to the glass of the central light; that is why there are only four lancets. A special local note of this Southwell work is fondness for fillets of various forms on the shafts and columns; they abound everywhere.

FIFTH PERIOD.—A little later, the eastern apse of the north transept was replaced by a double chapel (*c.* 1260). The shafts have the "keel-molding," both here and in the Chapter house.

SIXTH PERIOD.—Next was built the cloister—*i.e.*, the southern part of the passage leading to the Chapter house. Notice the lovely doorway in the north choir aisle. In this and the arcade is early naturalistic foliage, which fixes the date as *c.* 1280. Before the upper story was built, and when the eastern arcade was open, it must have been singularly beautiful. From the little courtyard between the cloister and the eastern transept the views are most picturesque.

SEVENTH PERIOD.—Next was built the Chapter house with its vestibule. If in window tracery and leafage it be compared with the Chapter house of York, it will be plain that the Southwell example is the earlier. Southwell Chapter house may be 1290, York 1300. York Chapter house is then but a copy of that of Southwell—and an inferior copy; both dispense with a central pier; but Southwell has a magnificent vault of stone, whereas York is vaulted in wood. The Chapter house of Southwell, not that of York, is "among Chapter houses, as the rose among flowers." "What Cologne cathedral is to Germany, Amiens to France," says Mr Street, "is Southwell Chapter house to England." Here English stone-carvers produced their best work; nowhere will you find such capitals or crockets or spandrels, nor such portraits—all, no doubt, here and in the cloister, representing people living at Southwell 1280-1300.

EIGHTH PERIOD.—But the wonders of Southwell do not end yet. Between c. 1315 and 1350 was erected quite the

DETAIL OF CARVING IN THE CHAPTER HOUSE

loveliest choir screen in England; next comes that of Lincoln, evidently by the same hand. Eastern and western sides are entirely different in design; on the western side the artist parts reluctantly with the beautiful geometrical design of the thirteenth century; on the eastern side he accepts unreservedly the reign of the ogee arch. Magnificent sedilia and stone stalls of similar character were erected, which only survive in part. Very charming, too, is the cusping of the reticulated windows inserted in the north transept chapel; and the doors of the north porch.

The upper parts of the Chapter house and the north transept chapel also were remodelled in this period.

For two hundred years or more, the highest and best of mediæval art found cultivated and wealthy patrons at Southwell; twelfth, thirteenth, and fourteenth century work are all seen here at their best. Few of our cathedrals, from the point of view either of architectural design or sculptured detail, can be mentioned in the same breath with Southwell. Nowhere will the architectural student find such a treasure of the best work of the best periods as in the sister churches of the canons of Beverley and Southwell. It is one of the greatest delights of Southwell that its lovely minster is little known and almost unvisited: one feels as if one were "the first that ever burst into this silent sea."

NINTH PERIOD.—Large windows with rectilinear tracery were inserted in the aisles (*c.* 1390) and the west end (fifteenth century) to light the nave; and a doorway from the choir to the archbishop's palace on the south. Between 1452 and 1480 the chapel of St. John Baptist, founded *c.* 1280, was enlarged by William and Laurence Booth, both archbishops of York. It adjoined the south-west tower and the two next bays of the south aisle. After the Reformation it was used as the Grammar School till 1784, when it was pulled down. In 1847 the adjacent aisle-wall fell down, and was re-erected with the present three sham Norman windows.

TENTH PERIOD.—There is an alabaster monument of Archbishop Sandys (*d.* 1588), of unusually good design. To the same century belongs the fine Renaissance glass (French) in the east of the choir.

The lectern was presented in 1805. Originally it belonged to Newstead abbey, and at the Dissolution was thrown into Newstead lake. Mention should be made also of the kneeling statue in bronze of Bishop Ridding, by Mr Pomeroy; one of the noblest memorials of ancient or modern times.

There were originally sixteen canons or prebendaries at Southwell in charge of the services. But as they habitually resided in their country parishes, they were allowed to appoint sixteen vicars or deputies, to do their work for them. These vicars choral, like the canons, formed a college or corporation. The vicars also found the work hard, and were aided by paid lay-clerks and choir-boys. Besides these there were thirteen chantry-priests. In later days there used to be in residence at Southwell only one canon out of the sixteen; he came into residence only once in four years, and only stayed three months. The handsome block of brick houses to the east of the minster was built in 1780: the eastern house for the canon in residence; the two houses on each side for four of the vicars. It should be added that the church, as at Ripon, had a very large parish attached to it. The whole of the nave was parochial, and at its east end was the parish altar, which was dedicated to St. Vincent.

BIBLIOGRAPHY.—J. F. Dimock's *Illustrations of the Collegiate Church of Southwell.*

G. M. Livett's *Guide to Southwell Minster.*

J. L. Petit in *Archæological Journal*, 1850, p. 208.

A. F. Leach's *Visitations and Memorials of Southwell Minster;* printed by the Camden Society in 1891.

THE CATHEDRAL CHURCH OF ALL SAINTS, WAKEFIELD

FORMERLY PAROCHIAL

THE see was founded in 1888. Like Manchester cathedral, the church is thoroughly parochial in appearance, inside and outside. But, archæologically, it is of exceptional interest. It is one of those numerous churches, every stone of the exterior of which is of late Gothic date, but which internally in their arcades reveal the existence of

THE NAVE

FROM THE SOUTH-WEST

much earlier building epochs. Like many others, though now a vast parallelogram, it was once a cruciform church in plan; and though now it has a western tower, its tower once stood above the crossing. Once its nave was aisleless; then it had narrow aisles; later on, these narrow aisles were replaced by broad ones. The piers and arches of the first aisles were low; afterwards they were heightened or rebuilt. Originally it had no clerestory; this was not added till the fifteenth century. When the central tower fell, the new tower was built 10 ft. west of the nave, so as not to interfere with the services. When it was finished, it was joined up to the nave by the addition of a new westernmost bay. The Norman chancel and its successor were short, and had neither aisles nor clerestory; the present chancel, the third, is long, having absorbed the space originally covered by the central tower; and it has a clerestory and aisles, and these have absorbed the transepts. Finally, the font, choir screen, and sounding-board are Jacobean. Wakefield cathedral is a typical embodiment of the history of the Church of England, with a personal identity undestroyed by its many transformations, like the boy's knife which had a new blade and a new handle, but was still the same old knife.

BIBLIOGRAPHY.—The architectural history of the church has been worked out in a paper by Mr J. T. Micklethwaite, forming a chapter in the *History of Wakefield Cathedral*, by J. W. Walker, Wakefield, 1888.

THE CATHEDRAL CHURCH OF ST. ANDREW OF WELLS

BUILT FOR SECULAR CANONS

"THE traveller who comes down the hill from Shepton Mallet," says Professor Freeman, "looks down on a group of buildings without a rival either in our own island or beyond the seas." "From a distance," says Mr Peabody, "the towers and lantern of the cathedral rise above rounded masses of green foliage. When we reach its walls, we find them springing from the azure depths of crystalline pools, from emerald lawns and arching trees, the home of cawing rooks and soaring pigeons. Close to the very walls of the ancient cathedral rises one of the noblest springs in the world, to which city and cathedral owe their name; an ever-abounding and magnificent outburst of waters at the side of the Lady chapel, surging up in a boiling heap in the midst of the unfathomed depths of a translucent pool; then bounding over in an impetuous cascade, which carries it into the Bishop's moat, to encircle palace and rampart and towers, till it rests in glassy clearness over many-coloured forests of branching or feathery or star-like water-weeds. Never did a Frenchman form such harmonies of church and scenery as one sees at Lichfield, at Salisbury, and at Wells, in their setting of close and cloister and lake, of brilliant garden and clipped green lawn and immemorial elms. Above rise three grey, time-worn towers; the music of the chimes vibrates and dies away:—

"'Lord, through this hour
Be Thou our guide,
That by Thy power
No foot may slide.'

WELLS CATHEDRAL

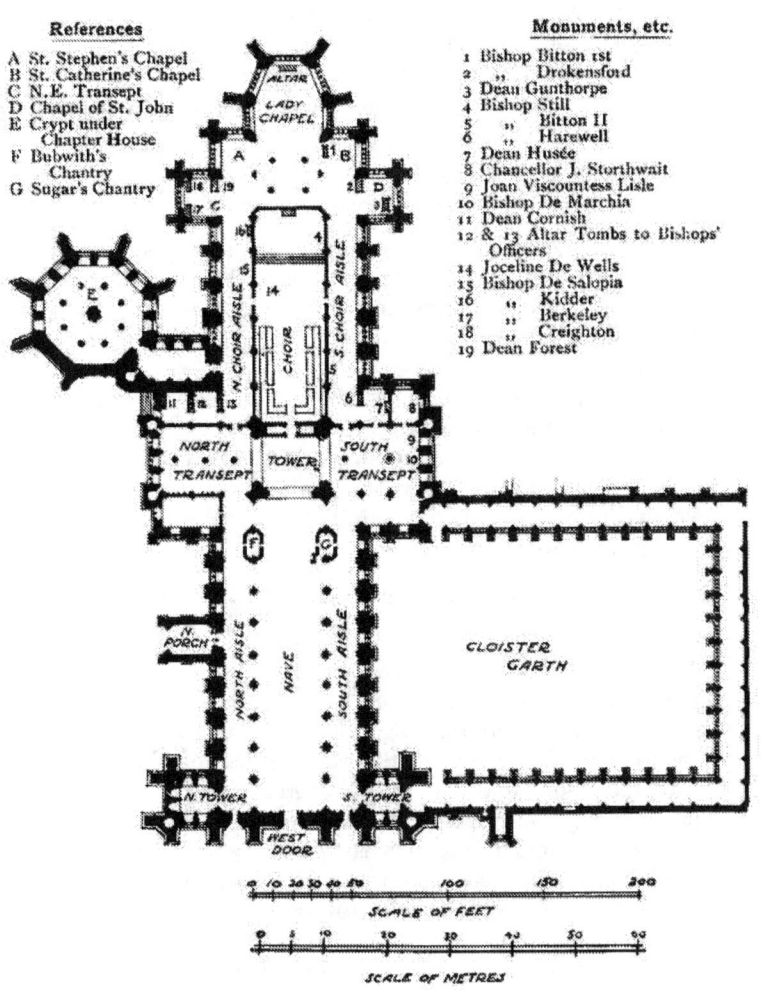

References

A St. Stephen's Chapel
B St. Catherine's Chapel
C N.E. Transept
D Chapel of St. John
E Crypt under Chapter House
F Bubwith's Chantry
G Sugar's Chantry

Monuments, etc.

1 Bishop Bitton 1st
2 ,, Drokensford
3 Dean Gunthorpe
4 Bishop Still
5 ,, Bitton II
6 ,, Harewell
7 Dean Husée
8 Chancellor J. Storthwait
9 Joan Viscountess Lisle
10 Bishop De Marchia
11 Dean Cornish
12 & 13 Altar Tombs to Bishops' Officers
14 Joceline De Wells
15 Bishop De Salopia
16 ,, Kidder
17 ,, Berkeley
18 ,, Creighton
19 Dean Forest

PLAN

So from hour to hour chant the bells over the peaceful beauty of the bishop's gardens and terraces and the ancient ivy-clad palace; while within the lonely nave, as the fading sunlight shines through the western window, and casts its coloured glories on sculptured tomb and carved boss and grey stone wall, the organ notes pulsate through the stony fabric :—

> "Through long-drawn aisle and fretted vault
> The pealing anthem swells the note of praise."

The great solemn place is filled with the thrilling sweetness of boyish voices, and we heartily join in their tuneful, long 'Amen,' as it rings and resounds down the empty nave, and echoes again and again from distant chapel and far-receding vaults.

"The bishop's palace is romance made tangible, even to 'spell-bound princes oaring their way as swans among the lilies of the moat.' In this home of peace good Bishop Ken led his simple, happy life, awaking with the sun and joining with the birds in their morning hymn, and each eventide singing to his lute :—

> "Glory to thee, my God, this night,
> For all the blessings of the light."

Beyond the gardens and the moat run avenues of stately elms; hard by, to the north, are the cathedral's triple towers, and, for background, the mighty range of the Mendips; all round is meadow-grass; to the west nestles the little town, with the stately tower of St. Cuthbert's church; and, five miles away, conical tors rise on either side of the isle of Avalon, the storied land of Glastonbury, where twice each year bloomed the sacred thorn struck by Joseph of Arimathea from a thorn in the Saviour's crown; where, too, lies King Arthur, borne thither after the fatal battle of Camelot, and buried in an unknown grave with the inscription, 'Hic jacet Arturus rex quondam rexque futurus.' This land of Somerset to the Englishman should be holy ground."

The peculiar charm of Wells lies, as Professor Freeman

WELLS CATHEDRAL 363

FROM THE SOUTH-EAST

remarks, in the union and harmonious grouping of the cathedral with its surroundings. It does not stand alone. On the other hand, it is not crowded by mean, incongruous buildings, like the great cathedrals of France. Nor, again, is it isolated from those buildings which are its natural and necessary complement—the palace of the Bishop, the Deanery, the residence of the Archdeacon, the Cathedral school, the Vicar's Close, the homes of precentor, organist, and architect. Nearly all the officials still live in the houses which Bishop Beckington built four centuries ago. And with the most perfect and picturesque of all these, "a double row of little ancient houses," the Vicar's Close, the north transept of the cathedral is connected by a delightful mediæval bridge.

The diocese of Wells is an offshoot of that of Winchester. When Wessex grew populous, the bishopric of Sherborne was split off from that of Winchester; and the shire of the Sumorsaetas was split off from Sherborne, perhaps in 904, and the men of Somerset got a bishop of their own. The diocese long had two cathedrals: one at Wells, served, as at this day, by Secular Canons; the other at Bath, served by monks of the Benedictine abbey. The latter was suppressed by Henry VIII., and ever since the bishop has been but in name Bishop of Bath.

FIRST PERIOD.—In 1148 there was a consecration of a Norman cathedral, built or repaired by Bishop Robert. Of this no certain traces survive, except the font. It may have occupied a different site, more to the south; on the other hand much of the walling of the present cathedral may be Bishop Robert's, unless indeed his church was entirely demolished, in which case much of his ashlar, being still in good condition, would be reused.

SECOND PERIOD.—In 1174 Reginald de Bohun or Fitz-Joscelinus became bishop, and is recorded to have made prior to 1180 a large grant "to the fabric fund until the work be finished"; the present cathedral therefore must have been begun in or soon after 1180. Another charter, recording a private gift, alludes to "the admirable structure of the rising church" and is attested by witnesses who appear elsewhere in 1206 and 1221. It appears therefore that by about the end of the twelfth century a considerable amount of work had been done. This documentary evidence is supported by architectural data at Worcester and Glastonbury. At

THE NAVE

Worcester the design of the ground story of the two westernmost bays of the nave resembles in many points that of the present choir of Wells, and may be dated back to 1175; its capitals are just as much behind those of Wells as might be expected in work five or ten years earlier in date. Still more behind Wells are the triforium and clerestory, in which the semicircular arch prevails and in which there is large use of the Romanesque zigzag ornament. At Glastonbury the Lady chapel (wrongly styled St. Joseph's chapel) is definitely known to have been begun after the fire of 1184 and to have been consecrated in 1186; its vault system is precisely that of Wells. It is true that much of its sculptured foliage is largely Romanesque in design, but it is deeply undercut, and evidently the work of exceptionally skilled masons; nor is there anything remarkable in the fact that the Glastonbury monks should be more conservative than the Wells canons. St. David's cathedral was also building at the same time as Wells cathedral, and is more retrogressive than either Wells or Glastonbury. So it may be taken that at Wells we see the first important English church ever built in the Gothic style, and that the primacy of English Gothic belongs to Wells, and not to Lincoln, which was not begun till 1192. Nor can priority be claimed for the Yorkshire Gothic, as seen at Roche abbey and Ripon minster; for in the Northern work the semicircular arch still lingers, whereas at Wells it is utterly exterminated; pier-arches, wall arcade, windows, doorways, vaults all have pointed arches and nothing else. Compared with Lincoln, Wells is vaulted throughout, whereas Lincoln choir originally had no vaults, nor was designed for vaults.

In plan Reginald's church consisted of an aisled nave of ten bays, of aisled transepts, and of a square-ended aisled eastern limb of four bays. The stalls of the choir, till the fourteenth century, were placed in the crossing, and the easternmost bay of the nave: marks where the choir screen was fixed may still be seen in the first pair of piers from the central tower and in the walls of the aisles; the ritual nave therefore consisted of nine bays. The transepts had both eastern and western aisles. In each eastern aisle was a couple of chapels; and adjoining the southern of these eastern aisles was a sacristy, very much as at Worcester. For a church so small as Wells to have western aisles to the transepts seems rather an extravagance; but a western aisle was necessary in the south transept, in order to get access to the eastern walk of the cloister; which walk could not be built further to the east because in the way was an early Lady chapel. As for the western aisle of the north transept, it may also have been used, as at present, as an additional sacristy; or as Chapter house till the present Chapter house was built. If the exterior of the present choir aisles be examined, it will be seen that the second buttress from the west is much more massive than the one east of it. This shews that the latter was in line with a thin and therefore a low wall, while the former lined with a thick and lofty wall. This latter therefore was the high end-wall of the presbytery, and the former the eastern wall of a low aisle running north and south; just as at the Cistercian abbey of Dore, which was building at the same time, and probably at Glastonbury. The presbytery would open into the aisle behind by two arches, as at Exeter, or three, as at Dore; the aisle would probably provide both a row of altars and a procession path. This leaves three bays for the presbytery; and if we pass within, we shall find all its three arches still in existence on either side. The easternmost of these arches would formerly rest to the east on very massive piers in a line with the bigger buttresses; these could not be allowed to remain when the presbytery was prolonged eastward in the fourteenth century; so they were replaced by fourteenth-century piers of more moderate dimensions, this being done without taking down the arches.

The Wells design deserves most careful study, both from the earliness of its date and from its great influence on the school of West Country Gothic. In the design the controlling factor is the vault and abutment system. The remarkable feature about the vault is that instead of adopting the usual Gothic method of making the diagonal arches semicircular, and pointing the transverse ones till they rose to the level of the central boss—the course taken in the westernmost aisle-vault of Worcester nave—the Wells architect determined to point the diagonal arches as well. The same course was taken in the choir and aisles of St. Cross, Winchester, which was probably built some twenty years earlier, and in the contemporary Lady chapel at Glastonbury. Vaults with pointed diagonal arches are of course easier to construct, the lower courses approaching

THE SOUTH AISLE AND SUGAR'S CHANTRY

the vertical to such an extent as to require little centering. A more important advantage is that the more pointed a vault, the more vertical are its thrusts, and the less abutment they require; probably this weighed most in the Wells design, which above all things aims at securing stability. But a vault with pointed diagonals has its defects. If the transverse arches are made as lofty as the diagonal ones, the whole vault will be very lofty and proportionately heavy and expensive. If, on the other hand, the former are kept low, the vault will be domical in form, *i.e.*, much higher at the centre than at the sides, and this is precisely the state of things at St. Cross. But in England the architects were all for non-domical vaults, *i.e.*, vaults with their longitudinal ridges level. They had indeed tried domical vaulting in Lincoln central transept and Southwell choir, but it was not satisfactory, and was abandoned. At Wells also it was determined to have a vault with level ridge. The difficulty was how to combine it with pointed diagonals without unduly increasing the height of the vault. This is how it was done. Let us imagine in the first place that the nave was to be vaulted in square bays, not as now in oblongs. The diagonals of a square would be longer than those of an oblong bay, and would rise to a very great height. But if we vaulted the nave in rather broad oblongs, the diagonals would not rise so high; and if for broad we substituted narrow oblong bays, the diagonals would be lower still. This is precisely what was done at Wells. The central aisle was set out in very narrow oblongs. But of course all the vaults require supports, and these supports are the piers down below. The result, therefore, of narrowing the bays of the vault was that more bays were required, and consequently more piers and arches were required also. This then is the reason why the short nave of Wells has actually nine piers and ten arches on each side. Lincoln nave has six piers and seven arches; and while the aisled part of Lincoln nave is 181 ft. long, that of Wells is only 161 ft.

Another important factor in the vault design was the lighting system. Much importance was evidently attached to good lighting at Wells. All the lancet windows are exceptionally broad, owning no kinship whatever to the slender, graceful lancets of Lincoln and Salisbury; but following the proportions of the round-headed windows in St. Cross choir and Worcester nave. But it would have been useless to put large lancets in the clerestory if they were to be obstructed by the vault; therefore, to unmask the clerestory windows, the side cells of the vault were tilted upward, as at Pershore, instead of having level ridges.

Then the serious question of abutment had to be considered. Here the builders shewed themselves thoroughly sceptical of new-fangled Gothic methods. Flying buttresses in the open air, like those going up simultaneously at Chichester, they would none of. They actually had little faith even in vertical buttresses; they put them up indeed; but both in the aisles and the clerestory, as at the east end of Pershore, they have little more projection than Norman pilaster strips. What they believed in, as the archaic Norman builders had done, was thickness of wall. Here, as at St. Cross, which seems to have been largely the prototype of the early Gothic of Worcester and Wells, the walls are very thick; those of the aisles being 5 ft. 3 in., those of the clerestory 6 ft. 2½ in. at the top. Though no flying buttresses were built outside, yet they are present inside the triforium chamber, their heads being about on a level with the corbels which support the vaulting-shafts within, the idea being, correctly enough, that the thrusts of the high vault would be exerted not at the level of its spring, but a little distance lower. And, curiously enough, their heads are also made to carry the clerestory buttresses; the latter are not, as in Lincoln choir, brought down to the floor of the triforium chamber to rest in "false-bearing" on the transverse arch of the aisle-vault.* Then, after all this engineering, to make things more stable still, the ground story was built exceedingly low.

As has been said above, the clerestory walls are very thick; it follows that the piers below, which carry them, have to be very massive also. And as they are also low, they are very squat piers indeed; so they are at Lichfield also. The next problem to be solved was how to make them look taller. The answer was—multiply the number of vertical lines by encircling the piers with all the shafts

* Pershore nave also was built with internal flying buttresses; and though the present ones are external, I discovered in the triforium chamber one flying buttress complete, and stumps of the others.

that can possibly be packed together. Accordingly in the presbytery the piers have sixteen shafts, while in the nave the number rises to twenty-four, which in the latter are all arranged in triplets. It is to be noted that the shafts are not detached and are not of marble. Here again the design hails from Worcester nave, where it appears in a less perfected form. These low massive piers, surrounded by triplets of shafts in coursed freestone, appear in the parish churches of St. Cuthbert, Wells; Llanidloes; St. Mary, Shrewsbury, and St. Sepulchre's, Northampton; and at Pershore, Lichfield, Dore, Chester cathedral, and Christ church, Dublin.

Another curious feature is the non-correspondence of the intermediate story externally and internally. If we pass outside, we shall find that the aisle roof rises up to the sill of the clerestory windows, leading to the expectation that inside the church we shall find a lofty triforium arcade. But on re-entering the transept and nave, we find that the triforium arcade is quite low. But though it is low, behind it there is a lofty triforium chamber, rising, as externally, up to the sill of the clerestory window. The clerestory string therefore does not tell the truth about the elevation; it pretends to demarcate the triforium from the clerestory, but it does nothing of the sort. This string is in reality not much more than half-way up the front of the triforium chamber. At Worcester the string is in its proper place, *i.e.*, just below the sill of the clerestory windows, and the vault springs from the top of a pier situated between the clerestory windows. But the Wells people did not care to spring their vault from piers, however broad, but preferred that the vault should spring from a broad surface of solid wall unbroken by any openings. Consequently in the nave all the wall from the sill of the clerestory window to the top of the triforium arcade was left solid, and against this the builders with confidence set their vaults. What space was left between this solid wall and the tops of the pier-arch was but inconsiderable, and it was this that was pierced with a low triforium arcade. This arcade differs from any other in England. Elsewhere, and at Wells itself in the transept, the triforium arcade is divided by piers into bays corresponding with those of the ground story and the high vault. In the nave of Wells on the other hand it is made to correspond with the broad strip of solid wall beneath the clerestory windows, extending all the way from the central tower to the west end without any relation as to the disposition of its arches either to the pier-arches below or to the clerestory and vault above.

From this curious treatment of the three stories a very remarkable internal elevation results; one with a clerestory made to appear nearly as tall as the ground story, and a low triforium arcade between. A similar elevation no doubt was once to be seen in Lichfield choir, but only its ground story survives. At Pershore, however, the whole elevation remains, but with further attenuation of the intermediate story; the arcade of the triforium chamber being there omitted altogether: the same treatment is to be seen in Southwell choir; both of them are later than Wells nave.

As to the order of all this work, it proceeded in the usual way from east to west. The first section of the work is that of Bishop Reginald, and was done between c. 1180 and his death in 1191; this would probably include only the presbytery and part of the eastern sides of the central transept; the plan of the piers and the archaic foliage of the capitals differentiate it from all the western work. The second section includes the rest of the central transept and about half of the nave, in which, half-way down, is a marked break in the masonry, as well as a change in the foliation of the capitals, which now swarm with grotesque birds and beasts; the lovely north porch probably belongs to this period. This section was probably put up between 1191, the year when Reginald died, and 1206. The work must now have been abandoned from 1206-1216, during which the income of the see was confiscated and the revenues were paid yearly into the king's purse; this was the wretched King John, who died in 1216. At length the works were resumed in 1220 by Bishop Joscelin, who found the church much dilapidated after fourteen years' stoppage of the works. To him may be attributed the western bays of the nave, which retain the indigenous Gothic style of the West Country, but banish the birds and beasts from the capitals. He is recorded to have consecrated the church in 1239. This must mean that the western bays of the nave were now finished; it does not necessarily imply that the west front was finished also, except so much as was necessary to close up the west end of the nave.

From the great diversity of style in the foliated capitals, it would seem that many of them, together with the corbels in the transept, were left in block and were not carved till much later; this is certainly the case with the capitals of the south transept—the finest of their type in England—on which are representations of the cure of toothache by Bishop Bytton or Button, who both in life and death achieved many cures, and who did not die till 1274.

As we have seen, the design of the nave of Wells has great archæological interest; it has also a decided artistic distinction of its own. In the first place, the interior looks taller than it is. It is but 67 ft. high, and is thus one of the lowest of our cathedrals; yet it looks sufficiently lofty. This is due to the narrowness of the bays, the great number of piers, and the multiplicity of shafts by which they are encircled. But the main impression is rather of great length than of great height. This is because the piers and arches are so numerous, and in the nave because of the obliteration of vertical divisions in the triforium and ground story, which are not separated off, as usual, into bays by vaulting-shafts. Here these are stopped just below the sill of the clerestory, and the triforium runs in an uninterrupted arcade the whole distance from west to east. And the free flow, east and west, of the broad horizontal band of the triforium is aided still further by designing it void of shafts, bases, and capitals alike.

THIRD PERIOD.—Then comes perhaps the most remarkable *volte-face* in the history of English mediæval design. All this fine church had been built in West Country Gothic.

But Bishop Joscelin was often at Salisbury (commenced in 1220), and no doubt had many a talk with Bishop Poore. Now Salisbury, except as regards its abutment system and thick walls, is not West Country Gothic; it belongs to the South-Eastern school, which had produced Canterbury choir, and Chichester and Winchester retro-choirs, and of which the sign manual is the profuse employment of detached

THE WEST FRONT

shafts of marble. Therefore, discarding local talent, he seems to have sent for masons of the alien school, and both in the west front of the cathedral and in his own palace followed the Lincoln and Salisbury manner; (in his palace it is curious to see how heavily he scores his buttresses in Salisbury fashion).

We may now pass out and survey this famous façade and its immense collection of sculpture—by far the best mediæval figure-sculpture in England, and only surpassed by the yet earlier sculpture of Chartres. The visitor will do well to study it in detail in the admirable series of photographs, taken when the scaffolding was up for the restoration of the façade. Much of the statuary must have been executed after the completion of the façade, and, in the opinion of Comte Robert de Lasteyrie, belongs to the closing years of the century. As for the composition of the west front, it has been severely criticised, but two things must be borne in mind. The first is, that the towers were probably designed for spires. Add the spires, and as Notre Dame, Paris, the squatness of the façade disappears. There are, however, no squinches for stone spires at Wells; if spires were intended, they would have had to be of wood.

DETAIL OF THE NORTH TOWER, NORTH SIDE

Secondly, it was designed for the sculpture—a sort of open-air reredos—and not the sculpture for the façade. Nevertheless, it is not good, even as a reredos. The windows are mere slits in the wall, the doorways mere "holes for frogs and mice." But it must be remembered that these doorways merely led to the cemetery in front of the façade;

the entrance for the town folk was through the south-west tower; that for the dean and canons was the north porch. The façade, however, certainly lacks variety: the six big buttresses project, but have all the same amount of projection. The arcading below the west window is confused and muddled, and, as in the south transept of York, is cut into anyhow by the central doorway. Nevertheless, its great breadth makes this façade of Wells more impressive than any other in the country, except that of Peterborough. What would it have been with the spires added!

The chapels of the western towers are of the same period as the west front, and are full of delightful detail; especially fine is the doorway into the cloister. It may well be that Bishop Joscelin commenced the west front before completing the western bays of the nave, employing in the latter the Somerset masons and in the west front outsiders. It is known that little was done at Wells from 1242-1268; we may therefore date the west front (except some of the statuary) between 1220 and 1242. It may be noted that the same flat-topped helmets occur as in the arcading inside Worcester retrochoir, which was begun in 1222.

INTERIOR OF THE CHAPTER HOUSE

FOURTH PERIOD.—While the west front was being

peopled with statuary, the undercroft of the Chapter house was built. A similar Chapter house, two stories high, once existed in precisely the same situation—*i.e.*, east of the north transept—at Beverley minster, the exquisite staircase to which still survives. Westminster has a vaulted undercroft, which was used as the Royal Treasury; at Wells the strong door and bars point to a similar use. The Wells treasury cannot be much later than 1286. The staircase or vestibule to the Chapter house, with simple tracery of cusped circles in its windows, is prior to 1292. The work here deserves the closest inspection. The naturalistic foliage of the capitals and corbels is superb: especially notice the first corbels, representing a monk and a nun treading on serpents. The staircase leads by the chain bridge to the vicars' close, as well as to the Chapter house. The Chapter house is one of the noblest in England. The long-lobed trefoils in the window tracery indicate that it is not earlier than the end of the thirteenth century; while the profusion of ball-flower round and beneath the windows, and the ogee dripstones outside the windows, indicate that it was not completed till later still. Canon Church has ascertained that the vestibule, floor, and temporary roof of the Chapter house were completed between 1293 and 1302, but that the outer walls, windows, stalls, central shaft, vault, and parapet were built between 1306 and 1319.

THE CHAPTER HOUSE VAULT

FIFTH PERIOD.—A much more important work remained, which had hitherto been postponed, owing perhaps to the great expense involved in the completion of the west front and the Chapter house. It was to extend the choir eastwards. The defects in the planning of Bishop Reginald's church were that the stalls were outside the eastern limb of the church, that there was no separate procession path, and that

THE RETRO-CHOIR, LOOKING EAST

the Lady chapel was outside the church. As usual, the easternmost part of the work, the Lady chapel, was started first; it was finished in 1326. Its windows have beautiful reticulated tracery of early type; and there is lovely carving in the capitals, bosses, reredos, sedilia, and piscina. Nowhere, not even in Lichfield, is there such an assemblage of Gothic capitals as at Wells; the development of the foliated capital should be studied successively (1) in the present choir and the eastern aisles of the central transept; (2) in the eastern nave; (3) in the western nave; (4) in the western aisles of the central transept; (5) in the west transept, west end and west front; (6) in the staircase of the Chapter house; (7) in the Chapter house; (8) in the Lady chapel, retro-choir, and the present presbytery.

The Lady chapel is polygonal and is flanked by two lateral chapels. In the retro-choir the vaults are planned most picturesquely; the controlling factors being the necessity to connect the broad central arch of the Lady chapel with the narrow central arch of the presbytery. This is achieved quite simply by forming the centre of the retro-choir into a square bay. It almost looks as if the central square was arranged for the shrine of some local saint, but there seems to have been no such saint at Wells. May it have been intended for the tomb of Bishop William de Marchia, for whose canonisation the canons made great but unsuccessful efforts at Rome, and whose tomb is in the south transept. In the Chapter house a single central stalk branches upward and outward in all directions, like some palm tree transmuted into stone. This beautiful effect is transferred to the retro-choir, but multiplied—six palm trees in place of one; for each of the six piers of the retro-choir emulates the Chapter house's central stalk. " It is difficult to determine whether the effect is more striking in the early morning, when the ancient splendours of the stained glass are reflected on the slender shafts of Purbeck marble and the clustered vault; or at the late winter services, when the darkened figures of saints and prophets in the clerestory combine with the few lights burning in the choristers' stalls to add something of mystery and solemn gloom to the maze of aisles and chapels, half hidden, half revealed." There is certainly no such lovely chevet in England; Salisbury perhaps exhibits the nearest approach to it: but at Wells the unsymmetrical arrangement of the piers of the retro-choir and those of the three arches opening into it from the presbytery open out vistas which are a veritable glimpse into fairyland. The delightsomeness of the planning is still further increased by throwing out little eastern transeptal chapels, as at Southwell. These make up for the four altars which had occupied the east end of Bishop Reginald's church. In this retro-choir of Wells

THE RETRO-CHOIR, LOOKING WEST

we have something really worthy of comparison with the intricate vistas and perspectives of Amiens and Le Mans.

The next thing was to remove Bishop Reginald's eastern aisle and to build three new bays connecting the retro choir with his presbytery. This done, new stalls were built, and were placed in the eastern limb, the three western bays now becoming choir, and the three eastern ones presbytery. (The present stalls are modern, but retain the ancient misericords, which are admirably carved.) Moreover, a new choir screen was added under the eastern arch of the central tower, against which the stalls were returned. Larger windows also were inserted in the aisles of the new choir. The vault, like the contemporary one of Gloucester choir, is a new departure. It is not really a vault whose web is supported by ribs, but a pointed barrel vault cut into by lunettes for the windows; on its inner surface are carved patterns ill adapted for the purpose. The thrusts of this vault are taken by external flying buttresses; the junction of the two systems of abutment is well seen from the graveyard to the south.

THE CHOIR, LOOKING EAST

So early as 1321 the central tower had been raised to its present height. As was so often the case, the additional weight "caused the four great piers, on which it rested, to sink into the ground. This, of course, tore away the masonry of the four limbs of the church from the piers, and yawning gaps began to appear between the tower arches and the main walls of the church." The piers had to be strengthened and the gaps filled up. This was done about 1338. At Canterbury the central piers were strengthened by running across a horizontal stone girder; at Wells, as at Glastonbury, the exceedingly strong and exceedingly ugly form of an arch carrying an inverted arch was adopted. This stone framework assumes something of the shape of St. Andrew's cross, by which name it is generally known. The eastern arch is not strengthened in this fashion, but by a massive screen, which is practically a solid wall, as at Canterbury, York, and Ripon. What makes the St. Andrew's cross more objectionable still is the large scale of its moldings, which dwarf everything in the cathedral into insignificance. Probably one of the last works of this period was to crown the whole exterior of the cathedral with a fine pierced parapet. These great works, beginning at the Lady chapel, may be said to have begun on the completion of the Chapter house in 1319, and were probably finished, or nearly so, by 1349, the year of the Black Death.

SIXTH PERIOD.—The central tower being saved, the next thing was to carry up western towers. Of these the southern was built after the year 1386; the northern tower is later than 1424. Moreover, rectilinear tracery was inserted in many of the early windows—*e.g.*, by Bishop Beckington in the clerestory and aisles of the nave (1443-1464). The same prelate built the three gatehouses, all of which display his rebus, a beacon in flames issuing from a barrel: viz., the Chain Gate, the Penniless Porch (opening to the Market Place), and Browne's Gate (at the end of Sadler Street). His magnificent canopied tomb, retaining much of the original colouring, was cut in two by the "restorers" at the time when they also restored the stalls out of existence; the tomb is in the south aisle of the presbytery, the canopy in the south transept.

The present cloister was built in the first half of the fifteenth century. Bishop Reginald had merely provided a covered walk to the external Lady chapel and his palace; its eastern wall was retained, but the walk was now vaulted; southern and western walks were also added, a three-sided cloister being thus obtained. The absence of a north walk indicates that the purpose of the cloister was to provide a path under cover for the processions on Sundays, Corpus

Christi Day, Palm Sunday, and other great feasts; the processional path in the cloister starts at the eastern and ends at the western processional doorway of the south aisle of the nave. From the presence of a music gallery in the south clerestory of the nave facing the northern entrance it may be argued that the Palm Sunday procession re-entered the church by the north porch.

In the nave are two large chantry chapels; on the north side that of Bishop Bubwith (*ob.* 1424), on the south that of Treasurer Hugh Sugar (*ob.* 1489).

The stone pulpit was put up by Bishop Knight (*ob.* 1547); the lectern by Robert Creyghton, who became dean in 1660.

BIBLIOGRAPHY.—Professor Willis in *Ecclesiologist*, xxiv. 303; and in the Bristol volume, 1853, of the British Archæological Association: and in the *Journal of the Somerset Archæological Society* for 1863.

J. H. Parker in *Gentleman's Magazine* (*Ecclesiology* volume), pp. 278 and 294.

Professor Freeman in *Somerset Archæological Society's Journal* for 1888, vol. 34.

Professor Freeman's *Cathedral Church of Wells*, London, 1870.

J. T. Irvine in *Somerset Archæological Society's Journal* for 1873, vol. xix.

Parker's edition of Rickman's *Gothic Architecture*, 1881, p. 167.

All the above need to be corrected in the light of the new evidence brought forward in Canon Church's *Early Charters of Wells*.

Messrs Hope and Lethaby on the "Statuary of the West Front," in *Archæologia*, lix. 143.

THE CATHEDRAL CHURCH OF THE HOLY AND INDIVISIBLE TRINITY AT WINCHESTER

BUILT FOR BENEDICTINE MONKS

THE present legal designation of Winchester cathedral dates only from the time of Henry VIII. It was originally the church of the abbey of St. Swithun; and, next to St. Swithun, its greatest patron was St. Birinus. Later on, an alternative dedication was to St. Peter and St. Paul.

It is the longest mediæval cathedral in Europe. Once it was surpassed by Old St. Paul's, London; now its only rival is St. Albans. But Winchester has an internal length of 526 ft. 6 in.; exceeding that of St. Albans by 5 ft. 4 in.; originally, before its Norman façade was pulled down, it was 596 ft. long externally. The nave, with its aisles, is 88 ft. wide; the Norman west front was 128 ft. from north to south; it therefore projected 20 ft. beyond each aisle; it is said to have contained two western towers, but the plan of the excavations shews that it may have been set out like Bury and Ely, with a single central tower flanked by chapels.

Vast as it is, no cathedral shews up so little. It has but one tower, and that barely overtops the roof; in outline it is depressed and monotonous; there are none of the double transepts, and lofty side-porches, which so picturesquely break up the lines of Salisbury, Lincoln, and Hereford. It has no conspicuous façade to give it grandeur to the west; it lacks the wide reach of open square and verdant close that delights at Salisbury and Wells. So far from dominating the city, like Lincoln or York, it hides

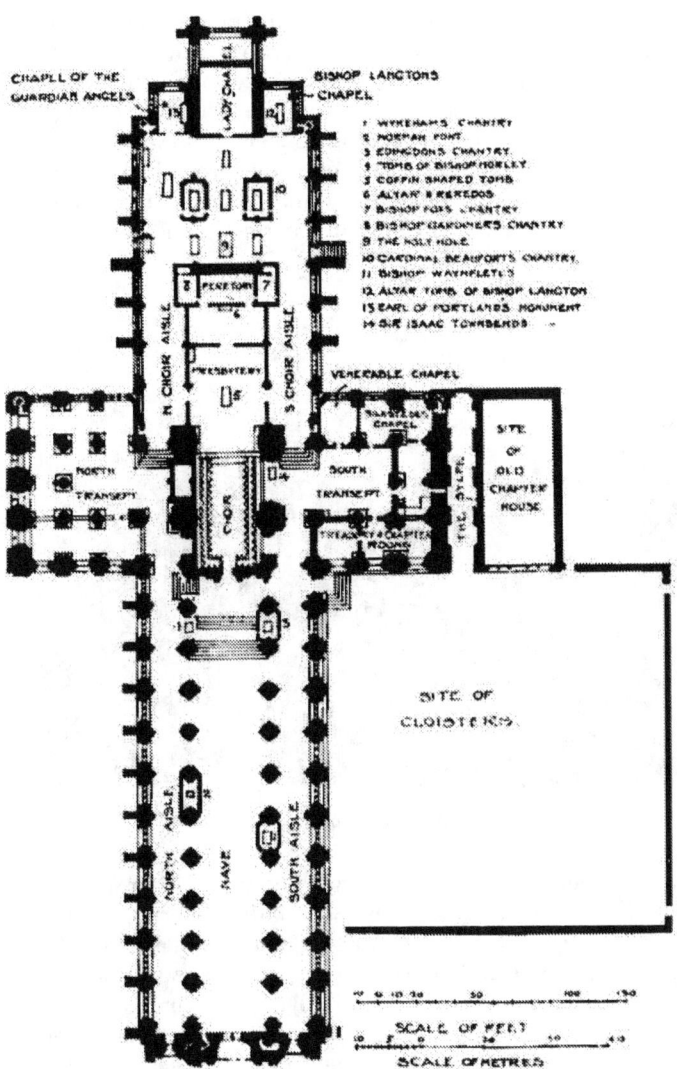

PLAN

out of sight. You walk all the length of the High Street and never get a glimpse of it; never was such a retiring cathedral. Generally, it is approached from the High Street through a hole in the wall; up a narrow passage, and down an avenue of obscuring elms. Slowly its huge mass uprears itself, sprawling over the ground like some stranded prehistoric monster. And, externally, it is as plain as it is huge: mainly an enormous bulk of blank

FROM THE NORTH-WEST

wall. Once it presented a better appearance; for though the Lady chapel to the east was rather shorter, to the west the nave was 40 ft. longer, and was flanked, like Southwell, by two Norman towers, or else was designed with a western transept, like Ely. The present west front does anything but prepare us for an interior so vast; as at Norwich and Gloucester, it seems rather the approach to some parish church of the second rank. All the more, perhaps, is one struck with the glorious interior. Only from St. Giles' hill, where Earl Waltheof was beheaded at dawn in 1076, can a comprehensive view of the vast cathedral be obtained; from this point in the early morning the view is one not to be forgotten.

FIRST PERIOD.—Bishop Walkelin began work in 1079; in 1086 a grant of oaks was made by the king, no doubt for the roofs, where several in good condition still remain in use as tie-beams, especially in the transept: this grant shews that the first part of the work was near completion:

FROM THE SOUTH-EAST

there was a consecration in 1093. Walkelin's eastern work has disappeared above ground, with the exception of the base of a cylinder inside Gardiner's chantry, a buttress on the north wall of the presbytery aisle near the north transept, and fragments at the eastern ends of the presbytery; but it remains in the crypt; from which it appears that the presbytery consisted of four bays and an apse, and was encircled by a procession path. From the latter a very long apsidal chapel of four bays projected eastward. Instead of the north-east and south-east chapels being tangential to the procession path, they are turned due east, probably to get proper orientation for the altars; from the thickness of their walls it is possible that they were crowned by small square turrets of the character of those at Canterbury. Walkelin also built a low central tower, and to abut it, he must have built most, if not all, of the transepts, and the eastern bays of the nave up to the Norman rood screen. Nothing is known of the building of the remainder of the long nave and the old west front; the work may have gone on, as at Ely and Peterborough, till the third quarter of the century. The crypt, as at Canterbury and Gloucester, was no doubt meant to be used; but there are no signs of altars, piscinas, or aumbries; probably from the very first it was liable to be flooded by water rising from the neighbouring stream, the Itchen.

In the north transept we are in presence of the earliest completed work in the cathedral. Much of it is the work of Bishop Walkelin (1070-1098); and, with the exception of some traceried windows inserted early in the fourteenth century to give more light to the eastern altars, it remains much as he left it. As his work is in the transepts, so once was the whole cathedral. As finished in the twelfth century, Winchester, in vastness of scale and stern power, must have been one of the most impressive cathedrals of England: more overwhelming than Ely or Peterborough; not inferior even to Durham. One is not sure that every change and transformation that took place at Winchester between the eleventh and the sixteenth century was not a change for the worse. For of the earliest temples of our race, torn as it were out of the solid rock, Walkelin's cathedral was one of the most awful and the most religious. The south transept of Hereford and the north transept of Chester are, in comparison, humble indeed. In colossal scale it finds one rival only—the mighty church of St. Alban. Artistically, they are miles apart; as far apart as two designs can be, one conditioned by the use of stone, the other of brick.

But not all the work of the Winchester transepts is by Walkelin; it is Norman, but part of it is a rebuilding rendered necessary by the fall of the central tower in 1107. The original work is readily distinguished. Those parts of the transept which are the nearest to the central tower have fine-jointed masonry; the vaulting of the aisles has ribs; the piers are larger. The further and earlier part of the masonry is much ruder, and the joints wider; the vaulting is without ribs, and the piers are smaller. In both parts the arches are square-edged, greatly adding to the peculiar severity of the aspect of this part of the church. The pier-arches are raised on stilts in order to get their crowns on a level with the intersection of the diagonal groins or ribs; for English builders in all periods, adhering to the Roman tradition, disliked domical vaults. The cushion or cubical capitals are of a simple type, little subdivided. Both transepts have double aisles. Lanfranc, in his metropolitan cathedral at Canterbury, was content with an aisleless transept; but Winchester cathedral was built on a scale befitting what was then the capital of the Norman realms; frequented all the more because it was a half-way house between London and Rouen. At the ends of the transepts the Norman aisles are returned, as at St. Stephen's, Caen, St. George de Boscherville, Cérisy-la-Forêt, and originally at Westminster and Ely. If the transept ends be examined externally and internally, it will be found that the two corner bays of each were intended for towers. Restore these in imagination and add another stage or two to the central tower, and there would be a central group of five towers, such as is unknown in England, but may be seen in the Romanesque cathedral of Tournai; with the addition of the great western tower, the exterior of Winchester would have been the most impressive, as it is now the most disappointing, in England. Partly no doubt from the extensive repairs necessitated by the fall of the central tower in 1107, partly from the great cost of a nave twelve bays long, transeptal towers were abandoned. Vast as this abbey of St. Swithun, there were two more abbeys, nearly as large, between it and the High Street; to the north that called the New Minster, to the south the nunnery of St. Mary. Adjoining New Minster to the north was the king's palace; altogether a marvellous group. Ultimately the New Minster was crowded out, and was replanted outside the town under the name of Hyde abbey; in its precincts were reburied the bones of King Alfred, no man knows where.

The Crypt.—From the north transept one descends to the crypt, which is well worth a visit, when not under water. The level of the river seems to have risen since the eleventh century, causing the crypt to be frequently flooded. It extends to the extreme east end of the present cathedral, and is in three parts. The first part, the western, consists of the substructure of the original presbytery. Secondly comes a very remarkable feature, of the same date—viz., a long aisleless chapel beneath the present retro-choir. Whether the chapel above it was a Lady chapel is a matter of uncertainty; for Lady chapels do not seem to have come into fashion till the thirteenth century. Thirdly, to the extreme east, comes the substructure of Courtenay's Lady chapel, built between 1486 and 1492. Most interesting of all is the sacred well, immediately beneath the High altar; far older than Norman crypt or Norman cathedral; the holy central spot of bygone Saxon and even British minsters.

South Transept.—Crossing the choir, we pass down a flight of steps to the south transept. At the top of these steps are the bolt-holes of the iron gates, which are now placed in the north-west corner of the nave, but which once stood here as a barrier to the pilgrims, who were allowed access to the north transept and choir aisles, but not to the choir itself, or to the south transept. They entered the cathedral by a doorway which may still be seen from the outside at the south-east corner of the north transept. In the south transept the same two periods of Norman work are recognisable which we saw in the north transept; but the aisles have been shut off by walls and screens, forming chapels on the east side and treasury on the west.

The central tower fell in 1107. Its fall was regarded as a judgment, William Rufus having been buried under it in 1100. The piers, as strengthened, are "most unwieldy and intrusive from their excessive size and squareness of form; the largest tower piers in England in proportion to the span of the arches that rest upon them." The tower windows could formerly be seen from below, as well as a grand specimen of late Norman arcading: now hidden from view by the wooden fan vault erected in 1634. The northern and southern sides of the piers were designed nearly flat, so as not to interfere with the stallwork of the monks. Originally the monastic choir of Winchester extended still farther to the west, being separated from the western bays of the nave by a stone screen. The old arrangement has been preserved at Norwich, Westminster, and Gloucester, and has been restored at Peterborough. Before leaving the south transept, the northern bay of the western triforium should be noticed. It has been only partially transformed into the style of the nave; for the semi-circular upper arch of the Norman triforium can still be seen. This helps us to restore in imagination the original triforium of the whole Norman nave. Near the steps leading up to the screen there remain some of the capitals of the Norman nave; from these it can be seen how low the Norman pier-arcade was.

SECOND PERIOD.—Of the period 1145-1190 only two traces seem to remain at Winchester. One is the doorway below the triforium bay mentioned above. Its zigzag ornament is of Norman character, but the obtusely pointed arch shews that it is subsequent, yet not much subsequent, to 1145. This doorway, with its queer fluted pilasters, may have been built by Henry de Blois (1129-1171) when he walled off this western aisle to serve as a treasury. If so, it is the only trace in the structure of this, the greatest of all Winchester's bishops. The other is the font, which like other fonts in Hampshire and those in Lincoln minster, Thornton Curtis, and Ipswich, is of black marble, brought from near Tournai. Among other subjects, there are representations of the legend of St. Nicholas.

THIRD PERIOD—*Retro-choir.*—Traversing the north choir aisle, we reach a large retro-choir; it consists of three bays, with an east end originally consisting of three chapels, of which the central one was a Lady chapel and projected slightly beyond the rest; this chapel was elongated still more in the fifteenth century. This retro-choir was built by Bishop Godfrey de Lucy, between 1189 and 1204, and therefore, with the Chapel of the Holy Sepulchre, is the earliest Gothic work in the cathedral, and contemporary with St. Hugh's work at Lincoln. De Lucy's work is not very ambitious, nor very rich, nor artistically on a plane with the Lincoln work. The object of the extension seems to have been to obtain a central Saint's Chapel surrounded by aisles, as well as more spacious eastern chapels. In the very centre, between the later monuments of Beaufort and Waynflete, would rise a pedestal supporting the shrine of St. Swithun. Over the shrine De Lucy seems to have built a tower, for in 1241 a *flabellum, i.e.*, a louvre board or shutter, fell down and damaged the shrine. It is quite impossible that the four slender piers now surrounding the

THE FONT

site of the shrine can have carried a tower; this central part of the retro-choir, however, seems to have undergone considerable remodelling, judging from masonry to be seen above the vault. The great defect is that, in relation to its area, it is so miserably low. To get it high, the architect would have had to sacrifice the east windows of the clerestory of the choir; and this he was not allowed to do.

The best part of the design is seen in the southern wall of the Lady chapel, and in the charming vaulted staircases which lead out of the side chapels to the roofs of the retro-choir and presbytery, and to the clerestory of the presbytery, from which a good view of the interior and of the interesting vault and glass of the presbytery is obtained. At the north-east corner of the retro-choir is an effigy in a vesica: it commemorates Bishop Ethelmar or Aymer, whose heart was buried at Winchester in 1261.

Chapel of the Holy Sepulchre.—Now we return to the north transept, which is cut off from the choir by a massive stone wall, the object being to keep the pilgrims out of the choir, to form a backing to the stalls, and, perhaps, to support organs. At the end of the twelfth century a curious chapel was built on to this wall: it contains frescoes representing the Passion of Our Lord.

THIRD PERIOD—*The Stalls.*—These were executed *c.* 1305. "The beauty and variety of the carvings are wonderful. There is no repetition; and the grace and elegance, as well as the fidelity, with which the foliage is represented, are nowhere to be surpassed. The human heads are full of expression; and the monkeys and other animals sporting among the branches have all the same exquisite finish." The misericords also are of great interest and beauty.

It was this period probably that the choir was removed to its present position from the nave. The reason probably was, as at Canterbury, that owing to the presbytery being raised high on a crypt, the High altar was barely visible to a choir placed in the nave.

FOURTH PERIOD.—All this time the Norman presbytery

remained standing; judging from the style of the new work, it was taken in hand c. 1320. At first all that was done was to pull down the apse and join up De Lucy's retro-choir to the Norman presbytery. De Lucy's central aisle, however, was narrower than that of the presbytery; the result was that the east end of the presbytery could not be made rectangular, but had to be polygonal.

THE CHOIR

Later on, the Norman presbytery itself was taken in hand, the work being done in very curious fashion. The templates of the 1320 work seem to have been used again, so that the work seems to be rather of 1320 than c. 1330–c. 1350. It consisted of substituting a two-story elevation, as in the choirs of Wells and Lichfield, for the three Norman stories. From the resemblance of some of the details of the work to that done in Edington church, Wiltshire, which was built by Bishop Edington and dedicated in 1361, it is probable that this bishop (1346-1366) completed the rebuilding, commenced by his predecessor. It would seem that the tracery of the windows had not been inserted when the Black Death attacked Winchester with frightful severity, leaving only some 2,000 alive out of a population of about 8,000; and that they remained without tracery and glass till late in the century.

The walls of the Norman aisles were not pulled down; it is probable therefore that their groined vaults were retained. If so, only the Norman piers, which supported the inner sides of these vaults, would probably be allowed to remain. But on the side next to the presbytery the piers and the spandrels of their arches were cut back, as may be seen near the tower, sufficiently to allow new piers and arches to be inserted in front of them.

To the same period belong the nine exquisite tabernacles in the retro-choir, on the wall at the back of the feretory; the naturalistic foliage of which is perhaps the best work in the cathedral. Below is an entrance to the crypt, now called the "Holy Hole." It can hardly be the original entrance. Above it is the inscription:—

"Corpora sanctorum sunt hic in pace sepulta
Ex meritis quorum fulgent miracula multa."

FIFTH PERIOD.—On his death in 1366 Bishop Edington left money for the work in the nave, which, he says, had been "begun by himself." It is usual to attribute to him the west front and the two western bays on the north side and the westernmost bay on the south side of the nave, where the windows are broad and low and the cusps of the panelling are foliated. Before commencing this work he pulled down 40 ft. of the Norman nave, either because the western tower was in a dangerous condition, or because so long a nave was not wanted after the stalls had been removed into the eastern limb. His work in the nave should be compared with that of Edington church, Wiltshire, which he commenced to rebuild in 1352 and which was dedicated in 1361. "The moldings at Winchester are largely the same as at Edington, but are more advanced, being much flatter, and more of the 'save-trouble' type; *e.g.*, the corresponding members of the great west window and the aisle windows are of the same dimensions, in the latter therefore being quite out of scale. It would seem that the bishop did not commence rebuilding the Winchester nave till he had completed or nearly completed Edington. Supposing him to have commenced the rebuilding of the nave *c.* 1360, the work would have gone on only for six years till his death in 1366; which together with the fact that he had to do so much demolition towards the west would explain why his work in the nave is so moderate in extent.

William of Wykeham, who succeeded Edington in 1367, resumed the work in the nave in 1371. It is to Wykeham that the upper part of the west front is probably to be attributed. To him belongs the transformation of the first eight bays of the southern pier-arcade, counting from the west. The greater part of the nave, including the magnificent lierne vault of stone, was completed by Wykeham's successors, as is shewn by the arms of Cardinal Beaufort and Bishop William of Waynflete on the bosses of the vault and in the string-course under the triforium. A curious feature of the high vault is that it is constructed without diagonal ribs. In the aisles the liernes are grouped into simple hexagonal or "stellar" patterns. The vault of the nave is often said to be unsupported by flying buttresses. They are there, however, between the vault and the outer roof of the aisles, sheltered from the weather, as are the flying buttresses of Durham nave, Wells, Worcester, and Salisbury.

This Winchester nave is of exceptional interest. In the first place, for its vast length of twelve bays of 250 ft. Norwich has fourteen bays of 230 ft. Secondly, because its Gothic vesture is little more than skin deep, the solid core of every pier and every wall, from pavement to roof, being Norman. It is just this combination of the massive solidity of Romanesque with the grace and elegance of

THE NAVE

Gothic which makes it what it is, the finest nave in the country. The walls are Norman; built, in Norman fashion, of rather small and square blocks; they are thick, nearly 10 ft. thick at the top; outside the south aisle may still be seen the flat Norman buttresses; hidden behind the balustrade of the clerestory are the upper arches of the Norman triforium, one of which we saw in the south transept. The vault rests on the original Norman vaulting-shafts, though they are stopped by Gothic capitals. They are not really stopped, however; for when we mount up to the back of the vault we find the vaulting-shafts, piercing *through* the vault, rising to the very top of the wall, to support, as they once did support, a wooden ceiling like that of Peterborough. The disposition of these shafts, as seen above the vaults, is very curious; it looks as if there was some intention to vault the nave in Norman days.

The casing of the Norman work is not merely skin-deep, as in Gloucester choir, where the Norman work can be seen at the back of the Gothic screens and panelling. The casing at Winchester goes at least one stone deep into the piers. But it was not executed all in the same way. William of Wykeham's work, in the seven western piers of the southern arcade, has the new moldings cut in the original Norman stones. But in the rest of the piers it was found simpler and cheaper to withdraw the Norman stones and replace them with new stones with Gothic moldings cut on them. In the former it will be seen that the blocks are usually small and rather square and with broad joints; in the latter they are large and with fine joints. The moldings of all this work are rather large and coarse; but we must remember that the architect was restricted at first to such moldings as could be developed out of the Norman detail, and in any case they had to be in harmony with the big and heavy Norman vaulting-shafts which were retained unaltered in the Gothic design.

The method adopted was similar to that which was employed in Waltham abbey, where the work was left half finished. At Winchester, first the Norman clerestory was pulled down altogether. Secondly the ground story was thrown into the triforium story by removing the arches of the former, together with the masonry in their spandrels. This left nothing standing but tall piers, connected by what had been the containing arches of the triforium; these arches still exist at the back of the panelled wall below the new clerestory windows. When this had been done, then everything, in the post-Wykeham work, was cased in Caen stone. It was a wonderful idea—this transformation of the stern old Norman nave into Gothic—but the idea came from Gloucester, where a similar, but less thorough, remodelling had been commenced c. 1330. In all probability the work in the nave was executed under the superintendence, not of William of Wykeham, one of the busiest men in the kingdom, and with no knowledge of the technique of building, but of William Wynford, who was Wykeham's master mason from 1394-1403. Begun by Bishop Edington c. 1360, the work in the nave was completed by Bishop Waynflete, who died in 1486; thus it occupied fully a century.

From the west door there is a superb view eastwards. The grandeur of the interior of the cathedral is much enhanced by the raising of the choir. This raising of the choir is due, however, to no æsthetic preferences on the part of the architects, nor to any wish to emphasise the importance of the clergy, but simply to the fact that, as at Canterbury, the choir is raised on a crypt. The vista, too, from west to east, is of great length.

Imposing, however, as the vista is, it is not so long as it might be, and it appears shorter than it really is. In the first place, out of the whole internal length of 526 ft., only 338 ft. come into the vista. This is because De Lucy kept his retro-choir so low. Far nobler would have been the interior of Winchester, if, as at Ely, York, Beverley, and Worcester, retro-choir and eastern chapels had been kept as high as presbytery and nave. Indeed, the Winchester vista of 338 ft. is surpassed even by that of the small cathedral of Lichfield. Secondly, owing to the destruction of screens, the apparent length has been greatly diminished. Formerly there were two solid screens: a rood screen in the nave, on the footpace of the second bay west from the tower; and a choir screen. Thirdly, as at St. Paul's, the great wall of the reredos is far too lofty, and is placed much too close to the east end of the presbytery, shearing off another 20 ft. of the apparent length of the interior. This reredos, indeed, beautiful as its detail must have been, is a vast mediæval

THE REREDOS

blunder — *i.e.*, from an artistic point of view; which point of view, to tell the truth, the mediæval architects cared little about in comparison with the religious purposes which they wished their architecture to subserve. Still here, as at St. Saviour's, Southwark, one cannot help wishing the reredos away; one would like to see once more behind and above the High altar, on their lofty platforms, the shrines of St. Swithun and St. Birinus, and on either side of them such delightful peeps as one has at Wells into retro-choir and eastern chapels. Beaufort's reredos has much to answer for.

In the south arcade of the nave are the two earliest of the magnificent series of chantries which are the especial glory of Winchester. They should be examined in chronological order. They are those of the following bishops: Edington, died 1366; Wykeham, died 1404; Beaufort, died 1447; Waynflete, died 1486; Fox, died 1528; Gardiner, died 1555. Thus they form a continuous record of the growth and development of our late Gothic architecture from 1366 to 1555.

SIXTH PERIOD.—Building activity now transfers itself to the eastern part of the cathedral. Prior Hunton (1470-1498) and Prior Silkstede (1494-1524) lengthened the Lady chapel and put in the admirable woodwork; their rebuses appear on the bosses of the vault. To Prior Silkstede is also due the fine pulpit and other work in the choir, and good screenwork in the south transept. In the Lady chapel are important wall paintings by an Italian artist, illustrating the life of the Blessed Virgin. Here also is the chair in which Queen Mary sat when she was married in this chapel to Philip

FOX'S CHANTRY

of Spain. The southern chapel was fitted up by Bishop Langton (*ob.* 1500) as his chantry chapel; here also is elaborate and beautiful woodwork. Between 1500 and 1528 Bishop Fox (1500-1528) set to work to complete the presbytery; and very likely every trace of early work would have been swept away from the transepts as well, had not building operations at Winchester been brought to a stop by the Reformation. As we saw above, the piers, arches, and clerestory of the presbytery had been rebuilt early in the fourteenth century. Fox rebuilt the gable of the presbytery, where his statue may be seen, and inserted the great west window. A second task was to rebuild the aisles of the presbytery, which, till now, had remained Norman. A third was to ceil the presbytery with a lierne vault. He built magnificent flying buttresses, evidently for a stone vault; but in the end put up a makeshift in wood; the emblems of the Passion, however, carved on the bosses, are of much interest, and should be inspected from the gallery. Fourthly, he built his own chantry

THE LADY CHAPEL AND BISHOP LANGTON'S CHAPEL.

chapel and tomb. Indeed, most chantry chapels were built during the bishops' lifetimes. Fifthly, he erected screens of stone between the presbytery and his new aisles. These Gothic screens were plainly wrought by English workmen. Just as plainly, the pretty Renaissance frieze which surmounts them was wrought by workmen imported from Italy. Sixthly, he constructed the Renaissance chests which stand on the screen. Bishop Henry de Blois (1129-1171) had collected from the crypt the bones of saints and kings buried there, and had transferred them, cased in lead, to the presbytery.

These sacred relics Fox placed in the present six chests. Among them are the bones of several Anglo-Saxon kings and queens; and of King Canute and William Rufus. The coffin shewn as the latter's is probably that of Bishop Henry de Blois.

In this cathedral, like that of St. Albans, the ritual divisions are very clearly marked and deserve attention. They consist of (1) the ritual nave, which extends up to the choir screen in the last bay but two; (2) the choir, in the westernmost bay of the nave and under the crossing; (3) a presbytery of three bays, extending up to the great reredos; (4) a feretory of one bay, for minor shrines, relics, and church plate in use; (5) the chief feretory between Beaufort and Waynflete's monuments, encircled by (6) the procession aisle; (7) a Lady chapel with flanking chapels.

So great is the wealth of minor work surviving in Winchester cathedral, so vast its scale, so impressive both the early Norman and the late Gothic design, so interesting its archæological history, that it stands almost unrivalled in the bede-roll of our cathedrals. It is not surpassed even by Lincoln; but to compare it with thirteenth-century Lincoln is to compare chalk with cheese; it is to be compared rather with the other Walkelin's vast cathedral at Ely; few will put Ely first.

BIBLIOGRAPHY.—Professor Willis in the Winchester volume of the Royal Archæological Institute, 1845.

Woodward's *History of Hampshire*.

Winchester Cathedral Records, edited by Dean Kitchin.

Winchester in "Historic Towns" series; by Dean Kitchin, 1893.

Diocesan History of Winchester, by Canon Benham.

Mr C. E. Ponting on Edington church in *Archæological Journal*, xlv. 43.

THE CATHEDRAL CHURCH OF CHRIST AND THE BLESSED MARY THE VIRGIN OF WORCESTER

Built for Benedictine Monks

AS is indicated by the form of dedication of 1218, "The cathedral church of the Blessed Virgin and Saint Peter and of the Holy Confessors Oswald and Wulfstan," Worcester is one of the pre-Conquest cathedrals; the present dedication dates only from the time of Henry VIII. With Hereford, Leicester, and Lindsey, the diocese of Worcester was carved out of the immense see of Lichfield, which was coextensive with the kingdom of Mercia, by Archbishop Theodore of Canterbury towards the end of the seventh century. Through the influence of Archbishop Dunstan, who had been Bishop of Worcester from 957 to 961, its Secular Canons were replaced by Benedictine monks by his successor, St. Oswald; and the cathedral was served by monks till the time of Henry VIII., when it was put upon the new foundation and reverted to Secular Canons. In 1062 St. Wulfstan became bishop. From his "great piety and dovelike simplicity" of character, he had great influence in the English Church, and was allowed by the Conqueror to retain his bishopric. He repaid William by beating off Robert Courthose, Duke of Normandy, when he attacked Worcester; he retained the see till his death at a great age in 1095. In the year 1201 miracles commenced at his tomb, "from fifteen to sixteen per diem being cured from every kind of sickness." In 1203 he was canonised.

WORCESTER CATHEDRAL.   405

St. Oswald, in 983, had rebuilt the cathedral in the style of his day. Of this Anglo-Saxon cathedral nothing is left, unless it be the balusters in the arcading of the slype. This

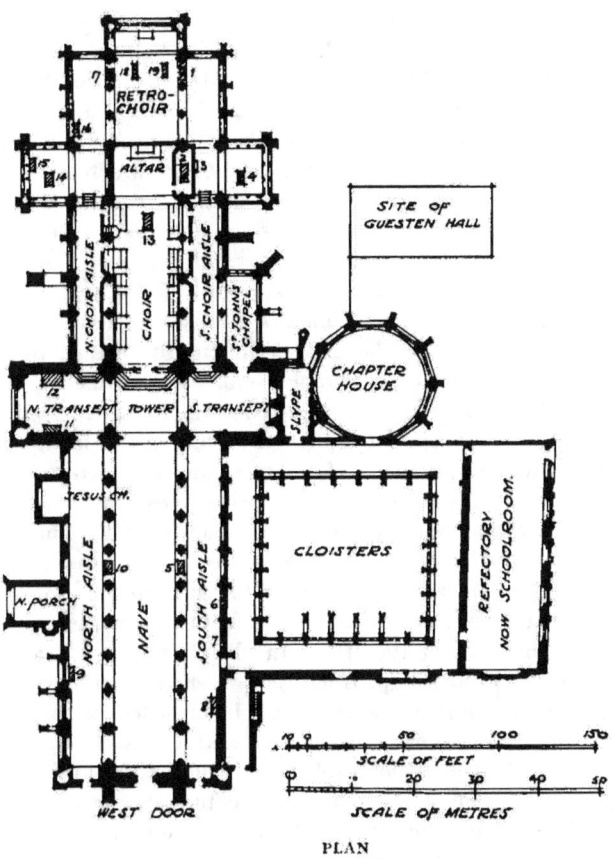

PLAN

work of the holy Oswald Wulfstan pulled down, with many searchings of heart. Almost he repented of his purpose and long stood silent in the churchyard, groaning. At last he burst into a flood of tears, "We wretches," said he, "pompously imagining that we do better work, destroy what the saints have wrought." Many centuries have passed since Wulfstan's day, and there have been many "restorations" of Worcester cathedral, but there is no record that anyone but Wulfstan commenced his work with tears and groans; modern "restorers" enter on their work with light hearts.

FIRST PERIOD.—Wulfstan commenced his cathedral in the new Anglo-Norman style in 1084, and in 1092 a synod met in the crypt, which had already been dedicated. The presbytery contained a shrine at the time of the fire in 1113; and was therefore probably finished by that year, together no doubt with much of the work to the west. Many fragments of Wulfstan's work remain above ground; e.g., the south aisle wall of the nave, with its tomb recesses;* the vaulting-shafts at the east ends of the two western bays of the nave; a shaft in the east of the north aisle of the nave; the two "vices," or circular staircases, in the west corners of the central transept; the arches which originally led from the central transept into elongated eastern apses, perhaps two stories high; and traces of his triforium and clerestory in the central transept and in the westernmost bay of the north side (on the inner face, near the junction of the choir to the tower) of the choir. Strange to say, the walls of the choir with the clerestory buttresses still exist; but they were faced internally with ashlar in the thirteenth century, except the part which is in the triforium chamber. Moreover so much of Wulfstan's crypt is left that we are able to restore the plan of the Norman presbytery. It consisted of three bays, ending in a semicircular apse, and encircled by a procession path, from which probably radiated three apsidal chapels, as at Gloucester. The nave was probably two bays shorter than the present one; and as its eastern bays were appropriated by the choir and the two screens, what remained to the west would be very short; it is likely therefore that it was not finished to the west. The transept was of the

* But this has been rebuilt or refaced in red sandstone.

same dimensions as at present. Since Bishop Samson, who died in 1112, was buried in front of the rood loft, and it was common to bury a builder in view of his work, it is probable that the eastern and central parts of the nave were built during his episcopate (1096-1112). Even when completed afterwards, the nave had but nine bays. The Norman churches of Worcester, Gloucester, Tewkesbury, Pershore,

FROM THE SEVERN

Leominster, and others belong to a western school of Romanesque quite distinct in origin from that which produced such churches as Ely, Norwich, and Peterborough: the western group is notable for the shortness of its nave and its employment of cylindrical piers, as well as for its predilection for the periapsidal plan. To simplify the vaulting of the crypt by making the compartments as small as possible, it was divided into more than a hundred

compartments. Owing to the curve of the apse many of
the compartments are not square; yet the difficulty of
vaulting triangles and trapeziums was successfully overcome,
even at this early date. When nearly all the other traditions
of Roman methods of construction had been lost, the
architects of mediæval Christendom still retained in their
crypts the traditions of Roman vaulting.

THE SOUTH TRANSEPT AND CHAPTER HOUSE

SECOND PERIOD.—To the first half of the twelfth century
belongs the circular Chapter house. Most monastic Chapter
houses were constructed in a rectangular form, which best
fitted on to the side of a cloister. But the cathedrals of
Secular Canons, when they built Chapter houses, usually
followed the Worcester precedent, except that they were
built polygonal instead of circular. Such was the beauty,
however, of the new form, that the monastic houses also, in

later times, themselves frequently adopted the polygonal form, as at Westminster, Evesham, Belvoir (Benedictine); Margam and Abbey Dore (Cistercian); Alnwick, Cockersand, Thornton, Carlisle, Bridlington, Bolton (Canons Regular). The polygonal Chapter house never appears in France; it is one of the most beautiful features in English Gothic.

THIRD PERIOD.—The fourth quarter of the twelfth century was occupied with much important work. Its commencement is marked by the record of the fall of the new tower, "nova turris corruit." What was this new tower? It may have been that Wulfstan's nave terminated in a single western tower, as at Ely and Hereford; but there is no record of the building of it, nor any traces of it. It is far more likely that this collapse in 1175 was of the central tower begun by Wulfstan, but probably not completed till the twelfth century. If so, it was at this time that the bays adjoining the crossing were rebuilt or remodelled. It was intended also to vault the whole of the central transept, for vaulting-shafts are to be seen in the centre of each arm of the transept and at the eastern corners. Now these vaulting-shafts are of the same curious design as those between the two western bays of the nave and its aisles; consisting of three shafts widely separated on either side from a quirked three-quarter bowtell. On the west wall of the south transept may be seen a trefoiled arch, which must have stood in front of the arcade of the wall passage; with this trefoiled arcade may be compared that of the north aisle of Lichfield choir.

At the same time the nave was completed to the west by the addition of two bays, which still remain. These two bays are a landmark in the history of English Gothic; but their great importance is hardly ever realised. We are constantly told that St. Hugh's work at Lincoln is the "first pure, undefiled Gothic" in England. But here at Worcester is work considerably earlier than that of Lincoln. And though in detail—*e.g.*, the sculpture of the capitals and the moldings—Lincoln is far ahead, yet, as has been shewn above, it was built without high vaults. The work at Worcester, on the other hand, was vaulted throughout. The vault of the south aisle remains, and the vaulting-shafts of that of the north aisle. Moreover, from the clerestory passage the marks of a high vault are clearly seen. This high vault no doubt remained till it was taken down by Bishop Wakefield; the tufa filling of the old vault seems, however, to have been reused in the present vault. While other builders were fumbling over vaulting problems, which they were to continue fumbling over for another half century, the whole theory was worked out at Worcester soon after 1175. The aisle is vaulted in oblong bays; the transverse arches are not broader than the diagonals, as they are in the contemporaneous vaults of Canterbury choir and in the aisle vaults of Lincoln choir, but are of the same section; the bays of the vault are not domed as in the choirs of Canterbury and Lincoln, but have level ridges; there are wall arches which, as in Lichfield choir, descend to the pavement without shafts or bases; most important of all, the narrow arches, the transverse ones, are pointed, while the wide diagonal ones are semicircular; it is a Gothic vault fully developed, except in the matter of the bosses; but even in the later work at Pershore the bosses are but tiny rosettes. All this perfectioning of the vault is seen in the Lady chapel at Glastonbury, begun in 1184 and consecrated two years later, and in Bishop Reginald's work at Wells, begun c. 1180. Of the three the work at Wells is the most advanced; at Glastonbury much of the detail is Romanesque, especially in the southern doorway. At Worcester, though the semi-circular arch is banished from the ground story, yet it reappears again and again in the triforium and clerestory, where also is much zigzag and other Romanesque ornament. At Wells the semicircular arch is expelled altogether. The capitals of the Worcester work are of great interest; by far the most common and characteristic is the "pollarded willow," very prevalent in St. David's cathedral, commenced in 1180; this capital appears not only in the piers and vaulting-shafts, but outside in the angle shafts of the buttresses, the doorway of the western slype, and that of the southern entrance to the cloister; it is common in the contemporary work at Lichfield, and appears, foliated, at Wells; the most magnificent example of all is seen in the east window of Pershore. Other capitals of this work at Worcester are a plantain leaf, symmetrical acanthus, and small knobby volutes. From the evidence of the capitals one would conclude that the work is earlier than that at Lichfield and Wells, and still earlier than that in the neighbouring abbey church of Pershore. The pier again has not been standardised as at Wells, Lichfield, and Pershore, to which therefore a later date than that of Worcester must be assigned. The Worcester piers indeed are ignorant of the Purbeck use; the shafts by which they are encircled are of coursed freestone; but they are not arranged in triplets, as in the other three churches; the bases also are without the water-holding molding, and the abaci are square. Externally, the elevation is wholly Romanesque; the clerestory windows and the west windows (restored) of the triforium are round-headed; the wall is very thick, and the buttresses run straight up into the parapet without any stages whatever. Both the work in the transept and that at the west end of the nave are of the same date, and none of it can be much later than 1175. This work included a west front; the wall passages into which from the circular turret staircases, at the levels of the triforium and clerestory respectively, remain, as also parts of the external ground course.

It is to be noted that this West of England Gothic is not only the earliest we possess, but is purely indigenous; there is not the slightest trace of French influence in it. Nor if there were any such influence, could it have been exercised at Worcester through copying the work of William of Sens at Canterbury; for the Worcester work and the Canterbury work were set out practically at the same time.

To the same period belong the vaulted slype or parlour in the west walk of the cloister, adjoining the church; the cellarage extending downwards towards the river; and the doorway leading from the college to the barrel-vaulted passage by which the cloister is reached from the south.

FOURTH PERIOD.—The above work can barely have been completed, when another calamity befell the church, viz., a great fire in 1202; it was not till 1218 that the church was re-dedicated. To have occupied sixteen years the repairs must have been on a very large scale. Yet there are no parts of the church now visible which bear indications of important repairs of the periods 1202 and 1218. If, however, we penetrate into the darkness and dirt of the triforium chambers, we shall find traces of flying buttresses. In most cases the pockets of the vault are filled with vast accumulations of powdery dust; but in some of the pockets are clearly seen stumps of masonry, the upper surface of which is not horizontal but skewbacked; plainly it is the springer of a flying buttress. Moreover, in the northern triforium there also remain the uppermost courses (skewbacked) of some of the flying buttresses. On the inner wall, moreover, behind the piers, are disturbed surfaces of masonry in which plainly were once bonded in the heads of flying buttresses. There must therefore once have been in each triforium chamber a whole row of internal flying buttresses, like those which still exist at Wells, and those which formerly existed at Pershore, but which, with one exception, have been removed. When were they put up? Certainly not in Wulfstan's church, for flying buttresses were not then known. Moreover, his clerestory buttresses are cut into to receive their heads. Nor did they belong to the present choir; for if they had been built to transmit the thrusts of its high vault, they would certainly not have been removed. It follows that since they do not belong either to the work begun in 1084 or to that begun in 1224, they must belong to that necessitated by the fire of 1202. On this evidence we conclude that the work done between 1202 and 1218 was none other than the repairing and vaulting of the Norman presbytery, central span as well as aisles. And it was this presbytery, finished in 1218, which controlled the design of that which was commenced some twenty years later, and which to a large extent is but the previous work recased.

FIFTH PERIOD.—At length the tide turned in the fortunes of Worcester. The body of St. Wulfstan, after lying dormant for more than a century, began to work miracles. Pilgrims came in crowds. It was the age of pilgrimages. Even King John came with offerings; and his body was brought here for burial in 1216. With the pilgrims came the need for more accommodation in the eastern limb of the church, and from the pilgrims no doubt came the money to provide it; in 1224 it was found necessary to make a final agreement between Bishop Blois and the convent as to equitable distribution of the receipts from the offerings at St. Wulfstan's shrine. It was resolved to wholly rebuild the eastern arm of the church, and to extend it to the east. Similar eastern extensions with funds provided from similar sources were going on elsewhere. Winchester cathedral was not long enough to provide for the crowds who resorted to the shrine of St. Swithun, the Healer; Rochester had turned a Scotch baker into St. William of Perth, and had to provide eastward extensions; Ely had to rebuild its presbytery to give room to the votaries who came from all East Anglia to venerate St. Etheldreda; Durham erected the Chapel of the Nine Altars to accommodate those who flocked from all northern England to the shrine of St. Cuthbert; Canterbury crypt—spacious as it was—was too strait for the pilgrims who came from all over Christendom to worship the relics of its murdered archbishop; both Lincoln and St. Albans were crowded out, and later in the century were to build eastward in honour of St. Hugh and St. Alban. St. Wulfstan, while his repute was fresh, was for a time exceedingly popular.

The new work is remarkable in plan. The Canterbury precedent of removing the stalls into the eastern limb, where they are now, was not followed; they remained in the crossing and the easternmost bay of the nave till the reign of Queen Mary. If the plinths of this eastern bay be examined, it will be seen that they are higher than those to the west; which argues that the pavement on which the stalls stood was at a higher level than at present. (The steps leading up to the present stalls are modern in arrangement.) The High altar stood in the same bay as at present, but further forward, occupying the same position as at Salisbury, Southwell, Beverley, and Pershore, *i.e.*, in a line with the eastern transepts. That the altar platform was at about the same height as at present is shewn by the level of the sill of the doorway leading on to it from Prince Arthur's chantry chapel. The presbytery consisted of no less than five bays, not including the space between the eastern tower piers. What did the monks want with so long a presbytery as this, and why did they keep their stalls out of it? The reason is that they had to provide space in it (1) for the High altar; (2) for the "medium" or matins altar, employed for other services than that of High Mass: (3) for the tomb of King John; and (4) for the shrines of two great local saints, St. Oswald and St. Wulfstan. It was no doubt the latter consideration which turned the scale. They might indeed, like other people, have built a Feretory for the local saints at the back of the High altar. But for more than a century St. Oswald and St. Wulfstan had been lying in front of the High altar, one on each side. In just the same position at Canterbury lay the bodies of two other local saints, the martyred Archbishop Alphege and St. Dunstan. When Canterbury choir was rebuilt in 1175, the bodies of the two archbishops were reburied in the same position: a Feretory indeed was built, but it was not for them, but for St. Thomas of Canterbury. So it was at Worcester. It was arranged to rebury its two bishops in the same relative position as before. If we could see Worcester presbytery again as it was finished *c.* 1260 we should find King John's tomb moved to the position now occupied by it; the effigy, however, painted, not gilt; on the north, attached to the corner pier of the eastern transept, we should see the shrine of St. Oswald, on the south, similarly placed, that of St. Wulfstan; both would have small altars at their west end, like that now attached to St. Edward's shrine at Westminster.

The bay east of that containing the High altar would be the procession path; and to the east of it was built a Lady chapel * three bays deep; it was flanked by aisles only two bays deep, each screened off from the Lady chapel and containing an altar; its own easternmost bay was not aisled, in order to get side light on the altar. Moreover, to obtain more altars still, eastern transepts were thrown out. All these eastern parts, instead of being low as at Pershore, Hereford, Salisbury, Wells, Winchester, rise to the same height as the presbytery, in this agreeing with Lincoln and Beverley. The plan much resembles that worked out a generation earlier at Rochester; but at Rochester the easternmost compartment was to be used as presbytery, and therefore the Norman crypt had to be extended eastward in order to keep it up to the level of the work to the west; otherwise the High altar would have been in a hole and invisible. At Worcester, on the other hand, the new presbytery was built on the top of the ancient crypt, which therefore did not need to be extended eastward. The result is that the Worcester Lady chapel and procession path are at a low level, to which one descends by a flight of six steps. Consequently the piers and arches here are considerably loftier than those of the presbytery, and proportionately more impressive. The arches are also of narrower span, because it was unnecessary to give the procession path the breadth of the bays of the presbytery. Consequently again the eastern are more acutely pointed than the western arches of the eastern limb, and proportionately more graceful; the latter tend to the proportions which prevail in the pier-arcade of Lincoln nave; the former to those of Westminster and Wells. Taking it as

* There is no documentary evidence as to the dedication or use of this chapel; but a chapel so spacious and dignified can hardly have been provided except for the services of Our Lady, which would be attended by the whole body of monks, and for which a large amount of accommodation would be required.

a whole, the design of the eastern bays of Worcester is one of the most successful in the Middle Ages. As at Beverley, the triforium chamber is masked by a solid wall ornamented by two arcades of unequal height; at Worcester both arcades are pointed; the more beautiful design of Beverley has a trefoiled arcade in front of a pointed one; at Worcester the solid wall of the choir triforium is that of the choir dedicated in 1218, masked and ornamented with a double arcade; the Norman piers and arches were taken out and replaced by new ones without taking down the Norman walling above them; a similar, but still more remarkable transformation was going on, almost contemporaneously, in Lincoln choir. Moreover the high vault at Worcester springs from the sill of the clerestory; while that of Beverley, springing at a higher level, greatly increases the apparent height and lightness of the design. But if the Worcester design must yield to that of Beverley, it yields to nothing else of the period.

There is documentary evidence that the eastern part of the work was begun in 1224. Moreover in that same year Bishop Blois built a charnel house north of the western bays of the nave; evidently because the first part of the work was built in the monks' cemetery, and it was necessary to provide for the reburial of bodies which had been disinterred. The date of the new work has sometimes been fixed at 1201, the year when the miracles at St. Wulfstan's shrine are recorded to have commenced; but the high vaults both of the Lady chapel and the eastern transepts have well-managed longitudinal ridge ribs, which, even at Lincoln, were not in use till c. 1230. It is not known when the presbytery was finished; but since there lie buried side by side in front of the altar of the Lady chapel Bishop Blois and his successor Bishop Cantelupe,* it is to be

---

* The authority for this is Noake in his *Monastery of Worcester*, p. 344, who merely says that these "two effigies on the floor of the Lady chapel are supposed to be those of Blois and Cantelupe." On the other hand Thomas, p. 134, says that Cantelupe was buried near the High altar.

concluded that they were regarded as co-founders, and that the presbytery was finished during the episcopate of the latter, *i.e.*, between 1237 and 1266. The fact also that sixty marks came from Bishop Nicholas in 1280 for the rebuilding of the tower looks as if at that date money were no longer required for the presbytery. We may take 1260 as an approximate date for the completion of the presbytery.

When the eastern portions were complete there would be for some time a stoppage of the works while the masons were taking down the upper portion of the presbytery of 1202-1218 to make room for the present one. That there was such a stoppage is proved by several differences of treatment; *e.g.*, the eastern portion has a roll, the western a hollow in the soffit of the transverse arches of the vaulting. One of the most marked features in the new work, as in Lincoln choir, Salisbury, and Beverley, is the great use of detached shafts of Purbeck marble. These were not added till the time of Bishop Giffard (1268-1301). If they had been added at the time when the piers were built, then, being monoliths, they would have settled much less than their central cores, which are in courses of freestone with mortar joints; and as more and more weight was superposed on them with the growing height of the building, would certainly have been shattered. As a rule marble annulets were constructed at the same time as the piers; and when the time came, the shafts were fitted into these. Where the Purbeck shafts consisted of more than one piece, it was customary, as at Waverley abbey, to insert a sheet of lead in the joints to give a certain amount of play; then the joints were encircled with copper rings; as at Salisbury. To keep the shafts upright, they were cramped to the freestone core by dowels with a tang. In the great use of Purbeck marble Worcester acknowledges the influence of the Canterbury school. But in its abutment system it is wholly Romanesque; for it is without flying buttresses, except those constructed between 1736 and 1789, and the external buttresses are vertical, without stages, and of little projection; the builders relied for abutment simply on the thickness of the earlier walls; it is surprising that a building of such unscientific construction should not have collapsed; old prints shew indeed that the east wall of the Lady chapel did fail, and was long propped up by flying buttresses.

Externally the influence of the Western school of Gothic is seen in the poverty-stricken ground course and windows, as well as in the unstaged buttresses and the absence of external fliers.

Internally the liberality of the pilgrims is shewn not only in the largeness of scale of the new work, but in the wealth of detail. Especially noteworthy is the lovely arcading running round the eastern walls; the sculpture in the spandrels, where genuine, is of exceptional interest; in addition to scriptural subjects there are many creatures from the Bestiaries, including the amphisbæna and the crocodile.

Externally the design reminds one of Salisbury, begun in 1220, in the studied avoidance of external detail; internally, *e.g.*, in the north aisle, the internal treatment of the windows is interesting and diversified; externally the windows are quite plain.

On the south side of the present choir is the Sacristy, and south of it, in 1377, was built a Treasury, approached from the Sacristy by a staircase. This sacristy has ignorantly been restored as a chapel, and has been given the name of St. John's chapel, simply because it contained an altar. But most sacristies, even in parish churches, contained an altar; sometimes the novices were taught the services at it; at St. Paul's cathedral such of the canons as were sick or desired to say their Hours privately were allowed to do so in the sacristy. There was a similar building on the north side of the present choir, the upper part of which was the sacrist's lodging. There still remains a pretty oriel window in the north aisle from which the sacrist commanded a view of the presbytery; his chamber therefore served as a Watching loft.

SIXTH PERIOD.—When the remodelling of the choir of 1202-1218 was complete, the next thing would be to rebuild the lower portion of the central tower. For this, as we have seen, money was left in 1280.

SEVENTH PERIOD.—The cost of the Novum Opus must have been very great, and may well have left the convent in debt. At any rate there is no record of any more building

THE NAVE

till the fourteenth century, when Bishop Cobham (1317-1327) commenced the reconstruction of the north side of the nave. For himself he built a chantry chapel and was buried therein. This chapel, afterwards styled the Jesus chapel, and the adjoining bays of the aisle are vaulted in tufa, as are the whole of the eastern limb of the cathedral and the two western bays of the nave.

After Cobham's death the polychromatic treatment of the arches ceases; the ugly design of his bases is abandoned; and the web of the aisle vault is built in ashlar, perhaps because the supply of tufa had come to an end. To the period between 1327 and the Black Death of 1349 may be assigned the whole of the ashlar vaulting of the north aisle of the nave, the third, fourth, fifth, sixth, and seventh bays of the ground story, counting from the east, and the third, fourth, and fifth bays of the triforium and clerestory. The sixth and seventh bays of the latter were left unfinished; it will be seen that in design these resemble the work on the south side of the nave; nor was the tracery inserted as yet in the clerestory windows. A curious mixture of work results. In the second pier from the west of the north nave there remain the vaulting-shafts of the Norman church; the two western bays are c. 1175; but in the adjoining two bays to the east the ground story is 1317-1327, while the triforium and clerestory are 1375-1394. Bishop Cobham's design is hardly typical of the period. With that tenderness for older design which one sees at this time at Ely, St. Albans, Beverley, and Westminster, the architect has suppressed his individual preferences, and designed his work so as to be a nice transition from the twelfth-century bays near the west front to the thirteenth-century bays of the presbytery; so his piers and clerestory are a version of the work immediately to the west of him, while his triforium is a repeat of that of the presbytery.

It is noteworthy that the fourteenth century was marked by the adoption of a new building material, red sandstone. The Norman builders up to c. 1150 had employed a grey friable sandstone; those of the last half of the twelfth and the first half of the thirteenth century both employed a freestone of uncertain provenance.

In the ante-room of the library is preserved part of a door of the cathedral (fourteenth century), under one of the hinges of which were authentic fragments of the skin of some poor wretch flayed alive for sacrilege; these are now in a glass case in the north-east transept. The great Guest Hall, now in ruins, had been built in 1320.

EIGHTH PERIOD.—Before the new work on the north side was joined up to the western bays of the nave money seems to have become scarce at Worcester. Perhaps pilgrims had begun to desert St. Wulfstan for newer if not holier saints. Hitherto St. Wulfstan had had a monopoly in the West country. There was not another saint of equal efficacy till you reached Winchester. But in 1287 Bishop Cantilupe began to bring the dead to life at Hereford; and in 1327 Edward II. was buried at Gloucester, and miracles soon followed there also. So Worcester now had rival miracle-workers on either side. Moreover, in 1349 came the Black Death, and little can have been done for several years after. At length, however, the work was resumed. First the cloister was rebuilt and glazed c. 1372; the bosses of the

THE NORTH-WEST CORNER
OF THE CLOISTER

vault are of singular interest; those in the south walk contain a Jesse Tree; the north walk is practically an open-air Lady chapel; for on the bosses are carved adoring angels turning towards the central boss, where sit the Mother and Child. The upper part of the central tower was built c. 1374; it is noteworthy that it is 196 ft. from the east and west ends of the church, and 196 ft. to the top of its pinnacles.

NINTH PERIOD.—Then came a vigorous bishop who greatly accelerated the work, Henry Wakefield, 1375-1394. The gaps in the triforium and clerestory of the north nave were filled up, and the whole of the south side, up to the two western bays of *c.* 1175, was rebuilt, and the west front remodelled ; in the southern clerestory are curious straight-sided arches, as in Boxgrove Priory church, the vestibule of the Westminster Chapter house and Hereford north transept. The south aisle has a rich lierne vault, pretty enough when set out on plan, but a failure when seen in perspective. The south aisle wall was now raised, and the present large windows were inserted. The high vault of the nave was also completed ; it is of the same type as that of Westminster choir. Since the stall work in the two easternmost bays of the nave was begun in 1375 and put up in 1379, it follows that at any rate the eastern part of the high vault was completed by the latter year ; this is borne out by the fact that there are records of vaulting going on in 1376 and 1377. It was in this period no doubt that the high vault of the two western bays of the nave was replaced by the present one ; partly perhaps because it was about 2½ ft. lower than the vault to the east, partly to get headway for the new west window, of which the date is 1380. The north porch was added in 1386. To the same period belongs the Watergate, built in 1378, leading down to the ancient ferry over the Severn, still in use (from the opposite bank is one of the finest views in England) ; also the Great Gatehouse or Edgar Tower was probably now remodelled. The Refectory, now the School Hall, is recorded to have been built with the cloister in 1372 ; the flowing tracery of its windows looks earlier, but much work at Worcester of the last half of the fourteenth century belongs in style to the first half. The east wall of the refectory, on which is a Majestas of the thirteenth and fourteenth centuries, is of Norman date. The refectory is built on the cellarage of the old Norman refectory; below is some groined vaulting, with barrel vaults to the east, and two fine Norman piers.

TENTH PERIOD.—By the end of the fourteenth century the great task of rebuilding the church had been completed, and little was done or needed to be done up to the dissolution of the abbey in 1540. The circular Chapter house was converted externally into a polygon in order to compensate for the weakening of the walls by the insertion of large windows. The chief work was the erection in 1504 of the magnificent chantry chapel of Prince Arthur, eldest son of Henry VII., who died at Ludlow castle in 1502, and was brought here for burial in what was regarded as one of the holiest spots in England, because of the neighbourhood of the shrines of St. Oswald and St. Wulfstan: the reredos of the chapel, though mutilated, is of much interest; indeed all the detail of this chapel is of fine design and execution, and merits careful study. King John had been reburied between the two patron saints, thereby fulfilling an old prophecy, "*inter sanctos collocabitur*"; probably his effigy was then flush with the pavement; the pedestal on which it now rests was erected between 1520 and 1522.

ELEVENTH PERIOD.—The chief Jacobean addition is the fine stone pulpit, formerly surmounted by a sounding-board. As it bears the arms of Scotland, it cannot be earlier than the Union of Scotland and England; it is probably *c*. 1640. It formerly stood in the nave, and the Mayor and Corporation bitterly complained when Archbishop Laud had it removed; it was placed in its present position between 1747 and 1756. The Worcester folk were at all times inordinately fond of preaching; and even in pre-Reformation days had open-air sermons at a preaching cross, which formerly stood north of the nave.

TWELFTH PERIOD.—In modern days Worcester has been embellished with various furniture by Sir Gilbert Scott—the reredos, the nave pulpit, the choir screen; to his credit it deserves to be recorded that what he wished himself was not the present flimsy screen, but a double screen carrying an organ. The font and font cover are by Mr Bodley. The Jesus chapel has a noble screen and rood by Mr R. A. Briggs. But the great "restoration"—the most drastic to which any of our cathedrals has been subjected—was that carried out by Mr Perkins from 1857 onwards. Internally many of the foliated capitals and much of the figure sculpture are modern; externally, as was inevitable from the decay of the soft red sandstone, the whole surface has been recased; it was not necessary, however, to recase it with horrible machine-dressed masonry. It is, however, when one looks at Britton's fine print of the exterior that one realises that the greater part of the external design, and not merely the masonry, has been swept away; all the four fronts, west, east, north, and south, are entirely modern compositions; all the pretty tracery in the lancet windows has, as in the west front of Ripon, been ruthlessly cut out: and though there was money galore for destruction and forgery and for gaudy abominations of alabaster and brass, there was not money enough to replace the cheap, mean, and contemptible roof of slate put up c. 1791, a disgrace to the cathedral and the city. But though much is lost, much remains; artistically as well as archæologically, the cathedral is of the very greatest interest: and it must in fairness be admitted that the eastern façade of the Lady chapel, and the northern and southern façades of the eastern transepts, all by Mr Perkins, are genuine successes.

TOUR OF THE CLOISTER.—Starting at the eastern procession door of the cloister we reach (1) the inner slype or parlour; (beyond which is the ruined Guest Hall, in whose windows beautiful tracery lingers; its fine roof has been put up in Holy Trinity church near Shrub Hill railway station); (2) the Chapter house; (3) the late twelfth-century entry to the cloister from the outer court, which contains to the east the Great Gatehouse or Edgar Tower, and to the west the Watergate; (4) the refectory, now the King's cathedral school, in the south walk; (5) the lavatory, in the west walk; (6) west of this walk, at right angles to it, and extending down to the river, was the monks' dormitory and rere-dorter on the first floor, with cellarage below: (7) at the end of this walk is the fine vaulted slype or outer parlour, with the night stairs in it from the dormitory; (8) hard by is the western door by which processions re-entered the nave.

BIBLIOGRAPHY.—Professor Willis' papers on the cathedral and monastery in vol. xx. of the *Architectural Journal*.

Littlebury's *Guide to the City of Worcester* contains a chapter on the cathedral by Canon Wilson.

Monograph by the Honourable Mrs O'Grady on the Sacristy; also paper on Bishop Cobham in the *Worcester Archæological Society's Transactions*.

Bloxam's paper on the monuments in *Gentleman's Magazine*, October 1862.

THE CATHEDRAL CHURCH OF ST. PETER, YORK.

BUILT FOR SECULAR CANONS

I. YORK Minster has had many predecessors—Romano-British, Saxon, Norman, and Transitional cathedrals. From the first period nothing survives, unless it be two walls of herring-bone masonry in the crypt. Little remains of Norman work except in the western portion of the crypt. In the centre of the crypt are fine fragments of the substructure of the choir of Archbishop Roger (1154-1181) whose work is seen at Ripon. The present cathedral is mainly of three periods. The great transept was built between 1230 and 1260; the nave, Chapter house, and vestibule between 1291 and 1324; the retro-choir, choir, and towers between 1361 and 1474. But though the work is of three periods, it is practically of only two designs, the choir and retro-choir being only a later version of the design of the nave.

II. As at Lichfield and Wells, the canons of York in the end left not a fragment of the earlier work visible above ground. They must have had vast resources at their disposal, in addition to what they received in offerings at the shrine of the local saint, St. William of York. He died in 1154, after working thirty-six miracles, a list of which used to hang up in the vestry; he was canonised in 1227. It was soon after the latter date that the rebuilding of the cathedral commenced; and it is not unreasonable to believe that the offerings from his shrine had something to do with the vastness of scale on which the new work was planned; the new transept being not only exceptional both in height

YORK CATHEDRAL

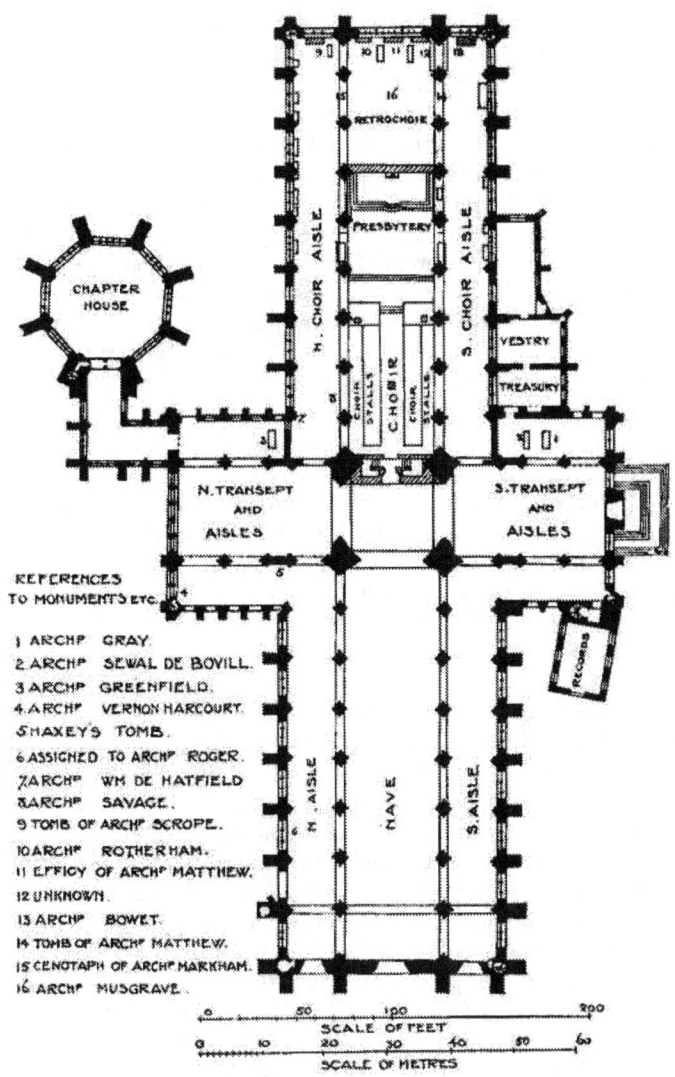

PLAN

and breadth, but also in having aisles on the western as well as on the eastern side—an extravagance unknown in our Gothic cathedrals, except at Wells and Old St. Paul's. It is amusing to find the double-aisled transept in the sub-cathedral of Beverley Minster. There seems to have been an internecine rivalry between the canons of Beverley and York. Both churches have double aisles to the central transepts; both continue in full height to the east end; both have western towers; and though Beverley has no central tower, it has by compensation an aisled eastern transept, where York has but transeptal aisles. Moreover, the high vaults of Beverley are of stone. In beauty of proportions and of detail—in everything but scale—Beverley has much the best of it.

FIRST PERIOD.—The south transept was built *c.* 1230-1241, the north transept 1241-1260. The façade of the south transept is confused and commonplace, overloaded with ornament, and cut up too much with windows; that of the north transept—with the Five Sisters—is of noble simplicity. In the south transept is the beautiful monument of Archbishop Gray (1216-1255), the builder also of Ripon west front and Southwell choir. "The view which is presented to the visitor on entering this transept is without doubt the finest in the cathedral. The magnificent spaciousness of the transept, the majesty of the lofty lancets which nearly fill the north gable, the solemn light struggling through their ancient diapered glass, the vastness of the central tower with its unrivalled lantern vaulted at a height of 180 ft. above the pavement, combine to produce an impression fully sustaining the great reputation of the minster." In proportions, the design of the transept is not a success; the elevation dwindles away upward, the triforium being made far too large at the expense of the clerestory. In itself the triforium is a very fine composition, only there is not room for it, nor is it in harmony either with the pier arcade below or the clerestory above. It is the largest and most complex triforium in the country; consisting of two pairs of acute lancets below, set under two acute lancet arches, which again are set under an outer arch almost semicircular. A similar design is seen in Whitby choir. This was the last big triforium arcade built in England (save the exceptional one in Ely choir). There had always been a feeling in favour of the diminution of the triforium. Even in the twelfth-century naves of Tewkesbury and Gloucester the triforium had been cut down to very small proportions; in Beverley choir the triforium is greatly attenuated; and very soon afterwards it is to be seen nearing extinction in Exeter choir and in the nave of York itself.

The proportions of the transept are ruined by the lowness of the clerestory; at Westminster the triforium is only half the height of the clerestory; here the triforium is the loftier of the two. Nor was it meant to be any higher than it is at present; for in the triforium spandrels there are the springers of a stone vault, which, if it had ever been put up, would have risen no higher than the top of the present clerestory wall. How the transepts were roofed at first is not known; probably with some form of roof resting on the clerestory walls. In the fifteenth century the present wooden ceiling was put up; its ribs are mainly decorative; it is in reality a pointed tunnel vault with lunettes cut into it to give passage to the light from the clerestory windows. Externally one sees traces of the influence of

THE NORTH TRANSEPT

Lincoln Minster; in the clerestory the abacus is continued so as to form a string-course, and each bay contains three lancet lights; while the bays of the aisle contain two lancets, separated by small chamfered buttresses receiving the thrust, as at Lincoln, of the intermediate rib of the quinquepartite vault of the aisle. Here, as at Lincoln and in the eastern transept of Durham, we see in the marble shafting the incursion of the south-eastern style of Canterbury choir.

SECOND PERIOD.—When the transept was completed, York minster consisted of a spacious transept, a late twelfth century choir of the character of that of Ripon, and a Norman nave. When the work of rebuilding was resumed, the choir, which was spacious, was spared once more, and the canons proceeded to take down and rebuild the Norman nave, laying the foundation stone in 1291, and beginning at the south-east. The new nave is so exceedingly broad and lofty that it may well have been built round and over the top of the old Norman nave. The money came from "indulgences, penances, briefs, bequests, and offerings at the shrine of St. William," which was at that time in the Norman nave, and which it would be very desirable not to disturb. The nave, like the whole minster, is exceedingly impressive in the vastness of its spaces: no building of such dimensions could fail to be impressive. Its proportions, however, are not good. The broadest cathedral nave in England (its span is 45 ft.), and the loftiest (it is nearly 100 ft. high), it ought to be one of the longest, which it is not. Matters are made worse, as in Lincoln nave, by the wide spacing of the piers, the result of which is to reduce the apparent length of the nave. It contains only eight bays. Had it been divided into ten or more bays, it would have looked far longer. It was designed not so much on architectural lines as a glass house. The canons wanted the greatest possible breadths of stained glass in aisles and clerestory. The error in the proportions was corrected in the choir, which, though no longer than the nave, has nine bays instead of eight. The exceptional height and breadth of the nave made it very costly; and the funds plainly ran short, for, though begun in 1291, it was not ceiled till c. 1354. To make matters worse, the canons were building a new Chapter house and vestibule at the same time as the

THE NAVE

nave: so that funds may well have failed. Nevertheless, at Ely equally large works were completed before 1360, though they were not commenced till 1321, and were executed with much greater richness of detail than at York.

Another feature which shows that the York canons had started their work without considering whether they would be able to finish it, is the omission of a stone vault, which was plainly contemplated at the outset; the pinnacles built for the purpose of weighting the buttresses against the thrusts of a stone vault still exist on the south side. When the north side was built, the canons had abandoned hope of vaulting the nave in stone, and so did not put up big pinnacles. It is well to remember, however, that the exterior of the nave was designed originally to have flying buttresses and big pinnacles on both sides. Flying buttresses have lately been built on both sides of the nave. In the end, as in Selby choir, a sham vault of wood was put up. One cannot help regretting these shams. It would have been Gothic to recognise honestly that the ceiling was wood, and to design it in wood and not in lithic fashion. Then we might have seen an English Gothic cathedral with such a hammerbeam roof as that of Westminster Hall: very magnificent it would have been.

The design of the nave is the very reverse of that of the transept. The Purbeck marble use disappears; and the builders reverted to the freestone clustered columns which no doubt were then standing in the choir of the minster, and which still remain in that of Ripon. And whereas in the transept the triforium had been important and the clerestory insignificant, in the nave the clerestory nearly crushes the triforium out of existence, as in the contemporary work at Exeter. To reduce the height of the triforium stage, the lean-to roof is much flattened; to minimise its importance, a blank wall is built in front of it, and the jambs and clerestory mullions of the windows are brought down to the sill of the triforium. A similar device had been adopted in the subcathedral at Southwell, *c.* 1233; and at St. David's, *c.* 1190. The result is, to the eye, to make the internal elevation one of two stories, instead of the traditional three. The nave was finished in 1324; its west window was not glazed till 1338; the wooden vault was not put up till c. 1354.

THIRD PERIOD.—Side by side with the nave went up the Chapter house. It is rather later in character than its sister at Southwell, and can be but little earlier than the Chapter house of Wells. Externally, it is provided with buttresses and pinnacles and flying buttresses and flying bridges to resist the thrusts of a stone vault. Yet no stone vault is there, but another sham vault of wood. The detail of the Chapter house, inside and outside, is of exquisite beauty.

THE NORTH ARCADE

At first the Chapter house was a detached building, but since some of its external moldings are now inside the vestibule, the latter must have been added later. The Chapter house is dated by Professor Willis at c. 1320; and Mr Charles Winston was of opinion that the glass in the Chapter house and vestibule was of the time of Edward II., and the early years of Edward III.; some of the glass, however, is earlier than 1307.

FOURTH PERIOD.—In 1361 the archbishop and chapter put it on record that "it is right that the choir" (*i.e.*, the presbytery) "where the holy sacrifice of the mass took place, should be especially rich in ornament." There were no doubt other reasons why an eastern extension was

FROM THE SOUTH-EAST

desirable. Archbishop Roger's choir did not contain a Lady chapel (there is some evidence that he built a Lady chapel detached from the church, as at Wells, on the north side of the Norman nave; and that this Lady chapel had to be pulled down to make room for the north aisle of the nave of 1291): also Archbishop William had been canonised in 1227, and a separate feretory was needed for him; moreover, procession path and eastern altars were mixed up in the eastern aisle.

At first only the eastern part of Archbishop Roger's work was pulled down, the services going on without interruption in the western bays. The four new eastern bays have the peculiarity of having an external instead of an internal arcade to the clerestory; this gives a fine play of light and shadow; the date of this part of the work is 1361 to c. 1370.

Then, between c. 1380 and c. 1400 the five western bays were built. Owing to the continuation of the high roofs to the extreme east end of the cathedral, there is little of the picturesqueness of the eastern terminations of Wells and Salisbury, but, as at Old St. Paul's, Ely, Lincoln, there is a lofty spaciousness that is wonderfully impressive. The design of the eastern limb is but a repeat of that of the nave, with the substitution of rectilinear for flowing tracery.

Over the new eastern limb the canons had not the money —or perhaps the courage—to put up a high vault of stone. Nave, eastern limb, and transept are all vaulted in wood. The punishment was long in coming, but it came at last. The wooden vault of the choir, the stalls, and the organ, were burnt down by a lunatic in 1829: and that of the nave by a plumber in 1840. The finest feature in the choir is the tall transeptal bays of the aisles, suggested by and built on the foundations of Archbishop Roger's flanking towers. Then came the central tower c. 1400-1423; the south-west tower, 1433-1447; the north-west tower, 1470-1474; the organ-screen, c. 1475-1505.

In 1472 the completion of the great works commenced c. 1230 was near at hand, and a solemn consecration of the rebuilt cathedral was held. The cathedral of the eleventh and twelfth centuries had disappeared; its successor had occupied two centuries and a half in building.

A very curious and bold specimen of mediæval engineering may now be mentioned. If the western bays of the great transept next to the central tower be examined, it will be seen that in the clerestory and in the triforium these bays are very narrow, but that in the ground story the narrow arch corresponding to the narrow bays of the triforium and clerestory has been moved, and a wider arch substituted. The fact is, when the transept was completed, the Norman nave, which was still standing, had a very narrow aisle. Consequently the builders of the transept built a pair of narrow arches, on either side of the central tower, leading from the transept into this narrow Norman aisle. Later on, as we have seen, the Norman nave and aisles were pulled down, and the present nave was built. Its aisles are exceptionally broad. The result was that the piers of the two narrow arches found themselves in the very middle of the new broad aisles of the nave—a most awkward obstruction to processions passing from aisle to transept, or *vice versa*. So the triforium and clerestory were underpinned, the piers next to the tower were taken down and rebuilt clear of the aisles, and the pair of arches also on either side of the tower were taken down and rebuilt, a narrow one where the broad arch had been, and a broad one in place of the narrow one. The result is that, counting from the end walls of the transepts, in the triforium and clerestory there are three of the bays wide and one narrow, while in the ground story there are two wide, one narrow, and one wide. Similar changes took place on the eastern side of the transept. It would appear that these alterations were not made till the central tower was rebuilt, when its great weight sank the piers on which it rests 8 in. into the ground, dislocating the adjoining masonry, and necessitating some amount of reconstruction in the adjoining bays. It should be added that it was found necessary also to block up the narrow bays of the ground story, triforium, and clerestory, and to rebuild the first pier from the north on the west side of the north transept.

As rearranged, the plan of York minster was as follows: (1) Lady chapel of two bays; (2) procession path of one bay, walled off to the west by the stone screen (restored after the fire of 1829). (3) The first bay west of this screen was "a chapel behind the High altar, called the Sanctum Sanctorum," *i.e.*, the chapel of the local saint, St. William; this Feretory was closed to the west by the oak reredos of the High altar. (4) The presbytery consisted of only two bays, and the High altar was one bay further west than at present, in a line with the eastern walls of the transeptal bays of the aisles, which no doubt were carried up high in order to give the altar abundance of light.* (5) Then came a choir of three bays; and (6) the crossing and a nave of eight bays.

Externally, York Minster, from its vast dimensions and the fine grouping of the towers, is exceedingly impressive. One realises its immensity best from the city walls, where it is seen "reflecting every change in the sky, and rising like a mountain above the parochial churches and houses of the city." The west front, in spite of overloaded and confused ornament, is of its type the finest in the country, with the one exception of that of Beverley minster; and the great west window in the fine contrast of the pointed arches and the free flow of the great ogee arches and the triple-heart centre-piece, surpasses its only rival, the east window of Carlisle. The central tower relies for effect on mass more than height, and thus contrasts strongly with the central towers of Canterbury and Lincoln. Gloucester tower is impressive equally from height and bulk. Shorn of its pinnacles, however, York central tower has not fair play. Very beautiful, too, is the play of light and shade in the double plane of tracery of the eastern clerestory. And very characteristic is the east façade: it may be all

---

* The oak reredos was pulled down and the High altar moved back one bay to its present position by Dean Finch, converting what had been the eastern screen of the Feretory into a reredos.

wrong, with its strong emphasis of horizontal lines and concealment of the gable, but it has distinction: one never confuses the east end of York with that of any other cathedral—one never forgets it. The weakest point in

THE WEST FRONT

York is what ought to be the source of the greatest beauty, the window tracery. Much of it, especially in the choir, is ugly in itself; even that of the great east window and of the windows in the transeptal bays is meagre and thin.

But what is worse, this poor tracery is repeated with wearisome iteration all over the flanks of the cathedral. Window after window of the nave, window after window of the choir, are monotonously alike. The imagination of the York people was singularly limited. What a contrast to the glorious series of windows of Exeter, contemporary with those of York nave!

But it is not from its architecture that York holds its paramount place as an exponent of mediæval art, but because its ancient glass is so largely intact. For a detailed account of it the reader should refer to Dean Purey-Cust's book. I will conclude by describing it in Mrs Van Rensselaer's words, which are as true as they are eloquent. "Most English cathedrals have been entirely reduced to architectural bone and sinew; they lack decorative warmth and glow, life and colour, and the charm that lies in those myriad accessory things which the lingering faith of Rome has preserved in other lands. All the varied tools and trappings, altars, shrines, and symbolic trophies of the rich Catholic ritual have been banished; much of the furniture is gone, the walls are bare of paint, scores of monuments and chantries have been shattered to bits, thousands of sculptured ornaments and figures have been swept away in dust; a painful cleanliness has replaced the time-stains which give tone to many Continental churches even when no actual colouring exists, and a glare of white light or hideous discord of modern hues fills the enormous windows. Columns and walls and floors are as barren at York as elsewhere; and although many tombs remain, without its glass it would seem even colder and emptier than most of its sisters, for it was built at a time when walls of glass had nearly replaced walls of stone. But it has its glass, and this means much more than that it has a richness of decorative effect which no other English church displays. It means that here alone we can really apprehend the effect of a late Gothic church, even from the architectural point of view. At York we can follow the development of the art of glass-painting through a period of fully four centuries. More delicate, clear, and exquisite fields of simple colour can never have been wrought than those which fill the Five Sisters with their sea-green purity. The west window, glazed a century later (1338), is a gorgeous mosaic of ruddy and purple hues, shining in the intricate stone pattern which shews black against the light, like a million amethysts and rubies set in ebony lace. The multicoloured eastern window, and its two mates in the minor transept, seem vast and fair enough for the walls of the New Jerusalem. And wherever we look in the lightly constructed eastern limb, it seems, not as though walls had been pierced for windows, but as though radiant translucent screens—fragile, yet vital and well equal to their task—had been used to build a church, and merely bound together with a network of solid stone. For the moment we feel that nothing is so beautiful as glass. After we have seen the glass of York, we never think again that stained glass was merely an adornment of Gothic architecture. The early Gothic architect demanded for his enlarged windows some filling which, as decoration, would take the place of the wide frescoes of former times, and which, from the constructional point of view, would justify to the eye that partial suppression of walls which he knew to be scientifically right. This filling the early glass-painter gave him; and it was so satisfying from the architectural standpoint, and so beautiful from the decorative, that he was ready and eager to carry on his architectural evolution to the farthest possible extreme. He felt that he could attenuate his constructional framework as far as the laws of gravity would permit, since the glazier stood ready to replace really solid wall-spaces by those which looked solid enough, and were more beautiful than any expanses of stone had ever been. No architect could have built as late Gothic architects did, if only white glass had been at his command. None would have made walls which are literally windows, unless strength of colour had come forward to simulate strength of substance. A late Gothic church was actually meant to look as the choir of York does look—like a great translucent tabernacle merely ribbed and braced with stone." The very best glass, however, is of later date than that of the cathedral, and the visitor should round off his education in mediæval glass by inspecting the late glass in which the parish churches of York abound. Perhaps the finest is that of All Saints', North Street, and St. Martin's church, Coney Street, near the interesting old Guildhall. Nowhere in England can stained glass be studied to such advantage as at York.

BIBLIOGRAPHY.—Thomas Gent, *History of York and York Minster*, 1730.
  Francis Drake, *Eboracum*, vol. ii., 1736.
  Joseph Halfpenny, *Gothic Ornaments in the Cathedral Church of York*, 105 plates, 1800.
  Charles Wild, *Plates and Perspectives*, 1809.
  John Browne, *York Minster*, 1840, 2 vols.
  Professor Willis on "York Minster" in *Archæological Journal*, 1845.
  Poole and Hugall, *York Cathedral*, 1845.
  Charles Winston on the "Stained Glass in York Minster" in *Art of Glass Painting*, 1865, p. 72.
  Canon Raines, *Fabric Rolls of York Minster*, Surtees Society, 1859.
  Dean Purey-Cust, *The Heraldry of York Minster*, 2 vols., 1896.
  Dean Purey-Cust, *Walks Round York Minster*, 1907.
  Excellent bibliographies both of the Minster and the City Churches are contained in the handbook prepared in 1906 for the meeting of the British Association.
  There are good handbooks to the cathedral by Mr G. Benson and Mr A. Clutton-Brock.

FROM THE CITY WALLS

THE WELSH CATHEDRALS

BANGOR

BUILT FOR SECULAR CANONS

THE work at Bangor falls into four periods. I. Originally the cathedral was a small Norman church, possibly without aisles, with nave, short transepts, choir of one bay, and apse. This was probably begun c. 1093. In recent restorations it was found that the bases remain of the piers of the central tower, and walling on both sides of the south transept; also portions of the ground courses of the latter, 12 ft. more to the north than the present end wall. Outside, there may still be seen a Norman buttress and a blocked window on the south side of the presbytery.

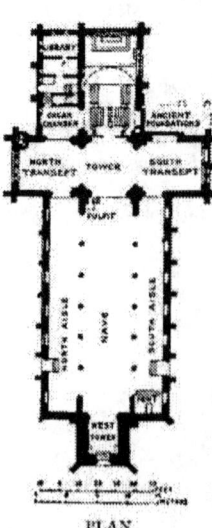

PLAN

II. In one of the many wars with the Welsh the Norman cathedral was burnt, possibly at the same time as that of St. Asaph; and in the time of Bishop Anian (1267-1305) was rebuilt. In 1284 the bishop received some £3,500 for damages done in the see during the war, and work is recorded as going on in 1291 and 1305. It is therefore probable that the rebuilding commenced c. 1284 and occupied over twenty years. Very little of Anian's work remains, though it was on a very extensive scale. But such large quantities of worked stones, used up as building material *temp.* Henry VII., were found in the walls by Sir Gilbert Scott that he demolished much of the work of the latter period, and rebuilt the central tower and transepts and to some extent the presbytery according to Anian's design, as far as it could be made out. The elevation of the south transept, with its triplet of windows and shafted buttresses crowned by gablets, is certainly a

FROM THE NORTH-EAST

noble design ; equally fine also is that of the north transept : the excellent corbel tables should be noticed. The buttresses are identical in design with those of the Lady chapel of Chester cathedral. It must be remembered, however, that up to 1866 the transepts in no respect resembled what we see now; in the end walls were huge windows with rectilinear tracery, and there were similar windows in the side walls. The transepts as rebuilt by Anian were 12 ft. longer than before. East of the south transept are foundations of an aisle, or a sacristy, of uncertain date. From Browne Willis's account, the piers and arches of the central tower seem to have been Anian's, and have been so rebuilt by Scott. On the north Anian built a chapel or sacristy of the length of the presbytery; this has been rebuilt by Scott as a library with Chapter house over.

It is not likely that the work would stop at the death

THE NAVE, LOOKING WEST

of Anian, leaving a ruined Norman nave. There is no documentary evidence available; but we may attribute to the first half of the fourteenth century the present aisle-walls and the pier-arcades; of the latter there remain but fragments of the eastern and western responds in the south aisle. No doubt Anian commenced, and his successors completed, both the existing aisles. In the south aisle the window tracery is of early fourteenth-century type; and in the north aisle the jambs of the windows are of the same period, though the tracery is later.

In 1404 the cathedral was once more utterly ruined by fire, this time at the hands of Owen Glendower: and is said to have remained in ruins till 1496. This is a mistake. In 1445 the choir at any rate had been restored in some measure, for services were then resumed in it. And in 1474 John Stanbery left in his will some £400 to be spent on the building of Bangor cathedral, where he had been bishop. The main work of restoration, however, seems to have been done by Bishop Deane (1494-1500) and Bishop Skivington (1509-1533). The western tower was certainly built by the latter, for in his will he left money to complete and roof it; this was in 1533. On the west wall of the tower is an inscription recording that he built this bell tower and the church; we may therefore conclude that Skivington rebuilt the nave and probably the transepts also. The reconstruction of the choir then may be assigned to Deane.

Internally, the restorers have done their utmost to make the cathedral look parochial. The altar is jammed against the east wall; the stalls are in the presbytery instead of in their proper position under the central tower; the return stalls are set diagonally after the foolish fashion of Worcester; and there is no screen between nave and presbytery.

BIBLIOGRAPHY.—Browne Willis's *Survey of Bangor Cathedral*, 1721.
Storer's *Cathedrals*, 1818.
Archæologia Cambrensis, New Series, i. 118, and Sixth Series, ii. and iv.
Sir Gilbert Scott's two *Reports*.

LLANDAFF CATHEDRAL

Built for Secular Canons

The cathedral of Llandaff, *i.e.*, the church on the Taff, which winds around it, is one of the most venerable in the British Isles, as is seen from its dedication in 1120 to Peter the Apostle and the Holy Confessors Dubricius, Teilo, and Oudoceus. The original dedication would be to Dubricius, the first bishop, Teilo, the second bishop, and Oudoceus, the third; the addition of St. Peter no doubt is due to Norman influence. Dubricius died *c.* 612, and seems to have sojourned at Llandaff with his little band of missioners before the end of the sixth century. Like St. David's and Bangor, and unlike the English sees, the bishops of Llandaff never removed to the refuge of a fortified town — though the mighty castle of Cardiff was hard by — from the site where Dubricius had built his little oratory near wood and water. After many mission journeys, he died in Bardsey island. His successor, Teilo, was the real founder of the see, and probably the first to erect a permanent church. On his death there was a dispute for his body, three places laying claim to it; but next morning three identical bodies presented themselves to view. The one

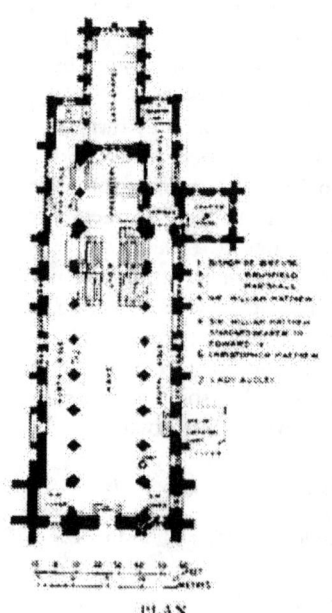

PLAN

which was carried to Llandaff was believed in later days to be the genuine body of St. Teilo, owing to the number of miracles which were wrought at the saint's tomb there. St. Teilo's remains were the one great treasure of Llandaff till between 1107 and 1120, when Bishop Urban brought the relics of St. Dubricius from Bardsey island.

FIRST PERIOD.—In 1120 the archbishop of Canterbury granted an indulgence to all who should aid in the rebuilding of Llandaff cathedral, and in 1125 the Papal Legate wrote that Bishop Urban had commenced work. What Urban's cathedral was like it is difficult to ascertain; the accepted view is that which was set forth by Professor Freeman. The only Norman work in the church which can be of Urban's time is to be seen in the presbytery, where there remain a noble eastern arch, and in the south wall portions of two Norman unglazed windows. This presbytery of two bays, with the addition of the next to the west, Freeman imagined to be the nave of Urban's cathedral. There is a solid wall on the south side of the presbytery; and a string course found at a restoration on the opposite wall at the level of the present piers shews that the north side was also solid; it follows that the imaginary nave was without aisles. A nave of only three unaisled bays is quite inconceivable for a Norman cathedral, however humble, begun so late as c. 1120; but even from these the westernmost bay must be lopped off. For where now stands the tall modern arch between the present choir and presbytery there were found at a restoration the bases of Norman shafts, which could only be the shafts of a Norman arch enclosing the present presbytery on the west, just as it is enclosed to the east by the existing Norman arch. Freeman's nave therefore is reduced to two bays. And what of its eastern arch? His theory was that it led into the eastern part of Urban's church, *i.e.*, his choir and presbytery. Not a scrap, however, of Norman work has been found to the east of the arch. The arch itself, moreover, is too narrow to have led into a cathedral choir.

The following explanation is suggested as an alternative.

It is based on a passage in the *Liber Landavensis*, written about 1133, which describes the Llandaff cathedral which was still standing between 1114 and 1122. It speaks of the "loci parvitatem, in longitudine xxviii pedum, in latitudine xv, altitudine xx, et cum duobus alis ex utraque parte admodum parvæ quantitatis et altitudinis, et cum porticu xii pedum longitudinis et latitudinis rotundæ molis"; *i.e.*, it was a little aisled church with a nave only 28 ft. long and 20 ft. high, and with an apse to the east. The width of the nave was 15 ft., and it had low and narrow aisles. If we assume each aisle to have been 6 ft. wide, the total width of nave and aisles will be 27 ft. The apse, we are told, was 12 ft. deep and 12 ft. broad. This then was the Llandaff cathedral which Urban set to work to replace in 1120. How would he begin? By demolishing the little church? That is unlikely; for then the congregation would have nowhere to worship in while the new church was being built. Moreover this old church and its predecessors for five long centuries had held the venerated bones of St. Teilo; the site was a most sacred one. At Glastonbury a similar case had occurred; in that far Somerset marsh there was a little church of wattles and mud which was believed to have been built by Joseph of Arimathea; in later days a church of masonry was built around and over the little osier church. Very much the same thing seems to have been done at Llandaff. For if measurements be taken, it will be found that the present presbytery is just wide enough to include the whole breadth of the nave and aisles of the early church, and is long enough to include its length with a few feet to spare. Moreover the present eastern arch is just of the span to provide an entrance into a new apse enclosing the little ancient one. Thus Urban's new presbytery and apse would include every inch of the ancient hallowed site. In that case the old nave would now become a presbytery, and the ancient apsidal presbytery would now become an eastern chapel. This was precisely the arrangement of the Norman cathedral at Hereford, where the presbytery, as at Llandaff, is square ended and led eastwards by a Norman arch, still standing, into a little apsidal chapel. The Hereford plan was set out between 1079 and 1095, and its presbytery and little eastern apse must have been completed long before Urban began to build. Nor can Urban have been ignorant of its existence; for Hereford and Llandaff are contiguous dioceses, and there were intimate relations between them. Indeed Urban and Reynelm, bishop of Hereford, were consecrated on the same day. The Hereford plan was not only one of the most advanced and most convenient of its day, but it had the special recommendation that it enabled the most sacred portion of the new Llandaff church to coincide with the site hallowed by the associations of Dubricius and Teilo, the latter of whom was buried within it. Only one important change would be necessary. That would be to transfer the High altar from the ancient apse to the eastern bay of the Norman presbytery. Where would it be placed? Not under the eastern arch as it is now; for then there would be no road into the eastern chapel. It must have been placed in the middle of the eastern bay, where it was still standing in 1718. For at that date a grand reredos, which had been put up behind the High altar in the fourteenth century, was still in existence, standing 5 ft. 3 in. in front of the eastern arch of the presbytery. Moreover, the modern sedilia are known to occupy the same site as the ancient ones, and they stand on the south side of the eastern bay of the presbytery.

Having settled the position of the altar and sedilia, Urban had then to settle the position of the tombs of Teilo, who had been buried in the old church for some five hundred years, and of Dubricius, whose body he had brought from Bardsey a few years before 1120. If he had had to find accommodation for one saint only, he might very well have converted the ancient apsidal presbytery into a Feretory. But there were two saints— of equal rank and importance. The same difficulty had arisen at Canterbury with the relics of Archbishops Alphege and Dunstan, and at Worcester with those of St. Wulfstan and St. Oswald. In both the difficulty was solved by burying both saints in the presbytery in the second bay from the east, one under the northern, the other under the southern arch. A similar course seems to have been adopted at Llandaff. Browne Willis, writing in 1718, says that in his time there was a tradition that Dubricius was buried on the north side of the presbytery, and Teilo on the south. Now in this western bay of the presbytery, on the south side, there actually is a sepulchral recess in which Wood, the Bath architect, in 1736 found a tomb. When he opened the tomb, the person buried in it from his pastoral staff and crozier appeared to be a bishop. The pastoral staff, when touched, dropped to pieces: the crozier was of pewter, almost perished, but would hold together; there was also a pewter chalice. The bishop was wrapped in leather (*i.e.*, in a hide for a coffin), and "the upper part was very sound." There can be little doubt that this recess marks the tomb of Teilo, and that his bones rest below. Now turn to the north side of the presbytery, exactly opposite. In 1496 Bishop Marshall died, and was buried opposite the tomb of St. Teilo. But curiously, Marshall's tomb, which still stands, is not immediately underneath the western arch on the north side of the presbytery, but most of it is in the aisle; yet in front of it, *i.e.*, on the presbytery side, is an unoccupied space large enough to hold it. Why then was it not placed in the space now unoccupied? Evidently, because when Bishop Marshall died, the space was then occupied. In all probability it was occupied in 1496 with the tomb of Dubricius. There was another point for Urban to consider. Every presbytery required two doorways, one to the north, one to the south, *ostia presbyterii*. It is very unlikely that they can ever have been placed in the third or fourth bays from the east of the presbytery; for ever since *c.* 1200 those bays have been separated from the aisles by solid walls. But in the present presbytery, west of the site of Teilo's tomb, there is a small doorway; this is modern, but Wood of Bath, writing in 1736, mentions a doorway in the same position, and the bases of the jambs of a Norman doorway were found there in 1857. Moreover, on the north side, Marshall's tomb is not placed centrally to the western arch, but to the east, leaving a passage to the west of it; this can only be because on the north side also there was a small doorway. In every respect then these two bays are built as a presbytery, and Freeman's theory that they represent Urban's nave may be finally dismissed.

Now we come to the great puzzle of Llandaff. In the south wall of the presbytery are the heads of two Norman windows. These, however, have no grooves for glass, and so are not windows; but openings into an enclosed space (*cf.* the unglazed openings in the central walls of Hereford retro-choir). What this enclosed space was is a mystery. It has been suggested that it was a porch; but it is in the wrong position. It is possible that it was a tower, which may have been completed; but of which it is more probable that only the lowest story was carried up. The other side of the presbytery has been so much altered that it is impossible to tell what was the plan of Urban's presbytery on the north. But assuming that the presbytery had a tower to the north and another to the south, we get two eastern towers. We know also that *c*. 1200 two western towers were erected. Thus Llandaff would possess no less than four towers *c*. 1200 and would be totally different from any church in England and Wales. It is a remarkable fact that a seal of 1234 actually does distinctly shew the church as having four towers.

Now how is the abnormal position of this pair of towers to be explained? Probably we must consider its relation to the general plan of the church. The salient feature of the plan is that alone of all the cathedral churches of England and Wales Llandaff has no transepts. And why not? The natural position for a transept would be in a line with the choir, with a central tower over the choir. But Urban had already built two towers in the adjoining bays to the east, and did not need any central tower. So he omitted central tower and transept also. Really, however, the ground story of the two eastern towers formed transepts. It is true that they do not project beyond the aisles; but precisely the same thing is seen in York minster, where the eastern transepts are nothing but single bays of the aisles carried up higher than the other bays. At York the object of this arrangement probably was, partly to give external prominence to the position of the High altar, partly to pour down on it a flood of light from the tall transeptal windows. At Llandaff it would rather be to mark externally the position of the two most cherished possessions of the church: the graves of Dubricius and Teilo. In later days the northern tower, if it existed, as was probably the case, was removed; but the ground story of the southern tower was retained, because its southern wall could be made to serve as the northern wall of a Chapter house. It is evident that this bay was regarded as something of exceptional character, because it is the only bay in the aisles that is vaulted.

But Urban would surely be able to build more than the short presbytery and eastern towers. It is not likely that he would stop till he had built a choir as well. The usual length for a choir was three bays. If this was so at Llandaff, Urban's choir would extend as far as the present small doorways on the north and south sides of the nave. It will be noticed on plan that these bays, which we will call the choir, are broader than those of the presbytery. The explanation probably is that the breadth of the former was regulated by the number of stalls it was to accommodate, while the presbytery was designed to enclose the precise site of the little old church.

The next question that arises is, Had Urban's choir aisles? All who have written on Llandaff seem to be unanimous in accepting Freeman's opinion that Urban's church had no aisles. If so, it was different from every cathedral church in the kingdom; even the little pre-Urban church had aisles. But assuming that Urban followed the normal practice, and built his choir with aisles, it does not follow that they opened into the choir by a pier-arcade. At

St. Albans and elsewhere there were no arches, but a solid wall between the choir and its aisles. That this was so at Llandaff also is probable; at any rate the supports in the centre of the northern and southern stalls look much more like fragments of a wall than like independent piers.

Then we come to the Norman nave. One would be commenced, though not perhaps till after Urban's time, for he died thirteen years after commencing his presbytery. Following the precedent of other cathedrals, the nave would have aisles, and therefore pier-arcades. Of the latter there is no trace whatever; it does not seem that the pier-arcades were even begun. It is probable, however, that the aisle-walls were begun; and to them we turn. Here again we have everybody's opinion against us; it seems not to have struck anyone that all the present aisle-walls west of the presbytery may be those of the Norman choir and nave, heightened indeed to admit the present windows in the fourteenth century, but in their lower part those which were begun by Urban and continued by his immediate successors. For they must be either the work of Bishop Uchtryd (1140-1147) and Bishop Nicholas (1149 or 1153-1183)—more probably of the latter, for he was a great builder—or they are contemporary with the pier-arcade and west front—*i.e.*, of the time of Bishop Saltmarsh (1185-1191) and Bishop Henry (1193 or 1195-1218)—more probably of the latter—or, lastly, they are of the same date as the windows in them in the fourteenth century.

They are not fourteenth-century walls; for in each aisle is a small fourteenth-century doorway. Now if the wall and the doorway in it had been built together, the doorway would, as usual, have been splayed; as it is, the opening is at right angles to the wall. Moreover, if the wall were fourteenth-century work, the doorway would have been placed so as to lead up to the centre of an arch, and not on to a pier. Secondly, the aisle-walls of the nave are 5 ft. thick; the existing fourteenth-century walls of the north aisle of the presbytery are considerably thinner than this.

Again, windows in an aisle-wall are intended to light not only the aisle but the nave as well. To accomplish the latter purpose adequately, each window ought to be placed exactly opposite the corresponding arch of the pier-arcade. Now if Mr James' longitudinal section of the south side of the nave be examined, it will be found that in only one case do window and arch centre accurately; this is in the fifth bay counting from the west end of the nave. Putting these considerations together, it may be taken as certain that the original aisle-walls were not built in the fourteenth century.*

It remains that they were built at the same time as the pier-arcades or earlier; in other words that they are the work of either Bishop Henry or Bishop Nicholas. Let us take the former case. The argument from the non-correspondence of arch and window again applies; for the position of the fourteenth-century windows was settled no doubt by the position of the earlier windows which they superseded. Moreover, if pier-arcade and aisle-walls were built together, each doorway into the aisles would have been so placed as to lead into the centre of an arch. But the large north doorway is not central; still less so is the corresponding doorway on the south. We have proved that the aisle wall is not contemporary with the pier arcade; we had previously proved that it was not posterior to it; it follows that it is of earlier date.

Can that date be fixed? The answer can be got out of the detail of the north and south doorways. They look far earlier than they actually are, and have usually been supposed to be. Of the two the northern is slightly later. Both of them contain a remarkable pattern; a double chevron or lozenge enclosing a roll. Now this is common on the pier-arches of the nave of St. David's, the choir of which was not commenced till 1180; also in the Glastonbury

---

* Freeman himself admits that though "the greater part of the aisle-walls was rebuilt from the ground in the Decorated period," yet "the lower part of the walls is in some cases original," *cf.* pp. 67, 73, and 75.

Lady chapel, begun in 1184 and finished in 1186; the north porch of Wells cathedral, *c.* 1200; in the doorway leading from the transept into the north aisle of Lichfield choir, *c.* 1200; and the doorway of the western slype of Worcester cloister, *c.* 1180. From these parallels it follows that we can hardly date the two doorways earlier than *c.* 1180. And this late date is confirmed by the fact that the hood-mold of the north doorway is actually composed of a band of tooth ornament. The character of the capitals also is important: both those of the north and those of the south doorway are the scalloped or subdivided cushion familiar in late Norman work. The northern base is worn and indistinct, but the southern is of a familiar Norman type.

Putting these considerations together we come to the conclusion that the north doorway is not earlier than *c.* 1180, and that the south doorway may be *c.* 1170. This difference of date furnishes a clue to the order of work; the south aisle must have been built before the north one. If we try to picture to ourselves what the aisles of the nave looked like when finished, we must imagine them lower than at present, and with a single light in each bay; which in the eastern bays—those of Bishop Urban—would have semicircular heads, but in the western bays might be lancets: the north and south doorways would be precisely as they are at present. Probably the work went on intermittently from the death of Urban in 1133; but if the date of 1180 ascribed above to the north doorway is correct, it would seem that the work was not completed till the last years of Bishop Nicholas, who died in 1183; and as he was bishop for no less than thirty-five years, and is recorded to have been a great builder, it is probable that the building of the aisles was commenced by him, and that his predecessor, Uchtryd, who was only bishop for seven years, had no part in the work. This is rendered the more probable by the fact that Nicholas was the son of Bishop Urban, and would naturally desire to help forward the great work set on foot by his father. It may be thought remarkable, as indeed it is, that no part of the walls of the central aisle or nave of the western bays was put up. But if any had been built, it would hardly have been pulled down; and if it had been demolished, it would have left some traces. So far from that, the pier-arcade of the four western bays is set out with symmetrical regularity, except so far as it disregarded the spacing of the bays of the aisle-wall and the position of the aisle doorways.

SECOND PERIOD.—Then came another long continued effort to complete Urban's church. It is easy to recognise,

LOOKING EAST

having the marked peculiarities of the early Gothic of the West of England. It occurs, with certain breaks, up the whole length of the church, from the west front as far as the entrance to the Lady chapel. Now where would the builders be likely to commence work, when once the aisles were finished? Obviously the first thing to do would be to complete the central aisle of the nave from the point where Urban had left off; viz., at the end of the third bay from the presbytery; in other words the first block of work would be the building of the western bays of the nave. Now these four bays are a homogeneous piece of work, and there are certain important differences between them and the similar work in the bays adjacent to the east; one is that the piers are much larger; another is that the roofing shafts are in triplets and are disposed on the face of the clerestory wall; whereas in the eastern bays they are single shafts in the clerestory, and are recessed in the wall, which is set back 4 in. The next point is, did the builders begin the western bays of the nave from the west or from the east? Not from the west, for the west front is not the earliest, but the latest in design of all this work. Moreover, of these western piers, the eastern centre more accurately than the western with the wall piers of the aisles.

This piece of work being completed, the question would arise—Should they or not remodel Urban's choir? Now if his choir had opened on its aisles by piers and arches, these would be likely to be retained. But we have suggested that his choir was separated from the aisles by solid walls. This unsightly arrangement it seems to have been decided to remove. Not all of it however. Between each pair of eastern bays, instead of building a new pier, they retained a piece of the old choir wall as a support for their new arches; partly because, then as now, it would be masked by stalls, and therefore escape notice. The rest of the choir walls would be pulled down, and in the place of each wall two piers built on either side. Urban's choir, however, was wider than the four new western bays of the nave; this was set right by gradually bringing in the two new piers on the north side of the choir. The fact that both the piers and the roofing shafts of the choir are of less bulk than those of the nave probably means that when the latter were begun, it was contemplated to put up a high vault; and that when the remodelling of the choir was taken in hand, the intention had been abandoned. The whole of nave and choir was provided with an identical clerestory; the design of which, with five arches, non-graduated, in each bay, points to the fact that when the clerestory was reached, the intention to vault had been abandoned; as also does the fact that the vaulting-shafts rise to the wall plate.

At present the nave has a high-pitched roof, and looks all the better for it; but the ledge above the great triplet of the west end looks as if originally it had a tie-beam roof.

Nave and choir completed, the next piece of work seems to have been to remedy a great defect in Urban's church, the absence of a procession path round the presbytery. The work seems to have commenced on the south side; the south aisle of the nave being carried through the southern choir-tower and round the presbytery. To this period belongs the vault of the so-called vestibule; the only example of West of England vaulting in the church, and of great interest. Its diagonal arches are semicircular; both the ridges are horizontal; there are no wall arches; the diagonal ribs are supported by shafts of coursed freestone; the web of the vault is plastered over. Of the capitals one has the incurved scallop or "pollarded willow"; the remaining three have rudimentary conventional foliage of rather lumpy character, such as is seen in the north aisle of Lichfield choir; two of the shafts are supported by corbels; the other two descend to the ground and have bases with a well-marked water-holding hollow. From the vestibule aisle-walls were carried on eastwards towards the modern doorway. Opposite the modern doorway the procession aisle turned northward. Of the eastern arm of the procession path only the supports of the southern and northern arches were built; the shafts are of the normal West of England type with the ogee keel; one of the capitals has no necking, and another is of the pollarded willow type. At the northern entrance the builders seem to have stopped; at any rate if they continued the procession aisle on the north side of the presbytery, there are no traces of it left; it seems not to have been completed till the end of the thirteenth century. It is not unnatural that funds should at last have failed; for in addition to all the other work which has been enumerated, two western towers were commenced, if not completed. Of the northern one there remain both the arches and the lower part of the walls except on the north side; this tower was vaulted; a fragment of one of the springers survives. The west front both externally and internally is a very fine composition; the doorway in it has no central shaft; and from the disposition of the masonry of the tympanum was evidently not intended to have one.

The whole of the West Country design as seen at Llandaff is of great interest. The curious little foliated bosses on the west front connect it definitely with the triforium of the west bays of Worcester nave, and with the exterior of the Galilee of Glastonbury. Shafts of coursed freestone surround the piers, and have the ogee keel. Two or three of the capitals, as at St. David's and Lichfield, have no necking. The characteristic capital is one which is very elongated and is nearly all stalk; this appears in Wells nave, Lichfield choir, and Dore retro-choir; in all cases *c.* 1200. The "pollard willow" cap occurs in the vestibule. The bases are of the water-holding type; those of the west end are of very advanced and late character. The ground course is very simple; consisting merely of a straight slope upon a vertical course, as at Pershore and the western bays of Worcester nave. The external corbels of the clerestory are designed as if in wood; corbels of similar design appear in Glastonbury Lady chapel and Pershore choir.

On the other hand there are marked divergencies. The designer, both in pier and arch, preferred chamfers to molds; in the arch there are none of those repeats of identical rolls which are common in West Country work elsewhere; and instead of the sixteen or twenty-four shafts of the Wells piers, there are at Llandaff only twelve. The most marked difference is that the clerestory has in each bay two windows widely spaced, shewing that no vault was intended when the clerestory was built. (At the time of the restoration only one bay of the clerestory survived—on the south side—the present clerestory is a reproduction of it; it is of identical design throughout, except in the presbytery, which was remodelled in the fourteenth century.

The east windows of the presbytery are wholly of modern design.)

THIRD PERIOD.—About the middle of the century a campanile was erected on the high ground to the southwest. In this campanile later was placed "Great Tom," which is now in Exeter cathedral, having been exchanged by Jasper Tudor for a ring of smaller bells. For detached campaniles compare Chichester, Salisbury, Westminster, Worcester, East Dereham. It is rather remarkable that Llandaff, having already two, if not four towers, should build yet another. But the cathedral is hidden away in a hole, and no doubt the sound of bells in its towers would travel but a little distance.

About the same time was built the Chapter house; it is of a rare type, being square with a vault resting on a central pillar, the object of which is to get a lower vault; of similar design was the large vaulted chapel built early in the fourteenth century at Pershore to the east of the south transept. The capitals and corbels of the Chapter house are molded, which points to a later date than the West Country work described above. The corners are filled up with large internal squinches, shewing that it was intended that the upper story should be octagonal, as it is now; a print of 1718, however, shews the upper story square. It was probably built as a Treasury; it has been restored as a library, and contains manuscripts of great interest.

FOURTH PERIOD.—The next work was to build an eastern Lady chapel of four bays. Here at last Purbeck marble is used for the shafting. On the north side of the altar is buried Bishop Bruse, its founder; he was bishop from 1266-1287. The whole east end is occupied by a most interesting stone reredos; the two end niches and part of the rest are fifteenth-century work; the central niche is a reproduction of the ancient one. The east window and sedilia are wholly modern. The chapel has a quadripartite vault with longitudinal ridge ribs, as in Worcester choir. To complete the westernmost bay of the vault, it was necessary to build the northern and southern arches of the procession path, thus completing the eastern walk. Before this was done, the eastern apsidal chapel of Urban's presbytery would have to be demolished.

At the same time the presbytery aisles were prolonged to the east, so as to form chapels flanking the Lady chapel.

FIFTH PERIOD. —The next thing was to continue the procession path on the north side of the presbytery till it met the choir aisle. Here the windows have flowing tracery of early fourteenth-century type, diversified in pattern and unusually good; it is such as we might expect to find c. 1340.

Then came an important set of changes, almost wholly directed, as at Hereford, the cathedral of the contiguous diocese, to improving the lighting of the cathedral. The darkest part of the church was the Norman presbytery, because it had no side windows; but merely openings looking into the presbytery towers, through which it obtained only borrowed light. The northern of these towers was pulled down, and the north wall of the presbytery with it, and for the latter a pillar and two arches were substituted; through these arches a considerable amount of light could be obtained from the large windows of the new north aisle. On the south side of the presbytery things were more difficult to arrange. However, one arch—the eastern one—was inserted, and in it no doubt were placed new sedilia. But in the western bay, above the tomb of St. Teilo, there was a large space of blank wall, which it was desired to preserve, and which has been preserved to this day: perhaps on it was some venerated wall painting depicting the miracles wrought by the saint buried below. Anyhow, the south side of the presbytery was left unfinished, with one new arch and part of another, and the heads of two unglazed windows, which from their sculptured ornament are of precisely the same date as Urban's eastern arch. In the upper walls of the presbytery, no doubt, to north, south, and east, large windows were inserted; these have perished, and the present ones are modern. This work may well have occupied the last years of the thirteenth and the early years of the fourteenth century.

SIXTH PERIOD.—The next business was to substitute for the small lights of Urban and Nicholas in the aisles large windows of flowing tracery with ogee dripstones; to get headway for these tall windows the aisle-walls had to be raised. Moreover, at some period, a square building had been erected in front of the south doorway of the nave, perhaps as a sacristy; (afterwards it became the Consistory Court; it has now disappeared altogether). A new south doorway was now built; and as it had to be cut between two neighbouring windows, it had to be narrow. A similar doorway was inserted in the same position in the north aisle; this was called St. Teilo's doorway, and, as at Peterborough, led to the cemetery. From the character of the window tracery, we may assign all this work to the second quarter of the fourteenth century.

To the same period probably belongs the reredos—once magnificent—now placed in the north-east chapel of the retro-choir. It formerly stood nearly in the centre of the east bay of the presbytery, with of course the High altar in front of it. Like the great reredoses of Christchurch, Winchester, St. Albans, and Westminster, it contained two doorways giving direct access from the presbytery to the procession path and Lady chapel. At a later period it was painted and gilded; among the patterns are white roses, which led Browne Willis to believe it to be of the time of Edward IV. or Richard III.

SEVENTH PERIOD.—By the end of the fifteenth century the north-western tower seems to have become unsafe, and to have been taken down, except some portions to the south-east. It was rebuilt by Jasper Tudor, son of Owen Tudor and Queen Catherine of France, widow of Henry V, and uncle to Henry VII. Originally it closely resembled the tower of St. John's, Cardiff; Mr Prichard has given it a still richer coronal of Somerset type.

A large window of five lights was inserted to give more light to the High altar in the presbytery, which on the south side has but one arch, and that partly blocked by the sedilia.

On the north side of the presbytery is the tomb of Bishop Marshall (1478-1496) in pontifical vestments. Opposite he built his throne; an interesting picture, probably formerly attached to it, depicts the Blessed Virgin in flight through the starry firmament, and the bishop beseeching her to open to him the gates of heaven. It is now in the bishop's palace: and might well be placed on the blank wall, facing the bishop's tomb, veiled so as to save it from undue exposure to the light.

FROM THE WEST

EIGHTH PERIOD.— In post - Reformation days the cathedral fell into the most dreadful state of disrepair and ruin; the south-west tower fell; the aisles and the western bays of the nave were long roofless; and in the eastern bays Wood of Bath erected a Roman temple of stucco. The whole restoration, including a fine southwestern steeple of the type usual in the early Gothic of Normandy, was directed by Mr Prichard; restorations seem to have been much more careful and successful, when, as at Llandaff, Gloucester, and Winchester, they have been entrusted to local men.

Behind the High altar is a picture of the Nativity by Rossetti; the altar frontal is by Messrs Morris & Marshall;

the candelabra in the presbytery and the font were designed by Mr Seddon; the statuettes on the nave pulpit are by Woolner; in the recess east of the north doorway is a sculptured memorial by Armstead of Henry Thomas, *ob.* 1863.

BIBLIOGRAPHY.—Browne Willis's *Survey of Llandaff*, 1718.
Dugdale's *Monasticon Anglicanum*, vol. vi., 1217.
Professor Freeman's *Llandaff Cathedral*, 1850.
Bishop Ollivant's *Llandaff Cathedral*, 1860.
Rev. E. Newell, *Diocesan History of Llandaff*.
John H. James, *Measured Drawings and Architectural Description of Llandaff Cathedral*, Cardiff, 1898.

ST. ASAPH

BUILT FOR SECULAR CANONS

THIS is the smallest of the Welsh cathedrals, and consists of an aisled nave of five bays, an aisleless transept, a central tower, and a chancel. The cathedral is finely situated on a ridge between the valleys of the Clwyd and Elwy; the massive central tower, 40 ft. square, is particularly impressive. The earliest part is the presbytery, of which, however, only the westernmost groups of lancets follow the original design; the work appears to belong to the second quarter of the thirteenth century. In one of the Welsh wars the cathedral was burnt by the English in 1282; and the rebuilding is said to have been begun by Bishop Anian in 1284; he died in 1293; in the present church there seems to be nothing

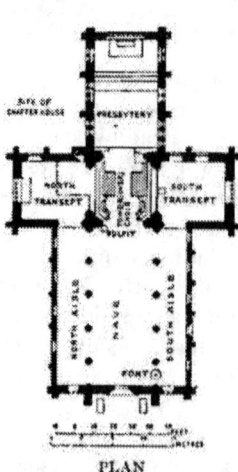
PLAN

of such early date; probably all that Anian accomplished was to restore the new presbytery. The ogee tracery of the windows of the central tower shews that it was not built before the first half of the fourteenth century. It is supported by arches whose chamfered orders, relieved by wave moldings, descend to the ground without capitals or bases. As all the arches of the nave and that of the west doorway repeat the design of the tower arches, they must all have been built together; probably in the time of Bishop David (1315-1352). It is possible that the aisle-walls

THE NAVE, LOOKING EAST

were commenced by Anian or Leoline (1293-1314). In 1402 the cathedral is said to have been "burnt and utterly destroyed": this, however, is an exaggeration; what perished was the roofs, stalls, etc. These were not replaced till the time of Bishop Redland (1471-1496), whose coat of arms may be seen on the stalls. The upper part of the tower was blown down in 1714, and was carefully restored. Internally, the most striking features are the square windows of the clerestory, which originally seem to have been taller, and the continuous moldings of the pier-arcade, which occur again at Tenby. There is an interesting incised slab, and an admirable effigy of a bishop, which would seem to be that of Bishop Leoline. The south transept originally contained two altars and was the Lady chapel. North of the presbytery, as at Bangor, was a chapel, sacristy, or Chapter house.

BIBLIOGRAPHY.—Browne Willis's *Survey of St. Asaph Cathedral*, 1729. 2nd edition by Rev. Edward Edwards in 1801.
Storer's *Cathedrals*, 1818.
Professor Freeman in *Archæologia Cambrensis*, 1854.
Archdeacon Thomas's *History of the Diocese of St. Asaph*, 1870.
H. Hughes in *Archæologia Cambrensis*, Sixth Series, i. 204, ii. 261, iv. 17.
See also the bibliography in Murray's *Welsh Cathedrals*, p. 251.

ST. DAVID'S

BUILT FOR SECULAR CANONS

FAR away in the extreme west of Pembrokeshire, sixteen miles from Haverfordwest, is one of the most interesting cathedrals in the British Isles. Dedicated to the great patron saint of Wales, it is as complex in plan as Winchester or St. Albans, and abounds in lovely detail of the twelfth and fourteenth centuries.

FIRST PERIOD.—The present church is stated in the *Anglia Sacra* to have been begun in the episcopate of Peter de Leia (1176-1198), and comprises parts of the presbytery, the western walls of the transept, the western piers and arch of the tower, and the whole of the nave except the outer portion of the west front (Sir G. G. Scott) and the south porch and the exterior of the south aisle (1328-1347). Though built quite late in the twelfth century, when Gothic architecture had got good hold in Ripon, Canterbury, and Wells, St. David's—partly perhaps from its remote situation—is still sternly Romanesque; for a parallel to such retrogressive design we must turn to Oxford cathedral or St. Bartholomew's, Smithfield, or to the western bays of the naves of Ely and Peterborough. The pier-arcade is low, the piers massive and squat; their arches are semicircular, as also the windows of the clerestory; there is a profusion of Norman zigzag ornament. On the other hand, pointed arches appear in the triforium and the wall arches of the clerestory, the bases have the water-holding hollow, and there are all sorts of beautiful varieties of Transitional capitals —from the incurved scalloped or "pollarded willow" capital, which is the normal capital of the church and which here abounds, to the minor capitals of rudimentary foliated character, of great diversity and charm, which testify to the late date of the work. Many resemblances in detail shew that the builders, though engaged on an old-fashioned Romanesque design, yet were in touch with the early Gothic which was going up in the West of England. It could hardly be otherwise; for the masons could not possibly have been got together from Pembrokeshire; most likely they would be Somersetshire men, shipped from Bristol, as were those who were engaged on Christ Church, Dublin. The "pollarded

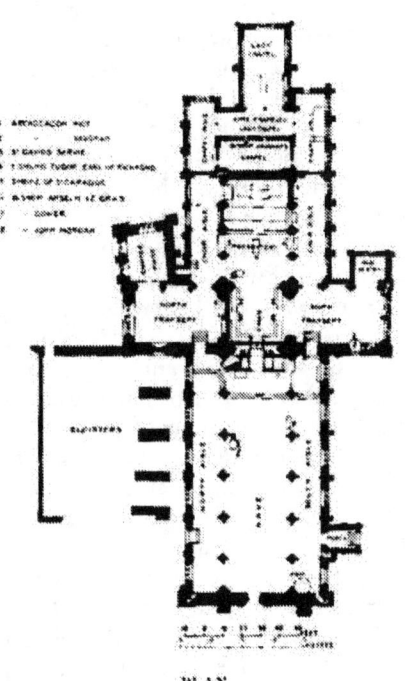

PLAN

willow" caps, bursting into foliage and sometimes into tiny figure-subjects, are repeated in the nave of Wells and the choir of Pershore; the caps without necking are characteristic of Llandaff, as also is the ogee keel of the filleted shafts; very frequent is the roll enclosed in the zigzag or diamond ornament, for which parallels are to be found at Wells and Lichfield: in fact for this complex ornament and for the "pollarded willow" cap St. David's must have been, with Worcester, one of the earliest centres.

The aisles of both presbytery and nave have vaulting-shafts, and some portions of them seem to have been actually vaulted. In the nave the vaulting-shafts rise from the string-course of the ground story, and are alternately triple and single, shewing that it was planned for a sexpartite vault. This type of vault was no doubt selected because of the exceptionally wide span of the pier-arches. If this vault had been built, its eastern bay would have been considerably lower than the western arch of the tower, and great complications would have arisen; that is perhaps one reason why it never was carried out. But an earthquake in 1248 did much damage, and may have deterred the builders. The triforium and clerestory, formed into a single member by a containing arch of zigzag, are a charming anticipation of the designs of Pershore and Southwell choirs. As in Rochester nave there is a passage in the thickness of the wall above the pier-arcade; which looks as if when they reached this point, they had abandoned their intention of vaulting the aisles, though they went so far as to prepare for a vault over the nave. In plan the presbytery is one of the most advanced of its day, consisting, as rather earlier at St. Cross, Winchester, of the square-ended aisled parallelogram which later on was to be the normal plan in our greater Gothic churches. The architectural was also the ritualistic nave; the stalls were in the crossing; the presbytery contained four bays.

SECOND PERIOD.—In 1220 the central tower fell, apparently in an eastern direction; and the presbytery and

the transepts appear now to have been rebuilt or remodelled; as much as possible of the older work being
retained and the new work assimilated to it. The old tower

THE NAVE ROOF

was taken down, with the exception of its western arch,
and was rebuilt, but only for one stage above the roof. The
three new tower-arches are all pointed; De Leia's arch is

semicircular. So also in the presbytery the new arches of the pier-arcade and the clerestory are pointed, and some of the abaci are circular. It was not intended to vault the aisles, and so the design of the nave, of which a triforium arcade forms part, was abandoned for one with pier-arches and clerestory only. The presbytery previously had a vault; the wall arches of which are cut through by the clerestory windows.

THIRD PERIOD.—The plan of De Leia's church was simplicity itself; it was indeed a good deal too simple, for it had neither procession path nor Lady chapel. It was resolved to add both. But the presbytery then was lighted by two tiers of lancets; an upper row, which has been restored by Scott; a lower row, now blocked, which was originally glazed. The upper windows were retained, which made it necessary that the eastern extensions should be low, as at Wells, Salisbury, Pershore, and elsewhere. But the canons contrived to keep the lower windows also—so valuable for light on the High altar and the celebrant—in a way which seems to have occurred absolutely to not a single soul elsewhere. Their plan was simply to build a sort of three-sided cloister, east of the church, with north and south walks forming prolongations of the presbytery aisles, and connected by an eastern walk. A similar design was carried out later at Wells; except that there the three-sided cloister abuts on the south side of the nave, and not on the east end of the presbytery. This left a narrow unroofed courtyard adjoining the east end of the church, and so there was no interference with "ancient lights." This open court or backyard was walled in all round, and no doubt became a receptacle for all sorts of rubbish. In fact in 1492 it cost some 4s. 6d. to clean it: and a little later it is described as the most filthy place in all the church, "vilissimus sive sordidissimus locus in tota ecclesia." Of three procession walks of the procession the northern and eastern still remain. From each angle of the eastern walk a little chapel was projected eastward—the central Lady chapel had to wait a little longer fo completion. The double arches leading into the eastern walk are of typical thirteenth-century design; the work generally may be attributed to the middle of the century.

FOURTH PERIOD.—In 1220 was the famous translation of the relics of St. Thomas of Canterbury; and at some period in the century later than this date the canons erected a chapel to St. Thomas the Martyr east of the north transept; its doorway and a beautiful double piscina remain.

To this period belongs the very remarkable pedestal of the shrine of St. David, canonised in 1131: a very plain structure, designed for use—for very strange uses. Down below in each side are three openings, allowing three sick people at a time to lie beneath. (Perhaps they lay there all night, waiting for the Saint to come and touch them, as was the case in some shrines of Pagan Greece.) On the side next to the aisle are two large and shallow upright openings, and three small circular openings—the latter, perhaps, as in St. Albans shrine, to allow the patient to insert a diseased arm. A parallel to the lower openings may be found in the remains of the shrine now inserted under the effigy of Lord Stourton at Salisbury. One would have expected a Feretory to have been built in the back-yard east of the presbytery; but here, as at Worcester and Llandaff, there was evidently a disinclination to remove the relics from a site long consecrated by their presence.

On the south side of the north transept is a smaller and ruder shrine-pedestal, probably that of St. Caradoc, who died in 1124 and was canonised by Pope Innocent III.

FIFTH PERIOD.—In 1302 Bishop Martyn founded an important chantry, and before his death in 1328 he completed the Lady chapel as his chantry chapel, and is entombed next to the sedilia in it as founder. It was probably at the same time that the northern flanking chapel of St. Nicholas was completed by Sir John Wogan as his chantry chapel.

SIXTH PERIOD.—Then came the great building prelate of St. David's, Bishop Gower (1328-1347). He seems to have remodelled the procession paths, to have built the chapel of King Edward the Confessor, south of the Lady chapel, and to have built the sedilia and tombs in the Lady chapel. (2) Like Abbot Thokey, at Gloucester, he transformed the Norman south aisle of the nave into the style of his day, and built a south porch. (3) He rebuilt the chapel of St. Thomas Martyr, *c.* 1329, except its south wall, considerably enlarging it, so as to support a Chapter house above it, and a Treasury above the Chapter house; this was done with the aid of a chantry endowment founded by Sir R. Symonds in 1329. (4) He raised the tower one stage, so that it now became two stories high. (5) He improved the lighting of the church by raising the aisle walls and inserting larger windows with flowing tracery. (6) To him probably is to be ascribed the existing oak screen between the presbytery and the choir; it is the only instance in England of a presbytery screen, except in three or four small parish churches. (7) He put up the bishop's throne, which, however, was reconstructed between 1496 and 1505. (8) He built for himself a magnificent palace across the Alan, and another at Lamphey, besides Swansea castle and church. (9) His most beautiful work is the choir screen, one of the grandest examples of mediæval art. It consists of three compartments of stone, surmounted by a modern cornice of wood. The southern compartment has two pointed arches, with compound cusping and rich crockets; and within, the tomb and effigy of the bishop, formerly surrounded by palisades of brass. The central compartment is occupied by the doorway and vaulted vestibule leading from the nave to the choir; on either side of the vestibule are effigies of priests. The northern compartment seems to consist of earlier arcading, which has been worked up to serve as a reredos to the altar dedicated to the Holy Cross. Above the tomb is the same skeleton vaulting as in the Bristol Sacristy, built by Abbot Knowle (*ob.* 1332). The bishop and he were friends, and the stone for Gower's work at St. David's came from the same quarries at Dundry, Somerset, as that for Bristol choir, and was worked by the same men, for the same masons' marks occur in both churches.

SEVENTH PERIOD.—The chief expenditure in the fifteenth century was on carpenters' work. The stalls, which have excellent bench ends and interesting misericords, are of the date 1460-1480. To about the same period belong the sedilia, of good design; like those in Beverley minster, they are of oak. The nave roof is ascribed to the years 1472-1509; the other high roofs may be of similar date. The nave roof consists simply of tie-beams resting on the walls, and carrying transverse beams. At their intersection pendant posts extend down for some distance, and arches are thrown across from the end of one post to the end of the next; the principle is the same as in the construction of the stone pendants of the fan-vault in Henry the Seventh's chapel at Westminster. About the end of the century the north wall of the nave, built too near the marshy bank of the Alan, was propped up by huge detached buttresses.

EIGHTH PERIOD.—The last great building prelate was Bishop Vaughan (1509-1523). He gave the tower the present third stage, and built a parvis over the south porch. His main work was to complete the eastern chapels and procession path. He vaulted the Lady chapel, previously recasing and rebuttressing it externally. He also vaulted the eastern walk of the procession path; his arms occur on a boss in the vault. Finally, he blocked the lower three lights of the east wall of the presbytery and covered the backyard with an unusually fine fan-vault: his altar platform remains; also squints looking on to the altars of the northeast and south-east chapels. The altar was dedicated to the Holy Trinity. A fine screen and doorways remain.

On the west side of the chapel, in the east wall of the presbytery, is a curious recess of De Leia's time; the sill of it is about 3 ft. above the floor of the chapel, and 1½ ft. above that of the presbytery. It contains a cross encircled by other crosses, the spandrels of the central cross being pierced right through the wall to the High altar on the other side. In the lower part of the recess human bones were found, which had been run into a solid mass with mortar; probably to preserve and conceal them when the order came down for the destruction of relics at the Reformation.

In the centre of the presbytery, as at Worcester and Gloucester, is a table tomb: it is that of Edmond Tudor, son of Owen Tudor and Queen Katharine, widow of Henry V., and father of Henry the Seventh; he died in 1456 and was buried at Caermarthen, but at the Dissolution his remains and tomb were removed to St. David's.

THE CATHEDRAL AND PALACE, FROM THE SOUTH-EAST

Externally, the cathedral is simple and plain, in harmony with its bleak and wild surroundings. The interior is very striking, as well from the unusual character of the design as from the complexity of the planning; it is rich also in admirable minor work and monuments; it yields in interest to no English cathedral and surpasses most. Entering the nave, the first thing that strikes one is the sharp slope of the floor; following the upward slope of the wooded dell through which the little stream runs, it rises 2 ft. as one advances from west to east. Next one notices that neither of the pier-arcades is vertical; both slope outwardly, perhaps as a result of the earthquake of 1248. The colouring too is quite unique; the local stone is of tones of purple absolutely unknown elsewhere; while the fourteenth-century work is in red stone from Dundry. In one respect it is far away the oldest cathedral in Great Britain, for the purple stone comes from local Cambrian beds, the most ancient sedimentary formation in Great Britain. Its situation too is extraordinary; it is approached from a high tableland to the west, and is invisible till one sees it close at hand sunk so low that it seems but a step from the high road on to the top of the central tower. Remote and inaccessible as it is, the little city was once crowded with life; it was on the main road to Ireland, and its famous shrine was the resort of pilgrims from all over Europe: it was visited among others by William the Conqueror, Henry the Second, Edward the First and Queen Eleanor. To St. David's, as to Wells, every architectural pilgrim will resort.

BIBLIOGRAPHY.—Browne Willis's *Survey of St. David's Cathedral*, 1717.
Bishop Basil Jones and Professor Freeman's *History and Antiquities of St. David's*, 1856.
W. L. Bevan's *History of the Diocese of St. David's*, 1888.
Architectural Review, Nos. 27, 28, 29.
There is a good handbook by Mr P. A. Robson, 1st edition, 1901.
See also the bibliographies in the prefaces of the books of Jones and Freeman and Mr Robson.

MODERN CATHEDRALS

THE following new dioceses were formed during the last two reigns: Birmingham, Liverpool, Manchester, Newcastle, Ripon, St. Albans, Southwark, Southwell, Truro, Wakefield. Of the cathedrals of these Manchester, Newcastle, Ripon, St. Albans, Southwark, Southwell, and Wakefield, have been described already. In only two dioceses, Truro and Liverpool, have new cathedrals been commenced. The bishops of Birmingham, Newcastle, and Wakefield are housed in parish churches; Manchester was a collegiate church.

BIRMINGHAM CATHEDRAL

THE episcopal chair, *cathedra*, of the bishop of Birmingham, is temporarily located in the parish church of St. Philip, built by Thomas Archer, a pupil of Vanbrugh, between 1711 and 1719, and a solid, stately example of the later English Renaissance. The chancel is a recent addition,

FROM THE SOUTH-WEST

separated from the nave by a fine iron screen by Jean
Tijou, from whose hand came the similar screens in St.
Paul's cathedral, London. The galleried interior, with its
fluted piers and classical entablature, is impressive and
satisfactory; the steeple one of the most successful
Renaissance examples in England. The great glory of the

THE INTERIOR, LOOKING EAST

church, however, is the stained glass, three great windows
at the east, and one at the west end; they should be seen
both by morning and afternoon light. They were designed
by Burne Jones, a native of Birmingham, a magnificent
collection of whose works is housed in the City Museum;
and executed by William Morris. It may be doubted if

nobler glass was ever executed, in modern or in mediæval days. The three eastern windows represent the Ascension, Nativity, and Crucifixion; the western window, the Last Judgment. "Standing before these great solemn angels," said a well-known architect to the writer, "my knees trembled under me."

LIVERPOOL CATHEDRAL

This cathedral was begun in 1904 from the designs of Mr G. Gilbert Scott. In 1910 the Lady chapel was opened, and at the present rate of progress the completion of the whole cathedral may be expected about 1932; (St. Paul's, London, occupied thirty-five years). Owing to exigencies of site, it is orientated, like Rievaulx abbey, from north to south. Its planning is remarkable. In the centre is an enormous expanse of unbroken space, such as exists in no cathedral in Europe; this in the centre is 80 ft. wide, while from east to west (speaking ritualistically) it is 200 ft. long. There are two transepts, but these are not arranged as at Salisbury or at Durham, but are of identical dimensions and flank the crossing to east and west; these steady the piers and arches of the crossing, which is to be covered with a vaulted lantern, somewhat after the manner of Ely, except that it is to be of stone, and not of wood. To the north and south of the crossing are great cavernous porches, forming the main entrances to the cathedral. To the west is an aisled nave; to the east an aisled choir and presbytery with ambulatory behind. East of the main wall of the church are vestries; to the north-east an octagonal Chapter house; to the south-east a Lady chapel. The length from east to west is, internally, 480 ft.; externally, including the Lady chapel, 600 ft. The choir is 47 ft. wide, *i.e.*, wider than our widest churches, Lincoln and York minsters. It will be vaulted throughout in stone; our highest cathedral vault, that of Salisbury, rises at the apex to 84 ft.;

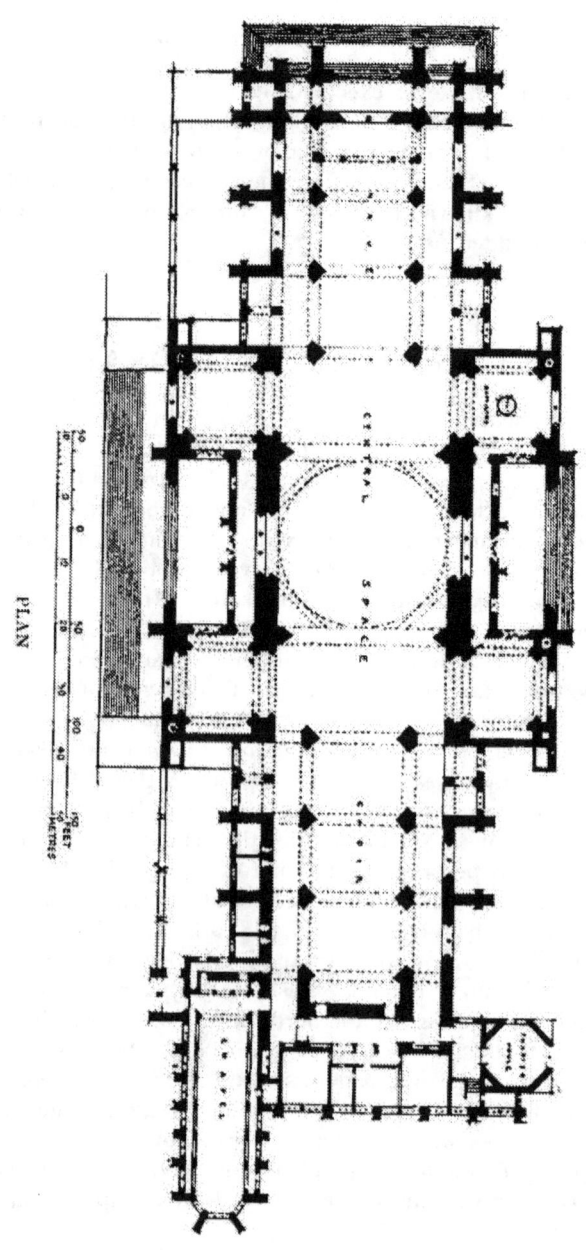

PLAN

LADY CHAPEL, LOOKING WEST

LADY CHAPEL, LOOKING EAST

at Liverpool the spring of the vault is 84 ft. above the pavement, and the vault itself being 31 ft. high, the total height of the interior will be 115 ft.; so that both in breadth and height it surpasses any mediæval cathedral in England. The high vaults are to have roofs of copper carried by fireproof material. Speaking generally, the plan serves three purposes; first it includes a comparatively small Lady chapel for services for which the choir would be too large; secondly, it provides a choir and presbytery for the daily choral services, surrounded by aisles, and in direct communication with vestries and Chapter house. The organ is placed on each side of the choir in the westernmost bay, with cases towards the choir and the central space. Finally, for great congregational occasions, such as a national festival, a meeting of diocesan choirs, &c., as well as for preaching, there is the vast central space, and in addition the transepts and nave. In design, as well as in plan, the cathedral is a revulsion from the "Imitative Gothic" which has been in vogue for more than half a century, and which found final expression in Truro cathedral; Liverpool cathedral cannot be labelled as "Early English" or "Decorated" or "Perpendicular"; it is none of them. It is too early to speak of the details of the design, which will be open to change and amendment as the building progresses; it can hardly be doubted, however, that its vastness of scale, the free handling of the masses, the depths of its shadow effects, the stern sobriety of the exterior, and the general absence of minute frippery, will make it one of the most grave, solemn, and monumental buildings in Christendom.

TRURO CATHEDRAL

TRURO cathedral, consecrated in 1887, is the first entirely new cathedral built in England since St. Paul's. In dimensions it ranks with Norwich and Wells; in plan it is as complex as any of the greater of our cathedrals. It was

designed for a central and two western towers, crowned by
spires, a south porch and a western narthex, an aisled nave
of nine bays, a central transept with eastern and western
aisles and baptistery, a choir, sanctuary, and eastern processional aisle, a square east end, and an unaisled eastern
transept, projecting slightly beyond the aisles; and below
the choir a crypt to be appropriated to vestries. Internally
it is picturesque, and admirably adapted for the ritual of the

GENERAL VIEW FROM THE NORTH-EAST

Church of England as it was in the thirteenth century. In
design it is as conservative as in planning; for everything
there is a precedent, if not in England, then in the North of
France; of freshness and originality there is little; that was
not desired or attempted. It is probably the last thing on
a large scale which we are likely to have in England in
imitative Gothic; and forms an enduring memorial to the
scholarship and cleverness of one of the many able architects

of the Gothic Revival. Because it is but a reproduction of the planning, construction, and detail of a bygone age, it does not follow that the design is unjustifiable or uninteresting. Mr Pearson was just as much at liberty to reproduce at Truro a thirteenth-century type of ecclesiastical architecture, as Alberti and Brunelleschi to resuscitate the art of Imperial Rome at Mantua and Florence for the edification, instruction, and delight of mankind.

At Truro there is real interest in tracing the meanders of Mr Pearson's scholarship. The crypt is in the massive style of the latter years of the twelfth century; the choir is supposed to have been commenced in the early years of the thirteenth century; but since, as in the transepts of Salisbury, the aisle windows are lancets, while

FROM THE SOUTH-EAST, SHOWING THE SOUTH AISLE OF OLD ST. MARY'S

those of the clerestory have early plate-tracery, we are to imagine that the upper part of the choir was not finished before the middle of the century. So again, in the half-century or so which might have elapsed between the commencement and the completion of the cathedral, the design is supposed to have been altered here and there as it passed through different hands; hence the rose windows, which are

unusually plentiful, are all different; the transept ends are
differently treated; the arches of the choir are narrow, those
of the nave are wide; the latter has coupled bays, the choir
has not; the quadripartite vault of the choir becomes more
complex in the nave, just as it does at Lincoln. And just as
the Lincoln architect dropped down fortuitous chapels at the
west end of the nave, so Mr Pearson purposely forgot to leave
room for a baptistery, and tacked it on, in a carefully casual
manner, to the south transept. A cloister, too, was designed
three-sided and lop-sided, as at Chichester. The south side
of the choir has the remarkable peculiarity of having three
aisles; so has that of Oxford cathedral. But it got its three
aisles in a different way from Oxford. Mr Pearson was
instructed to leave standing a piece of genuine mediæval
work, late and good—viz., the south aisle of the old church
of St. Mary's. The cathedral was placed to the north of it,
just so far off as to barely admit the buttresses supporting
the flying buttresses of the choir vault. The intervening
space Mr Pearson roofed over, thus obtaining a narrow intermediate aisle between the choir aisle to the north and
St. Mary's aisle to the south. Thus on the south side of
the choir there are three ranges of piers and three ranges
of arches, and the changing vistas and perspectives are
delightful. In this instance the architect was mediæval in
spirit as well as in the letter.

INDEX

ABBREVIATIONS—A. = *Abbot*; AB. = *Archbishop*; B. = *Bishop*; P. = *Prior*.

A

Acharius, A. of Peterborough, 265
Adrian IV., Pope, 298
Aidan, B. of Durham, 82
Alan, P. of Ely, 106
Alban (St.), 297, 308
Alcock, B. of Ely, 110
Aldred, B. of Gloucester, 136
Amphibalus (St.), 297
Andrew, A. of Peterborough, 265
Andrewes, B. of Southwark, 337
Anian, B. of Bangor, 442
Anselm, AB. of Canterbury, 24
Aquablanca, B. of Hereford, 164
Arthur, son of Henry VII., 423
Arundel, B. of Chichester, 79
Audley, B. of Hereford, 169
Audrey (St.), Abbess of Ely, 98
Augustine (St.), 82, 283
Augustinian Establishments:—
    Bristol, 9; Carlisle, 43; Oxford, 245; Southwark, 331

B

BANGOR Cathedral, 442-445
Barnett, B. of Ely, 106, 111
Bauchun Chapel, Norwich, 236
Beaufort, Cardinal, 396
Becket's "Corona," 30
Becket's Martyrdom, site of, 24
Bede, Venerable, 90
Bek, B. of Durham, 85
Benedict, A. of Peterborough 261, 264,
Benedictine Establishments:—
    Canterbury, 22; Chester, 52; Durham, 84; Ely, 96; Gloucester, 136; Norwich, 227; Peterborough, 257; Rochester, 284; St. Albans, 298; Winchester, 384; Worcester, 404
Berkeley Chapel, Bristol, 17

Bernardi's Paintings, Chichester, 81
Bethune, B. of Hereford, 161
BIRMINGHAM Cathedral, 477-479
Birinus (St.), 400
Bitton, B. of Exeter, 124
Black Prince's Chantry, Canterbury, 34
Booth's Porch, Hereford, 170
Boothby, Sir Brooke, 186
Boteler's (A.) Chantry, Gloucester, 154
Brandiston, A. of Bristol, 13
Brantingham, B. of Exeter, 133
BRISTOL—The Cathedral Church of the Holy Trinity, 9-21
    Augustinian Establishment, 9; FIRST BUILDING PERIOD (Norman Church), 10; Norman remains, 11; SECOND PERIOD, 12; Elder Lady Chapel, 12; THIRD PERIOD, 13; rebuilding, 13; lighting problems, 13; Vaulting, 14; Lady Chapel, 17; Choir, 17; Berkeley Chapel, 17; Chancel, 18; decorative detail, 18; Newton chapel, 19; FOURTH PERIOD, 19; Transepts remodelled, 19; FIFTH PERIOD, 20; modern executions, 20
Bronescombe, B. of Exeter, 119
Bruere, B. of Exeter, 118
Burton, A. of Bristol, 20
Butler, B. of Bristol, 19
Byzantine Font, Chester, 63

C

Caesar, Dean of Ely, 112
CANTERBURY—The Cathedral of Christ Church, 22-42
    FIRST PERIOD, 22; Pre-Conquest remains, 22; Lanfranc's Cathedral and Benedictine Monastery, 22; site of Becket's martyrdom, 24; SECOND PERIOD, 24; Anselm's

488 INDEX

CANTERBURY—*Continued*.
  work, 24; Chapels, 26; Presbytery, 27; the Choir, 27, 30; THIRD PERIOD, 28; Destruction and Restoration of Choir, 28; Becket's Corona, 30; French Influences, 32; Stained Glass, 33; FOURTH PERIOD, 34; Crypt, 35; FIFTH PERIOD, 35; Norman Work Removed, 35; Clerestory, 36; SIXTH PERIOD, 37; Cloisters, 37; SEVENTH PERIOD, 37; Central Tower, 37; Chapter House, 38; West Front, 40
Cantilupe (St.), 157
CARLISLE—The Cathedral Church of the Holy Trinity, 43-51
  Augustinian Establishment, 43; FIRST PERIOD, 43; the Norman Church, 43; SECOND PERIOD, 44; Gothic Chancel built, 45; THIRD PERIOD, 46; destruction by fire, 46; the East Front, 47; FOURTH PERIOD, 49; Central Tower and Nave, 49; FIFTH PERIOD, 50; Gondebour's illuminations, 50; SIXTH PERIOD, 51
Cathedrals, Ritualistic divisions of, 6
Chad (St.), 173
CHESTER—The Cathedral Church of Christ and the Blessed Virgin, 52-64
  Benedictine Monastery, 52; FIRST PERIOD, 52; Norman Work extant, 52; Cloisters, 55; SECOND PERIOD, 55; THIRD PERIOD, 55; Lady Chapel, 57; the Choir, 57; FOURTH PERIOD, 58; extensive rebuilding, 58; St. Oswald's Church, 59; Central Tower and Nave, 60; FIFTH PERIOD, 62; Nave, High Altar, and Cloisters, 62; Minor Works, 63; Stalls, 63
Chichester, B. of Exeter, 117
CHICHESTER — The Cathedral Church of the Holy Trinity, 65-81
  Foundation of the See, 66; the Norman Church, 68; the Lady Chapel, 70; destruction by fire and restoration, 71; the Towers, 76; Chapels, 76; Window Tracery, 78; detached Campanile, 79; Bernardi's paintings, 80; rebuilding of the Towers and Spire, 81
Cobham, B. of Worcester, 420
Conrad, P. of Canterbury, 24
"Corona," Becket's, Canterbury, 30

Cousin, B. of Durham, 94
Crauden's (P.) Chapel, Ely, 110
Cuthbert (St.), B. of Durham, 82

D

Dadderby, B. of Lincoln, 206
"Dark Entry," Canterbury, 42
David, A. of Bristol, 13
David (St.), 471
DURHAM—The Cathedral Church of Christ and the Blessed Virgin Mary, 82-95
  Foundation of the See, 82; Benedictine Establishment, 84; Episcopal Jurisdiction, 84; FIRST PERIOD, 86; the Norman Cathedral, 86; Vaulting, 88; Internal Elevation, 89; SECOND PERIOD, 89; Gothic spirit, 90; THIRD PERIOD, 90; "Chapel of the Nine Altars," 91; FOURTH PERIOD, 93; Window Tracery, 93; Altar Reredos, 93; FIFTH PERIOD, 93; the Central Tower, 93; SIXTH PERIOD, 94; the Sanctuary Knocker, 94

E

Eastry, P. of Canterbury, 34
Edington, B. of Winchester, 395
Edward I., 166
  „ II.'s Tomb, Gloucester, 144
Eleanor, Henry II.'s Queen, 17
Elliott, Dean of Bristol, 20
Elsinus, A. of Peterborough, 257
ELY—The Cathedral Church of the Holy and Undivisible Trinity, 96
  Benedictine Establishment, 98; FIRST PERIOD, 98; Plan and Construction of Norman Cathedral, 98; SECOND PERIOD, 102; the Galilee Porch, 102; Reconstruction of East End, 102; THIRD PERIOD, 104; the Lady Chapel, 105; Collapse of Central Tower, 106; Construction of the Octagon, 106; the rebuilt Choir, 108; Stalls, 110; FOURTH PERIOD, 110; Lighting Improvements, 110; Chantry Chapels, 110; FIFTH PERIOD, 111; Wren's Classical Doorway, 111; Minor Works, 111
Ely Porta, 110
Ernulph, P. of Canterbury, 24
Ethelbert (St.), King of East Anglia, 157
  „ King of Kent, 284

Etheldreda (St.), Abbess of Ely, 98, 100

EXETER—The Cathedral Church of St. Peter, 114
Foundation of the See, 114; FIRST PERIOD, 116; construction of the Norman Cathedral, 111; SECOND PERIOD, 118; the Chapter House, 118; THIRD PERIOD, 119; the Chapels, 119; FOURTH PERIOD, 121; various completions, 121; the Arcades, 122; FIFTH PERIOD, 123; the Choir remodelled, 123; SIXTH PERIOD, 124; completion of the Choir, 124; the Bishop's Throne, 125; the High Altar, 126; SEVENTH PERIOD, 127; the design of the Cathedral, 130; Interior problems, 130; Window Tracery, 131; symmetry of the design, 131; EIGHTH PERIOD, 133; the Chantries, 134

F

Fitzharding, A. of Bristol, 10
Fleming's (B.) Chantry, Lincoln, 20
Frideswide (St.), 243

G

GLOUCESTER — The Cathedral Church of St. Peter, 136-155
Benedictine Establishment, 136; FIRST PERIOD, 136; the Crypt, 136; SECOND PERIOD, 138; the rebuilding, 138; the Choir and Nave, 140; THIRD PERIOD, 142; Towers, 142; destruction by fires, 143; FOURTH PERIOD, 143; Strengthening by Buttresses, 143; Windows, 144; FIFTH PERIOD, 144; Tomb of Edward II., 144; SIXTH PERIOD, 146; Lighting Improvements, 146; South Transept, 146; Vaulting, 149; the East End, 150; SEVENTH PERIOD, 151; rebuilding of Cloisters, 151; EIGHTH PERIOD, 151; West Front, 151; NINTH PERIOD, 152; Central Tower, 152; TENTH PERIOD, 152; rebuilding of Lady Chapel, 152; the Cloister, Chapter House, etc., 153; Minor Works and Monuments, 154
Godfrey, B. of Chichester, 67
Goldstone, P. of Canterbury, 40

Goldwell, B. of Norwich, 238
Gondebour, P. of Carlisle, 50
Goodrich, B. of Ely, 111
Grandisson, B. of Exeter, 127
Grimthorpe, Lord, 304, 309
Grostete, B. of Lincoln, 201

H

Hacket, B. of Lichfield, 177
Haithwaite, P. of Carlisle, 49
Hatfield, B. of Durham, 93
Henry I., 43
„ IV.'s Chantry, Canterbury, 37
„ VIII., 254

HEREFORD—The Cathedral Church of St. Mary and St. Ethelbert, 156-171
FIRST PERIOD, 158; the Norman Church, 158; SECOND PERIOD, 160; Nave and renovation of Choir, 161; THIRD PERIOD, 161; the Chapels, 162; FOURTH PERIOD, 162; completion of Lady Chapel, 163; FIFTH PERIOD, 164; Lighting Problems, 164; SIXTH PERIOD, 164; North Transept rebuilt, 164; SEVENTH PERIOD, 165; St. Cantelupe's Shrine, 166; various improvements, 166; EIGHTH PERIOD, 167; Central Tower rebuilt, 167; S.E. Transept rebuilt, 168; NINTH PERIOD, 168; South Transept Windows, 168; Chantry Chapels, 169; TENTH PERIOD, 170; Modern Restorations, 170

"Holy Hole" (in Crypt), Winchester, 395
Hotham, B. of Ely, 111
Hugh (St.), B. of Lincoln, 196, 201
Humphrey, Duke of Gloucester, 308

J

John, King, Tomb at Gloucester, 154
Justus (St.), 283

K

Ken, B. of Bath and Wells, 362
Kilkenny, B. of Ely, 112
King John's Tomb (Gloucester), 154
Kirton, A. of Peterborough, 270
Knowle, A. of Bristol, 13, 17, 19

INDEX

L

Lanfranc, AB. of Canterbury, 22
Langley, Cardinal, Tomb at Durham, 90
Langton, B. of Lichfield, 176
  ,, B. of Winchester, 401
LICHFIELD—The Cathedral Church of St. Mary, 172-190
  Foundation of the See, 172; Story of St. Chad, 173; History of the See, 175; the Cathedral during the Civil War, 176; Puritanical Devastations, 177; Re-erection of Central Tower, 178; FIRST PERIOD, 178; the Norman Cathedral, 178; SECOND PERIOD, 179; the Norman Cathedral rebuilt, 179; THIRD PERIOD, 182; the Transepts and Chapter House, 182; FOURTH PERIOD, 183; the Nave, 183; FIFTH PERIOD, 185; the West Front, 185; the Lady Chapel, 185; SIXTH PERIOD, 186; St. Chad's Shrine, 186-187; Lighting improvements, 186; SEVENTH PERIOD, 187; Altar Screen, 187; Completion of St. Chad's Shrine, 188; Minor Works, 189
LINCOLN—The Cathedral Church of St. Mary, 191
  FIRST PERIOD, 191; Norman remains, 191; SECOND PERIOD, 193; the Towers, 193; THIRD PERIOD, 194; the rebuilding, 194; St. Hugh's Work, 196, etc.; FOURTH PERIOD, 198; FIFTH PERIOD, 198; the Nave, 198; the West Front, 201; SIXTH PERIOD, 201; collapse and re-erection of Central Tower, 201; Choir and Transepts, 202; SEVENTH PERIOD, 204; the Angel Choir, 205; the Central Tower and Spire, 205; EIGHTH PERIOD, 206; Bishop Dalderby's Shrine, 206; NINTH PERIOD, 207; Choir Stalls, 207; TENTH PERIOD, 207; West Windows, 207; Chantries, 208; ELEVENTH PERIOD, 209
LIVERPOOL Cathedral, 479-483
LLANDAFF CATHEDRAL, 446-464
  FIRST PERIOD, 447; Urban's Norman Cathedral, 447-456; SECOND PERIOD, 456; completion of Urban's Cathedral, 456; THIRD PERIOD, 460; Campanile and Chapter House, 460; FOURTH

LLANDAFF—Continued.
  PERIOD, 460; Lady Chapel, 460; FIFTH PERIOD, 461; Improvements to Lighting, 461; SIXTH PERIOD, 462; New Doorways, 462; SEVENTH PERIOD, 462; North-West Tower, 462; EIGHTH PERIOD, 463; Restorations, 463
LONDON—The Cathedral Church of St. Paul, 210-223
  Sir Christopher Wren, 210; the original design, 212; the Dome, 214-221; the Interior, 217; the Exterior, 217
Longland's (B.) Chantry, Lincoln, 209
Losinga, B. of Hereford, 158
  ,, B. of Norwich, 227
Luxemburg, Cardinal, 111
Lyhart, B. of Norwich, 237

M

MANCHESTER, The Cathedral Church of St. Mary, 224-5
Mare, A. of St. Albans, 308
Marshall, B. of Exeter, 119
  ,, B. of Llandaff, 463
Meopham, AB. of Canterbury, 128
"Minstrels' Gallery," Exeter, 133
Modern Cathedrals, 476
Monks' Infirmary, Canterbury, 41

N

Nailheart, A. of Bristol, 19
Napier, John Moore, Epitaph at Chester, 64
NEWCASTLE, the Cathedral Church of St. Nicholas, 226
Newland, A. of Bristol, 19
Nix, B. of Norwich, 236
Northwold, B. of Ely, 102, 112
NORWICH—The Cathedral Church of the Holy Trinity, 227
  The See, 227; commencement of present Cathedral, 227; the Plan, 229; damage by fire and storm, 234; improvements to Lighting, 235; making the Cathedral fireproof, 237; Vaulting, 238; the Interior, 240

O

Oldham, B. of Exeter, 134
Orleton, B. of Hereford, 167
Oswald (St.), 404

INDEX 491

Ovin's Cross, Ely, 113
OXFORD—The Cathedral Church of Christ, 243-256
 St. Frideswide, 243; FIRST PERIOD, 245; Saxon Remains, 245; SECOND PERIOD, 245; Augustinian Establishment, 245; the Twelfth-Century Cathedral, 246; the East End, 247; THIRD PERIOD, 250; Tower and Chapter House, 250; FOURTH PERIOD, 251; Lighting, 251; St. Catherine's Chapel, 252; FIFTH PERIOD, 252; Vaulting the Choir, 253; SIXTH PERIOD, 254; Foundation of Bishopric, 254; Chronological Notes, 255

P

Paul of Caen, 302
Paulinus (St.), 82, 283, 343
Pearson, B. of Chester, 63
PETERBOROUGH—The Cathedral Church of St. Peter, 257-271
 Establishment of the Monastery, 257; Legendary History, 257; FIRST PERIOD, 259; destruction of Saxon Church by Fire, 259; SECOND PERIOD, 260; commencement of present Cathedral, 260; THIRD PERIOD, 261; Transepts and Nave, 262; FOURTH PERIOD, 264; extension of Nave, 264; New West Transept, 265; FIFTH PERIOD, 265; SIXTH PERIOD, 265; the West Front, 266; SEVENTH PERIOD, 268; Lady Chapel, 268; EIGHTH PERIOD, 268; Norman Tower, 268; Lighting, 268; NINTH PERIOD, 269; Windows, 269; TENTH PERIOD, 270; Procession Path and Chapels, 270; ELEVENTH PERIOD, 271; Parliamentarian mal-treatment, 271

Plantagenet School, 16
Poore, B. of Salisbury, 312
Prince Arthur's Chantry, Worcester, 423
Pudsey, B. of Durham, 89

Q

Quivil, B. of Exeter, 121

R

Rede, B. of Chichester, 78
Redman, B. of Ely, 112

RIPON—The Cathedral Church of St. Peter and St. Wilfrid, 272-282
 FIRST PERIOD, 272; the Seventh-Century Church, 272; SECOND PERIOD, 273; the Norman Church, 273; THIRD PERIOD, 274; the Cathedral rebuilt, 274; St. Wilfrid's Shrine, 275; the Nave, 275; Central Tower and Choir, 276; FOURTH PERIOD, 279; the West Front, 279; FIFTH PERIOD, 279; the East End, 279; SIXTH PERIOD, 280; Sedilia and Lady Chapel, 280; SEVENTH PERIOD, 280; collapse of Central Tower, 281; Woodwork, 282; EIGHTH PERIOD, 282; addition of Aisles, 282; NINTH PERIOD, removal of Spires, 282

Ritualistic Divisions of Cathedrals, 6
Robert, Duke of Normandy, 154
ROCHESTER—The Cathedral Church of St. Andrew, 283
 St. Augustine's Mission, 283; FIRST PERIOD, 284; the Early Church, 284; SECOND PERIOD, 284; the Norman Cathedral, 284; THIRD PERIOD, 286; the Nave, 287; the West Front, 287; FOURTH PERIOD, 288; Eastern Limb rebuilt, 288; FIFTH PERIOD, 290; extension of Choir, 290; SIXTH PERIOD, 290; SEVENTH PERIOD, 290; Central Tower, 290; EIGHTH PERIOD, 290; NINTH PERIOD, 290; removal of Southern Tower, 290; St. William, 291; TENTH PERIOD, 292; various Works, 292; ELEVENTH PERIOD, 292; Lighting improved, 292; TWELFTH PERIOD, 293; Enlargement of Lady Chapel and South Transept, 293; THIRTEENTH PERIOD, 293; Tower and Spire replaced, 293

Roger, AB., 274
Russell's (B.) Chantry, Lincoln, 209

S

SAINTS—Alban, 297, 308; Amphibalus, 297, 308; Augustine, 283; Bede, 90; Birinus, 409; Cantilupe, 165; Caradoc, 471; Chad, 173; Cuthbert, 82; David, 471; Ethelbert, 157; Frideswide, 243; Hugh of Lincoln, 196; Justus, 283; Oswald, 404;

SAINTS—*Continued.*
Paulinus, 82, 283, 343; Swithun, 400; Thomas of Canterbury, 30, 471; Werburgh, 63; Wilfrid, 66, 272; William of Rochester, 289, 291; Wulfstan, 402, 413

ST. ALBANS — The Cathedral Church of St. Alban, 294
General Survey, 294; Benedictine Foundation, 298; the Ritualistic Divisions, 299; FIRST PERIOD, 301; Norman Work, 301; Norman Nave, 302; Aisles and Transepts, 303; SECOND PERIOD, 304; Arcade and Doorway, 304; THIRD PERIOD, 305; the West Front, 305; FOURTH PERIOD, 305; Westernmost Bays, 305; FIFTH PERIOD, 306; Sanctuary, 306; Chapels, 307; SIXTH PERIOD, 307; the Lady Chapel, 307; SEVENTH PERIOD, 307; collapse of Nave and restoration, 307; EIGHTH PERIOD, 307; Minor Works, 308

ST. ASAPH's Cathedral, 464

ST. DAVID's Cathedral, 466
FIRST PERIOD, 466; Commencement of the present Church, 466; the Aisles, 468; SECOND PERIOD, 468; Presbytery and Transepts remodelled, 469; THIRD PERIOD, 470; De Leia's Church, 470; FOURTH PERIOD, 471; Chapel of St. Thomas the Martyr, 471; Shrines, 471; FIFTH PERIOD, 471; the Chantry, 471; SIXTH PERIOD, 471; the Chapels, 472; SEVENTH PERIOD, 473; Woodwork, 473; EIGHTH PERIOD, 473; completion of Eastern Chapels, 473; Exterior, 474

St. Oswald's Church, Chester, 59
Sais (Séez), A. of Peterborough, 260
SALISBURY—The Cathedral Church of St. Mary, 310
The Norman Cathedral, 310; Commencement of the present Cathedral, 312; comparative Survey of the Cathedral, 312-316; the Plan, 316; the Tower and Spire, 317; the External Aspect, 320; the Lighting, 325; the Interior, 326; the East End, 328

Salkeld, P. of Carlisle, 51
Secular Canons, Foundations of:—
Bangor, 442; Chichester, 65; Exeter, 114; Hereford, 156; Lichfield, 172; Lincoln, 191; Llandaff, 446;

London, 210; St. Asaph, 464; St. David, 466; Salisbury, 310; Wells, 360; York, 426

Serlo, A. of Gloucester, 138
Sherborne, B. of Chichester, 80
Simeon, A. of Ely, 98
Snow, A. of Bristol, 13, 17, 19

SOUTHWARK — The Cathedral Church of St. Saviour, 331-341
Foundation of St. Mary Overie, 331; Establishment as Augustinian Priory, 331; FIRST PERIOD, 332; Norman remains, 332; SECOND PERIOD, 333; rebuilding Eastern and Western Limbs, 333; the Presbytery, 334; The Nave, 335; THIRD PERIOD, 335; FOURTH PERIOD, 336; the Lady Chapel, 336; FIFTH PERIOD, 337; Tracery, 337; SIXTH PERIOD, 338; Reredos and Western Façade, 338; Minor Details, 338

SOUTHWELL — The Cathedral Church of St. Mary, 342-356
Foundation of the See, 342; FIRST PERIOD, 343; SECOND PERIOD, 343; THIRD PERIOD, 344; the Norman Church, 344; FOURTH PERIOD, 348; the Exterior of the Eastern Limb, 348; the Choir, 349; FIFTH PERIOD, 353; SIXTH PERIOD, 353; Cloister, 353; SEVENTH PERIOD, 353; Chapter House, 353; EIGHTH PERIOD, 354; Choir Screen, 354; NINTH PERIOD, 355; Tracery, 355; TENTH PERIOD, 355; Minor Works, 355

Stafford, B. of Exeter, 134
Stanbury, B. of Hereford, 169
Stapledon, B. of Exeter, 124
Stephen Langton's Tomb, 41
Stretton, B. of Lichfield, 188
Strickland, B. of Carlisle, 49
Structural changes, causes of, 3-6
Sudbury, AB. of Canterbury, 35
Swinfield, B. of Hereford, 169
Swithun (St.), 400

T

Thokey, A. of Gloucester, 144
Thomas (St.), of Canterbury, 30, 471
Travenant, B. of Hereford, 169
TRURO Cathedral, 483-486; the Design, 483; the Interior, 484
Tyndall, Dean of Ely, 111

U

Urban, B. of Llandaff, 447

V

Vere, B. of Hereford, 161
Victorian Cathedrals, 476

W

Wakefield, B. of Worcester, 421
WAKEFIELD, the Cathedral Church of All Saints, 357-9
Wakelin, B. of Winchester, 387
Waking, B. of Norwich, 237
Walpole Gate, Ely, 110
Warelhurst, B. of Exeter, 115-116
Warrior's Chapel, Canterbury, 41
Waterville, A. of Peterborough, 261
WELLS—The Cathedral Church of St. Andrew, 360-383
  Its charming aspect, 360; FIRST PERIOD, 364; Norman remains, 364; SECOND PERIOD, 364; commencement of present Cathedral, 364; the Design, 366; Vaulting, 367; the Lighting System, 369; order of execution, 372; THIRD PERIOD, 373; the Western Façade, 374; Western Chapels, 376; FOURTH PERIOD, 376; the Chapter House, 377; FIFTH PERIOD, 377; extension of Choir, 378; Lady Chapel, 379; Central Tower heightened, 381; SIXTH PERIOD, 382; the Western Towers heightened, 382; the present Cloisters, 382

WELSH CATHEDRALS:—
  Bangor, 442; Llandaff, 446; St. Asaph, 464; St. David, 464
Werburgh (St.), 63
West, B. of Ely, 110
Whispering Gallery, Gloucester, 155
Wilfrid (St.) of Ripon, 66, 272
William de Luda, B. of Ely, 111
William (St.) of Rochester, 291
William Rufus, 391
William of Sens, 30
William of Waynflete, 396
William of Wykeham, 396
WINCHESTER — The Cathedral Church of the Holy and Indivisible Trinity, 384-403
  Proportions of the Cathedral, 384; FIRST PERIOD, 387; Remains of

WINCHESTER—*Continued*.
  the Early Church, 387; the Crypt, 390; South Transept, 390; the Central Tower, 391; SECOND PERIOD, 391; Norman Doorway and Font, 391; THIRD PERIOD, 392; Retro-Choir, 392; Chapel of Holy Sepulchre, 393; Stalls, 393; FOURTH PERIOD, 393; restoration of Presbytery, 394; FIFTH PERIOD, 395; Re-erection of Nave, 395; SIXTH PERIOD, 401; the East End, 401; Langton's Chantry, 402; the Ritualistic Divisions, 403

Wolsey, Cardinal, 254
WORCESTER — The Cathedral Church of Christ and the B'essed Mary the Virgin of Worcester, 404-425
  Establishment of Benedictine Order, 404; FIRST PERIOD, 406; Anglo-Norman Church, 406; SECOND PERIOD, 408; Chapter House, 408; THIRD PERIOD, 409; completion of Nave, 409; FOURTH PERIOD, 412; repairs to damage by fire, 412; FIFTH PERIOD, 413; St. Wulfstan, 413; the Presbytery, 414; Lady Chapel, 415; Completion of East End, 417; SIXTH PERIOD, 418; lower part of Tower rebuilt, 419; SEVENTH PERIOD, 419; Bishop Cobham's Minor Works, 428; EIGHTH PERIOD, 421; Cloisters and upper part of Tower rebuilt, 421; NINTH PERIOD, 421; Vaultings, 422; TENTH PERIOD, 422; remodelling of Chapter House, 423; Prince Arthur's Chantry, 423; ELEVENTH PERIOD, 423; Jacobean Pulpit, 423; TWELFTH PERIOD, 423 Modern Furniture, etc., 423; tour of the Cloister, 424

Worcester, Earl of, Tomb at Ely, 111
Wren, Sir C., 111, 209, 210
Wulfstan (St.), 402, 413
Wygmore, A. of Gloucester, 146

Y

YORK —The Cathedral Church of St. Peter, 426-441
  FIRST PERIOD, 428; South Transept, 428; SECOND PERIOD, 430; the Nave, 430; THIRD PERIOD, 433; Chapter House, 433; FOURTH PERIOD, 433; extensions to the East, 433; the exterior aspect, 437

www.ingramcontent.com/pod-product-compliance
Lightning Source LLC
Chambersburg PA
CBHW071431300426
44114CB00013B/1394